Greenberg's® Guide to Lionel® Paper and Collectibles

By Robert J. Osterhoff

Edited by Cindy Lee Floyd and Carole A. Norbeck

Front Cover Photograph: "The Giant of the Rails" Lionel store display from the collection of Fred Wasserman.
Rear Cover Photograph: 1953-1954 Lionel Service Station decal.

LIONEL® IS THE REGISTERED TRADEMARK OF THE LIONEL CORPORATION, NEW YORK, New York. Lionel® trains are manufactured by Lionel Trains, Inc. of Mount Clemens, Michigan, the licensee of the Lionel Corporation.

Copyright © 1990

**Greenberg Publishing Company, Inc.
7566 Main Street
Sykesville, MD 21784
(301) 795-7447**

First Edition

Manufactured in the United States of America

All rights reserved. No part of this book may be reproduced in any form or by any means including electronic, photocopying, recording, or by any information storage system, without written permission of the publisher, except in the case of brief quotations embodied in critical articles and reviews.

Greenberg Publishing Company, Inc. offers the world's largest selection of Lionel, American Flyer, LGB, Ives, and other toy train publications as well as a selection of books on model and prototype railroading, dollhouse miniatures, and toys. For a copy of our current catalogue, send a stamped, self-addressed envelope to Greenberg Publishing Company, Inc. at the above address.

Greenberg Shows, Inc. sponsors the world's largest public model railroad, dollhouse, and toy shows. The shows feature extravagant operating model railroads for N, HO, O, Standard, and 1 Gauges as well as a huge marketplace for buying and selling nearly all model railroad equipment. The shows also feature a large selection of dollhouses and dollhouse furnishings. Shows are currently offered in metropolitan Baltimore, Boston, Ft. Lauderdale, Cherry Hill in New Jersey, Long Island in New York, Norfolk, Philadelphia, Pittsburgh, and Tampa. To receive our current show listing, please send a self-addressed stamped envelope marked *Train Show Schedule* to the address above.

ISBN 0-89778-152-X (Hardbound)
ISBN 0-89778-077-9 (Softbound)

Library of Congress Cataloging-in-Publication Data

Osterhoff, Robert J., 1947-
    Greenberg's guide to Lionel paper and collectibles / by Robert J. Osterhoff; edited by Cindy Lee Floyd and Carole A. Norbeck; photographed by Maury Feinstein. — 1st ed.
      p. cm.
      ISBN 0-89778-152-X : $40.00 — ISBN 0-89778-077-9 (pbk.): $29.95

    1. Railroads—Models—Collectors and collecting. 2. Railroads—Models—Catalogs. 3. Lionel Corporation. I. Floyd, Cindy Lee. II. Norbeck, Carole A. III. Greenberg Publishing Company. IV. Title.
TF197.073 1990   8948795
625.1'9—dc20   CIP

TABLE OF CONTENTS

Acknowledgments iv

Foreword v

Chapter I   Introduction to Lionel Paper 07
                    Publishing Efforts
                    Stock Certificates

Chapter II   Prewar Paper: 1901-1944 16

Chapter III   Postwar Paper: 1945-1969 50

Chapter IV   Modern Era Paper: 1970-1990 89

Chapter V   Service Station Paper 117
                    Service Station Bulletins
                    Lionel Service and Parts Manuals
                    Approved Service Stations

Chapter VI   Instruction Sheets for Lionel Trains: 1901-1969 ... 125

Chapter VII   Billboards 133

Chapter VIII Service Station Tools 144

Chapter IX   Non-Train Collectibles 153
                    Non-Train and Nautical Products: Airex Fishing Equipment
                    Corporation Memorabilia: Clothing and Patches • Souvenir and Promotional Pins and Jewelry • Consumer Promotional Offers (Non-Paper) • Promotional Phonograph Records • Promotional Films • Miscellaneous

Chapter X   Dealer Displays 174

About the Author 183

DEDICATION

*To my father and mother, Joseph and Louise Osterhoff,
who had the foresight to introduce me to Lionel trains many years ago.*

ACKNOWLEDGMENTS

There are times when one can believe the study of Lionel's fabulous history and products has been exhausted. This certainly cannot happen when one considers Lionel's non-train products and the paper produced by Lionel in the form of marketing programs, catalogues, and communications to its dealers.

In 1985 I admired I. D. Smith's listing of Lionel paper, published in the then-current edition of *Greenberg's Guide to Lionel Trains: 1945-1969*. I suggested to Bruce Greenberg that a significant expansion to that listing could be made. The paper listing expanded to cover Lionel tools, displays, and non-train products. Eventually, the chapters evolved to this, the first edition of *Greenberg's Guide to Lionel Paper and Collectibles*. Here we provide, for the first time, studies on new aspects of the hobby encompassing 90 years of Lionel history. Due to the vastness of this project, this was a team effort. Had it not been for the following individuals, this Guide would not have been possible.

First I would like to thank **Mrs. Olive Fisk** and **Chuck Fisk**, wife and son of the late **Edward Fisk**, whose collection served as paper, tools, and Service Station references. **Alan Rubin** generously provided his outstanding collection of paper and collectibles for photographs. His support allowed us to fill information voids which can now be shared with our readers.

Bill Mekalian also shared his collection and patiently waited for me as I drove through the California mountain fog to his home, and then stayed up with me as we reviewed his collection into the early morning hours.

I could always count on **Ron Antonelli** for providing seldom-known information regarding Lionel paper, and **Pat Neil**, dba Collectible Trains & Toys, for his indirect assistance in the study of the 1960s era. Much information on the final days of pre-MPC Lionel was graciously shared by **Rod Haggard**, a former employee of the Lionel Corporation. Mr. Haggard's outstanding recollection and fascinating stories enabled us to learn even more about Lionel in the late 1960s. The area of Lionel test sets presented an interesting challenge, and I thank **Mike Bingaman**, dba Des Peres Hobby Shop, as well as **Gordon Bickle**, for their contributions. **Ed Holderle's** contributions to the display chapter allowed us to correctly identify and substantiate the existence of many of these scarce collectibles. **Sandra Beste, Kathleen Wade**, and **Mike Braga** of Lionel Trains, Inc., provided needed assistance in filling gaps in our knowledge of modern Lionel paper and collectibles.

We can thank **I. D. Smith** not only for his innovative listing of paper previously mentioned, but for his continued contributions to this book, especially in the area of Service Station bulletins, billboards, and paper in general. **Don Corrigan's** earlier studies on billboards, part of which is included in Chapter VII, provide insight into the collecting of this specialized paper category. Don graciously shared his research and his photographs. **Joe Muscanere** planted the seed for categorizing Lionel's stock certificates, and as a result we are able to provide for the first time a chronology of these colorful and important documents. **Fred Wasserman** generously lent the Lionel store display, "The Giant of the Rails", which graces the book's cover.

The following people assisted in the preparation of this volume as readers: **Ron Antonelli, Charles Leibrock, Gary Magner, Bill Mekalian, Fred Natoli, I. D. Smith, Alan Rubin,** and **Todd Wagner**. We also thank **Bob Spivock** and **I. D. Smith** for their suggestions in developing revised grading standards.

The production of this book, which spanned over five years, was initially managed by **Carole Norbeck**, with final editorial direction and book compilation under the supervision of **Cindy Lee Floyd**. Without their dedication and skills this book would not have become a reality. Cindy's continued assistance in adding new information up until the last days of production now allows our readers the most current information. **Wendy Burgio, Marsha Davis, Juanda Duley,** and **Tina Joyce** assisted with last minute corrections. **Maureen Crum** (staff artist) and **Sam Baum** were responsible for the design and layout of the covers, and **Dallas Mallerich** wrote the copy for the rear cover. **Donna Price** proofread the book for style and consistency. **Maureen** and **Donna** were also responsible for preparing the book for the printer. **Maury Feinstein** provided most of the photographs for this book. **Bill Wantz** assisted in printing photographs and making the necessary photostats and halftones.

Special thanks are extended to the numerous collectors who brought new listings to our attention, and who are specifically named in the item listings of each chapter. It is hoped no one is offended by a credit omission; with this edition, ownership of more common items was omitted by necessity. And most importantly, a deep sense of appreciation goes out to the numerous train enthusiasts who provided the interest and encouragement to continue developing what appeared to be a never-ending compilation. We hope it will meet your expectations.

Robert J. Osterhoff
January 1990

FOREWORD

WHY THIS GUIDE

Trains are synonymous with the name Lionel, and the pleasures of holding a 700E scale Hudson or the ever-popular Pennsylvania GG1 often bring back fond memories of childhood. Handling a toy electric train provides an appreciation for engineering and manufacturing quality. The actual operation of a Lionel train provides endless opportunities to dream of operating a vast railroad empire and controlling all railroads at will by the simple pushing of a button or tugging of a transformer handle. The Lionel layout is that railroad empire personified. But there is much more to the hobby of tinplate model railroading: It is the volumes of paper materials issued in conjunction with the toy trains. And there is also a lesser-known fact behind The Lionel Corporation: The company widely diversified, and provided the consumer a fascinating product array of which trains were only a part. Volumes have been dedicated to the study of toy trains. The other Lionel products also deserve study and a methodic product listing.

In addition to errors, several important people who lent their invaluable help must be mentioned. **Roland LaVoie** lent his considerable expertise in organizing and writing Chapter IV - Modern Era. He traveled to Sykesville with his entire modern era paper collection which was photographed for that chapter. **Tom Whelan** provided his Lionel Naval instrument to our staff in Sykesville for photographing. His courtesy is very much appreciated. **Bill Mekalian**, who is an expert on Lionel paper, rewrote his original article on *Model Builder* magazines which begins on page 10. The article had previously been published in the *TCA Quarterly*.

offered at a given train meet on a given day. If a case of two hundred recent Lionel catalogues, from a defunct dealer's inventory, is put on the market the price will temporarily decline. While this may present a temporary local price fluctuation, normally paper material **on the average** bring prices similar to those identified in this reference. A related source of variation is the **season** of the year. The train market is slower in the summer and sellers may at this time be more inclined to reduce prices if they really want to move an item. This phenomenon takes place more with items of common availability; material of a scarcer or rare nature, it should be emphasized, will be **highly sought after** regardless of the season. Another important source of price variation is the relative strength of the seller's desire to sell and the buyer's eagerness to buy. Clearly a seller in economic distress will be more eager to strike a bargain. A final source of variation is the personalities of the seller and buyer. Some sellers like to turn over items quickly and, therefore, price their items to move; others seek a higher price and will bring an item to train meet after train meet until they find a willing buyer.

CONDITION

There are generally four accepted standards of condition: Good, Very Good, Excellent, and Mint. These are defined as **Good** — Scratches, small dents, dirty; **Very Good** — Few scratches, exceptionally clean, no dents or rust; **Excellent** — Minute scratches or nicks, no dents or rust; **Mint** — Brand new, absolutely unmarred, all original and unused, in original box. The above grading is most appropriate to tinplate trains, as well as those items defined as "collectibles" in this Guide. However, a scratch, dent, or rust would seem inappropriate as it relates to the majority of items appearing in this reference, those items made of paper and paper by-products.

In grading paper, this Guide applies the following descriptions:

NEW — Complete, unused. No defects such as detached or loose covers or pages, no holes, tears, dirt marks, or stains. There is no evidence of having been bent or folded, or if folded by factory, not unfolded. Item may have store stamp appropriately applied.

EXCELLENT — Complete, little evidence of use. May have minor defects such as small paper tears closed with transparent tape; very light dirt marks or stains; minor creasing. There is some evidence of bending and folding, or unfolding if originally factory folded. Item may have store stamp appropriately applied.

VERY GOOD — Well used, with small defects such as tears greater than two inches, closed with tape; extensive rust on staple, heavier fold marks; quantity of dirt or stain marks, minor gouging of covers or inside pages with small pieces missing.

GOOD — Heavily used, with major defects including detached or loose covers and inside pages; tears in cover and inside pages that may be taped; missing and crumpled corners, extensive rust on staple affecting paper; heavier dirt marks and stains which do not obliterate printing or illustrations. A usable reference copy only.

This book does not apply the term "mint" condition to paper or paper-related items. The nature of "mint" condition takes on an entirely different context with paper material. Catalogues, flyers, and posters did not come in the familiar orange and blue boxes, so "in original box" would not be an appropriate requirement for this type of material. A mint catalogue must appear to be brand new and absolutely flawless. This is seldom seen with paper products, and is the primary reason why we believe "new" is a more appropriate description.

It is the nature of a market for the seller to see an item in a very positive light and to assign the most favorable description. In contrast, a buyer may see the same item in a less favorable light and will attempt to purchase the item accordingly. This Guide points out a relative price difference based on condition, and it is then up to the buyer and seller to negotiate price based on their individual set of values.

We receive many inquiries as to whether or not a particular piece is a "good value." This book will help answer that question; but there is **no** substitute for experience in the marketplace. That is especially true for the early catalogues and literature of the Lionel Corporation, where an abundance of reproductions have been made and many, unfortunately, have not been so marked. When in doubt, the wisest purchase just may be the reproduction for reference only. At least the value of the item would be clearly established! **Regardless, we strongly recommend that novices do not make major purchases without the assistance of friends who have experience in buying and selling train material.** If you are buying an item and do not know whom to ask about its value, look for the people running the meet or show and discuss with them your need for assistance. Usually they can refer you to an experienced collector who will be willing to examine the item and offer an opinion.

NO REPORTED SALES — In a field for which consistent buying and selling has not been established, there are clearly certain pieces that due to their unusual nature could not have an established market value. Over time an identifiable market may be established, but in the meantime where there is insufficient information upon which to determine the value of a given item, we show **NRS** in the price column. Here again we recommend that you rely on your **experience** or on the assistance of an experienced collector to determine what price you should pay for any of these items.

Chapter One
INTRODUCTION TO LIONEL PAPER

Background

In my collection of Lionel memorabilia sits a small accumulation of catalogues from 1953 through 1959, tattered, torn, and repaired with tape. On today's market, these catalogues are almost worthless, yet they would not be available for sale at any price. These catalogues were my dream books. As a youngster growing up in the 1950s the Lionel catalogue was anxiously awaited, and often signaled the beginning of the Christmas holidays. The catalogues even ranked "up there" with purchasing Elvis Presley records or finding a Mickey Mantle baseball card.

While the marketing direction of Lionel had been fairly chauvinistic, I recall my sisters looking over these very catalogues — certainly operating many of the Lionel trains that were illustrated. Unfortunately Lionel recognized this fact too late; that the "girls" enjoyed trains as much as the "boys" or "Pop," to paraphrase terms often used by Lionel.

The Lionel catalogue was an important piece of my life. I considered myself fortunate at Christmas to receive perhaps two or three of those items in the catalogue marked "NEW". This was the distinguishing characteristic identifying a product's initial introduction by Lionel for that catalogue year. Growing up in the Midwest, I never visited the famous Lionel showroom on Manhattan's East 26th Street, or the factories in Hillside or Irvington, New Jersey. My experiences as a youngster were limited to the great catalogues, plus one visit to the Chicago showroom in the Merchandise Mart — to see firsthand the catalogue actually come alive with products recently introduced.

A review of the changing prices in the seven editions of *Greenberg's Guide to Lionel Trains* provides strong evidence to the increasing value of Lionel trains. Many fortunate individuals have retained their childhood trains, and can again fulfill their early dreams. Others are not so fortunate, either because the trains were disposed of or trains could not be afforded in the first place. Of the latter, there are two choices: 1) invest a small fortune and purchase the trains one had always wanted or 2) continue the dream of yesteryear and turn each page of a Lionel catalogue with admiring glances. Many serious collectors combine both activities, and enjoy the best of both worlds.

Obtaining older Lionel catalogues is becoming increasingly difficult. Yet, in certain years, over a million consumer catalogues were printed and distributed. This statistic was even boasted of by Lionel in its advertising to dealers and the general public.

Generally, the metals and plastics used in the manufacture of model trains have held up well over the years and the toys can be handled in a rigorous manner. (I qualify that statement because some trains from the 1930s used die-cast parts which have crumbled. It is not uncommon to be able to literally crumble a metal locomotive wheel in your bare hands.) The handling of paper catalogues is another matter. A quick turn of a page or a slight fold can turn a new copy into a grading of good in a matter of seconds. While tinplate trains can be readily cleaned, tumbled, and restored to like-new condition, the so-called repair of paper is an exacting science, and fortunately has not found its way into the mainstream of the model railroading hobby. Therein lies a logical explanation for the increasing popularity of Lionel catalogues today: supply vs. demand.

Thousands of collectors are searching for ways to either purchase catalogues for occasional reference, or complete a set of catalogues for each year. Yet for many catalogue years the supply is becoming increasingly smaller. Why is this so, if in fact millions were produced and issued? Unlike Lionel trains, the catalogue was viewed as a disposable commodity. A well-used catalogue could easily be disposed of when the youngster grew tired of the trains, whose fate was perhaps somewhat more secure. In the early years even some dealers saw these marketing works of art as useful as outdated newspapers. On one occasion I happened upon a storage area of a defunct hobby shop, the contents of which were sitting undisturbed for over twenty years. In describing my experience, I can only recall the oft-repeated phrase, "I have good news and bad news." The good news was the fact I had stumbled upon an entire case of 1950 Lionel Golden Anniversary color consumer catalogues. The bad news —

more appropriately, tragic news, was the rapid realization these catalogues were sitting on a wet dirt floor, obviously attacked by creatures I guessed to be squirrels. The Golden Anniversary catalogues of Lionel were reduced to water-soaked images of what might have been.

General Categories of Paper Collecting

Paper collecting can be divided into three categories: 1) Consumer catalogues; 2) advance and dealer catalogues; and 3) any paper item associated with Lionel.

CONSUMER CATALOGUES: In addition to nostalgic value, the consumer catalogues issued each year (except the wartime years of 1943 and 1944, and 1967) provide an ideal reference to single merchandise and sets available for that year. The recently-published listing of Lionel's non-catalogued sets (reference *Greenberg's Guide to Lionel Trains 1945-1969, Volume II,* and the forthcoming Greenberg volume devoted solely to Lionel sets) substantiates that the Lionel consumer catalogues were not always complete. The sole purpose of the catalogue decades ago, as it is with Lionel Trains, Inc. today, was to sell trains.

Beginning in 1924, the consumer catalogues became colorful works of art. Although previous editions were printed in color, depicted now were boys at play with their Lionel electric trains, complete with the ever-present pet dog (1924-1926). The 1930s frequently featured the idol of boyhood, the railroad engineer, with sleek streamliners side-by-side with the traditional steam locomotives.

With a void during the 1943-1945 war years, in 1946 Lionel came out with its traditional color catalogue, proclaiming "the finest model electric trains in the World." The firm then proceeded to flood postwar America, hungry for toys, with catalogues as inserts to an edition of *Liberty* magazine. And Lionel made a great marketing coup with the December 1946 *Liberty* magazine front cover which illustrated a happy father playing with Lionel trains.

Many collectors believe some of the artistic classics of Lionel consumer catalogues were published from 1947 to 1960. All catalogues of this period share similar horizontal formats, with full-color artistic renderings of Lionel products. The 1949 catalogue, today one of the more popular and scarce editions, featured a first for Lionel, depicting model railroading as a family affair.

The evolution of the Lionel Corporation can be well understood in studying the firm's catalogues. The 1961 edition ushered in yet a new era, perhaps the beginning of the end. Trains were still featured on the cover, but shared equal space with Lionel's aggressive venture into science kits and other non-train merchandise. This venture was prompted by market concerns. With waning interest in electric trains, Lionel was forced to be competitive in the cut-throat toy business. A comparison of the 1964 A. C. Gilbert and Lionel catalogues demonstrates remarkable similarities. Gilbert brought out its new Son of Wing Thing, which competed with Lionel's Helios product. The two firms were also head to head in chemistry sets, microscope labs, and miniature auto racing. And both would in time suffer a similar fate.

In 1970, the Lionel Corporation licensed General Mills to manufacture Lionel trains. General Mills' subsidiary, Model Products Corporation, manufactured Lionel trains until 1985 when General Mills decided to leave toy manufacturing. Consequently, General Mills created a new company, Kenner Parker, to carry on toy manufacturing. General Mills' stockholders received shares of Kenner Parker. Kenner Parker, which included Lionel trains, then sold its Lionel trains manufacturing facility and license to Richard Kughn. Richard Kughn renamed the Lionel operation Lionel Trains, Inc. and is successfully manufacturing Lionel trains under license from the Lionel Corporation. And who could have dreamed that the Lionel and American Flyer lines would be contained in the same colorful media?

From the basic tinplate of the 1920s and engineers of the 1930s we see a treasure of artistic renderings in the Lionel catalogue. Today, Lionel Trains, Inc. continues the tradition and provides the 1949 equivalent in Lionel catalogues for the 1990s. Just as the 1946 edition introduces the state-of-the-art Electronic Control, the 1988 version features RailScope, which simulates a ride in the locomotive cab of a model train.

Collectors have recognized the valuable role that consumer catalogues play as a supplement to the trains themselves. A collector can, with relative ease and a reasonable investment, obtain a catalogue from each postwar year. The hunt is more difficult for certain years prior to 1942 back to the early 1920s, but certainly possible. With a complete collection of Lionel consumer catalogues, what is the next challenge for the collector? A logical step may be the scarcer advance or dealer catalogues.

ADVANCE AND DEALER CATALOGUES: Lionel's advance and dealer catalogues can best be described as similar to the consumer version and more. The exact terminology for these catalogues varies, and some collectors use "advance" and "dealer" descriptions interchangeably. These catalogues were issued prior to the consumer version and were usually timed for New York's annual February Toy Fair, where dealers placed their advance orders for the year's product line. These versions were reserved for Lionel's dealers, distributors, and/or Authorized Service Stations and were not available to the general public.

Yet another variety of dealer catalogues was produced by Lionel from the 1930s through the 1950s, and is classified as scarce and many times rare. These deluxe versions, identified as V.I.P. or Executive editions, often depicted the consumer version, with a notable difference. The catalogues were hardbound or spiral bound, and often the inside pages were printed on card stock rather than a more conventional bond of paper. The distribution of these editions was extremely limited, and often each copy included personalization on the cover. Recipients included Lionel's top executives, its largest distributors, and occasionally a large-volume dealer.

The conventional dealer or advance editions were published to present a view of the proposed product line. On certain occasions, Lionel was not able to produce previously-announced merchandise, or based on dealer

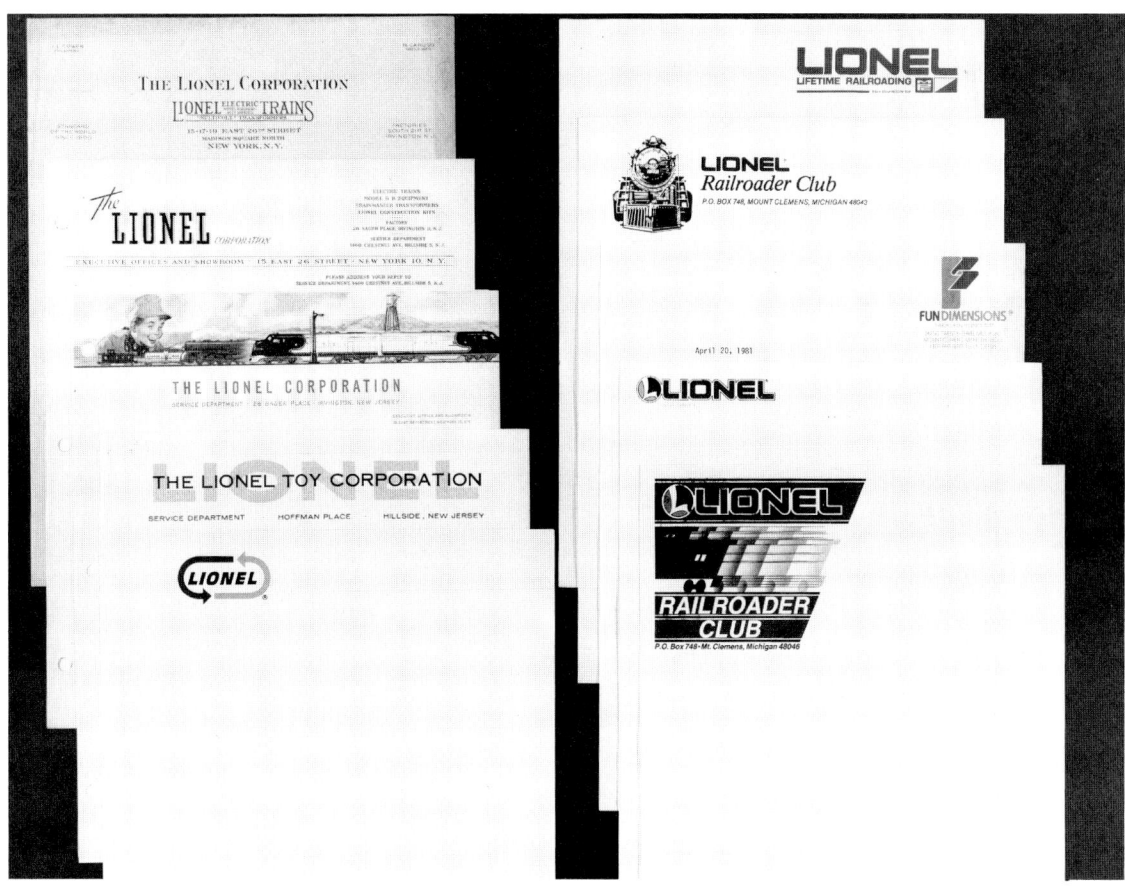

An assortment of Lionel stationery used over the years.

response at the Toy Fair, projected sales were not sufficient to make production of the item profitable.

A number of features differentiate an advance catalogue from that of the later consumer edition. The 1947-1949 advance catalogues are significantly larger than their consumer counterparts. Most advance versions are issued in black and white, while most (but not all) consumer catalogues were released in full color. As with other facets of Lionel collecting, there are exceptions, as evidenced by the 1965 catalogues. One of several differences between the advance and consumer versions is quite simple: page 38 contains information on the Helios 21 airship. After the Helios 21 heading, the advance version identifies the product as "Mark 2"; the corrected consumer version clearly labels the same item with a "Mark II". While the visual difference may be trivial, the astute collector can recognize a very significant price difference.

When in combination, Lionel's consumer and advance catalogues offer excellent references of the product array. Lionel produced non-catalogue paper in abundance, and this final category offers the collector an even more comprehensive understanding of the company, its history, and products.

OTHER PAPER ASSOCIATED WITH LIONEL: Catalogues offer a concise, organized view of Lionel's many products. But the company produced much more than just the annual catalogue. Posters, maps, face masks, art prints, easel displays, service manuals, and parts lists are only a fraction of what Lionel released to promote and support its products. Most collectors in this highly specialized collecting arena concentrate on those items issued directly by Lionel. The majority of material was focused on Lionel's Authorized Service Stations and distributors. However, there was an ample number of paper products such as billboards and the Bantam *Model Railroading* paperback series that were targeted for a general audience.

There is a growing number of collectors who attempt to assemble a collection of any Lionel-produced paper, regardless of its origin or content. Separately, this form of collecting raises one's curiosity. Collectively, such as all Service Station bulletins or letters from Lionel Corporation, it lends itself to a study of Lionel's intriguing history.

Lionel paper collecting can be further expanded by studying those items endorsing or referencing Lionel, but not actually produced by or for Lionel Corporation. Material in this category ranges from advertising (comics, newspapers, and magazines), place mats provided by McDonalds as part of a sales promotion, to paper trains found in Nabisco cereal boxes. These items may be a significant extension beyond the trains, but their association with the magical name of Lionel is unmistakably clear.

PUBLISHING EFFORTS

Several of the chapters that follow separate Lionel paper into distinct categories, such as prewar, postwar, and the modern era. Certain aspects of paper collecting, however, would be done an injustice if every item were classified into a singular narrow category. The best example is that of Lionel's many in-house publications, some continuing periodicals, and other general interest books, all published over a period of many years.

These periodicals came in many formats, and their study is really an in-depth analysis of the evolution of the Lionel Corporation. The evolution crosses the prewar and postwar era, and even leads us to the Lionel of today. For that reason, it was decided to exclude certain key publications from their respective chapters, and include them in a separate reference listing. Conversely, there are certain regularly-issued publications, such as *The Lionel Herald* of the Lionel Service Department, which can best be treated in more depth in a specialized chapter. And as with virtually all Lionel material, there still remains research to be done on this aspect of collecting. One point is clear: All the following items are highly sought after today, especially in excellent or better condition and in complete editions. First issues generally bring a significant price premium.

	G	VG	EXC	NEW

BOY'S RAILROAD MAGAZINE: A late 1920s flyer published by Lionel indicates that a "Boy's Railroad Magazine" would be published shortly. Was this magazine ever published? Reader information requested. Total issues released: Unknown.
Average value per issue: **NRS**

THE LIONEL MAGAZINE: Designated by Lionel as "the Model Railroad Magazine for Every Boy..." and published by the Lionel Engineer's Club, this profusely-illustrated two-color periodical made its debut in May 1930 with an issuance variation ranging from quarterly to ten times a year. Total issues released: 37.
Average value per issue:
(A) 1930-34.   6   8   12   16
(B) 1935-36.   3   5   8   10

MODEL ENGINEER: Volume 1, No. 1 for November-December 1936 was designated to be published bimonthly by the Lionel Corporation, according to a statement included in this sample — and only issue. A conflict in magazine titles with a British publication brought about an abrupt change in this Lionel publishing effort. Two varieties of this issue exist, one with "Sample Copy" on the front cover in black ink, and the other without any sample indication. It is believed the "sample" issue is the scarcer of the two. Total issues released: 1.
Average value per issue: 20   35   45   60

MODEL BUILDER: Came into existence as its own Volume 1, No. 1 (and not No. 2 as a continuation of *Model Engineer*). The quick change was due to the fact that a magazine entitled *The Model Engineer* was being published in England as early as 1898, and Lionel was threatened with litigation. Eighty issues of *Model Builder* were published in all; six issues were published annually from 1937-46. In 1946 the company began printing eight issues annually. At first, from 1937 through 1939, the magazine was published on a bimonthly basis; after that an issue was printed during the first three months and the last three months of the year. Beginning in 1946, a copy was issued the first four months and the last four months of the year. For no apparent reason, however, only five issues were printed in 1940. There was one other exception during this time — the November 1943 issue was never published due to a serious paper shortage during World War II.

When model railroaders learned that the *Model Builder* would cease publication with the eightieth issue in April 1949, many of them wrote to Joshua Lionel Cowen pleading with him to continue that magazine. Mr. Cowen indicated that Lionel had already reached a final decision. Following are a few excerpts from the April 1949 issue: "Suspending Publication — *Model Builder* Will No Longer Be Issued!" "*Model Builder* is being suspended for several reasons, but perhaps the most important is that it has served its major purpose. During the past two decades, a publication was greatly needed to insure the establishment of model railroading as a hobby. Now that has been done, and there are now three *other* publications in the field — all doing a good job. The need for *Model Builder* has changed completely, thus the decision was made.

MODEL BUILDER
Published by The Lionel Corporation

		Jan.	Feb.	March	April	May	June	July	Aug.	Sept.	Oct.	Nov.	Dec.
1937	Vol. 1		1		2		3		4		5		6
1938	Vol. 2		7		8		9		10		11		12
1939	Vol. 3		13		14		15		16		17		18
1940	Vol. 4		19		20						21	22	23
1941	Vol. 5	24	25	26							27	28	29
1942	Vol. 6	30	31	32							33	34	35
1943	Vol. 7	36	37	38							39		40
1944	Vol. 8	41	42	43							44	45	46
1945	Vol. 9	47	48	49							50	51	52
1946	Vol. 10	53	54	55	56					57	58	59	60
1947	Vol. 11	61	62	63	64					65	66	67	68
1948	Vol. 12	69	70	71	72					73	74	75	76
1949	Vol. 13	77	78	79	80								

Note: Shaded areas show that there were no issues for that month.

The April 1949 cover of this *Model Builder* shows the Bascule Bridge at Chesapeake Creek in northern New Jersey.

                                  G   VG EXC NEW

"Of course, other factors have entered as well, and rising prices and falling revenues have touched almost every magazine to a greater or lesser degree. *Model Builder* was *hard hit*, but the basic reason was that other publications could fulfill the needs of the readers.

"The editors of *Model Builder* have spent a great deal of time analyzing the various possibilities in concluding the existence of *Model Builder*.

"After careful consideration, it was decided that the magazine *Model Railroader* could best fulfill the needs and desires of the readers."

Although Lionel stated sound and logical reasons in the foregoing excerpts for withdrawing from the publishing business, it stands to reason that perhaps not all the facts were bared. Several possibilities have been bandied about. It is obvious that "the needs and desires of the readers are being fulfilled" by other publications — as evidenced by the fact that *Model Railroader* is still in existence. This does not, however, delve into Lionel's departure from the field. There is a distinct possibility that Lionel was actually involved with the manufacturing end of model railroading more so than reporting the news and ideas of manufacturers, even though they (Lionel) were included themselves. Possibly their staff was not on a par with other magazine staffs in that they did not have complete objectivity. Perhaps the staff members' background was geared more to the factory than reporting. Then again, Lionel may simply have felt the field slipping from them, as *Model Railroader* had a paid circulation of 83,000 by 1949. And advertisers have always shown a preference to deal with those publications showing a higher paid circulation figure. Perhaps Lionel's reasons were valid too, or there was a series of circumstances they did not mention that ultimately compelled Lionel to retire from the publishing field. Certainly there is always room for speculation. Total issues released: 80.

Average value per issue:

	G	VG	EXC	NEW
(A) 1937-42.	4	7	10	12
(B) 1943-46.	3	5	8	10
(C) 1947-49.	—	—	3	5

In this edition of the *Lionel Lines* (Vol. 6, No. 5, October 1943) Lionel proudly displays the "M" award they received from the government for their outstanding service manufacturing war supplies. W. Mekalian photograph.

                                  G   VG EXC NEW

LIONEL LINES: An internal publication issued for Lionel employees and the forerunner of the noted *All Aboard* magazine. Only one issue of this magazine has been observed by the editor, that being Volume 1 from 1938. Another issue, Volume 6, No. 5 (1943) is in the collection of W. Mekalian, and features Lionel executives receiving the wartime "M" award. Total issues released: Unknown.

Average value per issue: **NRS**

ALL ABOARD: An internal publication issued for employees of the Lionel Corporation and later expanded to Service Station owners, this glossy magazine provides the most significant insight into the Lionel family. The magazine combines feature stories on Lionel itself, its relationship with customers and suppliers, and its products. Each issue also contains personal anecdotes such as births, marriages, retirements, and deaths of employees. The later topics are generally featured in a special section titled "The Mainliner", and includes employees of Lionel and Airex.

Current information indicates *All Aboard* was first published in early 1947. A letter from James Limner, *All Aboard's* editor, dated February 17, 1954, states "Here it is — the first issue of *All Aboard at Lionel* to go to its new audience, the proprietors of the company's Approved Service Stations. This magazine came into existence seven years ago as a medium of communications between management and employees at the firm's Irvington, New Jersey plant. Now its circulation is being expanded to include another segment of the Lionel organization — its Service Station operators." It would therefore be assumed the March 1954 issue is the first to receive mass Service Station distribution, and it is no irony this issue is the most abundant, but for a different reason. The March issue, which illustrates Chicago's Michigan Avenue skyline on its cover and features Lionel's Chicago Showroom in that issue, often appears with a pink cover rather than the original issuance orange cover. This version is also missing a number of pages, and

In 1955 Lionel celebrated one of the greatest years in its history in the December issue of *All Aboard* magazine. The cover of this issue (pictured) was atypical as usually covers displayed country and town scenes and did not show trains. This cover has the added pleasure of children playing with Lionel trains.

	G	VG	EXC	NEW

printed on slightly smaller paper. It is no coincidence that the reprinted version contains the full feature story of Bill Vagell, then the noted proprietor of the Treasure House Hobby Shop in Garfield, New Jersey. It is not surprising therefore that the reprints originated with Vagell himself. Total issues released: Unknown.
Average value per issue: **8 12 20 25**

LIONEL ANNUAL REPORT: Since Lionel went public as a corporation in 1937, a requirement is to issue an annual report to its stockholders. As it did in virtually all its printed media, Lionel often took advantage of the Annual Report as an important marketing tool. While the reports of the late 1930s and into the 1940s were financially-oriented, their true purpose, the late 1940s brought publishing masterpieces to the Corporate annual report. Again Lionel was ahead of its time. Often the reports bore similar covers as the consumer catalogue for that year. In the 1959 Annual Report, for instance, in addition to containing the mandatory financial data, included was other information on Lionel products that border on being a dealer catalogue.

There is still a Lionel Corporation today, and annual reports are still published under the Lionel name, but with a noted difference: A recent annual report includes a one-paragraph narrative and occasional reference that "the Company also receives royalties under a license agreement...covering the manufacture and sale of *Lionel* trains and other toys." Total issues released: (Still being published).
Average value per issue:

	G	VG	EXC	NEW
(A) 1937-44.	—	—	—	40
(B) 1945-50.	—	—	—	60
(C) 1951-62.	—	—	—	20

Six major editions of *Model Railroading* — Bantam books. D. Corrigan photograph.

	G	VG	EXC	NEW
(D) 1963-70.	—	—	—	12
(E) 1971-present.	—	—	—	7

LIONEL INTERIM REPORT: Similar to the Annual Report, and issued as required by the Securities & Exchange Commission for publicly held corporations, such as Lionel. Current editions include very little, if any, reference to the manufacture of toy trains. Total issues released: (Still being published.)
Average value per issue: — — — **2**

MODEL RAILROADING: This popular reference, better known as "the Bantam series," was published by Bantam Books, Inc. of New York, but prepared by the Editorial Staff of the Lionel Corporation. We presume this staff was actually part of Lionel's advertising or sales department, and there was a point made in the first edition to dedicate the book to their leader, J. Lionel Cowen. This book is an extremely useful and fully illustrated reference, containing topics ranging from how to build tables to how to control several trains at one time. The first edition made its appearance in October 1950, with revised editions and nine printings appearing through September 1961. One cannot judge a book by its cover, however, as different printings retained the same cover design, as evidenced by the seventh (October 1957) and eighth (October 1958) printings, both assigned to the fifth edition. These books have always been popular with collectors, and are often found in rather poor condition, the result of frequent use. All known editions and varieties are listed below.

First Edition, First Printing, September 1950. Bantam Book number A-2, blue cover. **8 10 15 20**

First Edition, First Printing, September 1950. Bantam Book number A-2, purple cover. **10 15 20 25**

First Edition, Second Printing, December 1950. Bantam Book number A-2, blue cover. **10 15 20 25**

Second Edition, Third Printing, October 1951. Bantam Book number A979, white cover. **15 18 25 35**

Second Edition, Fourth Printing, March 1952. Bantam Book number A979, white cover. Existence of this printing has not been confirmed. Reader assistance requested. **NRS**

	G	VG	EXC	NEW
Third Edition, Fifth Printing, November 1953. Bantam Book number F1152, blue cover with 736 illustrated.	10	15	20	25
Third Edition, Fifth Printing, November 1953. Bantam Book number F1152, blue cover. "F1152" missing from front cover due to book cutting error.				NRS
Fourth Edition, Sixth Printing, October 1955. Bantam Book number F1430, dark blue cover with 2331 FM locomotive.	15	20	25	35
Fifth Edition, Seventh Printing, October 1957. Bantam Book number S1663, blue cover with 746 locomotive illustrated.	15	20	30	40
Fifth Edition, Eighth Printing, October 1958. Bantam Book number S1663, blue cover with 746 locomotive illustrated.	15	20	30	40
Sixth Edition, Ninth Printing, September 1961. Bantam Book number N2384, white cover with 746 locomotive illustrated.	15	20	25	35

Total issues released, all editions: 9 (excluding varieties).

HANDBOOK FOR MODEL RAILROADERS: Priced at 50 cents and published by Lionel, this 192-page work was often an advertised offer from *Model Builder* magazine. The publication was first announced in the December 1940 issue of *Model Builder*, at which time a two-page advertisement indicated that "20 men worked 3 years in planning, building and photographing models...." Deluxe clothbound editions were available at hobby stores for $1 each, the regular editions were available at 50 cents per copy or free with a two-year subscription to *Model Builder*. The paper-covered economy edition came in two versions, with yellow cover, inscribed "How to Assemble Your Trains and Tracks Into a Complete Model Railroad System"; and a red cover, inscribed "Fun and Facts for the Amateur Railroader". Total issues released: 1,(with 2 editions)

Average value per issue:	15	20	30	45

KEEP ON TRACKIN': After a 27-year hiatus from publishing a magazine for general consumption, this periodical, admittingly brief compared to its predecessors, can be loosely classified as the closest modern day version of the *Model Builder*. It was first published in 1976 and distributed to members of the Lionel Railroader Club. Total issues released: 19.

Average value per issue:	—	—	—	1

LIONEL RAILROADER CLUB: May 1982, Issue Number 20. This only issue includes a contest to name the newsletter. The name selected was "The Inside Track," which made its first appearance in August 1982. Total issues released: 1.

Average value per issue:	—	1	2	3

THE INSIDE TRACK: A continuation of Lionel's *Keep on Trackin'* periodical, and issued irregularly since August 1982. Generally four pages in length, and often includes a special offer for Lionel Railroader Club members. Total issues released: (Still being published).

Average value per issue:	—	—	—	1

STOCK CERTIFICATES

Lionel, in its marketing prowess, had always been successful in placing toy train images before the general public. It should be no surprise to see, in a fine engraved format, a boy overlooking a Hudson locomotive and tender on Lionel's first stock certificates as a public corporation.

To better understand this issuance, it is helpful to explore a portion of Lionel's fabulous history. There are three distinct periods in Lionel's business history. The first phase was the sole proprietorship of Joshua Lionel Cowen from 1900 through 1917. His trading name was "Lionel Manufacturing Company." It was a developmental phase for Lionel, which saw the evolution of a mass market for toy electric trains. The second period, circa 1918-1936, began with the legal incorporation of the growing toy train business as the Lionel Corporation. This is still the name under which the company does business, although not as the manufacturer of toy trains.

Our focus here, however, is on the third and current phase of Lionel's organizational life span. From 1900 through 1936, Joshua Lionel Cowen relied on internal financing and private funds for the research, development, production, and marketing efforts of his company. It was a significant decision in the mid-1930s, therefore, when Cowen took his company public and created what we know today as the Lionel Corporation.

In 1937 Lionel first issued public stock, 77,500 shares with a par value $10 per share but sold at a new issue price of $12. The earliest known sales of issued stock were to William Bonanno, brother of Lionel's Chief Engineer Joseph Bonanno, and were dated September 24, 1937. By offering public stock, Lionel gained immediate access to almost a million dollars in additional working capital, allowing for debt reduction and company expansion. It also opened the Company's books to public scrutiny and proxy fighting. Two decades after this initial stock offering, Lionel as a public entity began its gradual degradation in sales and earnings, and the saga even continues today as a modern Lionel Corporation has emerged successfully from a Chapter 11 bankruptcy filing.

Although there were relatively few different stock issuances, each represents an important piece in Lionel history. Unlike the railroading products of the company, there need not be a designation of prewar, postwar, or modern era assigned to stock certificates or related corporate memorabilia. For instance, General Mills or CPG Products Corp., as the parent companies of Fundimensions, was the licensee of the Lionel trademark. The original Lionel Corporation still acts as licenser of the electric train trademark to the present manufacturer, Lionel Trains, Inc. Paper relating to the Lionel Corporation is therefore very much a collectible to the paper collector today.

As a footnote to the listings below, "Stock Issue" refers only to the different stock certificates as printed, and does not necessarily relate to the Lionel Corporation's actual issuance of additional shares of stock for increased working

14 • Greenberg's Guide to Lionel Paper and Collectibles

issuance of additional shares of stock for increased working capital. In addition, the years given represent dates of certificates actually observed, and are not always the first year of issue.

Reader assistance in identifying actual first issuance dates is requested. Many certificates were in use for the time duration of the senior corporate officers designated to sign the certificates.

1937

FIRST STOCK ISSUE: Engraving features boy admiring Hudson locomotive and tender, and bears the signature of Mario Caruso and Joshua Lionel Cowen. Common par value $10.

		G	VG	EXC	NEW
(A) Blue color for 100-share denomination. Muscanere Collection.		—	—	60	75
(B) Orange color for less than 100-share denomination. Muscanere Collection.		—	—	60	75
(C) Orange color for less than 100-share denomination, first year of first issue. Muscanere Collection.					NRS

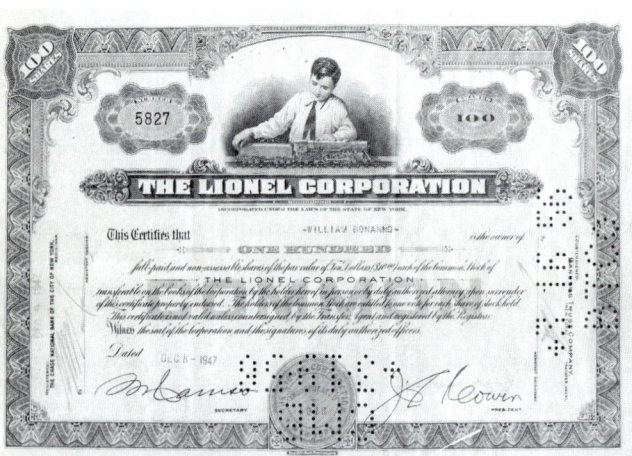

First Stock Issue, 1937.

1949

SECOND STOCK ISSUE: Engraving features boy admiring Hudson locomotive and tender, and bears the signature of Joseph Bonanno and Lawrence Cowen. Common par value $5.
(A) Green color for 100-share denomination. Muscanere Collection. — — 35 50
(B) Maroon color for less than 100-share denomination. Muscanere Collection. — — 35 50
(C) Maroon color for less than 100-share denomination, with red diagonal imprint, "This Certificate Represents Shares of $2.50 PAR VALUE", dated July 18, 1951. A. Rubin Collection. NRS

1955

THIRD STOCK ISSUE: Engraving features boy engineer overlooking diesel and steam locomotives, and bears the signature of Joseph Bonanno and Lawrence Cowen. Common par value $2.50.
(A) Orange color for 100-share denomination. Muscanere Collection. — — 10 15
(B) Blue color for less than 100-share denomination. Muscanere Collection. — — 10 15

1960

FOURTH STOCK ISSUE: Engraving features boy engineer overlooking diesel and steam locomotives, and bears the signature of Joseph Bonanno and Roy Cohn. This marks the first time Lionel leadership includes an "outsider," i.e. a senior officer not a part of the early Lionel organization. Cohn was a noted lawyer who gained fame in the early 1950s during the Joseph McCarthy Senate hearings. Common par value $2.50.
(A) Orange color for 100-share denomination. Muscanere Collection. — — 10 15
(B) Blue color for less than 100-share denomination. Muscanere Collection. — — 10 15

FIFTH STOCK ISSUE: Engraving features boy engineer overlooking diesel and steam locomotives, and bears the signature of Joseph Bonanno and John Medaris. Common par value $2.50.
(A) Orange color for 100-share denomination. Muscanere Collection. — — 10 15
(B) Blue color for less than 100-share denomination. Muscanere Collection. — — 10 15

Fifth Stock Issue, 1960.

1962

SIXTH STOCK ISSUE: Engraving features boy engineer overlooking diesel and steam locomotives, and bears the signature of W. T. Watson and John Medaris. Common par value $2.50.
(A) Orange color for 100-share denomination. Muscanere Collection. — — 8 10
(B) Blue color for less than 100-share denomination. Muscanere Collection. — — 8 10

SEVENTH STOCK ISSUE: Engraving features boy engineer overlooking diesel and steam locomotives, and bears the signature of Curtis E. Johnson and Melvin Rainey. Common par value $2.50.
(A) Orange color for 100-share denomination. Muscanere Collection. — — 8 10
(B) Blue color for less than 100-share denomination. Muscanere Collection. — — 8 10

1963

EIGHTH STOCK ISSUE: Engraving features boy engineer overlooking diesel and steam locomotives, and bears the signature of J. E. Donohue and Melvin Rainey. Common par value $2.50.
(A) Orange color for 100-share denomination. Muscanere Collection. — — 8 10

	G	VG	EXC	NEW

(B) Blue color for less than 100-share denomination. Muscanere Collection. — — 8 10

(C) Green color for 100-share denomination. No record of being issued, only specimen copies found. The only specimen observed is that of $20 par value preferred stock. Hollander Collection. **NRS**

1966

NINTH STOCK ISSUE: Engraving features boy engineer overlooking diesel and steam locomotives, and bears the signature of Richard R. Schilling and Robert A. Wolfe. Common par value $2.50.

(A) Orange color for 100-share denomination.
— — 6 8

(B) Blue color for less than 100-share denomination.
— — 6 8

(C) Aqua color for more than 100-share denomination. Muscanere Collection. — — 10 12

1970

TENTH STOCK ISSUE: Engraving features Classical God vignette, a significant printed message as a testimonial that indeed trains were no longer the integral product of the Lionel Corporation. Certificates bear the signature of Richard R. Schilling and Ronald Saypol.

(A) Orange color for 100-share denomination. **NRS**
(B) Blue color for less than 100-share denomination. **NRS**
(C) Aqua color for more than 100-share denomination. **NRS**

1973

ELEVENTH STOCK ISSUE: Engraving features Classical God vignette, and bears the signature of George R. Padgett and Ronald Saypol. Common par value $2.50.

(A) Orange color for 100-share denomination.
— — 10 12

(B) Blue color for less than 100-share denomination.
— — 10 12

(C) Aqua color for more than 100-share denomination.
— — 12 15

(D) Blue color for less than 100-share denomination; common par value 10 cents. There is no record of these shares being issued, as only specimen copies have been found. Muscanere Collection. **NRS**

1982

TWELFTH STOCK ISSUE: Engraving features Classical God vignette with 2-3/4" x 7-1/2" security design printed to the left of stock data on certificate. Certificate bears the signatures of George A.

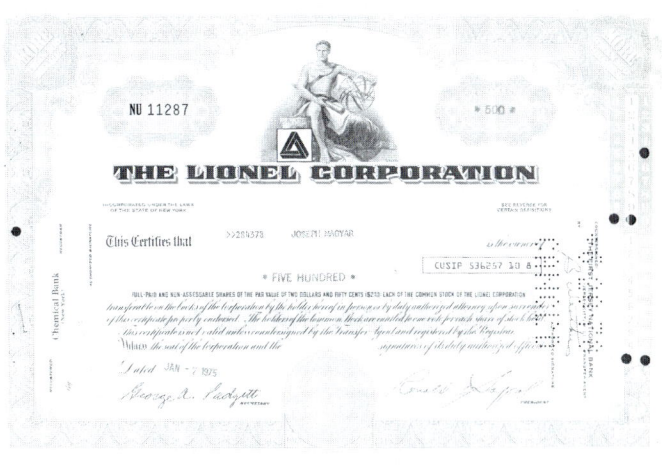

Eleventh Stock Issue, 1973.

	G	VG	EXC	NEW

Padgett and Michael J. Vastola. Common par value 10 cents. Blue color for less than 100-share denomination.
— — 5 7

1985

FIRST WARRANT ISSUE: Engraving features no pictorial vignette, only "The Lionel Corporation" and was issued to all stockholders of record on November 25, 1985. Certificate bears the signature of Michael J. Vastola and George A. Padgett. No par value. These certificates were issued under Lionel's Third Amended Consolidated Plan of Reorganization from bankruptcy, and allowed shareholders to purchase stock at specific prices during a specific period of time. These warrants, like Lionel stock itself, were regularly traded on the American Stock Exchange.

(A) Blue color for any number of warrants, with stock purchase of $8 per share to be exercised from December 4, 1985 through December 4, 1986. Designated Warrant A. — — 15 20

(B) Purple-red color for any number of warrants, with stock purchase of $12 per share to be exercised from December 4, 1986 through June 1, 1988. Designated Warrant B. — — 15 20

Note: Common Stock in "The Lionel Rail Road Company" was issued in 1960 to all who entered a track layout contest. The contest rules stated that "as an honorary stockholder you will receive your very own stockholder's certificate and the right to vote for *The Lionel Rail Road Company* Board of Directors..." Because this stock issuance was of a promotional rather that a legal nature, these certificates are listed in the postwar paper chapter of this *Guide*.

Chapter Two
PREWAR PAPER: 1901-1944

"State of New York
County of New York

We, Joshua L. Cohen, and Harry C. Grant, of the City, County and State of New York, Borough of Manhattan....Do hereby certify, that we are conducting and transacting the business of the manufacture of electrical novelties at No. 24 Murray Street, in the County of New York, and State of New York, under the name of the 'Lionel Manufacturing Company'...."

Perhaps the above extract represents the earliest document which could be considered media produced pertinent to the magic name of Lionel. The prewar era represents a fascinating period for paper, driven by the wide variability between the items produced. For instance, we can view the simple, crude flyer produced in 1905, which describes the "miniature electric cars, motors, etc. for holiday presents and window displays," and comments on the few products in minute detail. Or we can peruse the artful masterpiece catalogue produced in 1931 for the consumer market. Page ten illustrates in vivid color one of Lionel's engineering feats, described as "the largest and most powerful model locomotive ever built." The code word was "Mogul," and in 1931 the price of $42.50 for the 400E locomotive with tender was steep for a nation already in the throes of depression.

Previous listings of prewar Lionel paper concentrated more on sequential descriptions of catalogues. The following listing has now been expanded to include the many dealer-related items, such as display catalogues and advertising mats, which are now becoming visible on the collectors' market. The paper that follows in chronological sequence represents Lionel's longest defined era. The era spans well over four decades of start-up, fiscal disaster, a comeback to success, and interruptions with the outbreak of war. And this is all clearly depicted in the printed media of Lionel paper.

Study the available reprints of the early years. Admire the full-color catalogues in the glamorous late 1920s and 1930s. Learn how Lionel quickly and successfully adapted to wartime production in the service of one's country. Lionel Corporation was a blue chip company in the prewar era. The message communicated by the paper that follows is living proof.

Note: Dimensions are given with width followed by height unless otherwise noted.

G   VG   EXC   NEW

1901
CATALOGUE: Catalogue not confirmed for this year. Reader assistance requested. **NRS**

1902
CATALOGUE: 3-1/2" x 6-1/4" vertical format, 16 pages plus covers. Cover is light green paper printed with red ink. Text is black ink on white paper. Front cover reads "Miniature Electric Cars with full accessories for Window Display and Holiday Gifts". Cover portrays Converse trolley on track. Company address is 24 and 26 Murray Street. Items offered are 300 trolley, 200 powered gondola electric express, 400 unpowered gondola electric express.
(A) Original. One known copy. **NRS**
(B) Reproduction by E. A. Basse, Jr.
    1   2   3   5

1902 Catalogue cover.

1903
TYPE I: 6" x 9" vertical format, 16 pages. Cover reads "Electrical Novelties and Appliances for Boys, Ewing-Merkle Electric Co., Saint Louis, Mo. U.S.A." Cover shows portrait of young boy, dressed in cap and scarf, speaking into telephone. In Lionel's earliest years, it was apparently customary for large electrical supply houses like this one to promote Lionel products with their own names. See 1910 and 1912 entries for other examples. This is the only one in which the name "LIONEL" does not appear on the cover. Products shown: B & O tunnel locomotive, derrick motor-

1903 Type I Catalogue cover.

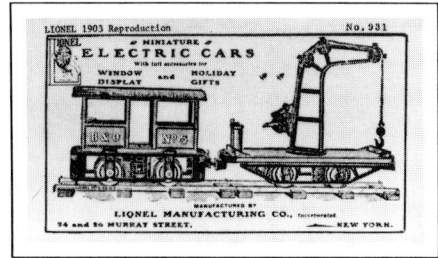

1903 Type II Catalogue cover.

                                                            G   VG EXC NEW

less trailer unit, wet cell glass jars, and batteries.
(A) Original.   NRS
(B) 1977 reproduction by Greenberg Publishing Company on plain paper.   1   2   4   5
(C) White paper reproduction by William Vagell on semi-translucent paper.   1   2   3   4

TYPE II: 6-1/4" x 3-1/2" horizontal format, 20 pages, same legends as 1902 predecessor and 24-26 Murray Street address. Lionel "lion" logo added to upper left corner. Cover shows 100 B & O locomotive and 600 derrick trailer. Also shown in catalogue: 200 powered and 400 trailer gondolas, 300 converse trolley track, and varied accessories.
(A) Original.   NRS
(B) Reproduction by Greenberg Publishing Company.
                                                             1   2   4   5
(C) Reproduction by William Vagell.   1   2   3   4
(D) Reproduction by Don LaSpaluto with light gray cover stock and without reproduction notice.   1   2   4   5

1904

CATALOGUE: 6" x 6-1/2" format, 12 pages. Cover legend reverses order of "Holiday Presents" and "Window Display", black print on white paper. Cover shows products within diagonal stripe running downhill. Countershafting apparatus in lower left corner; directly above it is legend "Manufactured By / Lionel Mfg. Co. Inc. / 4 & 6 White St. / New York" inside black border. New products: "Special Show Window Display", 300 and 3090 trolley and trailer, 800 and 900 boxcar and trailer, Type A and K miniature motors, and No. 2 countershafting apparatus.
(A) Original.   NRS
(B) Reproduction by Greenberg Publishing Company.
                                                             1   2   4   5
(C) Reproduction by William Vagell with blue and black cover.   1   2   3   4
(D) Reproduction by Don LaSpaluto. Some may not be marked as reproductions.   1   2   3   4
(E) 1959 reproduction by Train Collector's Association. "VALLEE BROS. ELECT. CO." in place of "MANUFACTURED BY LIONEL MFG. CO. INC."   1   2   3   4

1905

CATALOGUE: 6" x 6" square format, 12 pages. Black ink on white paper. Cover has same wording as 1904 catalogue, but pictures differ. 100 locomotive pulling 400 trailer gondola passes through 340 suspension bridge on its way around an oval of track supported by 380 elevated pillars. Below the lettering, the No. 2 countershafting apparatus is shown powering an unidentified set of toy saws and drills mounted on a platform. New products: 1000 and 1050 passenger car and trailer, a "new improved 1905" track, and a Type L power motor. This is the last catalogue showing 2-7/8" Gauge equipment.
(A) Original.   NRS
(B) Reproduction by Greenberg Publishing Company with heavy blue index stock cover.   1   2   4   5

Top row: 1904 and 1906 Catalogue reproductions. *Bottom row:* 1905 and 1905-06 Catalogue reproductions.

                                                            G   VG EXC NEW
(C) Reproduction by Greenberg Publishing Company with regular-weight paper printed cover.   1   2   4   5
(D) Reproduction by William Vagell on translucent paper.   1   2   3   4
(E) Reproduction by Don LaSpaluto on coated stock without reproduction notice.   1   2   4   5

1906

CATALOGUE: 4-1/2" by 6-1/2" horizontal format, 24 pages plus covers, black ink. Features completely new line of three-rail Standard Gauge trains. Front cover shows elevated trackage leading to ornate Victorian-style train station. In upper left corner is large sign with legend, "Look Out / for the / Third Rail". Lower right corner shows White Street address and Chicago sales office address.
(A) Original.   NRS
(B) Reproduction by Greenberg Publishing Company, black ink on plain white paper.   1   2   4   5
(C) Reproduction by William Vagell, blue ink on cover, translucent paper.   1   2   3   4
(D) Reproduction by Don LaSpaluto, may or may not be marked.
                                                            1   2   4   5

1907

CATALOGUE: Supposedly 6" x 9" format, 28 pages. No other details are available, and confirming evidence of this catalogue has yet to surface.   NRS

1908

CATALOGUE: Supposedly 6" x 9" format, 28 pages. Purported to show 5 and 6 locomotives and the 16 ballast car, the 17 caboose, and

| | G | VG | EXC | NEW |

the 29 day coach. Reliable evidence for this catalogue's existence is lacking. **NRS**

1909

CATALOGUE: 6" x 9" format, 32 pages plus covers. Cover is tan with black ink. Text is printed in black ink on white paper. Front cover: Lion logo in upper left and right corners; between them is legend "Standard Of The World". Center of cover: "LIONEL" in heavy black type above "Miniature Electric Trains / and / New Departure Battery Motors". Lower right has dealer's name and address. At lower left: "As superior to any on the / market as the telephone / is to the speaking tube" in three lines. Featured 1, 2, 3, 4, 8, and 9 trolleys, 10-series freight cars, and 29 day coach.
(A) Original. **NRS**
(B) Reproduction by Greenberg Publishing Company on plain white paper marked "REPRODUCTION" on rear cover and in some gutters between pages.   1   2   4   5
(C) Reproduction by William Vagell on translucent paper.
   1   2   3   4
(D) Reproduction by Don LaSpaluto with tan-colored cover, some rubber-stamped "ORIGINAL REPRINT" in red on rear cover.
   1   2   4   5

1910

CATALOGUE TYPE I: 8" x 10" vertical format, 28 pages plus covers, format, black ink on white paper. Front cover: Lion logo in all four corners. At top: "Standard of the World". Date below upper right logo. "LIONEL" in heavy boldface type. "Miniature Electric Trains and / New Departure Battery Motors" in two lines underscored by heavy double line. Lower half of catalogue cover has space for dealer name, in this case "Anderson Light & Specialty Co. / known as / LA SALLE LIGHT STORE / 140 N. La Salle St. / CHICAGO OPPOSITE NEW CITY HALL". Introduction on page 1 shows new address for Lionel Manufacturing Company: 381-383 Broadway. Next three pages detail motor and frame construction, track details, body construction, and patent lists. Extensive line of trolleys. Contains 5, 5 special, 6, and 7 steam locomotives, 10-series freight cars, 1910, 1911, and 1912 electric locomotives, and 18, 19, and 190 passenger cars.
(A) Original. **NRS**
(B) 1976 reproduction by Greenberg Publishing Company on plain paper.   1   2   4   5

CATALOGUE TYPE II: Same contents as Type I, but front cover has picture of Lionel factory at bottom center instead of dealer address.

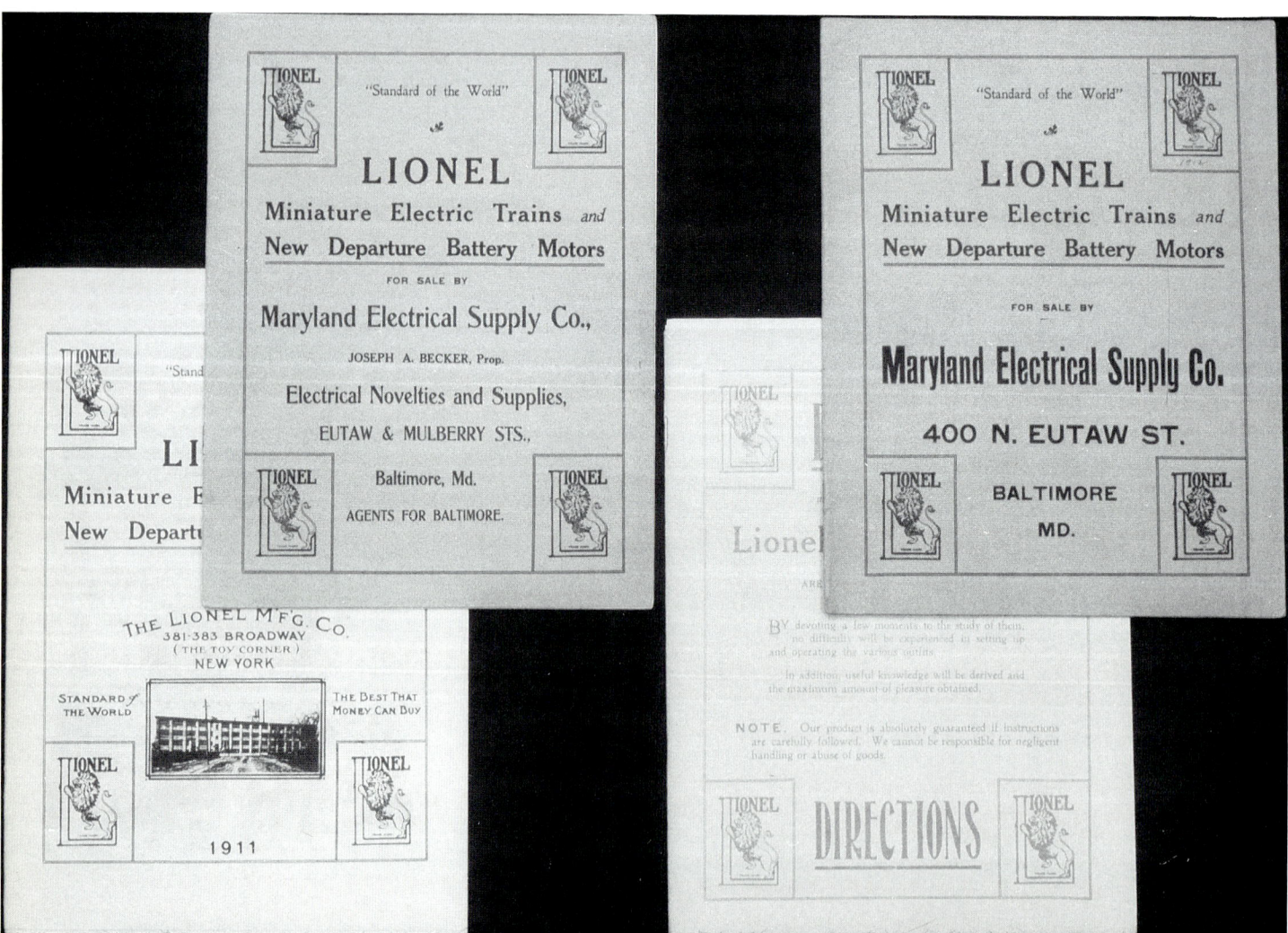

Top row: 1911 and 1912 Catalogue with overprint for Maryland Electrical Supply. Lionel produced a line of specially lettered streetcars for this Baltimore retailer. *Bottom row:* 1911 Catalogue with factory illustration and reproduction 1912 Catalogue Type II with train line.

	G	VG	EXC	NEW

(A) Original. **NRS**
(B) Reproduction by William Vagell on translucent paper.
    1   2   3   4

CATALOGUE TYPE III: Same contents as Type I, but cover is wraparound multicolored cover showing five rows of trains and sets. "The Lionel Mfg. Co." runs vertically along the right cover border, and "381 Broadway, New York" runs vertically along the left cover border. Original. **NRS**

1911

CATALOGUE TYPE I: 8" x 10" vertical format, 32 white text pages with black ink plus tan covers with black ink, pulp. Same general design as 1910 Type I but dealer name replaced by "Preserve This Book" and description of contents followed by bolder print: "DO NOT MISPLACE THIS BOOK". Lionel address at bottom center between two lion logos. First pages show five photos of Lionel Manufacturing Company factory. Original. A. Rubin Collection.
    —   —   150   —

CATALOGUE TYPE II: Same contents as Type I, but with multi-colored wraparound cover. Original. **NRS**

CATALOGUE TYPE III: Same as Type I, but space below double horizontal line, lists store name following "FOR SALE BY". Only known example lists "MARYLAND ELECTRICAL SUPPLY CO., JOSEPH A. BECKER, Prop." Red ink for numbers on page 4.
(A) Original. Weisblum Collection. **NRS**
(B) Reproduction by Greenberg Publishing Company.
    1   2   4   5
(C) Reproduction by William Vagell. Marked bottom of first page after opening cover "EARLY 1911 LIONEL CATALOGUE / REPRINTED BY WM. VAGELL'S TREASURE HOUSE".
    —   —   8   12

1912

CATALOGUE TYPE I: 8" x 10" vertical format, 36 white text pages with black ink, plus red ink on page 4, gray vellum cover with black ink. Lion logo in four corners of the front cover. Cover lettering: "Standard of the World / Lionel / Miniature Electric Trains and New Departure Battery Motors" followed by a double horizontal line. Then "FOR SALE BY / Maryland Electrical Supply Co." Text page 1 shows four interior factory views plus exterior facade. "FACTORY NEW HAVEN, CONN." Racing cars are offered on pages 16 and 17. Pages 34-36 are devoted to "DIRECTIONS".
(A) Original. Weisblum Collection. **NRS**
(B) Reproduction by Greenberg Publishing Company with tan cover stock, black ink on white-coated text pages and red ink on page 4.
    1   2   4   5

CATALOGUE TYPE II: Same as Type I but with different cover lettering. "DIRECTIONS / FOR THE USE AND CARE OF / LIONEL ELECTRIC TOYS / ARE GIVEN ON PAGES 34, 35 & 36".
(A) Original. **NRS**
(B) 1955 reproduction by J. C. Andrews and W. H. Kitchelt, Jr. in reduced size of 6-1/2" x 8-1/2".   —   —   5   8
(C) 1966 printing of (B) by Train Collector's Association.
    1   2   4   5
(D) Reproduction with gray cover and red ink and only 24 text pages. Pages were deleted without notice as were page numbers. Rubber-stamped on rear inside cover "REPRINT AS IS / NOVEMBER 1972". We would like to learn who published this reprint.
    —   —   1   2

CATALOGUE TYPE III: Color wraparound cover. Text pages probably the same as Type I. More information requested. Original. **NRS**

1913

CATALOGUE TYPE I: 8" x 10" vertical format, 36 white text pages with black ink, and gray vellum cover with black ink and lion logos in four corners, text page 1 shows four interior factory views plus exterior facade. On page 2 "the manufacture of electric toys thirteen years ago..." Original. **NRS**

CATALOGUE TYPE II: 6" x 6-3/4", 16 pages including cover. Cover is lettered "LIONEL ELECTRIC TOYS" with red "L", "E", and "T" and "ARE STANDARD OF THE WORLD". A boy and girl are playing on the floor with an elaborate double-tracked railway. Page 2: "the manufacture of electric toys thirteen years ago..." Left centerfold, page 8, shows 33, 38, 53, and 42 locomotives.
(A) Original. **NRS**
(B) Reproduction by Greenberg Publishing Company in black ink only, on plain white paper. On top of front cover lettered: "LIONEL 1913 CATALOGUE REPRODUCTION".   1   2   4   5
(C) Reproduction by Don LaSpaluto with blue and red outside covers. Coated stock pages. Some not marked as reproductions.
    1   2   4   5
(D) Reproduction in black ink only on translucent paper by William Vagell. Marked as reproduction on page 2.
    1   2   3   4

1914

CATALOGUE TYPE I: 8" x 10" vertical format, 32 white text pages with black ink and gray vellum cover with black ink; text page 2 "the manufacture of electric toys fourteen years ago". Original. **NRS**

CATALOGUE TYPE II: Same cover as 1913 Type II, 6" x 6-3/4", 16 pages including cover. Cover and text are printed in green and black with "L", "E", and "T" on front cover in green, light green screen behind cover image, and green text copy. Interior halftones are printed in black.
(A) Original. Weisblum Collection. **NRS**
(B) Reproduction by William Vagell in black with green and black front cover, translucent paper.   1   2   3   4

CATALOGUE TYPE III: Similar to Type II, but text is printed in brown ink and images are in orange ink.
(A) Original. L. Connors Collection.   —   —   150   —
(B) Reproduction by Jerry Rubenstein.   1   2   4   5
(C) Remaining Rubenstein reproductions were sold to Greenberg Publishing Company and rubber-stamped: "1975 REPRODUCTION GREENBERG PUBLISHING CO..."   1   2   4   5

1915

CONSUMER CATALOGUE TYPE I: 10" x 7" horizontal format, 40 pages including cover and color insert, but pages numbered only to 38. Printed in black and orange ink with orange used as a highlight primarily for headings. The center image on the front cover shows a 42 electric locomotive with two cars; four line drawings flank the center image. This catalogue introduces "A LITTLE TRIP THROUGH MY FACTORY" for the first time. The tour includes an extremely slanted comparison of Lionel and Ives production. The catalogue also contains the first catalogue photograph of J. Lionel Cowen. "250,000 Boys Now Operating Them" on all but front cover and centerfold. Page 2: "For fifteen years I have been making boys happy..." Page 24: "LIONEL FREIGHT CARS. PRICE LIST..." The catalogue centerfold was printed in color on heavier stock showing the 42 locomotive with 19, 18, and 190 cars on a Meccano bridge.
(A) Original. Weisblum Collection. **NRS**
(B) Reproduction; all-black ink on white slick paper. Bottom front cover printed "1953 Reprint of 1915 catalog. Distributed by J. C. Andrews & W. H. Kitchelt, Jr."   —   —   5   8

	G	VG	EXC	NEW

CONSUMER CATALOGUE TYPE II: Exactly the same as Type I, but the old price of $32.50 for outfit 421 on the left centerfold page is overprinted with a red line and a new price of $40. Original. Weisblum Collection. **NRS**

1916

CONSUMER CATALOGUE TYPE I: 10" x 7" horizontal format, 40 pages including cover and color insert, but pages numbered only to 30. Printed in black and orange ink with orange used primarily as a highlight for headings. This catalogue is very similar to 1915 Type I, but has "LIONEL FREIGHT CARS. PRICE LIST..." on page 23, and "LIONEL PULLMAN CARS..." price list on page 25. It does have "250,000 BOYS..." on all but front cover and centerfold. 1-3/8" diameter red label on front cover: "IMPORTANT / All prices in this / Catalogue are withdrawn. / See enclosed sheet / for revised figures." Enclosed in the catalogue is a 10" x 7" "SCHEDULE A" with new 1916 price list. On this sheet Cowen blames "Old Mister War" for the price increases on his entire line. Original. Weisblum Collection. **NRS**

CATALOGUE TYPE II: Reportedly same as Type I, but with "For sixteen years I have been making boys happy" on page 2, with new higher prices compared to Type I and "260,000 BOYS..." on all but front cover and centerfold, without separate "SCHEDULE A" and without red cover sticker. Verification requested. **NRS**

CONSUMER CATALOGUE TYPE III: Reportedly 6" x 9" folder with 16 pages; more details and verification requested. **NRS**

1917

CONSUMER CATALOGUE TYPE I: 40 text pages with pages 17-24 in full color and balance black and red ink only; front cover is printed in red and black with white block with ornate red and black lettering: "LIONEL ELECTRIC TRAINS / & Multivolt Transformers". Below is a picture of Lawrence Cowen, Joshua Cowen's son, posing as the "Happy Lionel Boy" operating a 420 passenger set. Plant pictures are on the inside and semaphores are portrayed on the back cover. Introduces O Gauge series. Text page 1 "STANDARD of the WORLD for 17 YEARS" with page entirely in black. Text page 2: "Seventeen Years Ago I Started To Make'"; pages 3-19, 22-40, back covers with heading "Over 300,000 Boys Are Now Operating Them". Original in mailing envelope labeled "Boys — Here's Fun"; letter insert erroneously refers to 1916. R. Otten Collection.
— 200 — —

CONSUMER CATALOGUE TYPE II: Similar to Type I, but without extra four color pages, wraparound cover, and text page 1 has "LIONEL" and "TRAINS" in red and black lettering. It is possible that the Type II is simply a Type I without a cover. Reader confirmation requested.
(A) Original. Fitchett Collection. **NRS**

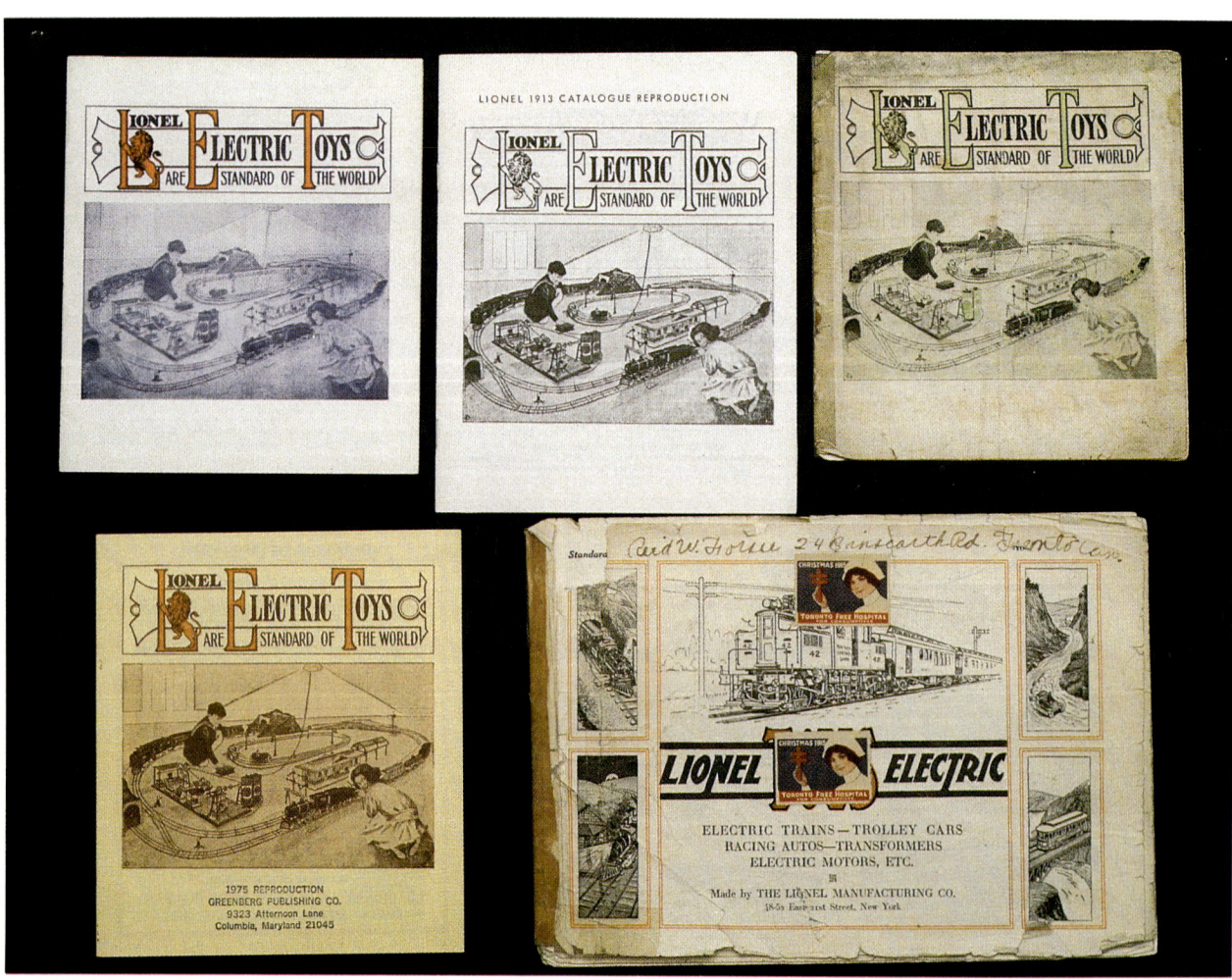

Top row: Red and blue 1913 Catalogue reproduction by D. LaSpaluto, black 1913 Catalogue reproduction by Greenberg, green and black 1914 Catalogue original. *Bottom row:* Orange and brown 1914 Catalogue reproduction, and 1915 Catalogue original. The 1915 Catalogue original has two stickers applied many years ago: "Christmas 1915 / Toronto Free Hospital / for Consumptives".

Top row:. 1916 Consumer Catalogue original which is the same as 1915, except for the red notice label on the cover and the insert sheet "Boys Here's My New 1916 Price List." The price increases were blamed on "Old Mister War." *Bottom row:* Color centerfold from 1916 featuring the 420 deluxe Pullman train.

	G	VG	EXC	NEW

(B) 1971 reproduction by Greenberg Publishing Company as all-black catalogue bound by a staple at the edge rather than through the centerfold as in the original. Picture quality is modest at best.
— — 1 2

(C) 1977 reproduction by Greenberg Publishing Company as all-black catalogue bound by a staple through edge. Much better picture quality than (B). 1 2 3 6

CONSUMER CATALOGUE TYPE III: Same as Type II, but text page 1 entirely in black. The original catalogue examined gives no evidence that the center color section has been removed. L. Connors Collection. — 100 — —

CONSUMER FOLDER TYPE IV: 6" x 9" vertical format, eight pages on each side, unfolds to 24" x 15" horizontal format, black and red ink on coated stock with red ink used only for headings and outlines. Side 1: front cover with Lawrence Cowen with arms spread wide over 42 passenger set. Cover lettering: "1917 / CATALOGUE OF / LIONEL / ELECTRIC / TOY TRAINS / And Multivolt Transformers". Upper left panel with transformer chart with B, S, T, and K transformers. Side 2 lower center right panel with illustration of 121 and 121X station as well as tunnel.
(A) Original. NRS
(B) 1967 Gordon Reproduction. 1 2 3 4

CONSUMER FOLDER TYPE V: Similar to Type III, but significant differences. Front lettering: "1917 / CATALOGUE OF / LIONEL / ELECTRIC / TOYS". Front panel is outlined by solid red rule. Side 1 upper left panel with transformer chart with S, T, and K transformers. Side 2 lower center right panel with illustration of tunnel only.
(A) Original. Weisblum Collection. NRS
(B) Reproduction on coated stock by Greenberg Publishing Company. Extremely close match to original, but with extra outlining added around panel. Reproduction printed by Collins Lithography, Baltimore. 1 2 3 5

DIRECTIONS FOR OPERATING...: 4-9/16" x 5-1/8", 20 pages, black ink on white paper, "The Lionel Manufacturing Co. / 48 East 21st Street New York City" on page 1. Operating instructions, lubrication points, voltage specifications, packed with each train set. Pages 4-5 the same as 1918(B) entry. Transformer prices on page 13: "B", - $3.40; page 14: "S", - $5.00; page 15: "T", - $6.50; and page 16: "Kg", - $8.00. L. Bohn comments.
(A) Original. Weisblum Collection. 5 10 15 20
(B) Reproduction by Greenberg Publishing Company, slightly reduced size. — — 1 2

1918

CONSUMER FOLDER: 6" x 9" vertical format, eight pages on each side, unfolds to 24" x 18", black and red ink on coated stock with red ink used only for headings and outlines. Side 1: front cover panel

| | G | VG | EXC | NEW |

with boy (Lawrence Cowen) with arms spread wide over a 42 set. Cover panel is outlined with a thin red rule enclosed in a triangular rule. Lettering: "LIONEL / ELECTRIC / TOY TRAINS / And Multi-volt Transformers / SOLD BY / MANUFACTURED AND GUARANTEED BY / The Lionel Manufacturing Company, 48-52 East 21st Street, New York". Side 1 upper left panel with transformer chart with B, T, and K transformers. Side 1 lower center left panel: "PLAY WAR!" Shows armored locomotive and armored locomotive with two sets. Side 2 lower center right panel without illustrations of tunnels or station. (Compare with 1917 folders.) Side 2, lower right edge: "NOTE — All locomotives...equipped with 3-1/2" volt bulbs".
(A) Original. Weisblum Collection. **NRS**
(B) Reproduction on coated stock by Greenberg Publishing Company. Printed by Collins Lithography, Baltimore.
  1 2 3 5
(C) 1955 black and white reduced size reproduction by Andrews et al. 18-1/2" x 29". **1 2 3 4**
(D) Reproduction, red and black on non-slick white paper. Front cover is rubber-stamped below "SOLD BY": "REPRINT OF ORIGINAL / LIONEL CATALOG / BY SANDERS". Printed as two pages instead of one. C. Weber Collection. **NRS**

CONSUMER CATALOGUE: 10" x 8" horizontal format, probably 40 pages. We suspect that this catalogue exists but have no confirmed reports. **NRS**

TYPE I DIRECTIONS FOR OPERATING: Directions for Operating..., 16 pages, black ink on white paper, "The Lionel Manufacturing Co. / 48 East 21st Street New York City" on page 1. Page 3: "Standard Gauge brushes are known as No. / 74. / Price...Per pair $.25". Transformer prices: "B", - $4.25; "S", - $5.00; "T", - $6.50; and "K", - $8.00 all on page 13. Page 15 advertises transformers B, T, and K as "high duty." L. Bohn comment.
(A) Original. Weisblum Collection. **5 10 15 20**
(B) Reproduction by Greenberg Publishing Company.
  — — 1 2

TYPE II DIRECTIONS FOR OPERATING: 16 pages, black ink on white paper, "THE LIONEL CORPORATION / 48 East 21st Street, New York City". L. Bohn comment.
(A) Original. **5 10 15 20**
(B) Late 1918, Directions for Operating Lionel Electric Toy Trains... 4-9/16" x 5-1/8", 16 stapled pages including covers, shows sliding shoe Standard Gauge motor on page 4 and on page 5 shows four dry cells wired in series and labeled "LIONEL MFG CO. DRY BATTERY". The product is undated but by inference we have dated it late 1918. The inference is based on the prices of the B, T, and K transformers shown on page 13 and priced respectively at $4.25, $6.75, and $8.00. These prices are shown in the February 18, 1919 trade price list (reproduced by Knoecklein). The address shown for shipping goods for repair is "603 to 619 SOUTH 21st ST. IRVINGTON, N.J." The company name

Left: L. Gordon 1917 Type IV Consumer Folder reproduction. *Top center:* 1917 Type I original. *Bottom Center:* 1917 reproduction of Type II. It is possible that the Type II is simply a Type I without the front and rear covers. Reader comments requested. *Right:* Type V Consumer Folder reproduction.

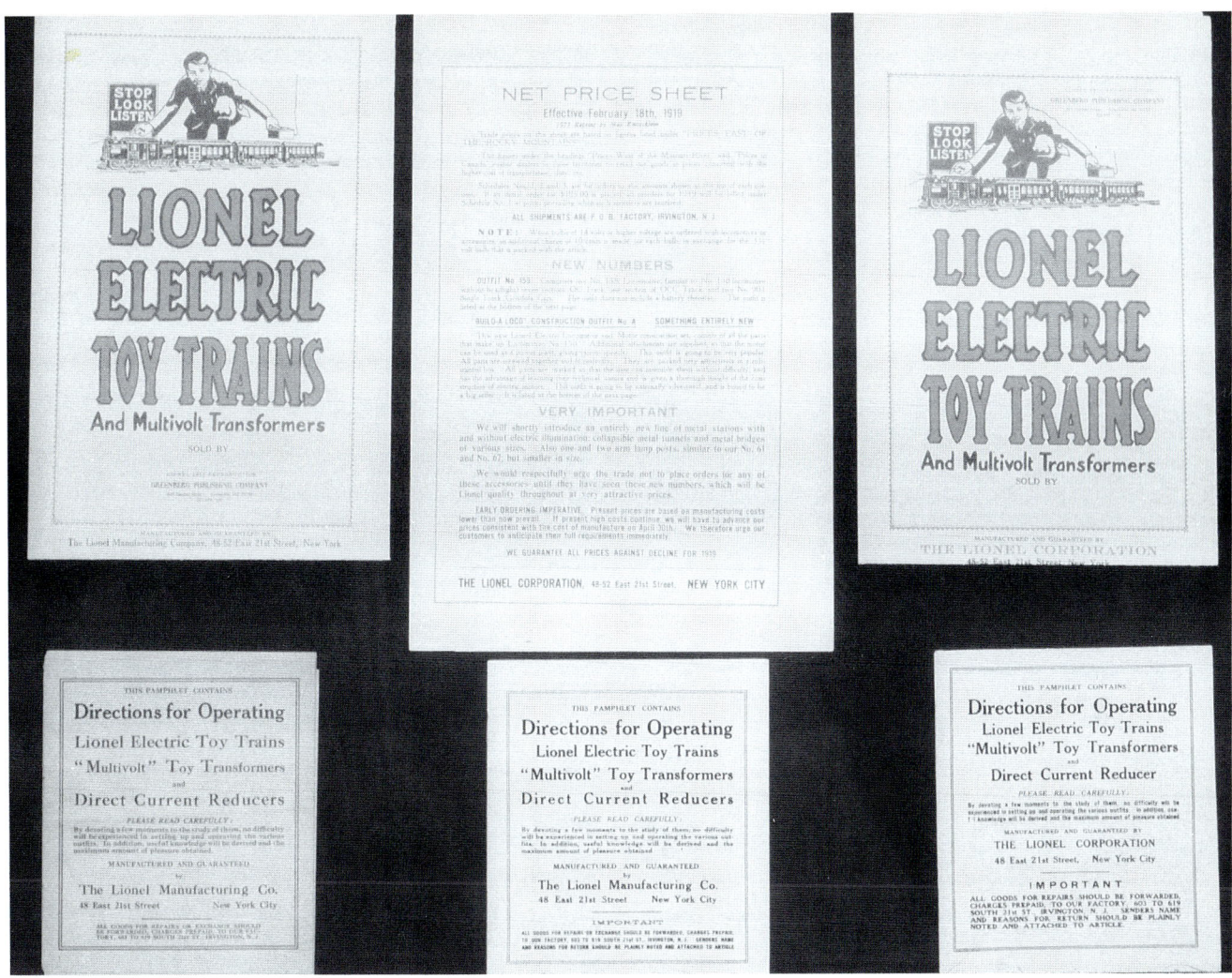

Top row: 1918 Consumer Folder reproduction, 1919 Net Price Sheet reproduction, 1919 Consumer Folder reproduction. *Bottom row:* 1917 Directions for Operating with 20 pages, 1918 Type I Directions for Operating with 16 pages and "B" transformer priced at $4.25, 1918 Type II Directions for Operating and "The Lionel Corporation" rather than "The Lionel Manufacturing Co." as on two other versions.

                                                                              G   VG   EXC NEW   G   VG   EXC NEW

and address is shown as "THE LIONEL CORPORATION 48 East 21st Street, New York City". A. Weaver and L. Bohn Collections.   **NRS**

1919

CONSUMER FOLDER: 6" x 9" vertical format, eight pages on each side, unfolds to 24" x 18", black and red ink on coated stock with red ink used only for headings and borders. Side 1: front cover with Lionel Cowen with boy (Lawrence Cowen) with arms spread wide over 42 set. Cover is outlined with a thin red rule enclosed in a triangular rule. Lettering: "LIONEL / ELECTRIC / TOY TRAINS / And Multivolt Transformers / SOLD BY / MANUFACTURED AND GUARANTEED BY / THE LIONEL CORPORATION / 48-52 East 21st Street, New York". Note change of company name compared to 1918 consumer folder. Side 1 lower center left panel shows Standard Gauge 5 and 51, and 6 and 7 locomotives. (Compare with 1918 Folder.) Side 2 lower right corner panel shows illustration of single tunnel. (Compare with 1917 and 1918 folders.) New listing of Lionel 158 locomotive on side 2, lower left corner. Price of 420 and 421 outfits in Canada is $77.55 and $85.70 respectively.
(A) Original. Weisblum Collection.   **NRS**
(B) Reproduction By Greenberg Publishing Company.
                                                        1   2   3   5

NET PRICE SHEET: 7" x 10-1/2"; "Effective February 18, 1919", four-page folder, black and red ink on coated stock with red ink used only for border rule and headings. Announces new 158 locomotive (outfit 159) and "BUILD-A-LOCO". The 158 was produced, but the "BUILD-A-LOCO" was not produced until 1928. It also announced the discontinuation of the 53.
(A) Original.   **NRS**
(B) 1971 reproduction by Max Knocklein.
                                                  —   —   **1   2**

DIRECTIONS FOR OPERATING LIONEL ELECTRIC TRAINS: 4-9/16" x 5-1/8", 16 pages, shows sliding shoe Standard Gauge motor on page 4 and on page 5 shows four dry cells wired in series and labeled "LIONEL MFG. CO. DRY BATTERY". The product is undated and exactly similar to 1919 Directions (A) except for the prices shown for the B, T, and K transformers on page 13 of $6.25, $9.75, and $11.25 respectively. Another 1919 publication, a black and red folder entitled "LIONEL ELECTRIC TOY TRAINS and Multivolt Transformers", shows "East of Missouri River" prices of $6.35, $9.65, and $11.30 respectively. Since this catalogue evidently was originally published later in 1919 our best hypothesis is that this Directions pamphlet is also 1919, but later in the year than the sheet cited earlier. L. Bohn comment. Original.   **8   16   20   25**

| | G | VG | EXC | NEW |

AN APOLOGY: 11" x 17" page and 6" x 9" apology folder with 16 pages are listed as 1919 in *Lionel Trains: Standard of the World* edited by Donald Fraley. Our reading of both sheet and folder suggests 1920 based on the side 1 text of the 11" x 17" sheet: "A Twenty Year Record / Lionel Trains have been on the market for twenty years..." The 16-page folder cites the sheet as accompanying it on side 1, lower left panel "...there you will also find explained the cause of my not being able to send you the big Lionel Catalog..."
NRS

1920

AN APOLOGY: 11" x 17" page printed both sides in red and black with red used only for headings and borders. Came with 6" x 9" 16-page folder. (See next item.) There is some question about the dating of this item. See 1919 listing for explanation. Side 1 shows 156 passenger set on top and carries the explanation of how a New York printers' strike prevented the printing of the "wonderful big Xmas catalogue". The text is a real piece of advertising bravura which captures the essence of Joshua Lionel Cowen's excellence as a salesman. It is appropriately signed "J. LIONEL COWEN / friend of the boys". The second side of this sheet provides detailed drawings and explanations of the Standard and O Gauge chassis and motors.
(A) Original. **NRS**
(B) Reproduction in black and red on coated stock by Greenberg Publishing Company shows wear and tear of original with one damaged line of type on side 1. — — 1 2
(C) Reproduction in black only on translucent paper by William Vagell, but not marked. The picture reproductions are poor.
— — 1 2

CONSUMER APOLOGY FOLDER: 6" x 9" vertical format, eight pages on each side, unfolds to 24" x 18", black and red ink on coated stock with red ink used only for headings and borders. Side 1: front cover panel: boy (Lawrence Cowen) with arms spread wide over a 42 set. Cover panel is outlined with a thin red rule enclosed in a triangular rule. Lettering: "LIONEL / ELECTRIC / TOY TRAINS / And Multivolt Transformers / SOLD BY / MANUFACTURED AND GUARANTEED BY / THE LIONEL CORPORATION / 48-52 East 21st Street, New York". Side 1, lower left panel contains a message to "BOYS" to see the enclosed 11" x 17" Apology sheet; side 2 lower right center panel shows illustration of single tunnel. The 1920 16-page folder appears identical to the 1919 except for the message to the boys. The likely explanation is that the 1919 type and cuts were rerun when the 1920 printers' strike prevented the new 1920 catalogue from being produced.
(A) Original. **NRS**
(B) Reproduction by Greenberg Publishing Company in black and red ink on coated stock. 1 2 3 5
(C) Reproduction by William Vagell as two 11" x 17" sheets reduced in size from the original. The 11" x 17" sheet side with the front folder

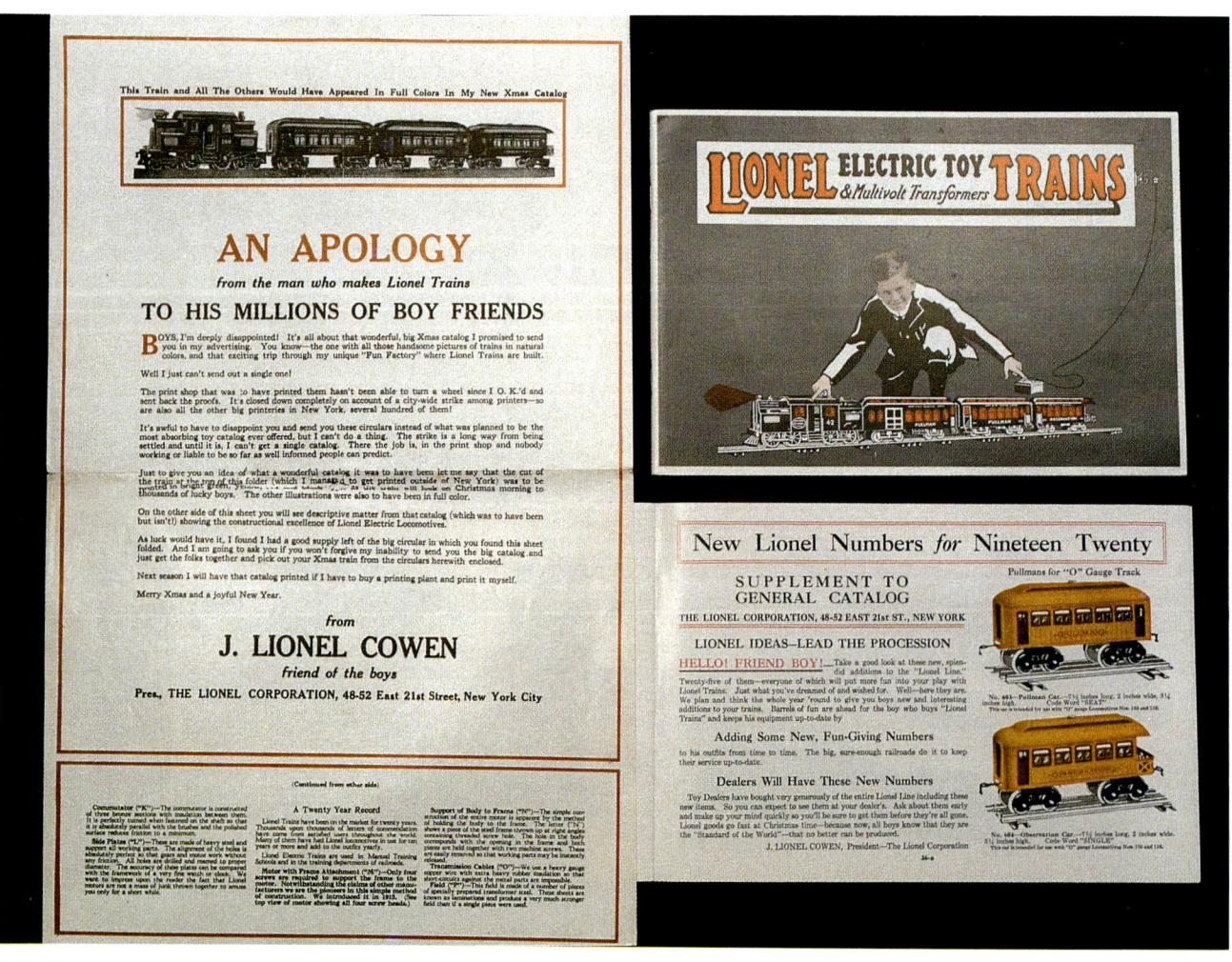

Left: "An Apology" folder. *Top right:* 1920 Consumer Catalogue reproduction. *Bottom right:* 1920 Catalogue interior page.

| | G | VG | EXC | NEW |

panel is printed on red and black; the second side is black only. The second 11" x 17" sheet is printed in black ink only on translucent paper.   1   2   3   4

CONSUMER CATALOGUE: 10" x 6-3/4", 46 pages plus unnumbered front cover. Gray front cover with white rectangular block with red and black lettering: "LIONEL ELECTRIC TOY TRAINS & Multivolt Transformers", boy with arms spread over 42 set. We have only examined the TCA reproduction and do not have access to an original for details of the use of color. It is likely that the inside front cover showing a claimed 120,000 square foot plant was in color. Text page 1 shows in red ink "STANDARD of the WORLD FOR TWENTY YEARS" and Uncle Sam holding a boy and a girl and a rhyme urging "Buy Toys Made in U.S.A." This text was probably in response to the expected resumption of German toy imports with the war's end. Page 2 "...Trip Thru My Factory". Most text pages carry heading "Standard of the World for 20 Years...500,000 Boys Enjoying Them" except for inserts 36a-36h. It is very likely that many if not most sets were in color. Reproduction illustrations on pages 18 and 19 appear to be translations of original color printing into reproduction black and white images. Rear cover shows Nos. 88, 107, and 170. L. Bohn comment.

The TCA reproduction insert pages 36a-36h is headed "New Lionel Numbers for Nineteen Twenty" on page 36a, but pages 36b-36h all have heading "Standard of the World for 21 years...550,000 Boys Enjoying Them". The full-color reproduction insert implies issuance for the 1921 season. It is therefore possible that the 1920 TCA reproduction is actually a 1921 consumer catalogue which was constructed from the strike-delayed 1920 catalogue updated with the 1921 insert. It is also possible that Cowen was hedging his bets and making a late 1920 catalogue also available in 1921. The insert shows the new 603 Pullman and 604 observation in dull orange with brown window inserts and doors. These cars are not shown in the 16-page 6" x 9" 1920 folder. Weisblum comments.
(A) Original.   NRS
(B) 1969 reproduction by TCA. See comments above.
      3   5   8   12

CONSUMER FOLDER: 7" x 5", 32 panels (16 panels on each side), opens to 40-1/2" x 20" sheet, full color. Front cover panel, side 1, black rectangle with white lettering "All Aboard — Boys!" and to left of rectangle there is a boy wearing conductor cap. Beneath the boy is black lettering: "BE AN / ENGINEER / CONDUCTOR / STATION MASTER / TRAIN DISPATCHER / SWITCHMAN, ETC." Below these words is Lionel boy with arms spread over 42 set and words "Watch Fellows!" Upper left panel, side 1, red words: "STANDARD of the WORLD / FOR TWENTY YEARS" and in black "TWENTY YEARS AGO I STARTED TO MAKE LIONEL ELECTRIC TRAINS". And "...over 550,000 sets are in daily use..." New stations and bridges shown on side 1, lower left side. Also new 62 semaphore, new 60 telegraph post, and new 65 railroad warning sign are shown on right center lower panel. On side 2, lower right panel, the same "120,000 Square Feet" factory is shown in color. This is the same image shown in black and white in the 1920 46-page catalogue.
(A) Original. L. Connors Collection.   60   125   175   —
(B) 1976 full-color reproduction by House of Heeg. Very small reproduction notice appears on lower left corner of side 1.
      —   —   10   12

DIRECTIONS BOOKLET: Nearly identical to 1921 Directions, but does not include "A" transformer. L. Bohn Collection.   NRS

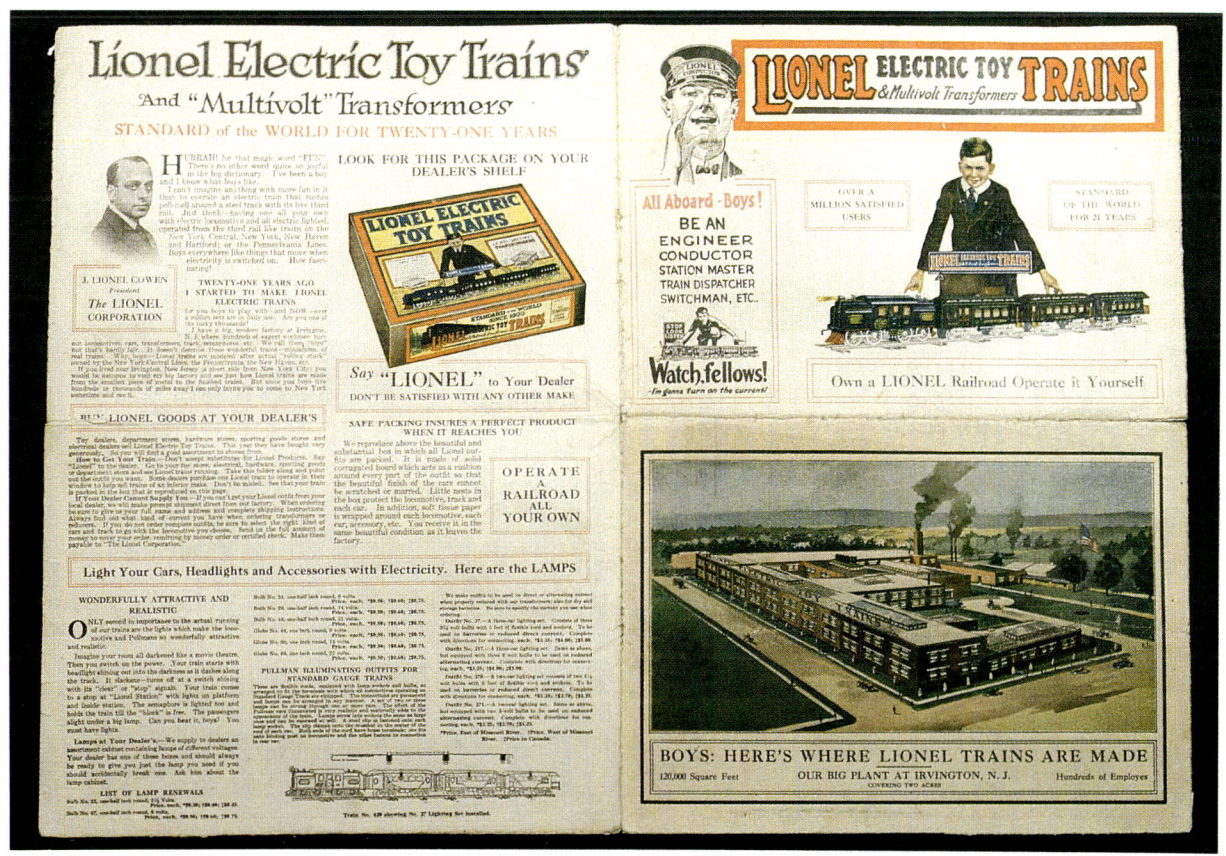

Four pages from one side of the 1921 Consumer Folder. There are 16 pages on each side of this very large folder.

	G	VG	EXC	NEW

1921

CONSUMER FOLDER: 7" x 5", 32 panels (with 16 panels on each side), opens to 40-1/2" x 18" sheet. Front cover panel somewhat similar to 1920 folder, but "LIONEL ELECTRIC TOY TRAINS" inside orange rectangular box replaces "All Aboard — Boys!" Center of panel has boy with arms stretched over 42 set. Upper left panel on side 1 "STANDARD of the WORLD FOR TWENTY-ONE YEARS". Side 1, lower left panel shows new 69 and 069 warning signals. Side 2, lower center left panels shows new 71 telegraph post outfit and 70 semaphore-lamp signal outfit. Original. Weisblum Collection. **NRS**

DIRECTIONS: "This Book Tells / HOW TO GET THE MOST FUN / Out of LIONEL ELECTRIC TOY TRAINS". 5-7/16" x 8-5/8", 12 stapled pages including covers. Page 3: Voltage obtainable from LIONEL "MULTIVOLT" TRANSFORMERS, Types A, B, T, and K. Centerfold shows a chart for "PROPER LAMP RENEWALS" both for battery and house current operation. The outfit numbers shown date the booklet as 1920-1921. However, the rear page shows the new 069 and 69 electric warning signals introduced in 1921. There is a 1921 edition which differs from this one only in type style. L. Bohn comment.
(A) Original. A. Weaver Collection.   8   12   15   20
(B) 1977 reproduction by Greenberg Publishing Company.
—   —   1   2

TRADE PRICE SHEET: February 1, 1921, 7" x 10-9/16".
(A) Original.   **NRS**
(B) 1974 reproduction by Max Knoeckllein.
—   —   1   2

CATALOGUE PROOF SHEET: 9" x 12", single sheet, used by printer in preparing catalogue and other promotional material.
NRS

1922

CONSUMER CATALOGUE: 10" x 6-3/4", 40 pages including covers, gray front cover with white rectangular block containing: "LIONEL ELECTRIC TRAINS..." Boy with arms stretched over 42 set. "Standard of the World for 22 years...Over Two Million Happy Users" as heading for most pages. Lionel claimed 500,000 users by 1920, 550,000 users by 1921, and this copy claims 2,000,000 by 1922. 1921 must have been a great year!
(A) Original. Weisblum Collection.   50   100   150   200
(B) 1974 black and white reproduction by Bruce Greenberg with full-color front cover and "1922" added to the cover. The original catalogue was printed in color. Printed by Bendix Field Engineering, Columbia, Maryland from negatives prepared by Photo Offset Service. Reproduction logo is on lower left corner of inside front cover.
3   4   5   6

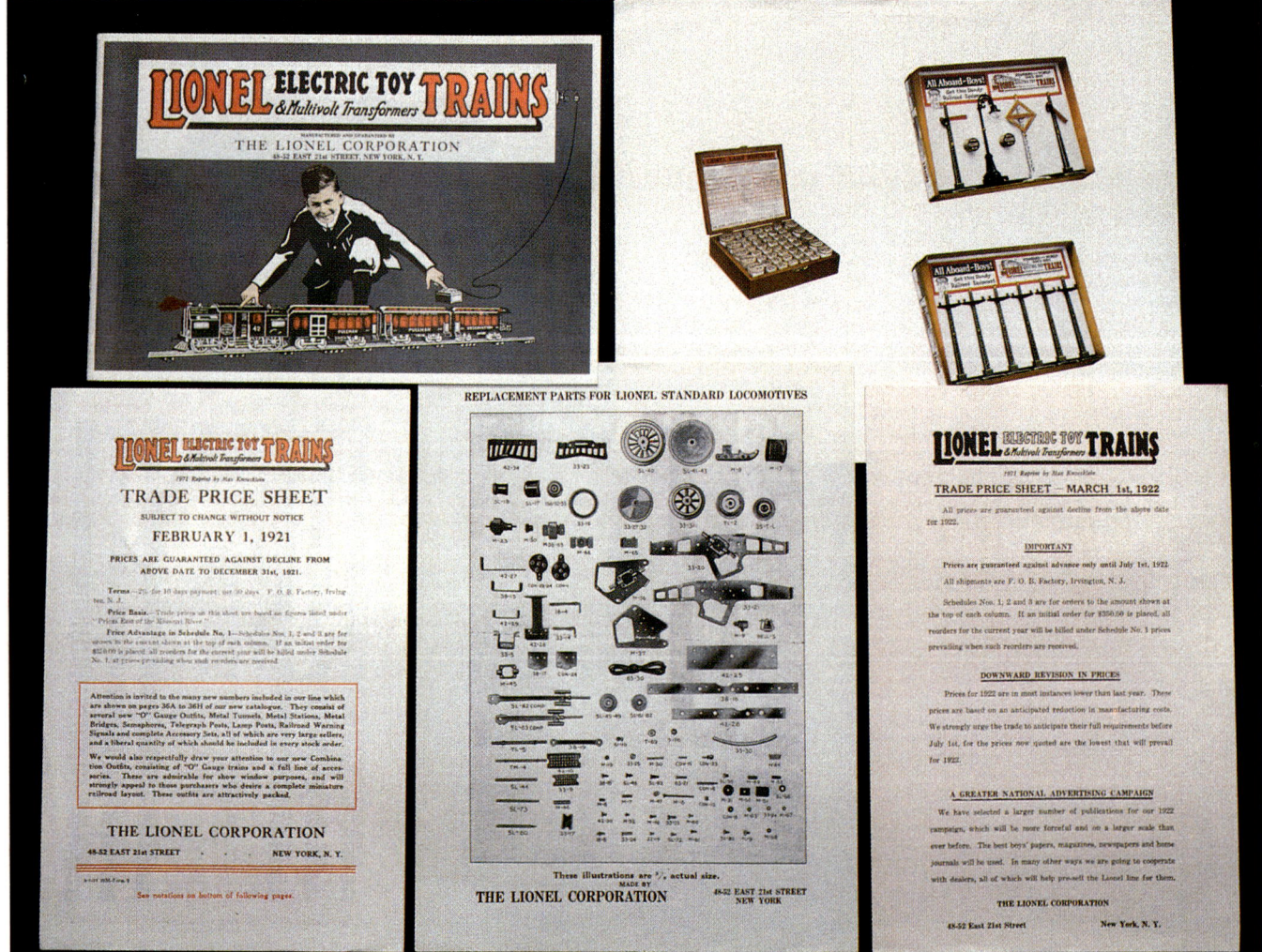

Top row: 1922 Consumer Catalogue; original press proofs of 1921 color images. *Bottom row:* 1921 Trade Price Sheet, 1922 Replacement Parts List for Lionel Standard Locomotives, 1922 Trade Price Sheet.

Top row: 1923 Catalogue centerfold featuring the new 402 set. *Bottom row:* 1921 Directions with instructions for new 069 and 69 electric warning signals, 1923 Consumer Catalogue reproduction, 1923 Directions.

	G	VG	EXC	NEW

(C) 1976 full-color reproduction by House of Heeg. The House of Heeg was the Pittsburgh area partnership of Robert Schnitzer and Frank Heeg. "REPRODUCTION" appears on the lower left corner of all even pages except the rear cover.   —   7   10   15

TRADE PRICE SHEET: "MARCH 1st, 1922", 7" x 10-9/16", four pages, black ink on white paper. Prices were reduced from 1921 reflecting the national business downturn.
(A) Original.   **NRS**
(B) 1974 reproduction by Max Knoecklein.
  —   —   1   2

1923

CONSUMER CATALOGUE: 10" x 7" horizontal format; 48 pages including covers; four-color picture measuring 5" x 5" dominates center of cover; background is light blue-gray; two black-printed drawings of train scenes flank center picture; "Lionel Electric Toy Trains" logo in red and black on bottom. The center picture is highly significant. It shows a man in his easy chair captivated by his son's trains, which appear to cover the whole living room floor and vanish into the parlor. The man's newspaper, symbolic of the "real world," falls carelessly to the floor. This father-son theme, appearing on a catalogue cover for the first time, would be trumpeted ceaselessly in years to come. Contents: pages 4 and 5 show amusing — and phony! — comparisons with "inferior" makes. The "other" passenger car appears to have been blown up by a firecracker. Rear cover has four-color somewhat fanciful picture of gigantic Irvington factory. The 402 and 380 locomotives are shown for the first time. All trains are illustrated in full color.
(A) Original.   50   80   120   150
(B) 1974 black and white reproduction by Bruce C. Greenberg, printed at Bendix Field Engineering, Columbia, Maryland; color front cover only with "1923" added for identification. The cover was printed on heavier stock than inside pages.   3   4   5   6
(C) 1975 full-color reproduction by House of Heeg, Pittsburgh. The remaining inventory and negatives were purchased by Greenberg Publishing Company. The inventory has been sold out; however, the negatives were used in printing *Greenberg's Lionel Catalogues: 1923-1932.*   —   7   10   15

DIRECTIONS: 6-1/4" x 9-1/2", eight-page folder made from single folded sheet, no staples. More outfit numbers added to Lamp Renewal Guide. Rear cover shows transformers A, B, C, K, T, and DC reducers 107 and 170. No date but believed to be 1923. L. Bohn Collection.
  5   8   12   15

1924

CONSUMER CATALOGUE: 10-1/2" x 8" horizontal format, four-color cover, "LIONEL ELECTRIC TOY TRAINS" logo at top. The entire remaining cover has a four-color portrait which is one of the great Lionel masterpieces of advertising art. Two boys, dressed immaculately in coats and ties, mischievously cheer on a speeding

Top row: Front and rear covers of 1924 Consumer Catalogue. *Bottom Row:* 1924 Miniature Consumer Folder and 1923 Trade Price Sheet.

	G	VG	EXC	NEW

passenger express pulled by a 402 electric as it chases the terrified family dog down the track. This triumvirate of boy, dog, and train would reappear (in somewhat less perilous circumstances for the dog).
(A) Original. **25 50 75 100**
(B) 1971-72 black and white reproduction by Bruce C. Greenberg in Galesburg, Illinois. 11" x 8-1/2" pages bound by staples on left edges. **— — 1 2**
(C) 1974 black and white reproduction with full-color cover only, by Bruce C. Greenberg. "1924" added for identification to the front cover. The cover is printed on heavier stock than inside pages. Printed by Bendix Field Engineering, Columbia, Maryland from negatives supplied by Photo Offset Service, Baltimore. **3 4 5 6**
(D) 1975 full-color reproduction by House of Heeg, Pittsburgh. The negatives were purchased by Greenberg Publishing Company and used in printing *Greenberg's Lionel Catalogues: 1923-1932*. **— 7 10 15**

MINIATURE CONSUMER FOLDER: 3-5/16" x 6-1/4", six panels each, printed in orange and black duotones. Front panel: "BOYS — YOUR LIONEL TRAIN IS HERE" with space for store name below. Second side with three panels shows a single image — the 1924 image of the two boys with train and retreating dog PLUS the continuation of the picture story. Note the track to the left of the 78 signal on the left side of the cover. On the folder the track continues with another train being urged on by another boy to a potential collision unless the signal stops the train in time! Weisblum comment. Original with store name: "GOLDENBERG BROTHERS / 717 NORTH GAY STREET / Baltimore, Maryland". Weisblum Collection. **— — 20 30**

DIRECTIONS: 6-14" x 9-1/2", eight-page folder made from single folded sheet, no staples. Same as 1923 version, except Lamp Renewal Guide says "For All O Gauge outfits" instead of numbering them. Page which describes cleaning and lubricating adds "The New Lionel Super Motors". Believed to be 1924. L. Bohn Collection. **5 8 12 15**

1925

CONSUMER CATALOGUE: 10-1/2" x 8" horizontal format, 44 pages including covers, four-color cover on white. Lionel logo at top changed to read "LIONEL ELECTRIC TRAINS / Model Railroad Accessories / Multivolt Transformers"; red and black paint on light brown. Cover painting, signed by Walter Beach Humphrey, has a Norman Rockwell "Americana" quality to it. A well-dressed boy runs a big 402 passenger express while his curious, but fearful, terrier looks on. (At least the dog is not running away!) In the background, both boy and dog sit in the cab of a real NYC S-class electric locomotive. The artist is suggesting that the boy imagines himself in the real locomotive cab while operating his Lionel trains! Complete scenic railroads are offered on pages 42-43. Factory pictures are on rear cover.
(A) Original. Prendergast Collection. **25 50 75 100**
(B) 1971-72 black and white 11" x 8-1/2" reproduction by Bruce Greenberg in Galesburg, Illinois. Bound by a staple along left edge. **— — 1 2**

	G	VG	EXC	NEW

(C) 1974 black and white reproduction with full-color front cover only, by Bruce Greenberg. Printed by Bendix Field Engineering, Columbia, Maryland from negatives made by Photo Offset Service, Baltimore. "1925" added to front cover to aid identification.

| | 3 | 4 | 5 | 6 |

(D) 1975 reproduction in full color by Robert Schnitzer and Frank Heeg (House of Heeg). Negatives were purchased by Greenberg Publishing Company and used in printing *Greenberg's Lionel Catalogues: 1923-1932*.   — 7 10 15

MINIATURE FOLDER: We believe this exists but have not been able to locate one to describe. Reader assistance requested. **NRS**

DIRECTIONS: For the use and care of Lionel electric trains, 5-1/4" x 8", 12 stapled pages, black ink on white paper. No dates appear in the pamphlet. We have dated it based on a diagram on page 7 showing the later Super Motor with small gears on the wheels and the listing on page 12 of 337, 338, 339, and 341 which were first offered in 1925. Service Department is 605 South 21st Street, Irvington, New Jersey. L. Bohn Collection.   5 8 12 15

1926

CONSUMER CATALOGUE: 10-1/2" x 8" horizontal format, 48 pages including covers, four-color cover. Cover painting, again signed by Humphrey, shows a boy operating an elaborate railroad using levers behind a power station. This time, his terrier looks as interested in the trains as he does. The 402 again pulls a fast passenger express, but the freight cars are the new 200-series freights, introduced this year. The 219 crane dominates the spur siding. Notice that crane and dump cars are not shown as produced. Electric locomotive reversing is introduced on page 3. On page 17, a boy is shown using a rheostat control to reverse a locomotive. Electric switches are introduced on page 39. Factory pictures are on a rear cover, and a Newark, New Jersey warehouse address has been added. L. Bohn comment.

(A) Original.   35 60 75 90

(B) 1969 black and white reproduction by Richard Rex. Reproduction logo is on the top left corner of page 2.   2 3 4 6

(C) 1974 black and white reproduction with full-color front cover only, by Bruce Greenberg. Reproduction logo is on the top left corner of page 2. Printed by Bendix Field Engineering, Columbia, Maryland with negatives prepared by Photo Offset Service, Baltimore.

| | 2 | 3 | 4 | 6 |

(D) 1975 full-color reproduction by Robert Schnitzer and Frank Heeg (House of Heeg). The negatives were purchased by Greenberg Publishing Company and used in printing *Greenberg's Lionel Catalogues: 1923-1932*.   — 7 10 15

MINIATURE FOLDER: Unfolded size, 21" x 5-3/4", orange and black duotone. Folds to 5-3/4" x 3" and shows a miniature image of 1926 catalogue front cover. A white block on the front cover was provided for the store name. Features new 437 tower, 436 and 435 power stations, as well as numerous sets. The folder offered the larger

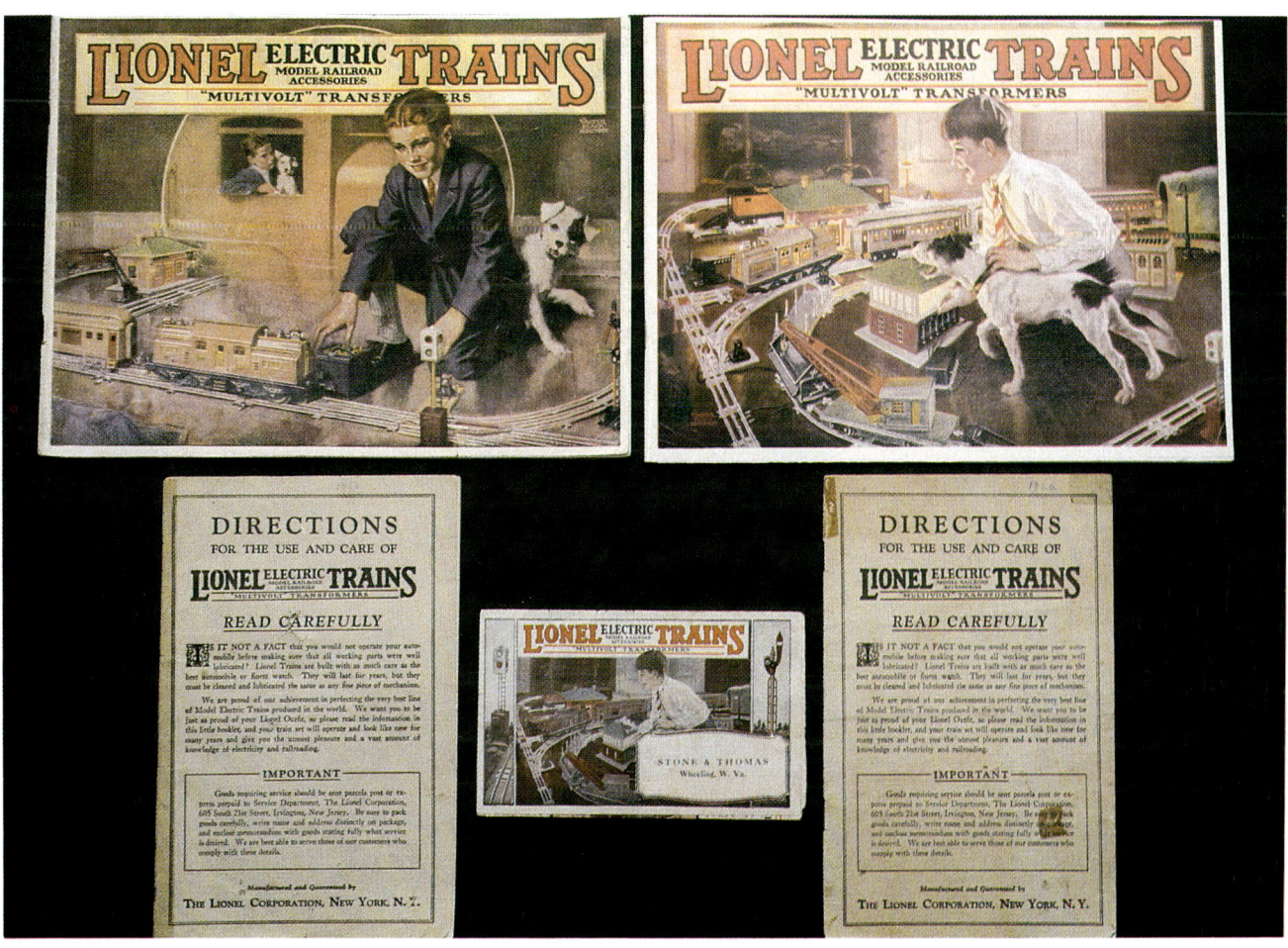

Top row: **1925 Consumer Catalogue with train image in background and 1926 Consumer Catalogue.** *Bottom row:* **1925 Directions, 1926 Miniature Folder and 1926 Directions.**

	G	VG	EXC	NEW

consumer catalogue for 10 cents. Weisblum comment. Original. Weisblum Collection. **10 15 25 30**

DIRECTIONS: 5-1/4" x 8", for the use and care of Lionel trains, 12 stapled pages, black ink on white paper. Dating based on page 12 parts list which includes Standard Gauge 211, 712, 213, 214, 215, 216, 217, 218, 219, 428, 429, and 430 cars. It also includes O Gauge 811, 812, 813, 814, 815, and 817 cars. These were all first issued in 1916. Identical to 1927 Directions, but it does not include 816 (1927), and no reference on page 11 to Nos. 210 and 222 Standard Gauge switches. L. Bohn comment. Original. Weisblum Collection.
5 8 12 15

POSTAL CARD: 6-3/4" x 3-1/2" printed two sides in color; address side illustrates 1926 catalogue; reverse side illustrates Type B transformer. R. Otten Collection. **— — 30 —**

1927

CONSUMER CATALOGUE: 11-1/2" x 8-1/2" format, 46 pages including covers, four-color cover. Cover has Lionel rectangular logo in red and black on light blue-gray background. Entire cover dominated by ballast-eye view portrait of new dual-motored 408E in mojave color. Also introduced are 500 freight series for Standard Gauge and 800 and 810 series O Gauge freights. Magnificent center fold-out shows 409E "Lionel Limited" passenger set: 408E locomotive pulls 418, 419, 431, and 490 passenger cars. Train is portrayed in brown against a dramatic black background. The centerfold ink coverage was only possible because of development in printing technology. The back cover shows two factory complexes.
(A) Original. **35 50 75 90**
(B) 1974 black and white reproduction with full-color front cover, by Bruce C. Greenberg. "1927" added to the cover for identification. Cover stock is heavier than inside pages. Reproduction logo on page 2 center bottom. 600 copies printed by Bendix Field Engineering, Columbia, Maryland from negatives made by Photo Offset Service, Baltimore. **2 3 4 6**
(C) 1975 full-color reproduction by House of Heeg. The negatives were purchased by Greenberg Publishing Company and used in printing *Greenberg's Lionel Catalogues: 1923-1932*.
4 8 12 15

MINIATURE FOLDER: Unfolded size 21" x 5-3/4", orange and green duotone. Folds to 5-3/4" x 3-1/2". Side 1 has front panel with miniature version of 1927 consumer catalogue 408 image with 78 signal and 82 semaphore. Panel provides block for store name and address. Other panels show new 83 traffic blinker and 87 crossing signal and other accessories as well as eight sets.
(A) Original with "STONE & THOMAS / Wheeling, W.Va." as listed store. **NRS**

Top row: 1927 Consumer Catalogue and 1927 Consumer Catalogue with discontinued items label. *Bottom left:* 1927 Directions with small "Lionel Corporation" lettering. *Bottom center:* 1927 Miniature Folder. *Bottom right:* 1927 Directions with large "Lionel Corporation" lettering.

| | G | VG | EXC | NEW |

(B) 1976 reproduction by House of Heeg. This item is still available from Greenberg Publishing Company or Iron Horse Productions.
— — 1 2

DIRECTIONS: 5-1/8" x 8", 12 pages, for the use and care of Lionel electric trains, "IS IT NOT A FACT..." with very elaborate "I", black ink on white paper. Dating based on page 12 list which is similar to that for 1926 Directions and to page 11 Lamp Renewal chart. The chart lists the following new accessories which were introduced in 1927: 82, 84, 83, 87, and 438. We have therefore dated the booklet as 1927 early. Original. Weisblum Collection.
— — 1 2

DIRECTIONS: 5-1/4" x 8", for the use and care of Lionel trains, 12 stapled pages identical to 1926 but page 11 adds 210, 222 Standard Gauge switches; 80, 82, 84, 08C, 082, and 084 semaphores; 83 and 87 signals; and 438 tower. 1927 early. L. Bohn Collection. **NRS**

DIRECTIONS: For operating Lionel O Gauge electrically-controlled locomotives, one page describes operation of early E locomotives, has picture of transformer-rheostat-track wiring at left, and diagrams of hand-reverse and E-unit connection levers at right. 1927 early. L. Bohn Collection. **NRS**

DIRECTIONS: 5-1/4" x 8", 16 stapled pages. Page 6 has first note of electrically-controlled locomotives, describes pendulum or "flip-top" reverse. Also contains first instructions for 80/080, 78/078, 82/082, 83, and 87 signals. 1927 late. L. Bohn Collection. **NRS**

POSTAL CARD: 6-3/4" x 3-1/2" printed two sides, red and black on white card stock, requesting Lionel to "kindly send me free of all cost the Lionel catalog in colors, showing the full line of wonderful automatic accessories." Illustrates 1927 consumer catalogue. A. Rubin Collection.
— — — 30

1928

CONSUMER CATALOGUE: 11" x 8-1/2" horizontal format, 46 pages including covers, four-color cover. Cover has Lionel rectangular logo in red and black type on cream background edged in orange. Catalogue is dated "1928" in right lower side of rectangle. Cover painting signed by Fernando E. Ciavatti shows two boys using a peacock and red 219 crane to load lumber onto a 211 flatcar. Page 13 explains new "Bild-A-Loco" outfits Nos. 4, 9E, and 381E. The "Lionel Limited" 408E-powered fold-out is repeated. Page 42 introduces the 300 "Hell Gate" bridge. Page 40 shows the new 200 turntable. Rear cover introduces the 840 power station, probably Lionel's most magnificent accessory.

(A) Original. 35 50 75 90
(B) 1974 black and white reproduction with full-color front cover by Bruce Greenberg. Cover stock is heavier than inside pages.

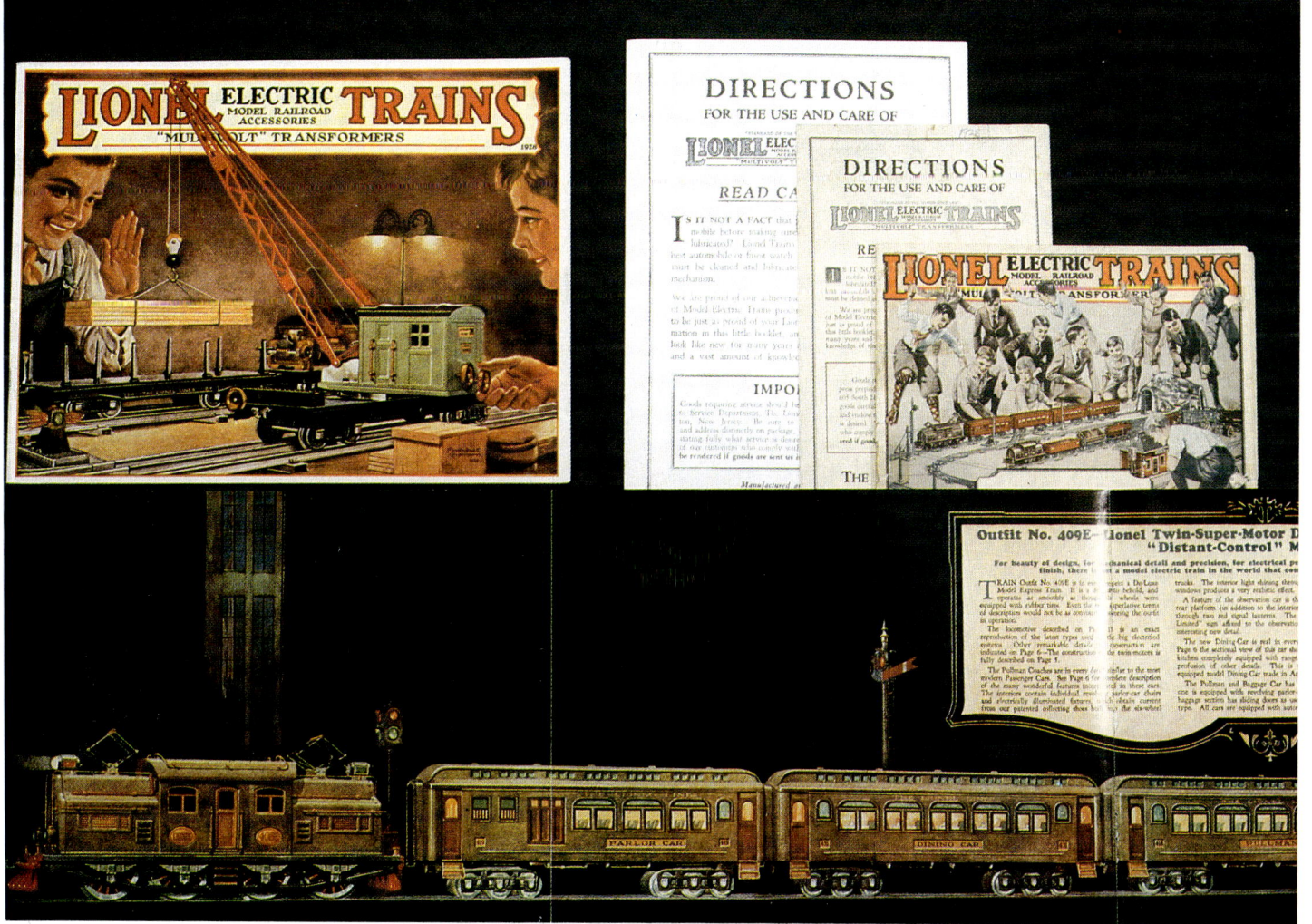

Top row: 1928 Consumer Catalogue, two 1928 Directions booklets, 1928 Miniature Folder with boys and girl on cover. *Bottom row:* A portion of the magnificent centerfold from the 1928 Consumer Catalogue.

| | G | VG | EXC | NEW |

Reproduction logo is on page 2, lower right corner. 600 copies printed by Bendix Field Engineering, Columbia, Maryland from negatives made by Photo Offset Service, Baltimore. **1 3 5 6**
(C) 1975 full-color reproduction by Robert E. Schnitzer and Frank E. Heeg. The negatives were purchased by Greenberg Publishing Company and used in printing *Greenberg's Lionel Catalogues: 1923-1932*. **4 8 12 15**

MINIATURE FOLDER: 7-7/8" x 5-5/8", orange and green duotone, 32 pages. This catalogue has a different format from those used in 1924-27. It also differs from its predecessors in that its front cover shows 12 boys and one girl rather than reproducing a miniature version of the consumer catalogue front cover. Pages 2 and 3 of the miniature catalogue are slightly modified reductions of pages 2 and 3 of the consumer catalogue. Original. **15 30 25 30**

DIRECTIONS FOR THE USE AND CARE OF LIONEL ELECTRIC TRAINS, TYPE I: 7" x 10-1/4", 16 stapled pages, black ink on white paper; dating based on page 12, Price List of Parts, 516 (1928) and 816 (1927) are listed for the first time. 437 (1926) is added to the Lamp Chart on page 15. Bottom of page 1: "Manufactured and Guaranteed by / THE LIONEL CORPORATION / 15-17-19 EAST 26th STREET NEW YORK". 1927 Directions do not have street address at the bottom of the page.
(A) Original. **NRS**
(B) T.T.O.S. reprint; rubber-stamped "A T.T.O.S. / REPRINT" on rear cover. **— — 1 2**

DIRECTIONS FOR THE USE AND CARE OF LIONEL ELECTRIC TRAINS, TYPE II: 5-1/4" x 8", 16 stapled pages, black ink on white paper; similar to Type I but smaller in size with changes in text. Page 1: "IS IT NOT A FACT" with "I" in white inside a block with fine black lines. Inside "IMPORTANT" block address is "Service Department, The Lionel Corporation, 605 South 21st Street, Irvington, New Jersey". Adds 437 signal tower to Lamp Replacement. Type I has "Sager Place" address. Original. L. Bohn Collection. **NRS**

DIRECTIONS FOR THE USE AND CARE OF LIONEL ELECTRIC TRAINS, TYPE III: 5-1/4" X 8-1/8". Identical to Type II, but does not include 437 signal tower on Lamp Replacement chart. Came in 1928 boxed set. Original. C. Rohlfing Collection. **NRS**

OIL INSTRUCTIONS: 5-1/2" x 6-1/2", four-page folder. First page is printed in red and black and has a picture of a 253 and three passenger cars. Top line in red says "ALL ARE OILED WITH '3 IN 1'". Below this is the "LIONEL ELECTRIC TOY TRAINS" logo, followed by "PROPER LUBRICATION / INSURES PERFECT OPERATION / AND LENGTHENS THE LIFE OF / YOUR LIONEL TRAIN". The picture is below this. Below the picture is the admonition to "BE SURE / TO READ AND FOLLOW / DIRECTIONS", followed in red by "WE USE AND RECOMMEND YOUR USING 3-IN-1 OIL". All printing is in black except the two lines mentioning "3 in 1". Pages 2 and 3 are a clock showing 12 uses for "3 in 1" with a bottle in the middle, and a calendar showing 12 uses for "3 in 1". Page 4 says in fancy red script "Oilright / Oilright". Came in 1928 boxed set.
(A) As described above. C. Rohlfing and A. Rubin Collections. **NRS**
(B) Page with Lionel illustration begins with heading "Very Important". L. Connors Collection. **NRS**

POSTAL CARD: 6-3/4" x 3-1/2" printed two sides in blue on cream stock, illustrates the 1928 catalogue; card is mailed to request consumer catalogue. W. Mekalian Collection. **NRS**

1929

CONSUMER CATALOGUE: 11-1/2" x 8-1/2" format, 46 pages including covers, four-color cover edged in yellow on white. Cover painting shows speeding steam and electric trains hurtling toward viewer against a dark blue background. A smiling boy towers over them from behind. Page 8 introduces several new O Gauge electric locomotives. Page 9 shows new 267 passenger outfit, and page 17 shows its 349 Standard Gauge counterpart. Pages 18 and 19 show the 390 steam engine and sets pulled by it. Center fold-out now shows two classic sets: the 409E "deluxe express" pulled by a 408E electric locomotive and the new 411E "Transcontinental Limited", which has the new 412, 413, 414, and 416 "State" passenger cars pulled by a 381E electric locomotive. Page 36 shows the 128 station and its matching 129 terrace.
(A) Original. Weisblum Collection. **40 65 90 125**
(B) 1968 black and white reproduction with full-color front cover by Lester T. Gordon. **1 3 4 6**
(C) 1973 full-color reproduction by Max Knoecklein. Still available from M. Knoecklein. **5 10 15 20**
(D) The catalogue is also reprinted in full color in *Greenberg's Lionel Catalogues: 1923-1932*.

MINIATURE CATALOGUE: 7-5/8" x 5-3/4", 32 pages, red and blue duotone. This catalogue has an unusual page layout being composed of sheets of paper 3-1/2" x 5-3/4". Many of the Miniature catalogue pages are miniature versions of the consumer catalogue. Original. Weisblum Collection. **7 12 18 25**

DIRECTIONS FOR THE USE AND CARE OF LIONEL TRAINS: 6" x 9", 16 stapled pages, black ink on white paper, page 14 contains first reference to 402E and 408E. L. Bohn Collection. **3 5 7 10**

PROMOTIONAL FLYER: 8-1/2" x 11", five-page flyer with cover letter from "Uncle Don, Chief Engineer, Lionel Engineer's Club", acknowledging request for membership details. Inside pages, in red and black, are rules of club membership, a description of what a member receives, and an announcement of a layout contest with the prizes being a share of $1,000 in gold! Membership benefits include a membership badge, an engraved certificate, plans for Lionel model railroads, and a *Lionel Magazine for Boys*, the latter proposed "to be issued next year." A. Rubin Collection. **NRS**

MEMBERSHIP CERTIFICATE: Issued 1929-30 to members of Uncle Don's Lionel Engineer's Club. Center of 8-1/2" x 11" certificate features frontal portrait of Uncle Don, who is described as the Chief Engineer of the Club. A. Stewart Collection. **— — 50 75**

1930

CONSUMER CATALOGUE: 11-1/2" x 8-1/2" horizontal format, 48 pages including covers, four-color front cover. Cover is an excellent example of the "art deco" motif of 1930s popular art; it is signed by Ciavatti and shows a highly stylized "Lionel Electric Trains / Model Railroad Accessories" in red and black on top of cover with no rectangle or borders. Cover painting shows busy yard scene with pink-toned Hell Gate bridge and power station in background. Two electric passenger trains head towards viewer; one is headed by an orange-tinted 381 while a smoking steam engine awaits clearance on siding. Sky and clouds are highly abstracted in dark blue and white. A village is portrayed at the left. All pages of this catalogue have a half-inch red lower border. Page 9 introduces the 260E O Gauge steam locomotive. Many sets are now hauled by steam locomotives rather than electrics. Page 26 introduces the Standard Gauge "Blue Comet" set. Pages 30-31 introduce new accessories and the 810 O Gauge crane car. Back cover introduces Lionel electric stove for girls.
(A) Original. **35 50 80 100**
(B) 1974 black and white reproduction with full-color front cover by Bruce C. Greenberg. **1 3 4 6**
(C) 1974 full-color reproduction by Iron Horse Productions. IHP notice on lower rear cover and on page 2. **4 8 12 15**

MINIATURE FOLDER: Folded size 3-1/2" x 6-1/8", opens to 14" x 12-1/4", full-color. Front panel shows 390 Blue Comet locomotive with

Top left: 1929 Consumer Catalogue. *Top right:* Pages 24 and 25 from 1929 Miniature Catalogue with 1929 Miniature Catalogue cover on top. *Bottom left:* Promotional Flyer for Lionel Engineer's Club. *Bottom right:* 1929 Directions.

	G	VG	EXC	NEW

green flags and green pilot marker lamps. Rear panel shows electric range.
(A) Original. 10 15 25 30
(B) T.T.O.S. reproduction. Marked "A GENUINE / T.T.O.S. / REPRINT" on front panel. 1 2 3 4

WINNER LINES FOLDER: 11-1/2" x 8-1/2"; four pages, plain gray cover with black "art deco" lettering; "WINNER TOY / CORPORATION" separated by heavy black line at upper left; text on cover reads "ANNOUNCING / A COMPLETE ELECTRIC TRAIN / AND TRANSFORMER / TO RETAIL AT / $3.95". Winner passenger train with 1000 electric locomotive shown inside.
  10 17 25 35

WINNER DEALER BROCHURE: 11-1/2" x 17". Eight panels, red and blue ink on white paper. Illustrated in accompanying plate. **NRS**

MINIATURE FOLDER: Front panel is 3-7/16" x 6-1/4"; folder opens to 13-7/8" x 12-3/8"; full-color, front panel shows 390E.
(A) Original. 15 20 25 30
(B) Reproduction by T.T.O.S. 1 2 3 4
(C) Crude reproduction. Front cover says "DAVEGA / 125 West 125th St." C. Weber Collection. **NRS**

DIRECTIONS, FOR THE USE AND CARE OF LIONEL TRAINS: 6" x 9", 16 stapled pages, black ink on white paper, adds 91 circuit breaker. L. Bohn Collection. 3 5 7 10

TRADE PRICE LIST AND DEALER HELP PORTFOLIO: Effective February 1930, measures 8-1/2" x 11-1/4", printed in black and red on white paper, 12 unnumbered pages also includes dealer ad cuts and displays available for purchase. A. Rubin Collection. **NRS**

POSTAL CARD: 6-3/4" x 3-1/2" in blue on cream card stock, illustrates the 1930 catalogue, and card is to be mailed as request for the consumer catalogue. R. Otten Collection.
  — — 15 25

MARKETING SURVEY FORM: Folded 5" x 7-3/8" format, four pages with cover stating "Free! How to get a wonderful, new railroading book". The questionnaire even asks "Your Dad's Name" and "What Kind of Work Does He Do?" R. Otten Collection. **NRS**

1931

CONSUMER CATALOGUE: 11-1/2" x 8-1/2" horizontal format, 52 pages including covers, four-color front cover on white. Radical change in cover layout; top of cover shows white and black sans-serif lettering within red rectangle: "LIONEL ELECTRIC TRAINS / The Trains That Railroad Men Buy For Their Boys". Cover shows engineer holding 400E locomotive for two boys dressed in white suits (looking as if they have just stepped out of a boys' choir). In the background is the gigantic valve gear and one driver of a New York Central 4-6-4 Hudson locomotive. At lower right is a red rectangle containing the black-printed legend "Just Like Mine" Says Bob Butterfield, Engineer of the 20th Century Limited. (See Page 3)". The first two pages contain sepia photos and testimonials from railroad men. Contents introduce several steam locomotives, including the

| | G | VG | EXC | NEW |

huge 400E. There is a noticeable increase in the appeal to realism in this catalogue. Page 46 introduces the non-derailing 222 and 012 remote-control switches. Page 48 shows new "silent track bed." Rear cover introduces issues of *Lionel Magazine*, published every other month.

(A) Original.   35   50   80   100
(B) 1973 black and white reproduction with color front cover by Bruce C. Greenberg. No reproduction markings.   1   3   4   6
(C) 1975 full-color reproduction by Iron Horse Productions. Marked as reproductions in gutter between pages.   4   8   12   15

IT'S FUN TO BUILD YOUR OWN RAILROAD: 8-7/16" x 11", four pages, black and light orange ink on white paper, light orange ink used only for the border. Shows 9" x 16" Standard Gauge and 5-1/2" x 6" O Gauge railroad. Shows new 94 high tension tower, new 99 automatic train control (three-light head), and lists new 223 Standard non-derailing switches. Also shows many other accessory items. Weisblum comment. Weisblum Collection.
—   —   10   15

WINNER SALES FOLDER: 8-1/2" x 11-1/8" but opens to 14-1/4". Four pages, black ink on white paper. Gives firm name and address as "WINNER TOY CORPORATION / 15 EAST 26th STREET / NEW YORK CITY", but does not indicate that Winner has any relation with Lionel. Shows sets 1000, 1001, 1002, and 1003. Weisblum Collection.
10   15   25   35

MINIATURE FOLDER: Folded size, 2-13/16" x 5-3/4", unfolded 17-1/2" x 11-1/2", red and yellow front panel, "Oh Boy! HAVE THE FUN OF YOUR LIFE with LIONEL..." Shows new 396E Blue Comet set with 400E locomotive, new silent track bed, and the new *Lionel Magazine*. A. Rubin and Weisblum Collections.
15   20   25   30

INSTRUCTION BOOKLET: 6" x 9", 16 stapled pages, for the use and care of Lionel, black ink on white paper. First use of "INSTRUCTION BOOKLET" in title, 92 floodlight shown on page 10, "BILD-A-LOCO" motor on page 11. Quantity and date code, bottom of page 15 "8-3-110M". *Lionel Magazine* advertised on rear cover. Weisblum and Bohn Collections.
2   4   6   8

DEALER SALES LETTERS: Letters typed (printed) on Lionel red and black letterhead outlining the availability of three new train outfits and the issuance of the 1931 advance catalogue. It is not known if these letters were sent under the same cover, but the letter identified by "Subject: 1931 Advance Catalog" did refer to an enclosure of a Winner Trains circular. A. Rubin Collection.   NRS

POSTAL CARD: 6-3/4" x 3-1/2", blue ink on white card stock, illustrates the 1931 Consumer Catalogue; card is used to request the consumer catalogue.
4   8   12   15

1932

CONSUMER CATALOGUE: 11-1/2" x 8-1/2" format; 52 pages including covers, four-color front cover has same logo as 1931. Blue area with red border contains black print: "A Boy's Dream Come True". Red circle contains "$.10 / A / COPY". Page 3 carries heading: "Take Your Dad Into Partnership — Make Him Your Pal". The

Top left: 1930 Consumer Catalogue. *Top right:* Circa 1931 Winner dealer brochure. *Bottom left:* 1930 Miniature Folder reproduction.

Top center: Centerfold of 1931 Consumer Catalogue. *Top right:* Postcard to request Consumer Catalogue. *Bottom left:* 1931 Miniature Folder. *Bottom center:* 1931 Instruction Booklet, 1931 Consumer Catalogue. *Bottom right:* 1931 Winner Sales Folder.

                              G   VG EXC NEW

"Pennsylvania Limited," pulled by a 392E steam locomotive, is introduced on page 23. It is outdone by the "20th Century Limited" shown on page 25. On page 24, the Milwaukee "Olympian" is introduced. Many new signaling accessories are introduced on pages 30-31. Miniature railroad figures appear for the first time on page 35. On page 47, a new 444 roundhouse and a 441 weighing scale are introduced. The Lionel 455 electric range now appears on page 51, with the line, "There's lots of fun in playing housewife". The rear cover is devoted to membership in the Lionel Engineer's Club.
TYPE I: As described above.
(A) Original.   **25   40   55   70**
(B) 1975 full-color reproduction by Greenberg Publishing Company, date added to lower right-hand block by publisher.
                                       4   8   12   15

TYPE II: As above, but with four-page Winner insert included.
(A) Original. Graves Collection.   **35   55   80 110**
(B) 1974 black and white reproduction with full-color front cover on heavy stock by Bruce Greenberg.   **2   3   4   6**

EXECUTIVE CATALOGUE: Same as Type II consumer catalogue as described above, but blue-green card stock over inscribed "Executive Edition — The Lionel Catalog". Also includes four-page Winner insert. A. Rubin Collection.   —   —   — **225**
COMPACT CATALOGUE: 8-1/4" x 10-7/8", vertical format, eight pages. Black and white with orange border. C. Weber comment.
(A) Original.   **NRS**

                              G   VG EXC NEW

(B) 1974 reproduction by Ladd Publications. C. Weber Collection.
                                            —   —   —   **7**

WINNER CONSUMER FOLDER: 11-1/2" x 8-1/2"; four pages, front cover is black and orange on gray background. Legend: "And Now! A Real Electric Train / For LITTLE BROTHER". Boy plays with Winner train against half-circle orange background.
(A) Original.   **10   15   25   35**
(B) 1974 black and white reproduction by Greenberg Publishing Company.   —   —   1   2
(C) Orange and black reproduction by Les Gordon.
                                            —   —   1   2

INSTRUCTION BOOKLET: 5-1/2" by 8-14" format, 16 stapled pages, black ink on white paper. This is the last booklet of its kind issued with the cover printed on the same paper as the inner pages. Beginning in 1933, the covers of such booklets were of heavier stock and usually colored. "Interesting Track Layouts" shown on pages 12-13 and a long parts list on pages 14-15. Rear cover announces "NOW 3 Service Stations to give you quicker and better service". The 1932 Ives instruction booklet closely resembles this one except for the large "IVES" on its cover. L. Bohn and M. Ocilka comments.
(A) Original. L. Bohn Collection.   **2   4   7   10**
(B) Reproduction. No identification. The first page has the following erroneous inscription: "REPRINT / This is an exact photographic reproduction / of the instruction booklet given with Lionel / equipment between the years 1927 to 1933". C. Weber Collection.   **NRS**

| | G | VG | EXC | NEW |

MINIATURE FOLDER: Original size and colors not known, reader assistance requested, shows closeup of boy in locomotive cab as illustrated on consumer catalgoue. **NRS**

1933

CONSUMER CATALOGUE: 11-1/4" x 8-3/8" format; 52 pages including covers, four-color front cover shows boy atop pedestrian bridge waving to engineer in a Pennsylvania K-4s Pacific steam locomotive 3759. Same logo as 1931 against red rectangle; zig-zag line lightning bolt added to emphasize "electric". Page 1 advertises Lionel radio program "True Railroad Adventures". Page 3 introduces the "Chugger" steam locomotive sound. Pages 1 to 10 done in monotone green on white paper, pages 11-42 are in color, and pages 43-50 are in monotone. Pages 12-15 introduce the inexpensive Lionel-Ives mechanized and electric trains. Lionel downplays this tremendously significant development. Rear cover shows new Lionel speedboat.

TYPE I: As described above.   35   50   70   85

TYPE II: Same as Type I, but National Recovery Act price increase information inserted in red-bordered block on page 11 and "Pennsylvania Limited" lettering and Keystone emblem added to page 24.
(A) Original. **NRS**
(B) 1971 xerographic reproduction by Bruce C. Greenberg, printed in Galesburg, Illinois at the Knox College Printing shop from an original lent by Rev. Robert Prendergast. Press run of 100 copies. Does not have a reproduction logo. — — 1 2
(C) 1974 black and white reproduction by Bruce C. Greenberg. Printed in Columbia, Maryland by Bendix Field Engineering. Press run of 600. — — 3 6
(D) 1975 full-color reproduction by Greenberg Publishing Company. Printed by Barton and Cotton, Baltimore, Maryland. Reproduction logo on page 2 and at the bottom of some pages. Press run of 3000. The color separations were used in 1982 in producing *Greenberg's Lionel Catalogues: 1933-1942*. — — 1 2

CONSUMER EXPORT CATALOGUE: 8-7/8" x 6" fully illustrated, Spanish edition "Trenes Electricos Lionel", 16 unnumbered pages, green on white.
(A) Original. **NRS**
(B) 1970, reprint by Max Knoecklein. — — — 10

DEALER PROMOTIONAL CATALOGUE: 9" x 12", "Lionel Revolutionizes the Toy Train Industry", includes set and product descriptions, dealer displays, advertising mat illustrations, and descriptions of Lionel's advertising campaign. The inside cover prominently announces "Lionel Absorbs Ives Corporation" and proudly boasts she is now the oldest and foremost manufacturer of high quality mechanical trains. Catalogue is printed in black ink on an inexpensive buff paper, and came with an introductory letter on Lionel

Top left: Mailing envelope for 1932 Consumer Catalogue. *Top center:* 1932 Compact Catalogue reproduction in black and orange. *Top right:* 1932 Instruction Booklet. *Bottom left:* 1932 Winner Consumer Folder, 11-1/2" wide x 8-1/2" high, which came inserted in the 1932 Consumer Catalogue. It may also have been distributed independently. *Bottom center:* 1932 Consumer Catalogue reproduction with date added. *Bottom right:* Photocopy of 1932 Miniature Folder.

Prewar Paper: 1901-1944 • 37

"1933-34 Dealer Dealer Promotional Catalogue.

                                                    G   VG   EXC NEW

letterhead, dated June 23, 1933 and signed by A. Raphael. R. Otten Collection.   **NRS**

INSTRUCTION BOOKLET: 6-1/16" x 9-1/16", titled "How to Build a Model Railroad", vertical format, orange wraparound cover with blue lettering, 32 white pages with black lettering. Page 23 has first instructions for the chugger. Back cover has "1B-100-10-33". C. Weber and M. Ocilka Collections.

(A) As described above.   **5   10   15   20**
(B) Correction insert on page 23, "The Chugger".
                                                      5   10   15   20

PRICE LIST: 8-1/2" x 11", "Prices, Code Words, Shipping Weights", four-page brochure, black and white; effective October 2, 1933. I. D. Smith Collection.   **NRS**

REPLACEMENT PARTS: "FOR LIONEL ELECTRIC TRAINS AND ACCESSORRIES", 12-7/16" x 9-1/4", ten pages green ink on cream stock.   **NRS**

1934

CONSUMER CATALOGUE: Smaller 11-1/2" x 7-1/2" format, 36 pages including covers. Same logo as 1931 in red rectangle; black and white lettering at top of page. Four-color cover shows father and son looking at Union Pacific M-10000 and steam freight passing through signal bridge against a navy blue background. Pages 8 and 9 show the renamed Ives electric sets as "Lionel Jr." Page 13 introduces the streamlined M-10000 and O72 Model Maker's track. Mechanical trains and boats are described on pages 34-35. Back cover gives details of the *Lionel Magazine* and the Lionel Engineer's Club.
TYPE I: As described above.

Top left: "IT'S FUN TO BUILD ...". *Top center:* 1933 Consumer Catalogue. *Top right:* Circa 1933 Replacement Parts booklet. *Bottom left:* Circa 1930 Marketing Survey form. *Bottom center:* 1930s (undated) Replacement Parts catalogue. Reproductions of English market and Spanish market Consumer Catalogues.

	G	VG	EXC	NEW

(A) Original; "LIONEL TRAINS" along top of cover.

          35   50   70   85

(B) 1971 xerographic reproduction by Bruce C. Greenberg. Printed at Knox College Print Shop, Galesburg, Illinois.

          —   —   —   1

(C) 1974 black and white reproduction with full-color front cover by Bruce C. Greenberg. Reproduction information appears on page 2 in the upper left-hand corner. The cover stock is heavier than the text pages and "1934" was added by the publisher to the upper right-hand corner.   2   4   5   6

(D) 1975 full-color reproduction by Greenberg Publishing Company. Reproduction information appears on the upper right-hand corner of page 2 as well as on pages 4, 9, 12, 16, 17, 29, 32, and 35. Date was added to the cover by the publisher. The negatives for this reproduction were used in printing *Greenberg's Lionel Catalogues: 1933-1942*.

          4   8   12   15

TYPE II: Same as Type I, but logo and red rectangle at bottom of page. Reported but not confirmed. Reader comments invited. **NRS**

ENGLISH CONSUMER CATALOGUE: 9" x 6", 16 pages, black ink on white-coated stock; cover shows father and son constructing Standard Gauge layout. Railroad rolling stock and accessories are described by their English names, for United Kingdom market.
(A) Original. **NRS**

(B) 1970 reproduction by Max Knoecklein.

          2   4   6   8

DEALER PROMOTIONAL CATALOGUE: 8-7/8" x 11", "A Sales Plan to Increase Your Profit on Lionel Trains and Accessories — 1934", 24 unnumbered pages printed in black and red on white paper. Includes much information on dealer displays, newspaper advertising campaigns, advance illustrations on trains and accessories, and even mentions the fact the *Lionel Magazine* is regularly sent to 170,000 subscribers. The copy examined came with a May 1933 Retail Price List and introductory letter dated June 1934 from Arthur Raphael, Lionel's General Sales Manager. R. Otten Collection. **NRS**

PROMOTIONAL BOOKLET: "4-1/2" x 5-3/4", "Handbook for Model Railroad Engineers", published by Lionel Engineers Club, and printed in black on orange (cover) and white paper throughout.
(A) Original, contains no Table of Contents. A. Rubin Collection. **NRS**

(B) Reprint, contains Table of Contents, numbered sequentially on the front cover, pages hand-numbered.   —   —   —   5

PRIVATE ISSUE CATALOGUE: 6" x 8-1/4" format, 24 pages, "1934-1935 Catalog and Price List No. 25" issued by The Model Railroad Shop, Dunellen, New Jersey. Black on buff paper.

          —   —   10   15

Top left: 1934 Mickey Mouse brochure. *Top center:* 1934 Retail Price List. *Top right:* 1935 Instructions for Assembling and Operating Lionel Trains. *Bottom left:* 1934 Consumer Catalogue front cover. *Bottom right:* 1934 Consumer Catalogue rear cover advertising the Lionel Engineer's Club.

Prewar Paper: 1901-1944 • 39

                          G   VG   EXC NEW

PRIVATE ISSUE CATALOGUE: 6" x 8-1/4" format, 20 pages, "Special 1934 Catalog and Price List of Lionel Trains No. 31", issued by The Model Railroad Shop, Dunellen, New Jersey. Black on buff paper with white Lionel price change notice.
                          —   —   10   20

MICKEY MOUSE BROCHURE: "TOY SENSATION OF 1934", red and blue ink on white paper. **NRS**

RETAIL PRICE LIST: "for LIONEL TRAINS AND ACCESSORIES" black ink and white paper. **NRS**

1935

CONSUMER CATALOGUE: 11-1/4" x 8-3/8" format, 44 pages. Four-color front cover shows "LIONEL TRAINS" in large block letters at top. An engineer points to a real Milwaukee Hiawatha locomotive as a boy holds his Lionel model up to compare it. At left in white is legend, "Announcing / The First / MODEL RAILROAD WHISTLE". Page 4 introduces the new DC-triggered whistle. Page 5 shows the new O Gauge Commodore Vanderbilt and Hiawatha streamlined steam locomotives. Great proliferation of O Gauge and decline of Standard Gauge is very evident in this catalogue. On page 18, the Standard "Washington Special" uses former Ives passenger cars. Automatic Gateman appears for the first time on page 31. Mickey Mouse circus train shown on page 40, as well as Santa and Mickey Mouse handcars. Other Mickey Mouse mechanical sets on page 42, and a second Lionel boat is on page 43. Rear cover devoted to the *Lionel Magazine* and the Lionel Engineer's Club. **NRS**

TYPE I: One train set, 1535, on page 41, caption "With Brilliant Chromium Finish" beneath the locomotive, three red lines at the bottom and three at the top of page 4.
(A) Original. Prendergast Collection.   35   65   80 100
(B) 1974 black and white reproduction by Bruce C. Greenberg with color front cover. There is a gray screen background on all other pages. Cover stock is the same weight as interior pages. No reproduction notice. Press run of 600 copies, printed in Mason City, Illinois.
                          2   3   5   6

TYPE II: One train on page 41, no caption beneath locomotive. Three red lines at the bottom and at the top of page 4. Original. M. Weisblum Collection.   35   65   80 100

TYPE III: Three train sets on page 41: 1535, 1521, and 1523, red lines are missing from the top and bottom of page 4.
(A) Original.   35   65   80 100
(B) 1975 full-color reproduction by Iron Horse Productions. Reproduction logo found in center gutter.   4   9   12   15

TYPE IV: One train on page 41, no caption beneath locomotive. No red lines at top or bottom of page 4.   35   65   80 100

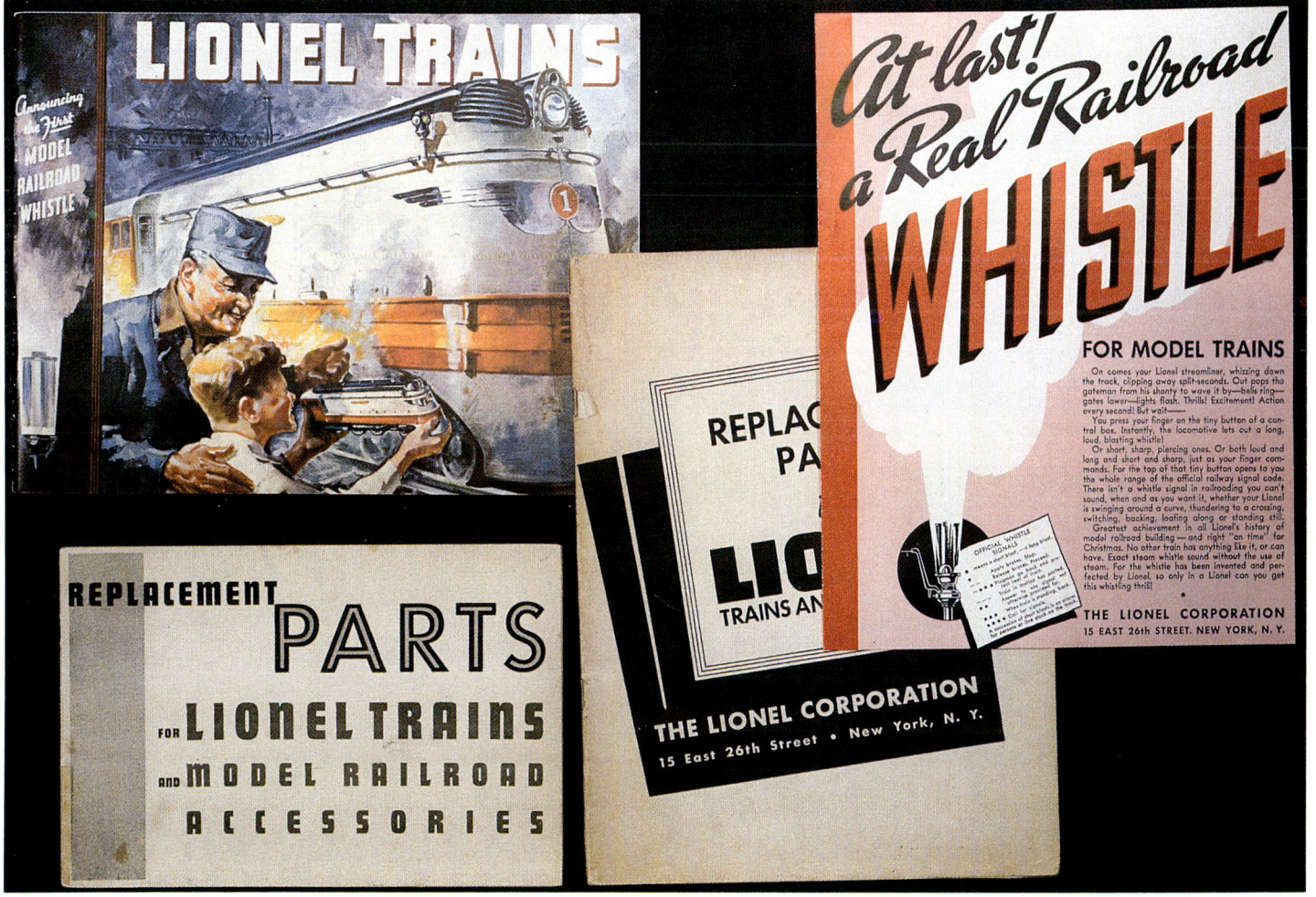

Top left: 1935 Consumer Catalogue. *Top right:* At Last! a Real Railroad WHISTLE. *Bottom left:* Horizontal format 1935 Replacement Parts For Lionel Trains. *Bottom center:* Vertical format 1930s (undated) Replacement Parts for Lionel Trains.

| | G | VG | EXC | NEW |

TYPE V: One train on page 41, with caption beneath locomotive. No red lines at top or bottom of page 4.   **35   65   80   100**

TYPE VI: Same as Type I described above, but all set prices on pages 10-20 are overprinted in a circular or rectangular gold ink, obliterating the price. Included in the copy examined in the A. Rubin Collection was the 1935 Retail Price List, described in a separate listing. The exact purpose of the gold overprinting is not known, and two theories are this catalogue version was for export purposes, or a rather expensive method of price changes for the domestic market.   **NRS**

INSTRUCTIONS FOR ASSEMBLING AND OPERATING: 6" x 9", 32 pages plus covers, orange cover stock with blue ink, "STREAMLINER INSTRUCTIONS" for Flying Yankee and Union Pacific on page 19; advertisement for Lionel Engineer's Club on page 32.
(A) No date or quantity on page 32. Weisblum Collection.   **2   4   6   8**
(B) "100M-8-35" on page 32. Weisblum Collection.   **2   4   6   8**

AT LAST! A REAL RAILROAD WHISTLE: 8-1/2" x 11", four-page, red and black ink, shows O Gauge streamline trains, new automatic gateman, invites readers to write for 1935 consumer catalogues.
(A) Original.   **10   20   25   30**
(B) 1977 reproduction by T.T.O.S. Reprint notice on bottom of page 2.   **—   —   1   2**

RETAIL PRICE LIST: 8-1/2" x 10-7/8" printed vertically, four pages price list printed in black on white glossy paper, and dated July 1, 1935. A. Rubin Collection.   **NRS**

1936

CONSUMER CATALOGUE: 11-1/4" x 8-1/2" format, 48 pages including covers. Four-color cover increases Lionel's appeal to realism. It shows large "LIONEL" white letters bordered in red against a blue-gray blueprint background. Precision instruments lie atop the full-page locomotive blueprint, and a die-cast steam engine, the Pennsylvania "Torpedo" and a New York Central Hudson (a harbinger of what is to come in 1937) dominate the left and center of the cover. Pages 2 and 3 explain whistle and automatic reversing. Solid "T" rails (Model Builder's Track) introduced on page 26. Page 43 relates details of magazine *Model Engineer*. Mechanical trains, now with whistles, are on pages 45-46. Rear cover introduces Lionel airplane.

TYPE I: Page 14 "The LIONEL / Union Pacific / CITY OF DENVER" above train; page 20: blocks to left of locomotive are blank; page

Top left: 1936 Consumer Catalogue. *Top right:* 1936 Advance Catalogue. *Bottom left:* Photocopy of 1936 English Consumer Catalogue. *Bottom center:* 1937 black and white Catalogue with UP streamliner and Hudson locomotive. *Bottom right:* 1936 Instructions for Assembling and Operating.

	G	VG	EXC	NEW

3: "This catalogue is effective July 1, 1936..." Original. J. Smith Collection. **40 65 80 100**

TYPE II: Page 14: "The / LIONEL / Union Pacific / CITY OF DENVER" above train; page 20: blocks to left of locomotives are numbered "No. 377W / WHISTLER / $32.50" and "No. 366W / WHISTLER / $30.00", page 3: "This catalog is effective July 1, 1936..."
(A) Original. **40 55 70 80**
(B) 1974 black and white reproduction with color front cover by Bruce C. Greenberg. Reproduction identification on page 2; cover stock is heavier weight paper than interior pages; date added to front cover by publisher. **— — 3 6**

TYPE III: Page 14: "the / LIONEL / Union Pacific / OVERLAND" above train set; page 20: blocks to left of locomotives have set numbers and prices; page 33: 46 automatic grade crossing does not appear.
(A) Original. Weisblum Collection. **40 55 70 85**
(B) 1974 full-color reproduction by Greenberg Publishing Company. Date added to cover by publisher. The negatives were also used in producing *Greenberg's Lionel Catalogues: 1933-1942*. **4 9 12 15**

TYPE IV: Same as Type II, but no line on bottom of page 3. Further information requested. **NRS**

TYPE V:
(A) Page 14: "the LIONEL Union Pacific OVERLAND" above train set; page 20: blocks to left of locomotives have set numbers and prices; page 33: Automatic Grade Crossing is present. Original. **40 55 70 80**

(B) Identical catalogue to the consumer catalogue described above, but covers and each page are in a thicker card stock and staple bound. The origin of these catalogues is not known, but one examined came in an original streamliner envelope with bulk rate mailing. R. Otten Collection. **— — — 300**

ENGLISH CONSUMER CATALOGUE: 9-7/8" x 6-15/16", 24 pages, shows Hiawatha on cover and lists address "LIONEL SERVICE DEPT. / 35 / 36, ALDERMANBURY, LONDON, E.C.2." Trains are priced in pounds, shilling, and pence with English rolling stock names. We do not know in what colors the catalogue was printed as we have only a xerographic copy. Shows several devices not appearing in U. S. version: a special transformer and a rotary convertor for changing DC current to AC. Foster Collection. **NRS**

INSTRUCTIONS FOR ASSEMBLING AND OPERATING: 6" x 8-7/8", 32 pages plus covers. Light blue cover stock printed in blue ink on front outside cover only. Page 32 at bottom: "PRINTED IN

Top row: 1937 Consumer Catalogue, 1937 Lionel Sales Aids. *Center left:* 1937 Lionel Track Layouts. *Bottom left:* 1937 Lionel Hudson 5344 J-1E booklet. *Bottom center:* Reproduction of 1938 Instructions For Assembling Lionel No. 700KW. *Bottom right:* 1937 Instructions for Assembling and Operating.

	G	VG	EXC	NEW

U.S. OF AMERICA-97M-8-36". Page 32 also carries introductory subscription offer for *Model Engineer*. Weisblum Collection.

| | 2 | 4 | 6 | 8 |

DEALER PRICE LIST: 8-3/8" x 11", "Lionel Sales Aids and Complete Retail Price List", eight pages, dark blue on light blue paper, includes two pages on dealer display material. A. Rubin Collection.
NRS

PRIVATE ISSUE CATALOGUE: The Model Railroad Shop, Dunellen, New Jersey, 25 pages, black on white pulp paper, includes two pages on Lionel replacement parts. R. Otten Collection.

| | 4 | 8 | 12 | 16 |

ADVANCE CATALOGUE: 10" x 7-1/2", black ink on white stock.

| | 45 | 65 | 80 | 100 |

1937

CONSUMER CATALOGUE: 11-1/4" x 8-3/8" format, 48 pages including covers. Front cover shows "LIONEL" in white lettering against rust background in upper right corner. To the left and beneath "LIONEL" are white outlines of locomotives against terracotta background. Entire remainder of cover has front 3/4 view of 5344 Hudson scale steam engine. Pages 2-3 give details of "Dispatcher Control". Pages 4 and 5 introduce 700EW Scale Hudson locomotive. Page 9 introduces 1668E PRR "Torpedo" six-driver engine. Catalogue clearly divided into O27, O, O72, and Standard sections. New 1121 switches for O27 shown on page 11 and page 30. The 636W City of Denver shown on page 16. The 763E Hudson appears on page 22, the magazine is on page 47, and the airplane is on page 48, the back cover.

TYPE I: Two tan boxes, page 39; no caption bottom left corner page 22.
| | 30 | 40 | 55 | 65 |

TYPE II: No tan boxes, page 39; caption "Six Wheel Drivers — Worm Gear Operations", page 22.
| | 30 | 40 | 55 | 65 |

TYPE III: Same as Type I, wrong colors on signal, page 38.
| | 30 | 40 | 55 | 65 |

TYPE IV: No tan boxes, page 39; no caption bottom of page 22.
| | 40 | 50 | 60 | 75 |

TYPE V:
(A) Same as Type II, but caption erronously reads "...worn gear", page 22.
| | 40 | 50 | 60 | 75 |

(B) 1975 full-color reproduction by Greenberg Publishing Company. "1937" added to the upper right corner of the front cover. The negatives for this reproduction were used in printing *Greenberg's Lionel Catalogues: 1933-1942*.
| | 4 | 9 | 12 | 15 |

CONSUMER CATALOGUE, PULP: 10-1/2" x 7-1/2", titled "Lionel Trains", 24 pages, black ink on pulp paper which has yellowed and dried out. Slightly reduced size and substantially edited version of consumer catalogue.
(A) Original
| | 4 | 6 | 8 | 10 |
(B) T.T.O.S. reproduction on coated stock, lettered "A GENUINE / T.T.O.S. / REPRINT" on lower right front cover.
| | 1 | 2 | 3 | 4 |

CATALOGUE: 10-1/2" x 7-1/2", 24 pages, black ink on newsprint stock, featuring UP Streamliner and Hudson locomotive. **NRS**

LIONEL ADVANCE CATALOG / COMPLETE PRICE LIST / 1937 DEALER DISPLAYS: 10-1/8" x 7-1/2", 28 pages, black ink on off-white stock. Includes dealer displays: 930 accessory stand, 7 display, 3 plane mural (each 4" x 13"), Lionel trains conductor. Also shows net (dealer cost) price for 1100 Mickey Mouse, dozen $7.50; 1105 Santa Claus, dozen $7.20; and 1107 Donald Duck, dozen $8.40. Original. Weisblum Collection.
| | 45 | 65 | 80 | 100 |

Lionel's catalogue marketing expertise began with the mailing cover. Lionel did not use a plain Manila envelope. *Top row:* Chug, Chug, Chug, probably 1933; Model Railroad Whistle, 1935; Lionel Trains, 1936. *Bottom row:* Lionel Streamliners, 1936; green and yellow Lionel Trains, 1939; orange and blue Lionel Trains, probably 1939.

| | G | VG | EXC | NEW |

INSTRUCTIONS FOR ASSEMBLING AND OPERATING: 5-7/8" x 8-5/8", 32 pages plus covers. Light tan cover stock printed in brown ink on front outside cover only. Page 32 at bottom on right: "No. 267E-1-100X-1-8-37". Compared to 1936 book printing quantities rose from 97,000 to 100,000, a reflection of slowly returning prosperity. Page 32 also offers subscriptions to *Model Builder* which replaced *Model Engineer*. Weisblum Collection.

| | 2 | 4 | 6 | 8 |

LIONEL TRACK LAYOUTS: 8-1/2" x 5-1/2", 24 pages, black and blue ink on white paper; cover shows boiler front of 5344 surrounded by a circle of track.

| | 2 | 5 | 7 | 10 |

LIONEL HUDSON 5344 J-1E: 8" x 5-3/8", 16 pages printed in blue and black ink on white paper, introduces scale Hudson.
(A) Original. 8 12 18 25
(B) 1975 reproduction by Schnitzer and Heeg. 1 2 3 5
(C) Reproduction by TTOS, over-sized, 6-3/4" x 9-1/2". 1 2 3 5

ACCESSORY BROCHURE: 8-3/8" x 11", four pages, yellow and black on white glossy paper, includes caption "Any Boy Can Build a System Like This!", and illustrates an attractive 9' x 16' Standard Gauge layout. A. Rubin Collection. **NRS**

LIONEL SALES AIDS and Complete Retail PRICE LIST: 8-3/8" x 11", 12 pages, blue ink on white paper. **NRS**

CHEMCRAFT EXPERIMENT BOOK: Booklet No. 1, 46 pages illustrated, measures 5" x 7-7/8", red and black cover, printed on white pages. This booklet was produced by the Porter Chemical Company, Hagerstown, Maryland and is actually a forerunner of when Lionel purchased the company. A. Rubin Collection.

| | — | — | 20 | — |

1938

CONSUMER CATALOGUE: 11-1/2" x 8-1/2" format, 52 pages including covers; front cover has very large "LIONEL" in red and white against sky blue background. An array of O Gauge locomotives emerges from between the letters, while the Lionel plane executes a loop above them. On the most common version, prices are printed for each entry. Pages 2 and 3 illustrate new electric remote controls for uncoupling new automatic box couplers, loading and unloading. Pages 6 and 7 introduce OO Gauge. Page 4 shows new 1664E locomotive. Also new in O Gauge are 1666E, 224E, 225E, and 226E. Pages 21 and 22 include special tear-out note from son to father, a classic example of Lionel's marketing prowess. Center fold-out for accessories and track layout plans. New 97 coal elevator and 3659-3859 automatic coal cars on page 39. Electric couplers on passenger cars described on page 40. Automatic flagman introduced on page 45. Lionel airplane on rear cover.
TYPE I: As described above.
(A) Original. Weisblum Collection. 25 40 50 65

Top row: 1937 Replacement Parts Catalogue and reproduction of 1938 Consumer Catalogue with date added to upper right corner.
Bottom row: 1938 Instructions for Assembling and Operating, 1938 pulp Consumer Catalogue, and photocopy of 1938 English catalogue.

| | G | VG | EXC | NEW |

(B) 1974 black and white reproduction with full-color front cover by Bruce Greenberg. Cover is printed on heavier stock and has date added to the cover for user identification. Reproduction logo on inside front cover. 600 copies. Printed by Bendix Field Engineering, Columbia, Maryland. Subsequently 100 copies were used in a special hardback book: *Lionel Catalogue Reproductions: 1938-1942* by Greenberg Publishing Company. Price for a single catalogue only.
2   3   4   6

(C) 1975 full-color reproduction by Greenberg Publishing Company. Date added to cover. Negatives subsequently used in printing *Greenberg's Lionel Catalogues: 1933-1942*.
4   9   12   15

TYPE II: Same as Type I, but with new page "CANADIAN RETAIL PRICE LIST 1938" glued to inside rear cover. Weisblum Collection.
40   55   70   80

TYPE III: Same as Type I, but with 6-15/16" x 3-7/16" white paper insert "NOTICE OF CHANGE IN PRICES" glued to inside rear cover. Weisblum Collection.
30   40   55   70

TYPE IV: Same as Type III, but with price change insert glued to page 9. R. Otten Collection.
30   40   55   70

MINI CATALOGUE: "10-1/4" x 7-1/2", "Lionel Trains", black and white pulp catalogue like that issued in 1937. 32 pages including covers.
4   6   8   10

MASTER CATALOGUE: 58-page catalogue bound in aluminum-coated fibre board stock, black plastic spiral binding with heavy stock pages. Includes pages in full color similar to the consumer catalogue, in addition to a Complete Retail Price List of six pages. Attached to the colored (inside) cover is a 7" x 5" Notice of Change in Prices. A. Rubin Collection. **NRS**

ADVANCE CATALOGUE: 8-1/2" x 10-7/8" vertical format, 20 pages, black and white with blue front and back cover. The format of this catalogue is completely different than that of the full-color consumer version, and in addition to featuring sets with prices, also includes one page on dealer displays and two pages identified as a "Complete Retail Price List". A letter dated May 19, 1938 from A. Raphael, Vice President and General Sales Manager of Lionel, accompanied each catalogue, describing the fact that, "never before in our history has our product been received with such unbridled enthusiasm (at the New York Toy Fair)". A. Rubin Collection. **NRS**

ENGLISH CONSUMER CATALOGUE: 10" x 7-1/6", page count unknown, shows 700 and 752 on front cover. We do not know the colors or page count as we only have a xerographic copy of the front cover. **NRS**

INSTRUCTIONS FOR ASSEMBLING LIONEL NO. 700KW: 7" x 9-1/2", 24 pages, (although numbered only to 22), black ink on white paper, inside front cover at bottom: "Form No. 700K-75X-7-38".

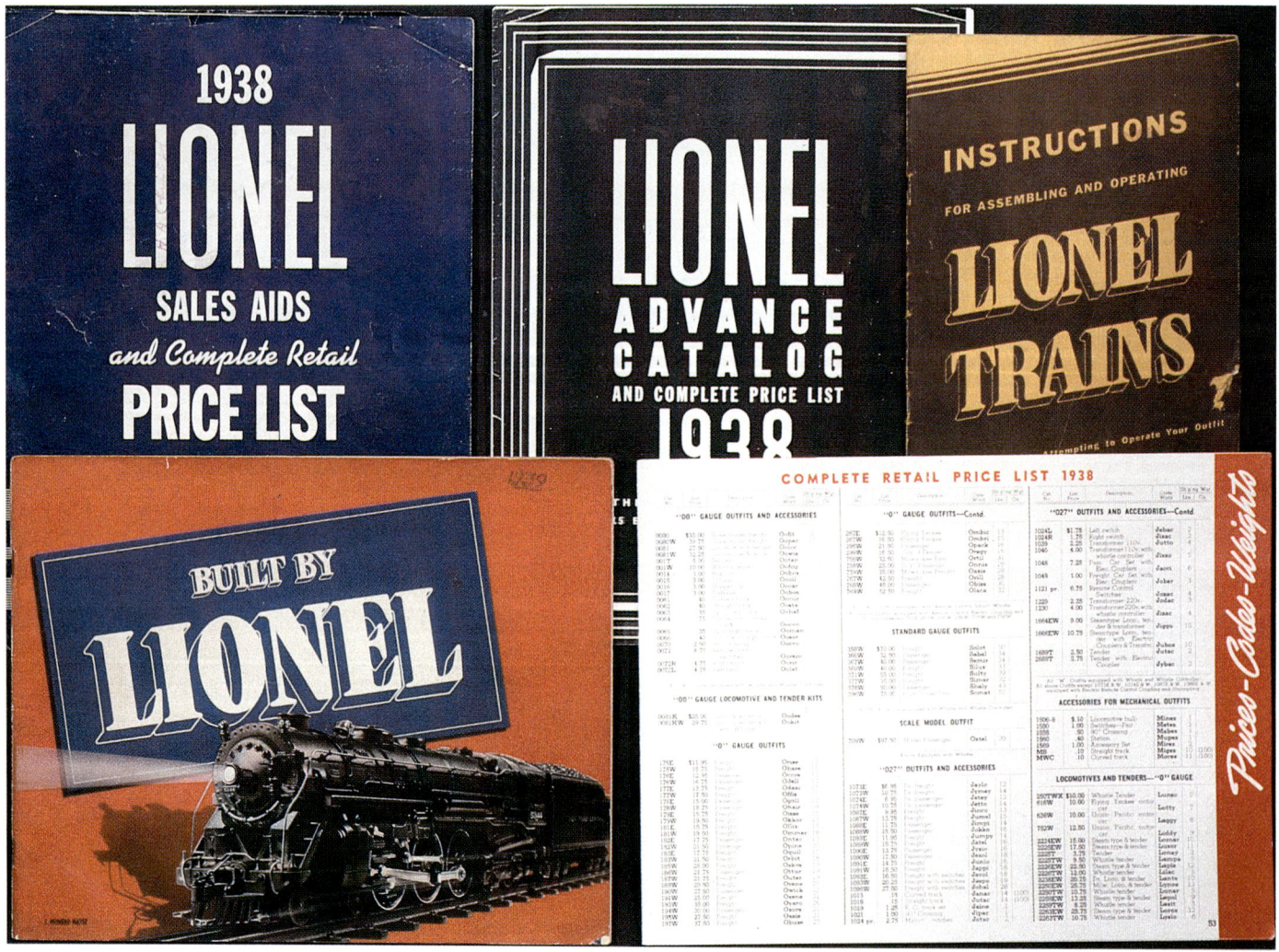

Top row: 1938 Lionel Sales Aids, photocopy of 1938 Advance Catalogue, 1938 Instructions For Assembling and Operating. *Bottom row:* 1939 Consumer Catalogue, 1938 Complete Retail Price List, as illustrated in Executive Catalogue.

Prewar Paper: 1901-1944 • 45

	G	VG	EXC	NEW
(A) Original. Weisblum Collection.	10	15	30	40
(B) 1977 reproduction by Greenberg Publishing Company, 6-11/16" x 9-7/16". Reproduction notices on front and rear covers	—	—	2	3
(C) Reproduction by Harry Gordon, 7" x 9-1/2", marked "REPRINT" on front cover.	—	—	2	3
(D) Reproduction by Dan Moss, 5-1/2" x 8-1/2", marked "Reprint by / Dan Moss" rubber-stamped on rear cover.	—	—	1	2
(E) Reproduction by Bruce Greenberg, 5-1/2" x 8-1/2".	—	—	1	2

HOW TO BUILD A MODEL RAILROAD: 5-15/16" x 9", 32 pages plus covers, orange cover stock printed with blue ink on both outside front and rear covers. This marks the first use of this famous Lionel color scheme on an instruction booklet. This booklet also has a different name from those immediately before and after it, as well as the booklet that follows. Lower rear cover: "1B-100M-10-38". Weisblum and I. D. Smith Collections.   **7   10   15   20**

INSTRUCTIONS FOR ASSEMBLING AND OPERATING: 5-13/16" x 8-5/8", 32 pages plus covers, but text pages numbered 3-33 (with 34 unnumbered). Gray cover stock printed with blue ink on front outside cover only. Page 34 lower right corner: "Part No. 267E-1-110X-10-36-TT". Weisblum Collection.   **2   4   6   8**

LIONEL SALES AIDS AND COMPLETE RETAIL PRICE LIST: Effective September 1, 1938, measures 8-3/8" x 10-7/8" vertical format, red and blue front cover, 12 pages, blue on white glossy paper, includes a price list plus two pages of illustrated dealer displays. A 6" x 2" correction sticker in red ink should also be attached to page 9, correcting assortment prices listed on that page. R. Otten Collection.   **20   25   30   40**

COMPLETE RETAIL PRICE LIST: 11-1/4" x 8-3/8", printed in red and black.   **NRS**

1939

CONSUMER CATALOGUE: 10-3/4" x 8-3/8" format; 52 pages including covers, front cover in red with large gun-metal blue rectangle bordered by white line. "BUILT BY / LIONEL" in white inside rectangle. Design patterned after steam locomotive builder's plate. Lower right part of cover shows 700E Hudson in three-quarter, fireman's side view. Use of electric remote-control couplers universal except in lowest-priced O27-series sets. Scale and semi-scale 708, 227, and 228 locomotives appear on pages 20 and 21. Scale Hudson kit shown on page 25. New two-rail OO sets introduced on pages 26-29. Standard Gauge sets appear for the last time on pages 30-31. Dial-type rheostat transformers introduced on pages 36 and 37. Rear cover gives details of free "Locoscope" with subscription to *Model Builder* magazine.

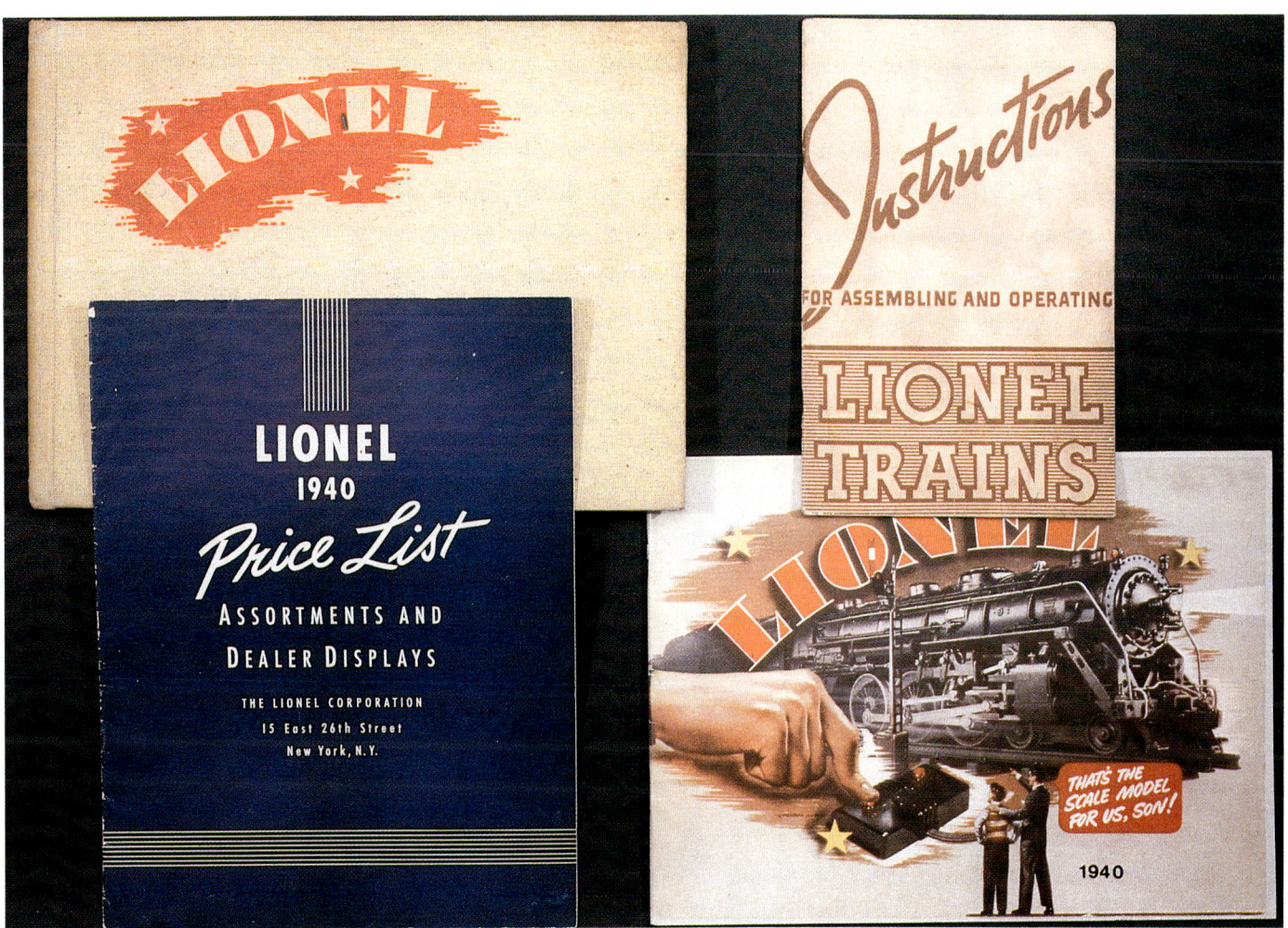

Top row: 1940 Executive Catalogue, 1940 Instructions For Assembling and Operating. *Bottom row:* 1940 Price List, reproduction 1940 Type I Consumer Catalogue with date added to cover by publisher.

| | G | VG | EXC | NEW |

TYPE I: On page 49 captions beneath 56 and 57 lamp posts illustrations are reversed.
(A) Original. **10 20 30 40**
(B) 1973 xerographic black and white reproduction by Bruce Greenberg. **— — 1 2**
(C) 1974 black and white reproduction with full-color front cover printed on heavier stock by Bruce Greenberg. No reproduction logo but "1939" added by publisher to upper right-hand corner of front cover. Printed by Bendix Field Engineering, Columbia, Maryland. Press run, 600. **— — 1 2**
(D) 1975 full-color reproduction by Greenberg Publishing Company. Date on cover added; slightly reduced in size from original. Color separations and printing by Barton and Cotton, Baltimore. **4 9 12 15**

TYPE II: Captions on page 49 are corrected. Original. **— — 30 75**

MASTER CATALOGUE: 68 pages with 52 pages identical to the consumer catalogue, but many other notable differences including heavy cardboard front and back covers in bright red with "Lionel" on front, and red spiral bound. Also includes an eight-page Classified Retail Price List plus several pages on dealer displays with full illustrations. A. Rubin Collection. **25 35 50 75**

EXECUTIVE CATALOGUE: Pages identical to the consumer catalogue, Type I, but released by Lionel with red plastic spiral binding. A. Rubin Collection. **NRS**

INSTRUCTIONS FOR ASSEMBLING AND OPERATING LIONEL TRAINS: 5-15/16" x 8-7/8", 40 pages plus covers, gold cover stock printed with brown ink on front outside cover only, white text pages with black ink; lower right side of page 40: "Form No. 267E-1-75X 10-39 TT". Original. Weisblum Collection. **2 3 5 7**

PROMOTIONAL BROCHURE: "19-3/8" x 5-7/8", The Romance of Lionel Trains", single sheet, two pages, printed in black and red on white paper. Advertises the "new 1939-40 fleet" and announces that the 1939 catalogue has just been issued. The example examined by the author, from the A. Rubin Collection, was found in the contents of a boxed World's Fair version of the Lionel Locoscope. **NRS**

PROMOTIONAL FEATURE: Three-page illustrated article appearing in December 1, 1939 issue of *People and Places*, monthly publication of the DeSoto Division of the Chrysler Corporation. Although this was not a Lionel publication, it provides significant insight into the prewar Lionel New York showroom, and is listed for information purposes. **NRS**

1940

CONSUMER CATALOGUE: 11-1/4" x 8-1/8" format, 64 pages including covers. Front cover shows white and red "LIONEL" in arch above 700E Hudson against buff- and slate-colored background. On left, a large hand pushes a remote-control button; next to button is a five-pointed yellow star. A minuscule father and son (comparatively

Top row: 1941 Price List without revision sticker, 1941 Price List with revision sticker, later 1941 Price List. *Bottom row:* Reproduction 1941 Consumer Catalogue with year added to cover, 1941 Instructions For Assembling and Operating.

| | G | VG | EXC | NEW |

speaking) stand at lower center. The father's remarks are in white lettering within a red balloon: "THAT'S THE / SCALE MODEL / FOR US, SON!" Extensive appeal to scale model railroading and realistic detail on pages 2 through 11 ... the longest introduction in any Lionel catalogue. "Magic Electrol" uncoupling system introduced on page 17. The scale and semi-scale freight cars are introduced on pages 42 and 43. New automatic signals make their first appearance on pages 52 and 53. The 313 bascule bridge appears for the first time on page 56. The back cover shows an old 5 locomotive against the legend "40 YEARS of Leadership!"

TYPE I: With all-white "LIONEL" letters on cover; page 20 caption beneath bottom train set describes 2651 lumber car as automatic unloading. The car did not have this feature. Original. Weisblum Collection.   **30   45   60   75**

TYPE II: Red "LIONEL" letters edged in white on front cover; same caption error on page 20 as Type I.
(A) Original. Weisblum Collection.   **25   40   50   60**
(B) 1975 full-color reproduction by Greenberg Publishing Company. Color separations and printing by Barton and Cotton, Baltimore, Maryland. Reproduced slightly smaller than original; date on cover added by publisher; reproduction logo on page 64.
   4   9   12   15

TYPE III: Red "LIONEL" letters edged in white on front cover; caption error corrected by removing caption, *Model Builder* premium inside front cover.
(A) Original. Weisblum Collection.   **25   40   50   60**

(B) 1975 black and white reproduction with full-color front cover by Bruce Greenberg. Date on cover added by publisher. Printed by Bendix Field Engineering, Columbia, Maryland; press run of 600. 100 copies of 1940 were used in producing limited edition book *Lionel Catalogue Reproductions: 1938-1942* by Greenberg Publishing Company.   **2   3   4   6**

TYPE IV: Same as Type I, but caption on page 20 is removed.
   30   45   60   75

EXECUTIVE CATALOGUE: Same as Type I consumer catalogue, but printed on heavy stock with metal spiral binding and heavy cloth-covered board covers.
(A) Contains additional pages 65-80 with dealer displays and pricing information. A. Rubin and Weisblum Collections.
   —   —   275   300

(B) Similar to Type I consumer catalogue, 64 pages bound in wire spiral, and printed in full color on heavy card stock. Does not include any dealer information. A. Rubin Collection.   **NRS**

ADVANCE CATALOGUE: "Lionel Trains and Accessories — Climb Aboard...", 14 unnumbered pages in full color illustrating products and dealer displays, with the first page a message to Lionel dealers. Printed on glossy red and light blue paper.
(A) Measures 8-1/2" x 10-7/8". There is a possibility this edition was cut down from a larger version, however the printing on the two versions, when placed together, does not line up. A. Rubin Collection.   **NRS**

Top row: 1942 Advance Catalogue, 1941 Chem-Lab folder. *Bottom row:* 1942 Consumer Catalogue, Consumer Catalogue mailing envelope.

	G	VG	EXC	NEW

(B) Measures 10-1/2" x 11". A. Rubin Collection. **NRS**

INSTRUCTIONS FOR ASSEMBLING AND OPERATING: 5-9/16" x 8-9/16", 48 pages plus covers. Light tan cover stock printed in brown ink on front outside cover only. Unnumbered page 2 lists three Lionel addresses: Irvington, Chicago, and San Francisco. Page 5 carries copyright notice and 1940 date. Pages 43-48 list "APPROVED SERVICE STATIONS".
(A) Smooth cover. M. Ocilka and Weisblum Collections.
                                           2   4   6   8
(B) Grained leather-like cover. M. Ocilka Collection. **NRS**

PRICE LIST: 8-3/8" x 10-7/8", 16 pages fully illustrated, printed in dark blue on white glossy paper. Catalogue features a Complete Retail Price List for 1940 and four pages of dealer display illustrations. A. Rubin Collection.   10 15 25 30

INSTRUCTIONS FOR ASSEMBLING LIONEL NO. 700 KW: Form No. 700K-7-UJX-10-40 NPCO. Similar to 1938 listing with inscription.   10 15 30 40

1941

CONSUMER CATALOGUE: 11-1/4" x 7-3/8" format; 64 pages including covers. Front cover: medium blue background, stripes at top in red-white-red pattern, single row of small white stars, large "LIONEL" in ribbed light yellow letters. Appeals to patriotism increased as World War II loomed. Below "LIONEL" in red in one line: "ELECTRIC TRAINS FOR THE YOUTH OF AMERICA". Lower left shows mid to front boiler of 700E Hudson; lower right has Navy shield in white rectangle and legend below it: "PRECISION INSTRUMENTS / for the / UNITED STATES NAVY". Chem-Lab Chemistry sets are introduced on pages 61 through 63. Rear cover devoted to *Model Builder* magazine and 192-page *Handbook For Model Builders*.
TYPE I: As described above.
(A) Original. Weisblum and I. D. Smith Collections.
                                    25 40 50 60
(B) 1974 black and white reproduction by Bruce Greenberg with full-color front cover printed on heavier stock. Date added to the cover to aid user identification. Printed by Bendix Field Engineering, Columbia, Maryland. 600 were printed and 100 of these were used in *Lionel Catalogue Reproductions: 1938-42*, a limited edition hardback.   2 3 4 6
(C) 1975 full-color reproduction by Greenberg Publishing Company; reproduction logo on page 2, date added to cover; press run of 3000. Negatives subsequently used in printing *Greenberg's Lionel Catalogues: 1933-1942*.   4 9 12 15

TYPE II: Same as Type I, but yellow "LIONEL" letters are edged in black. Graves Collection. **NRS**

DEALER CATALOGUE: 8-1/2" x 11" vertical format, 16 pages, "Lionel Trains and Accessories — Nothing Else Like Them in the World" on cover, and all pages in splashy red, white, and blue with stars. Includes full-color illustrations of dealer displays; on "Lionel Accessories" (unnumbered) page, a 2-5/8" x 3" gummed label is affixed designating "Revised Prices Effective June 14, 1941". R. Otten Collection. **NRS**

ADVANCE VIP CATALOGUE: Same as Type I consumer version, but all pages are printed on a thicker card stock glossy paper. A. Rubin Collection. **NRS**

LIONEL CHEM-LAB: 8-1/2" x 11", four pages, red and black ink on heavy white-coated stock. Brochure intended for dealers, rear cover reports: "A NATION-WIDE / ADVERTISING / CAMPAIGN / PLUS STORE HELPS". Weisblum Collection.
                                          5 9 12 15

INSTRUCTIONS FOR ASSEMBLING AND OPERATING: Forty pages plus covers, covers orange with blue lettering, un-numbered page 2 says "All contents copyrighted 1940 by / ... / Reprinted 1941".   3 4 6 8

PRICE LIST: Red and blue cover, 16 pages, blue on white paper, includes price list, availability of dealer displays, and a two-page chemistry spread, "A new field of scientific adventure for boys". R. Otten Comment.
(A) Blue center box on front cover, undated.
                                    9 18 25 35
(B) Same as (A), but with "REVISED PRICES" sticker, dated June 14, 1941.   9 18 25 35
(C) Red center box on front cover, list dated June 14, 1941.
                                  9 18 25 35

1942

CONSUMER CATALOGUE: 11" x 8-1/2" format; 32 pages including covers. Front cover has red, white, and blue American flag design with white "LIONEL TRAINS" lettering where stars would be on blue field. The 700E Hudson goes across entire lower third of cover. Page 2 details Lionel's war contracts for the Navy — "LIONEL GOES TO SEA" in white on blue banner at top of page. On page 3 in small agate type, consumer is told that many trains will be in short supply

Top row: 1942 Price List and 1943 Wonder Book of Railroading cover. *Bottom row:* Interior pages from 1943 Wonder Book of Railroading.

	G	VG	EXC	NEW

due to exigencies of national defense. Train sets greatly reduced throughout catalogue.

TYPE I:
(A) Bottom right layout on page 20 is horizontal.

	10	18	25	35

(B) 1974 black and white reproduction with full-color front cover by Bruce Greenberg. Cover printed on heavier stock; date added to lower right cover. Reproduction logo inside front cover, lower left corner. 600 copies printed by Bendix Field Engineering.

	2	3	4	6

(C) 1983 full-color reproduction as part of *Greenberg's Lionel Catalogues: 1933-1942*. This was not published separately. **NRS**

TYPE II:
Bottom right layout on page 20 is vertical. **10 18 25 35**

ADVANCE CATALOGUE: 10" x 11" red and black on white glossy paper, 12 unnumbered pages, features trains, accessories, and chemistry sets. Unlike prior advance catalogues, for the first time there is no reference to dealer displays. A. Rubin Collection. **NRS**

ADVANCE CATALOGUE: 16 unnumbered pages in full color, printed on white paper. **NRS**

INSTRUCTIONS: Same as 1941 instructions, but bottom line on page 2 says "Reprinted 1942". **3 4 6 8**

LIONEL TRAINS 1942 PRICE LIST: 8-1/2" x 11", blue ink on white stock. **NRS**

LIONEL CHEM-LAB — A MANUAL OF EXPERIMENTS: 320 pages, hardbound book containing over 900 experiments, and available with the four larger Lionel chemistry sets. Some illustrations included, this book came with a blue and red bound cover, measuring 5" x 6-3/4". Although this book was not available for separate sale, it did receive a notable write-up, with illustrations, in the 1942 Lionel consumer catalogue. R. Otten Collection.

	—	—	15	20

1943

LIONEL WONDER BOOK OF RAILROADING: 8-3/8" x 11-3/8", 48 pages plus cover, not paginated, color front and rear cover with drawing of 5344 front end. Consumer planning book, trains not offered for sale in this book. Contents also include "WILL TRAINS OF THE FUTURE LOOK LIKE THIS?", "WHAT MAKES A LOCOMOTIVE GO?", "LANGUAGE OF THE RAILS", "100,000 FOR A MODEL", "ALBUM OF ENGINE PORTRAITS". It also contains pictures of the Lionel showroom layout which included an 840 power house and 129 terrace. Came in black/red illustrated envelope.

	10	12	16	22

NAVIGATIONAL INSTRUMENTS: 8-1/2" x 11", 24 inside pages, light and dark blue ink on white glossy paper. Illustrations in significant detail identify Lionel's products for the U. S. Navy during World War II, including compasses, binnacles, peloruses, and taffrail logs. This booklet, Lionel's only true "catalogue" for 1943, was spiral bound with a dark blue card stock front and back cover. W. Mekalian and A. Rubin Collections. **NRS**

1944

LIONEL RAILROAD PLANNING BOOK: 6-1/16" x 9", four-color front cover, red and black interior pages, 40 pages plus covers; illustrates prewar equipment in layout settings, designed to keep children interested in trains during production hiatus of World War II, copyright 1944.
(A) 5-15/16" x 8-15/16". L. Connors Collection.

	8	12	16	22

(B) 6-1/16" x 8-15/16". **8 12 16 22**

Chapter Three
POSTWAR PAPER: 1945-1969

Lionel carefully prepared for the pent-up demand for model trains, brought about by the World War II interruption. The 1946 catalogue announced new and exciting developments: remote electronic control, puffing smoke, and operating knuckle couplers. The catalogue was the catalyst for the frenzied buying of toy trains immediately following the war.

But Lionel did not only issue annual product catalogues. Store posters described the "ideal Lionel model layout" in 1947 and beckoned customers in 1954 to realize that "you're the boss with Lionel trains and accessories". A booklet, the "official book of rules for model railroading", was distributed to thousands of youthful engineers and certificates were granted to those enrolling in Lionel's own Railroad Company.

Year after year, paper fueled the interest of children brought up in the railroading era. Adults, too, were specifically targeted with publications such as the 1949 layout planning book "for Pop". Lionel's products shifted from its operating milk cars and cattle cars to rockets and military equipment. Lionel paper reflected these major changes.

But the public did not realize that the Lionel corporation was faltering. Lionel created many new products: space products, racing sets, science kits, and even helium-filled airships. The catalogue and dealer flyers were produced by the hundreds of thousands, but Lionel's marketing efforts failed.

The demise of Lionel is depicted in an interesting and important 1967 document. This item was not produced by Lionel's creative Marketing Department. This item was the August 7-11, 1967 auction catalogue produced by Samuel L. Winternitz Company of Chicago. The auction sold the "machinery and equipment used to manufacture the products of the Lionel Toy Corporation." The curtain was closing on what collectors identify as the postwar era.

Note: Dimensions are given with width followed by height unless otherwise noted.

                                                    G   VG   EXC NEW

1945

ADVANCE CATALOGUE: Confirmation and description requested. **NRS**

CONSUMER CATALOGUE: 8-1/2" x 11", four-page folder, "The Lionel Line for Christmas 1945".

                                                    G   VG   EXC NEW
(A) Original, page 1, "suprises".   **NRS**
(B) Original, page 1 corrected, "surprises".   **NRS**
(C) Lester Gordon reproduction, red or red-orange, black ink on white-coated stock, reproduction logo on top of page 1: "Original printed black and red ink. Reproduced April 1, 1969 by LESTER GORDON". 2   3   4   6
(D) Greenberg reproduction on uncoated paper, cover states "1974 Reproduction" with Columbia, Maryland address, page 2 with same address. —   1   2   3
(E) Greenberg reproduction on coated stock, cover states "1974 Reproduction" with Columbia, Maryland address, but page 2 has Sykesville, Maryland address. —   1   2   3
(F) Unmarked reproduction, and similar to original. Buyers should exercise caution in purchasing originals of this year. —   —   3   5

CANDID CAMERA SHOTS — LIONEL TRAINS IN ACTION:
(A) 5-7/8" x 8-3/4", 20 pages, black and white with red caption backgrounds, no printing on inside covers. Note that 226 locomotive on trestle on cover is pulling an American Flyer gondola! Page 3 bottom "Entire Contents Copyright 1945..." 8   10   15   18

(B) Same as (A), but inside stapled upside down; there is no indication the staples in this booklet were tampered with, and the only example viewed came with the original envelope, imprinted *All Aboard*. A. Rubin Collection. **NRS**

STORE NOTICE: Small card stock notice "Due to the war emergencies and the scarcity of certain materials, Lionel reserves the right to make substitutions for any car, locomotive or other component part of any electric train outfit." Printed in red ink on cream stock, measures 9" x 6". Date confirmation requested; perhaps early 1946. R. Osterhoff Collection. —   —   —   70

PLANS AND BLUE PRINTS FOR LIONEL MODEL RAILROADERS: 5-7/8" x 8-13/16", 20 pages. Front cover shows block signal and what appears to be a 700E. Front cover is printed in yellow, black, and blue ink on white paper. Unpaginated centerfold, interior printed in black ink, pages 8 and 9 show four different layouts and 12 different track plans. G. Salamone Collection.
(A) As described above. **NRS**
(B) Inside pages ragged, uncut at top. Printers error. R. Otten Collection. **NRS**

PROMOTIONAL FLYER: 8-1/2" x 13-7/8", two pages, red and black on smooth paper, advertising "Every Model Railroad Engineer. . . needs *Model Builder* magazine." With coupon on reverse side for subscription. The copy examined came in "All Aboard" envelope with 1945 booklets, but this could be an early 1946 item. R. Otten Collection. **NRS**

Top row: 1945 Candid Camera Shots, 1945 Consumer Catalogue, and 1945 Promotional Flyer for *Model Builder*. *Bottom row:* 1945 Catalogue interior pages, 1945 Plans and Blue Prints for Lionel Model Railroaders.

	G	VG	EXC	NEW

1946

ADVANCE CATALOGUE: 1946, 10-1/2" x 8-5/16", 24 pages, "World's Finest Lionel Trains for 1946", red and black, includes "Price Sheet May 1, 1946" with brown ink on yellow paper. Features 671 steam locomotive on cover. All pages printed on heavy uncoated stock.
80   100   140   175

ADVANCE CATALOGUE: 21-3/4" x 10-1/2", eight pages, large size so-called Spring Catalogue, with the inscription "Trains for Spring 1946", black and red on white paper. **NRS**

CONSUMER CATALOGUE:
(A) 8-3/8" x 11-1/4", 16 pages plus four-page cover, full color, cover illustration shows trains and boy holding gray work caboose.
15   20   25   30
(B) 8-1/4" x 11-1/4", 16 pages, full color, similar to (A). Page 1 "Which LIONEL do you want, Son?" with father with arm around son. Son is wearing plaid shirt. I. D. Smith Collection.
15   20   25   30
(C) Reproduction of (A) by Greenberg Publishing Company, with "1946" on cover; and "1975 Reproduction" with Columbia, Maryland address on inside cover. **—   1   2   3**

(D) Reproduction of (B) by Fundimensions on heavier stock than original, inside cover states "Reproduced by Lionel of Fundimensions...1975" at lower left corner.
3   4   6   8

PRICE SHEET — LIONEL TRAINS: 7-1/4" x 8-3/8", one sheet printed both sides, plain white paper, black ink. Inserted in general catalogue.
3   5   8   10

PRICE SHEET #2: April 1st, 1946; 8-1/2" x 11", four black and white pages; begins with O27 outfits. Shows price increases. W. Mekalian Collection. **NRS**

PRICE SHEET: May 1st, 1946; 8-1/2" x 11"; four pink pages with black print. This price list shows further price increases. W. Mekalian Collection. **NRS**

PRICE SHEET: May 1st, 1946; 8-1/2" x 11"; yellow sheet with brown ink. W. Mekalian Collection. **NRS**

INSTRUCTIONS FOR ASSEMBLING AND OPERATING LIONEL TRAINS: 5-1/2" x 8-1/2", 40 pages plus covers, black ink on white paper.
(A) Dark and light blue cover, no printing on inside back cover.
3   4   6   8

| | G | VG | EXC | NEW |

(B) Dark and light blue cover, *Model Builder* ad on inside back cover.
                                                                      3   4   6   8

(C) Green and orange cover. This is the version which contains an unusual Lamp Replacement Chart showing lamps for items never made, such as the 703 Hudson and the Sager Place Madison-style observation car.   3   4   6   8

(D) Red and yellow cover, inside cover pages blank, otherwise similar to (C).   NRS

(E) Black and white cover, black ink only on interior pages.
    3   4   6   8

(F) Orange and black cover, Greenberg Publishing Company reproduction, page 1 (inside) states "1975 Reproduction" with Columbia, Maryland address.   —   —   1   2

(G) Same as (B), but numbered "No. 497" on back cover. M. Ocilka Collection.   —   2   3   5

INSTRUCTIONS FOR ASSEMBLING AND OPERATING ELECTRONIC CONTROL LIONEL TRAINS: Twelve pages, black and white.
(A) Original.   10   15   20   25
(B) by Greenberg Publishing Company.   —   —   1   2

SCENIC EFFECTS FOR MODEL RAILROADS — LIONEL TRAINS: 6" x 9", 24 pages, including covers. Front cover printed in black and red ink on white paper. Interior pages printed in red and black ink on white paper. Information on table building, mountain building, right of way scenery, and cutaway view of new Atomic motor with double worm-gear drive. Piker and G. Salamone Collections.
    8   10   15   20

ADVERTISING MAT: 8-5/8" x 12", made of papier-mache, cream color, illustrating Lionel logos, Service Station newspaper inserts, etc. Mat was sent in 1946 to Service Stations, accompanied by a 10-3/8" x 12-1/8" glossy paper sample with letter from Lionel requesting a list of Standard Gauge items in dealer's stock. L. Connors Collection.
    NRS

PRICE LIST: March 11, 1946, 8-3/8" x 10-7/8", four pages, black ink, begins with O27 outfits.   NRS

LIBERTY MAGAZINE: November 23, 1946 issue featuring 1946 catalogue insert of 16 pages, and does not include four-page cover found on consumer catalogue, nor a price sheet.
(A) Subscription edition, color outline of "Liberty" on front cover, top left is purple. In several observations this particular variation has always been found with an address label.   30   45   75   125
(B) Newsstand edition, color outline of "Liberty" on front cover, top left is blue. In several observations this particular variation has always been found without an address label.
    30   45   75   125
(C) Canadian edition, Lionel catalogue insert same as (A) and (B) above, but some advertising in magazine is different to meet the Canadian media requirements.   NRS

DEALER PROMOTIONAL POSTER: 14-7/8" x 10", "Lionel Electronic Control", black and white single page with suggestions to toy departments for display of set 4109WS. This example was found as an insert in the booklet "Facts for the Man Who Sells Lionel Trains", but it is not known if this sheet was sent to dealers in this manner. A. Rubin Collection.   NRS

Top row: 1946 Greenberg Publishing Company reproduction Consumer Catalogue, 1946 Advance Catalogue, 1946 Scenic Effects for Model Railroads. *Bottom row:* 1946 Price Sheet, 1946 Consumer Catalogue (16-page version), 1946 Instructions for Assembling and Operating Lionel Trains, 1946 Instructions for Assembling and Operating Electronic

1947 Price List, Consumer Catalogue, and Fun with Lionel Model Railroading.

	G	VG	EXC	NEW

DEALER SALES BOOKLET: 5-3/4" x 8-3/4", "Facts for the Man Who Sells Lionel Trains", blue cover on gray card stock. The purpose of this 24-page booklet is described in the opening paragraph: "We have forgotten how to sell electric trains. There have been none on the market for four years, and a refresher course for everybody is essential." Inside pages are black ink on an off-white glossy paper. A. Rubin Collection. **NRS**

PRICE SHEET: May 1, 1946, 10-1/4" x 8-1/4", one sheet printed two sides, black ink on blue-green paper.
(A) Original issue. **NRS**
(B) Corrected issue, (e.g., "page 12" has three listings). A. Rubin Collection. **NRS**

"HELLO POP — POP'S BREAKFAST PLATE": 6-7/8" x 8-7/8", two-page promotional card, "Check List for Dad". Printed in red and black on light gray card stock. **NRS**

1947

ADVANCE CATALOGUE: 14" x 11", 22 pages including tan, red, and black cover; "The Lionel Line for 1947", red, black, and white interior. G. Salamone and J. Zydlo Collections.
| | 75 | 100 | 135 | 160 |

CONSUMER CATALOGUE: 11-1/4" x 7-5/8", 32 pages, full color, cover shows 6200 passing crossing shanty.
(A) Page 6, No. 1431, $19.95; page 19, GG1 6-8-6, $29.95.
| | 20 | 25 | 35 | 40 |
(B) Page 6, No. 1431 $22.50; page 19, GG1 6-8-6, $29.95.
| | 20 | 25 | 35 | 40 |
(C) Page 19, GG1 6-8-6, $32.50.
| | 20 | 25 | 35 | 40 |
(D) Page 19, GG1 4-6-6-4 $32.50.
| | 20 | 25 | 35 | 40 |

INSTRUCTIONS FOR ASSEMBLING AND OPERATING LIONEL TRAINS: 5-1/2" x 8-1/2", 40 pages plus covers, black and white pages, red and yellow wraparound cover, number "No. 497" on back of cover.
| | 3 | 4 | 6 | 8 |

FUN WITH LIONEL MODEL RAILROADING: 32 pages, red, black, and white.
(A) 8-1/2" x 5-3/8", dark red. Back cover with *Model Builder* coupon.
| | 5 | 7 | 10 | 13 |
(B) 8-1/2" x 5-3/8", light red. Back cover with *Model Builder* coupon. B. Munn Collection.
| | 5 | 7 | 10 | 13 |
(C) 10-3/4" x 8-1/4". Back cover "coin for the club coffers..." J. Zydlo Collection.
| | 7 | 9 | 12 | 15 |

LIONEL RAILROAD GUIDE: 16-1/2" wide x 10-1/2" high, wall poster, printed on one side in yellow, black, and red ink on white paper, shows 0-6-0 switcher numbered "8976" and five other locomotives. Advertising copy reads "LIONEL R. R. GUIDE". For another variety, see next entry. G. Salamone Collection.
| | 10 | 15 | 20 | 25 |

LIONEL RAILROAD GUIDE: 20-3/4" wide x 15-3/4" high, wall poster, printed one side only in yellow, black, and red ink on white paper. Shows 0-4-0 switcher numbered "1662" and five other locomotives. Advertising copy reads "LIONEL R. R. GUIDE". For another variety, see previous entry. G. Salamone Collection.
| | 7 | 10 | 15 | 20 |

INSTRUCTION MANUAL FOR LIONEL CONSTRUCTION SETS: 10-5/8" wide x 7-5/8" high, red and black cover.
(A) Cover states "All models herein can be made with Lionel construction Kit No. 121". However, interior pages show parts for sets 111 and 222 and illustrate more elaborate sets 333 and 444. The 1947 consumer catalogue lists sets 111, 222, 333, and 444. Was there a 121 set, or was the cover information in error? Reader comments invited. B. Stekoll Collection.
| | 3 | 5 | 7 | 10 |
(B) Same as (A), but no reference to kit No. 121 on cover.
| | 2 | 3 | 5 | 10 |

ADVERTISING MAT: 40" x 40", printed on glossy white paper, black ink with heading "These Striking Ads Free — Promote Lionel Trains!"; many train illustrations and includes construction kits. These were proofs for the actual mats but depending on printing methods used, could actually be used for advertising purposes. R. Otten Collection. **NRS**

PRICE LIST: 8-3/8" x 10-7/8", five pages, "Lionel Trains Price Sheet, March 1947", black ink on blue-green paper, no illustrations. **NRS**

PRICE LIST: 8-3/8" x 10-3/4", 16 pages, effective August 1, 1947, black, gray, and red ink on dull white pages including illustrations of Lionel dealer displays. This item appears closer to a catalogue than a price list. M. Meters Collection. **NRS**

DEALER PRICE SHEET: 6-7/8" x 8-3/8", single sheet, "Correct Price Sheet for the 1947 Lionel Catalog", red ink on white paper, dated August 1947. Mentions "due to changing manufacturing conditions, certain prices have been altered since this catalog was printed." This sheet is seldom seen with the 1947 consumer catalogue. A. Rubin Collection. **NRS**

LIONEL TRAINS PRICE SHEET: January 1947; 8-1/2" x 11"; six pages, black ink on blue-green paper; no illustrations. W. Mekalian Collection. **NRS**

LAYOUT POSTER: "An Ideal Lionel Model Layout", designed by Robert M. Sherman, illustrating in "blueprint" drawing a 12' x 12' layout, printed on one side.
(A) 14-3/8" x 10-3/8".
| | 5 | 10 | 15 | 20 |
(B) 21-1/4" x 16".
| | 8 | 15 | 20 | 30 |

PRIVATE ISSUE CATALOGUE: "UNEEDA APPLIANCE CO.", 11" x 8-1/2"; 16 pages; Lionel throughout. Red and black on tan covers, black and white within. **NRS**

1948

	G	VG	EXC	NEW

ADVANCE CATALOGUE: "LIONEL FOR 1948", 14" x 11", 20 pages including cover. Cover has picture of 6200 in black and white plus red circle. Interior black, red, and white. Advance catalogue does not show F-3s. J. Zydlo Collection. **75 100 135 150**

CONSUMER CATALOGUE: 11-1/8" x 8", 36 pages, cover illustration shows PRR turbine passing streamline passenger train, with overpass in the background.

(A) Page 15, outfit No. 2140WS, locomotive keystone is tuscan red; page 16, outfit No. 2143WS, locomotive keystone is tuscan red. **20 30 40 45**

(B) Page 15, outfit No. 2140WS, locomotive keystone is tuscan red; page 16, outfit No. 2143WS, locomotive keystone is scarlet. **15 22 30 35**

(C) Page 15, outfit No. 2140WS, locomotive keystone is scarlet; page 16, outfit No. 2143WS, locomotive keystone is scarlet. **15 22 30 35**

EXPORT CATALOGUE: 16 pages, cover reads "Trens Lionel para 1948". Cover and contents similar to advance catalogue. Entire contents in Portuguese. Additional information requested. B. Bokelmann Collection. **NRS**

INSTRUCTIONS FOR ASSEMBLING: 5-1/2" x 8-1/2", 40 pages, black ink on white interior coated, plus yellow wraparound cover, with blue ink on front outside cover, black ink on inside front and rear covers, and "Form No. 703" on inside front cover.

(A) Model Builder ad on rear outside cover. **3 4 6 8**

(B) No printing on rear outside cover. **NRS**

MAKE THESE REALISTIC MODELS FOR YOUR LIONEL RAILROAD: 23-1/4" x 25", coated paper, printed one side in red, green, and blue ink. Models include grocery store, cottage, service station, country house, church, and garage. "Copyright 1948 by The Lionel Corporation". I. D. Smith Collection. **10 15 20 25**

3D POSTER: 18" x 19", printed in red and blue ink on coated stock with red ink printed from 5/16" to 7/8" to the right of the blue ink, three images, top image captioned "Away they go! Magnificent LIONEL TRAINS — So Real, So True to Life". Included is a pair of glasses with left red and right blue lens (card stock 3D viewer by "American Colortype Co.") often came with *Model Builder* subscription envelope as promotional insert in 1948 consumer catalogue. Schreiner and I. D. Smith Collections. **8 10 15 20**

FOR THE MAN THAT SELLS LIONEL TRAINS: 5-1/2" x 8-1/4", 35 pages plus red cover printed on heavy yellow stock; dealer guide, includes information on the 1948 Lionel line. L. Connors Collection. **NRS**

INSTRUCTION MANUAL: 10-1/2" x 7-3/8", 28 pages, for Lionel construction, No. 121, black and red on white uncoated paper. **3 5 7 10**

INSTRUCTIONS FOR ASSEMBLING AND OPERATING ELECTRONIC CONTROL LIONEL TRAINS: 5-1/2" x 8-1/2", 12 pages, blue cover with green inside pages. Form ECU-50. The sample examined also came with a single-sided separate sheet

Top row: 1948 Lionel Construction Kit Chart and 1948 3D Poster. *Bottom row:* 1948 Paper City, 1948 Instructions, and 1948 Consumer Catalogue.

	G	VG	EXC	NEW

"Wiring Diagram for No. 4110WS Electronic Outfit", form 763. L. Connors Collection. — — 30 45

PRIVATE ISSUE CATALOGUE: Madison Hardware Co. mailer opens into two-sided, 17" x 22" broadside. Black and white throughout. **NRS**

PRICE LIST: 8-1/2" x 11", black ink on blue paper, six fold-out pages printed on single sheet, dated February 1, 1948. includes retail information on entire product line. — — 25 35

PRICE LIST: Effective August 1, 1948, 8-3/8" x 10-7/8", 12 pages; black, light red, and dark red ink on white paper, features trains, accessories, construction kits, and dealer displays. R. Otten Collection. 20 25 35 45

LIONEL TRAINS PRICE SHEET: January 15, 1948; 8-1/2" x 11"; six pages, black on yellow paper. **NRS**

COLOR TRAIN POSTER: 3' x 6', full color, pictures locomotives, with the caption "Lionel Trains Puff Smoke / Whistle". Poster was silk-screened and available for $1.00 in 1948 together with four streamers. Information and confirmation of these streamers requested. L. Connors Collection. — — 600 800

LIONEL CONSTRUCTION KIT CHART: 23" x 16-7/8", two-page chart, "Actual size reproduction of all parts contained in Lionel Construction kits", red and black ink on white paper. 7 10 15 20

ORDER FORM: 6" x 10-1/2", one page, "Extra Parts for Lionel Construction Sets (Nos. 111 and 222)", black ink on white glossy paper. — — 2 —

INSTRUCTION MANUAL: 10" x 7", 67 pages, for Nos. 232, 343, and 454 construction kits, fully illustrated, features a 675 locomotive with tender in advertisement on last page; yellow, red, and black front cover. — — 10 13

1949

ADVANCE CATALOGUE: "LIONEL ADVANCE CATALOGUE FOR 1949", 17" x 8-1/4", 24 pages. Gray and white cover with silhouette of Hudson in yellow, blue, red, and black. Interior pages blue, yellow, and black and white. Shows Lionel construction sets on rear covers. G. Salamone and J. Zydlo Collections. 80 110 160 185

CONSUMER CATALOGUE:
(A) 11-1/4" x 8", 38 pages, cover illustration shows family viewing Lionel layout with Santa Fe twin diesels in foreground. Primary background is blue. Top locomotive on page 11 is 622 with headlight beam completely white. 50 80 110 135
(B) Same as (A), but top locomotive on page 11 is 6220. 50 80 110 135
(C) Same as (A), but top locomotive on page 11 is 6220, and "O27 Gauge" is imprinted in headlight beam. 50 80 110 135

Top row: 1949 Lionel Comic Section Advertisement, Instructions, and Consumer Catalogue. *Bottom row*: 1949 Lionel Train Layout Planning Book for Pop and Track Layouts. The Comic Section is from the F. Wasserman Collection.

	G	VG	EXC	NEW

(D) Same as (C) in content, but cover background is a distinct purple. L. Connors Collection. **NRS**

(E) Same as (A) in content, but certain pages inserted loose-leaf, with no staple holes. R. Otten Collection. **NRS**

(F) Same as (A) in content, but the entire catalogue is printed on a thicker card stock rather than the usual paper. It is not known whether this is a form of advance or dealer catalogue, but it appears to be even scarcer than the regular 1949 advance catalogue. A. Rubin Collection. **NRS**

INSTRUCTIONS FOR ASSEMBLING AND OPERATING LIONEL TRAINS: 5-1/2" x 8-1/2", 56 pages, black ink on white coated stock, No. 926-49.
(A) Light blue and blackish-blue wraparound cover. 3 4 6 8
(B) Two-tone blue wraparound cover. 3 4 6 8

TRACK LAYOUTS: 11" x 8-1/2", 16 pages, printed in green and black on coated white stock. Cover is photo of a section of the New York Lionel showroom layout. Contains tips, drawings, and photos of Lionel accessories. C. Weber Collection. 5 7 9 12

LIONEL TRAIN LAYOUT PLANNING BOOK FOR POP: 5-1/8" x 7-1/16", 16 pages, front cover shows pipe-smoking pop. Printed in multiple colors on white paper, black and red printing on interior white paper. Shows 15 different train layouts. G. Salamone and Weisblum Collections.
(A) As described above. 5 8 12 15
(B) Black and white reprint by The Old Venice Lionel Train Store. 1 2 3 4

RETAIL PRICE MAINTENANCE AGREEMENT: 8" x 12-3/4", two-page Lionel Corporation "Notice" legal document, with facsimile signature of Lawrence Cowen. Identifies that the price agreement is in force in certain states. R. Otten Collection. **NRS**

PRICE LIST: Effective August 1, 1949, 8-3/8" x 10-7/8", 12 pages, red and black on white rag paper. Includes many illustrations of dealer promotional material and a 6-1/2" x 4-1/2" red and black order blank for free poster and window streamers. R. Otten Collection. **NRS**

PRICE SHEET: February 1, 1949; 8-1/2" x 11"; six gray pages, rust color ink. Begins with Scout Line. W. Mekalian Collection. **NRS**

COLOR TRAIN POSTER: 4' x 7', full-color silk-screened poster, features Lionel GG-1 locomotive and Irvington passenger car. The poster came with four window streamers without charge. In 1948 Lionel charged $1.00. L. Connors Collection. — — 600 800

FACTS FOR THE MAN WHO SELLS LIONEL TRAINS: 5-3/8" x 8-1/4", 40 pages, contains "vital information relating to Lionel trains, Lionel accessories, and Lionel construction kits". Cover is black and red on yellow paper; inside pages are white paper. R. Otten Collection. 25 30 40 50

PROMOTIONAL SHEET: 8-1/4" x 10-7/8", one page, "New! Lionel Lamp Post No. 71", black ink on white. R. Otten Collection. — — 15 20

COUPON OFFER FORM: 7-3/8" x 11", one-page sheet, red ink on yellow paper, to order the booklet *Lionel Track Layouts* for 10 cents. There is some evidence that this sheet was issued again in 1951; reader confirmation is requested. A. Rubin Collection. **NRS**

INFORMATION FOR LIONEL APPROVED SERVICE STATIONS: 5-3/8" x 8-1/2", eight pages, illustrates No. 5C test set and provides background to being a Lionel Service Station. Designated Form 932, the booklet is black ink on white paper for inside pages, and cream card stock cover. R. Osterhoff Collection. 10 20 25 35

INSTRUCTION MANUAL: 12" x 8-3/8", for Lionel construction sets; 66 pages, yellow, red and black front cover. Fully illustrated and back cover illustrates a 675 locomotive and tender. A. Rubin Collection. — — 10 15

PRIVATE ISSUE CATALOGUE: "UNEEDA 1949-50 CATALOGUE" 11" x 8-1/2", 16 pages, Lionel throughout, blue and black covers (four pages), black and white elsewhere. **NRS**

1950

ADVANCE CATALOGUE: 11-3/8" x 8", gold cover with "Lionel Trains 1950", black and white inside pages. "Bigger values than ever before" imprinted in white oval on inside cover. 40 60 80 90

ADVANCE CATALOGUE: Same as listing above, but 1950 on cover replaced by "1951" as a pasteup, with other minor alterations. The origin of this piece is not known, but it is believed to be a prototype for the 1951 edition. H. Carter, Jr. Collection. **NRS**

CONSUMER CATALOGUE:
(A) "Golden Anniversary Year", 11-1/4" x 8", 44 pages full color, page 30 not numbered. 25 40 55 65
(B) Same as (A), but page 30 numbered. 25 40 55 65
(C) "Sorry! ...We are substituting this complete catalogue in 2 colors", 11" x 8", 40 pages, red and black on white-coated stock, 2343 shown on cover. 40 50 70 85
(D) Same as (C), but "Bigger values than ever before" imprinted in white oval on cover, Canadian edition. 55 80 120 160

INSTRUCTIONS FOR ASSEMBLING:
(A) 5-1/2" x 8-1/2", 64 pages plus dark blue and light yellow cover; "256 Pages — Hundreds of Pictures Just Published 25 cents", "No. 926-50" on inside front cover. Dixon and Smith Collections. 3 4 6 8
(B) 1/8" dark blue bar atop front cover. **NRS**

ART PRINTS OF 19TH CENTURY LOCOMOTIVES PRESENTED BY LIONEL: As part of Lionel's 50th Anniversary Celebration (1950), Lionel published four handsome color prints of historical locomotives. "The Best Friend of Charleston", "Civil War Period 1860-1875", "The Famous 999-1893", and "The Big Mogul — 1900". 6 8 10 15

THE MAGIC OF LIONEL MAGNETRACTION: 5" x 7", 16 pages including covers, front cover printed in red and black ink on white paper, interior pages printed in black and red on white paper.
(A) As described above. 5 7 9 12
(B) Twenty-four pages including eight-page center insert with excerpts from Lionel 1950 consumer catalogue. Cover marked 'The Hobby House, Inc." R. Spivock Collection. 2 3 4 7

LIONEL RAILROADING IS FUN: 17-1/4" x 23", poster printed in green and black ink on both sides, with prices. Features ideas for layouts, product information and a coupon for ordering the *Model Railroading* Bantam book. 4 6 9 12

DEALER PROMOTIONAL BROCHURE: 8" x 11-7/8", "Lionel Displays for 1950 — The Golden Anniversary Year"; red, black, and white cover. Colorful brochure folds out into six illustrated pages and features dealer displays of the era. — — 30 40

DEALER SALES BOOKLET: 5-1/2" x 8-3/8", 40 pages plus cover, "Facts About Lionel Trains for the Man Who Sells Them", Golden Anniversary Edition, described by Lionel as "a booklet of vital information relating to Lionel trains, Lionel accessories and Lionel construction kits." This edition of one of Lionel's more creative sales aids was issued with an attractive gold and red glossy cover, interior printed in green and black ink on a quality white glossy paper. A. Rubin Collection. — — 50 65

CONSUMER PRICE LIST: 6-7/8" x 9-7/8", single sheet, "Price List for 1950", black on light green paper, printed two sides. Came as an insert for black and white "Sorry..." replacement catalogue. 6 9 12 15

Top row: 1950 Railroading is Fun and Consumer Catalogue. *Bottom row:* 1950 Consumer Catalogue (C), the replacement catalogue, The Magic of Lionel Magnetraction, and the Advance Catalogue.

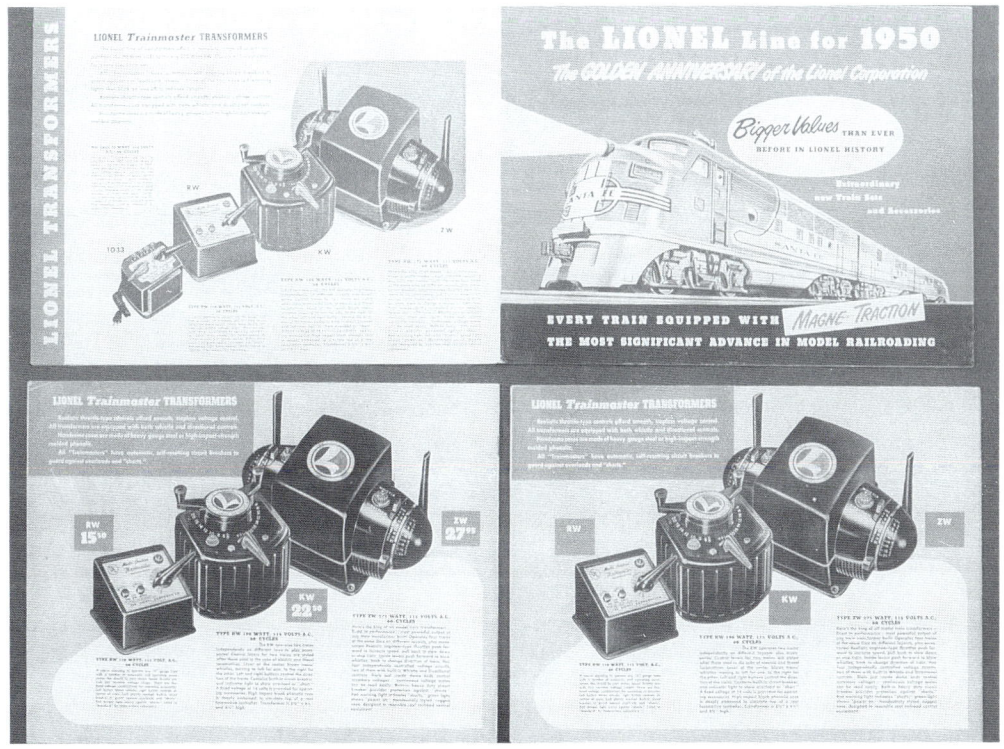

Top row: 1950 Advance Catalogue rear cover and front cover. *Bottom row:* Comparing United States edition *(left)* with Canadian edition *(right)*. Note absence of prices on Canadian edition.

	G	VG	EXC	NEW

LIONEL PRICE LIST: Dec. 26, 1950; 8-1/2" x 11"; three-page folder; black on green paper. W. Mekalian Collection.   **NRS**

PRIVATE ISSUE CATALOGUE: 8-3/8" x 11", 46 pages, "Revere Proudly Presents The Lionel Line for 1950", issued by Revere Electric Supply Co., Chicago, Illinois, a Lionel distributor. Black and white reprint of the Lionel Golden Anniversary advance catalogue. A. Rubin Collection.   **NRS**

PRIVATE ISSUE CATALOGUE: Model Railroad Equipment Corp., 25 pages of Lionel.   **NRS**

COUPON FLYER: 7-5/8" x 11", one page, advertises first edition of Bantam Book, *Model Railroading*, which could be ordered via coupon from Lionel's advertising department. Black and two shades of red on white paper. L. Connors Collection.   —   —   **20**   **25**

PRIVATE ISSUE CATALOGUE: 17" x 22", Madison Hardware Co. Mailer opens into a two-sided, broadside, black and white throughout, similar to 1948 format.   **NRS**

PRIVATE ISSUE CATALOGUE: "5-1/2" x 8-1/2" "950 MODEL R.R. EQUIPMENT CORP." 78 pages tinplate, 28 pages of Lionel, black and white throughout.   **NRS**

PRICE LIST: Effective December 26, 1950, 8-1/2" x 14", one page, black ink on white paper. H. Carter, Jr. Collection.   **NRS**

1951

ADVANCE CATALOGUE: 11" x 8", 24 pages, "1951 Lionel Trains Advance Catalog", red, black, and white cover; black, white, yellow, and red interior. G. Salamone and J. Zydlo Collections.
   5   **10**   **25**   **40**

CONSUMER CATALOGUE: 11-1/8" x 7-3/4", 36 pages, full color, cover illustration shows family in column at left and five trains to the right.
(A) Lower right corner of page 25 is green.   **NRS**
(B) Lower right corner of page 25 is brown.
   15   **25**   **35**   **45**
(C) Same as (B), but 2" white "stream" mark extends over coal loader on front cover. R. Otten Collection.   **NRS**
(D) Same as (A), but paper fold in printing caused 5" white streak through color, page 23.   **NRS**

INSTRUCTIONS FOR ASSEMBLING AND OPERATING LIONEL TRAINS: 5-1/2" x 8-1/2", 64 pages, black ink on white-coated paper. This is the first appearance of changing service station years in an instruction book. For instance, the light green/green variety comes with either a 1950-51 or a 1951-52 service station listing within.
(A) Light green/green, 1950-51 (Service Station listing); "Model Railroading" ad on rear cover.   **3**   **4**   **6**   **8**
(B) Light green/green, 1951-52 (Service Station listing); "Model Railroading" ad on rear cover.   **3**   **4**   **6**   **8**
(C) Light green/green, 1951-52 (Service Station listing); "Model Railroading" ad on rear cover w/red overprint.
   3   **4**   **6**   **8**
(D) Tan-gray/green, 1951-52 (Service Station listing); "Romance" ad on rear cover.   **3**   **4**   **6**   **8**
(E) Gray/green, 1951-52 (Service Station listing); "Romance" ad on rear cover.   **3**   **4**   **6**   **8**
(F) Gray/blue, 1951-52 (Service Station listing): "Romance" ad on rear cover.   **3**   **4**   **6**   **8**

ROMANCE OF MODEL RAILROADING WITH LIONEL TRAINS: 9" x 6", 32 pages including covers, front cover shows

An assortment of Lionel's mailing envelopes. *Top row*: 1952, 1951, and 1950. *Bottom row*: 1949, 1947, and 1948.

	G	VG	EXC	NEW

and orange ink on white paper. G. Salamone and J. Zydlo Collections.

	2	3	5	9

LIONEL RAILROADING IS FUN: 17-1/4" x 23-3/4", poster printed on both sides in blue and black ink on white paper. Shows track plans and accessories inside. G. Salamone and I. D. Smith Collections.
(A) Dark blue and black.   4   6   8   10
(B) Light blue and black. L. Connors Collection.   NRS

ADVANCE CATALOGUE SUPPLEMENT: Two-page flyer folds open to 22" x 11" poster-type sheet, printed in black ink on yellow glossy paper. Flyer features Nos. 1477S, 1479WS, and 1481WS freight sets, with illustrations of each.
(A) Inscription "This set does NOT have Magne-Traction".   NRS
(B) Inscription "This set equipped WITH Magne-Traction". A. Rubin Collection.   NRS

COUPON ORDER FORM: 6-1/2" x 8-3/4", two-page sheet, blue ink on white paper includes a coupon to order a free set of billboards, some of which are illustrated on the form. The reverse side printed in red contains a coupon to order the booklet *Romance of Model Railroading* for 25 cents. A. Rubin Collection.
                     —   —   20   25

POSTAL CARD: Standard United States Post Office card, Lionel acknowledges receipt of a request for the 1951 catalogue and special offer. Indicated "there will be a delay of several weeks in sending this to you" with no explanation as to the delay. Black printing. R. Osterhoff Collection.   NRS

PRIVATE ISSUE CATALOGUE: Fifty-two pages, black ink, issued by Model Railroad Equipment Corp., New York City, with seven pages devoted to Lionel. A. Rubin Collection.
                     —   —   10   15

PRIVATE ISSUE CATALOGUE: The House of Trains, Model Railroad Supply, 1951-52, eleven pages of Lionel trains and track diagrams.   —   —   7   10

PRICE LIST: 8-1/2" x 11", three-page folder, black ink on white paper, "Price List Effective January 12, 1951". R. Otten Collection.
                     5   10   15   20

PRICE LIST: Effective May 1, 1951, 8-1/2" x 11", two pages horizontal, black ink on white paper. The list examined is imprinted Hall's Hobby House, which indicates it could be a private issue.   NRS

PRICE LIST: 8-1/2" x 11"; three-page folder, black ink on ivory paper, no change in prices from January 12, 1951 price sheet, new items added. W. Mekalian Collection.   NRS

PRICE LIST: Aug. 10, 1951 (O.P.S.); 8-1/2" x 11", three-page folder, black on white paper; "Retail Ceiling prices pursuant to office of price stabilization ceiling price regulation 7 Sec. 43 special order 396". W. Mekalian Collection.   NRS

THE LIONEL CORPORATION: 7" x 9"; white enamel paper with black print. Economic stabilization agency "Statement of Considerations". W. Mekalian Collection.   NRS

DEALER SALES BOOKLET: 5-1/2" x 8-1/2", 34 pages, "The Answer Book on Lionel Trains is For the Man Who Sells Them." Illustrations, blueprints and sales hints. R. Otten Collection.
                     20   25   30   40

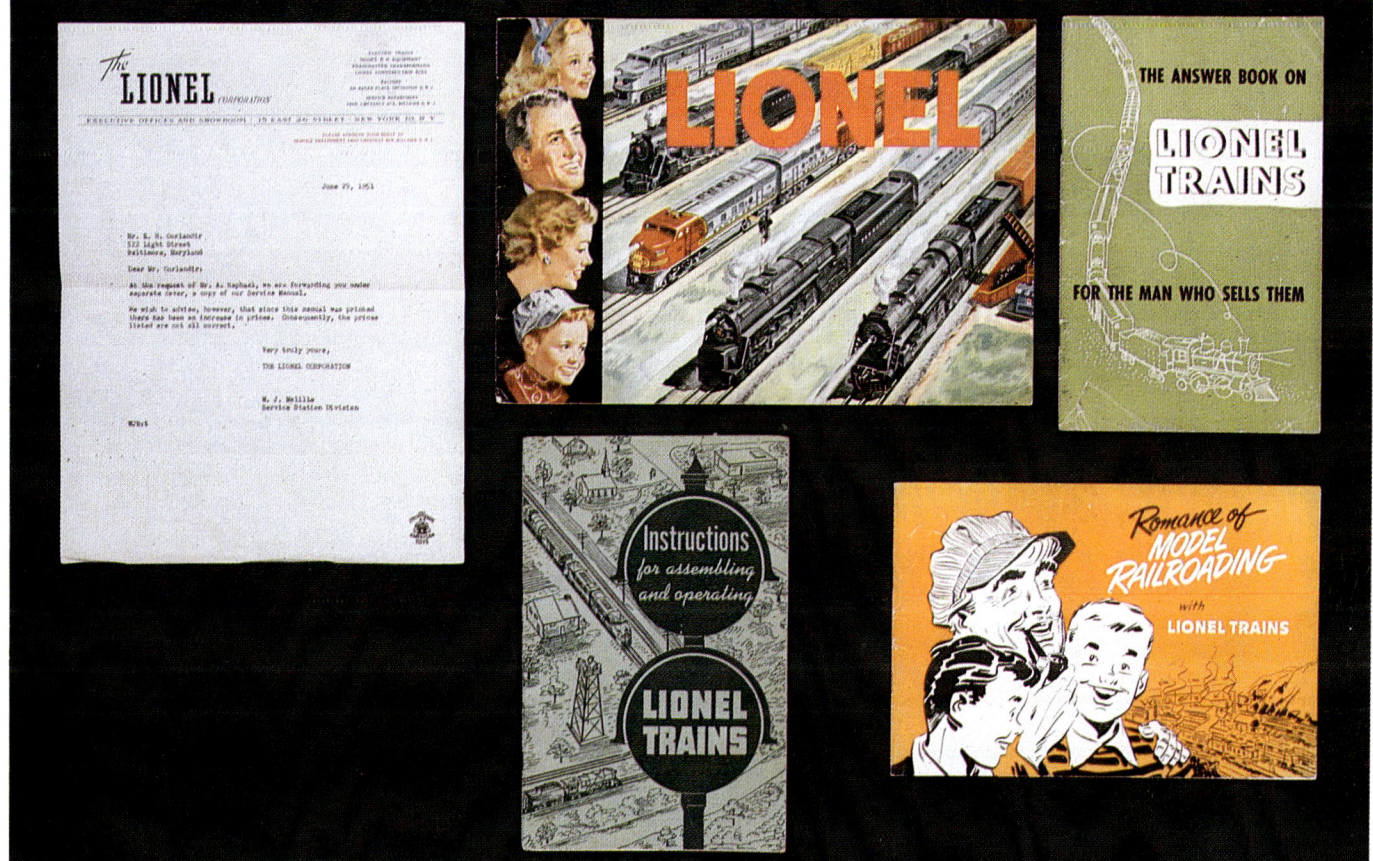

Top row: 1951 Lionel Stationery, Consumer Catalogue, and Dealer Sales Booklet: The Answer Book on Lionel Trains. *Bottom row:* 1951 Instructions and Romance of Model Railroading with Lionel Trains.

	G	VG	EXC	NEW

DISPLAY STICKERS: 5-1/2" x 5-3/4" glassine envelope of stickers, printed in red on yellow peelable adhesive paper. Front of envelope inscribed "use enclosed self-adhering stickers wherever Lionel Merchandise and Displays are shown". L. Connors Collection. — — 30 40

PRICE LABELS: Labels 1-3/16" square printed in sheets of various sizes. Sheets came in envelope marked "This is in accordance with section 43. Office of Price Stabilization". The labels were to be affixed to Lionel merchandise covered by the 1951 current price list.
(A) Assortment of separated labels. — — — 3
(B) Complete set of labels in sheets. — — — 50

COUPON ORDER FORM: 7" x 9" form, "NEW! JUST OFF THE PRESS", to order new 35 cent Bantam *Model Railroading* edition. NRS

PRIVATE ISSUE CATALOGUE: "8-1/2" x 11", The House of Trains MODEL RAILROAD SUPPLY MANUAL 1951-52" edition: 48 pages including current line, track diagrams and excerpts from *Model Builder*, black and white throughout. NRS

1952

ADVANCE CATALOGUE: 11-1/8" x 8", 40 red, black, and yellow pages, red and black cover. Cover carries only inscription "Lionel trains for 1952 — Advance Catalog".
(A) With product prices. 15 25 35 45
(B) Without product prices. Canadian edition. L. Connors Collection. NRS

CONSUMER CATALOGUE: 11-7/8" x 7-3/4", 36 pages, cover illustration shows boy overlooking Lionel arch bridge; Santa Fe switcher with train is crossing bridge and six locomotives are lined up beneath it.
(A) Back cover (page 36) has full-page illustration of three Trainmaster transformers. 7 15 25 35
(B) Same as (A), but cover has violet background, with partial dark blue background in upper right corner only. R. Otten Collection. NRS
(C) Back cover (page 36) has partial page illustration of three Trainmaster transformers, plus space for a store imprint. Inscribed in the space is "Hi fellers: Here's where to get Lionel Trains!" 7 15 25 35
(D) Same as (C), but combination Lionel and private issue catalogue. "The House of Trains", Chicago, Illinois overprinted in black on cover, plus a private issue black and white 16-page catalogue has been stapled into the center. A. Rubin Collection. NRS
(E) Same as (C), but cover has violet background. L. Connors Collection. NRS

INSTRUCTIONS FOR ASSEMBLING:
(A) 8-1/2" x 5-1/2", 64 pages, black ink on white interior coated pages plus yellow and dark blue wraparound cover, "Form 926- 52". Dixon and Smith Collections. 2 3 5 7

Top row: 1952 Paper City and Distributors Advertising Promotions Catalogue. *Bottom row*: 1952 Advance Catalogue, Consumer Catalogue, Official Book of Rules, and Railroading Is Fun poster.

	G	VG	EXC	NEW

(B) 8-1/2" x 5-1/2", 64 pages, black, white, and green on gray-brown cover, No. 926-51. **2 3 5 7**

DISTRIBUTORS ADVERTISING PROMOTIONS: 9-1/2" x 11", color cover, inside pages are either red and black or blue and black, printed on pulp paper, cover language, "1952 Lionel Trains with Real Puffing Smoke, Built in Remote Control Whistle, and Sensational new Magnetraction in all Diesel Locomotives". This catalogue was printed for dealer distribution and contained a block on the rear cover for dealer name and address. Bryan Collection.
5 10 15 20

LIONEL TRAIN CATALOGUE: 11-1/4" x 7-5/8", 36 pages including covers and interior pages printed in full color on coated paper; this catalogue shows retail prices; was probably a Lionel authorized reprinting in conjunction with a distributor. The retail store name appeared on the front cover; sample observed marked, "Playworld Toy Shop, Utica, N.Y." G. Salamone and I. D. Smith Collections.
3 5 7 10

PAPER CITY: 42" x 22", full-color printing, includes two oil trucks, two passenger automobiles, service station, packing plant, pump station, and other items. Available as part of coupon offer. C. Lang and Schreiner Collections. **10 15 20 25**

OFFICIAL BOOK OF RULES FOR MODEL RAILROADING: 4-3/16" x 6-1/8", 16 pages, blue cover, inside pages have blue ink with red and green ink on signals. Available as part of coupon offer.
(A) As described above. **4 6 20 25**
(B) Same as above, but printing error; pages 7 and 10 have blue printing shifted approximately 1/2", causing mis-registration of red and green signals. L. Connors Collection. **NRS**

RAILROADING IS FUN: Fold-out poster, 17-1/4" x 22-3/4", printed in black and white on both sides with orange background. M. Ocilka and Salamone Collections. **4 6 9 12**

MINIATURE CATALOGUE: Front and back in color with inside pages black and white, printed one side only on paper stock. Measures 7-7/8" x 5-1/2". It is believed this was a pre-production mock-up copy. W. Mekalian Collection. **NRS**

PRIVATE ISSUE CATALOGUE: 8-3/8" x 11", 48 pages, "Billy and Ruth — America's Famous Toy Children", toy catalogue, in full color, of which four pages are devoted to Lionel. A. Rubin Collection.
NRS

PRIVATE ISSUE CATALOGUE: 8-1/2" x 11", 36 pages, "Reference Guide to Electric Trains", 36-page catalogue issued by The Hobby House, Cleveland, Ohio, devotes eight illustrated pages to Lionel, in addition to several pages of Lionel track layouts. Blue and yellow front cover. A. Rubin Collection. **3 5 7 10**

PRIVATE ISSUE CATALOGUE: 8-1/2" x 11", 52 pages, "Model Railroad Equipment Corp.....1951-1952", all tinplate, seven pages Lionel current line, black and white throughout. **NRS**

CATALOGUE ACKNOWLEDGMENT: 8-1/2" x 11", one page, form letter from Dan Magee, The Lionel Engineer, confirming enclosure of the 1952 catalogue, "hot off the press".
— — 7 15

PRICE LIST LIONEL TRAINS: July 18, 1952; 8-1/2" x 11"; blue print on white paper. W. Mekalian Collection. **NRS**

CUSTOMER SURVEY: Form letter from Dan Magee, the Lionel Engineer, acknowledging completion of a special Lionel survey, and indicating a copy of the *Romance of Railroading* booklet is enclosed. Printed on Lionel stationery with Brooklyn, New York return address.
— — 7 15

CAVALCADE OF TRAINS: 8-1/2" x 5-1/2", 40 pages, private issue catalogue by Model Railroad Equipment Corp., New York, three colors. This was actually a distributor catalogue and could include other store names as well. **— — — 8**

DEALER SALES BOOKLET: 5-1/2" x 8-1/2", 32 pages, "The Answer Book on Lionel Trains...For the Man Who Sells Them". Yellow and black cover, inside pages creatively arranged with tabbed pages, layout ideas, and many illustrations. W. Mekalian and A. Rubin Collections. **15 20 30 40**

PROMOTIONAL FOLDER: 15-1/2" x 11-1/4", "Here's Your Christmas Sales Ticket". Large glossy folder with 726 locomotive with freight set being admired by a man and boy. The boy is wearing an engineers cap with pins attached. Full color highlighted by bright yellow. It is believed this is the dealer promotional pack envelope; one sample included the 1952 catalogue, hat (without "Lionel"), pins, and other consumer promotional items. **NRS**

LIONEL ENGINEER'S CAP LEAFLET: Actual hat accompanied by 7-7/8" x 4-7/8" sheetlet entitled "Dear Railroad Fan" and glassine packet of tin lapel buttons with railroad insignias. R. Otten Collection. Price for sheet only. **— — 20 25**

"HOW TO HAVE FUN WITH YOUR LIONEL MODEL R. R.": 8-1/4" x 10-3/4", two pages, promotional flyer in black and red on white paper. Consumer coupon flyer. L. Connors Collection. **NRS**

DEALER POSTER: 3-1/2" x 7", color paper poster, pictures boy viewing a Santa Fe AA diesel unit with silver liner cars. A. Rubin Collection. **NRS**

PROMOMOTIONAL FLYER: 7" x 10", one page, "Here it is!", red and black on white paper advertising new consumer catalogue. R. Stidd Collection. **NRS**

PROMOTIONAL FLYER: 7-3/4" x 10", one page, "We are now ready to go to press...", red and black ink on white paper advertising consumer catalogue. R. Stidd Collection. **NRS**

ORDER BLANK: 7" x 10", one page, red and black on white, coupon for dealer orders of consumer catalogue. R. Stidd Collection.
NRS

1953

ADVANCE CATALOGUE: 11-1/4" x 7-5/8", 44 pages, color cover with Santa Fe 2343 diesels, black and white inside pages with red and orange backgrounds and headings.
(A) Cover includes inscription "Advance Catalog for 1953", inside pages include prices. **20 30 40 55**
(B) No inscription on cover, and inside pages contain no prices, Canadian edition. Includes two-page Canadian Price List 1953, printed in blue ink on white glossy paper, illustrating 2333 Santa Fe diesel. A. Rubin Collection. **NRS**

CONSUMER CATALOGUE: 7-5/8" x 11-1/4", 40 pages, full color. Cover features steam and diesel locomotives heading in opposite directions.
(A) Page 8, "No. 2046 Lionel Steam Loco (above)" and "No. 2055 steam loco (right)"; page 14 "Lionel New No. 685 Steam Loco."
10 15 20 25
(B) Page 8, "No. 2046 Lionel Steam Loco and Tender (above)" and "No. 2055 Steam Loco and Tender (right)"; page 14 "Lionel New No. 685 Steam Loco". **10 15 20 25**
(C) Page 8, "No. 2046 Lionel Steam Loco (above)" and "No. 2055 Steam Loco (right)"; page 14 "Lionel New No. 685 Steam Loco and Tender". **10 15 20 25**
(D) Page 8, "No. 2046 Lionel Steam Loco and Tender (above)" and "No. 2055 Steam Loco and Tender (right)"; page 14 "Lionel New 685 Steam Loco and Tender". **10 15 20 25**

MINI CATALOGUE: 5-5/8" x 7-7/8", 32 pages, full-color cover similar to large size listed above. Some inside color pages, mostly black and pale colors. Came with imprinted outer envelope. Price with envelope. **7 9 12 15**

TEMPLATE SHEET: 8-1/2" x 11", "Templates of Lionel Accessories", Form 1364 8-53. Adhesive backed to cut and plan layouts.
— — 4 7

DISTRIBUTOR'S ADVERTISING PROMOTIONS CATALOGUE: 8-1/2" x 11", 16 pages, usually imprinted with store adver-

Top row: 1953 Consumer Catalogue, Canadian Advance Catalogue, and Dealer Sales Book. *Left center:* Mini Catalogue with mailing envelope. *Bottom row:* How to Operate Lionel Trains, Distributor's Advertising Promotions Catalogue, and How to Operate Lionel Trains.

	G	VG	EXC	NEW

tising, pulp paper, color covers, red, black, and blue interior pages, "New Lionel Trains for 1953" on cover. 7 9 11 14

PRIVATE ISSUE CATALOGUE: 8-1/2" x 11", 16 pages full color, known as UNEEDA Catalogue. M. Ocilka Collection.
  3 5 7 10

PRIVATE ISSUE CATALOGUE: 8-1/2" x 11", 16 pages, covers are white heavy stock and show "UNEEDA TRAIN TOWN" store front, 736 steam engine, "Trains Are Our Business, Not a Sideline". I. D. Smith Collection. 3 5 7 10

HOW TO OPERATE LIONEL TRAINS AND ACCESSORIES: 8-1/2" x 5-3/8", 64 pages, black ink, plus wraparound cover, No. 926-53.
(A) Black and yellow wraparound cover. M. Weisblum Collection.
  2 3 5 7
(B) Orange and black wraparound cover. M. Ocilka Collection.
  2 3 5 7

LIONEL ACCESSORIES: 9" x 6", 16 pages, "Give you true Railroading Realism and Operating Excitement", coated stock, red and black print on white paper. Bryan Collection.
  2 3 5 9

ADVERTISING FLYER: 7" x 10", "Lionel Trains for Fun and Excitement" printed in black and red on glossy paper; four sets on front, accessories on back with prices. Schreiner Collection.
  1 2 5 6

DEALER SALES BOOK: 5-3/8" x 8-3/8", "At Your Service, the Answer Book on Lionel Trains", orange and black see-through cover. Inside pages are tabbed for reference purposes. R. Otten Collection.
  10 20 30 40

STORE DISPLAY CATALOGUE AND PRICE LIST: 12" x 9", 12 pages, white-coated paper, printed black and red, front cover includes "1953 Price List — Store Displays — Merchandise Assortments — Special Catalog". L. Connors Collection.
  15 25 40 50

THE GOLDEN BOOK OF TRAINS: 8-1/4" x 10-1/2", 88 pages, by Jane Werner and published by Simon & Schuster, New York. Full-color cover features 2333 Santa Fe diesel, inside color illustrated drawings. This book was prepared "with the cooperation of the Lionel Corporation" and sold for 50 cents in 1953.
  — — 15 20

CAVALCADE OF TRAINS: 8-1/2" x 5-1/2", 40 pages, private issue catalogue by Model Railroad Equipment Corp., New York, three colors. — — 7 10

EMPLOYEE HANDBOOK: 5-5/8" x 7-3/8", 45 pages, titled "Life at Lionel", issued to Lionel employees in the 1950s to explain the company, its management, and benefits. Printed on a high quality high gloss paper, in four colors on the cover, blue and black on white paper on the inside pages. This informative piece of literature bears a remarkable resemblance to copy layout and certain articles found

| | G | VG | EXC | NEW |

in the employee publication, *All Aboard*; this is no small coincidence, for both publications were issued under the direction of Philip H. Marfuggi, Lionel's Industrial Relations Director. As a leader in progressive employee benefits in its day, Lionel provided ample benefits such as group insurance, paid holidays, and a health clinic, all of which is thoroughly explained in this unusual document. W. Mekalian Collection. **NRS**

REFERENCE CHART: "Chart of Lionel Replacement Lamps", one page, Form No. 1292 May 15, 1953. Black on white paper, with attached price increase note. — — 2 4

PARTS ORDER FORM: Nine-page pre-printed Form No. 1302 3-53, begins with part No. 1-92 brush. Printed in black on pink paper. 4 8 12 15

1954

ADVANCE CATALOGUE: 11-1/4" x 7-5/8", 44 pages, color cover with Lackawanna 2321 FM diesel, red and black on white-coated inside pages. Cover states "Advance Catalog 1954".
(A) Prices included on inside pages, frequently came with one- page "boxcar" insert (see separate listing). 15 25 35 45
(B) No prices on inside pages, Canadian edition. Included Canadian Price List 1954, two pages printed on white glossy paper. This edition also came with the one-page "boxcar" insert. A. Rubin Collection. **NRS**

MASTER CATALOGUE: Consumer 44-page catalogue, 11-1/4" x 7-5/8", in full color, but spiral bound in white and thick clear acetate cover on front and back. Sometimes referred to as the Executive Advance Catalogue. A. Rubin Collection. **NRS**

CONSUMER CATALOGUE:
(A) 11-1/4" x 7-5/8", 44 pages, full color, coated stock, yellow cover with four locomotive fronts. 5 10 15 20
(B) 8-1/8" x 5-3/4", 32 pages, color covers like (A), red and black interior printing, coated stock. Identified as "Special Lionel Dealer Catalogue", also known as a mini catalogue. Came with imprinted outer envelope. Price with envelope. 5 10 15 20

NEW LIONEL BOXCARS: Supplement to advance catalogue, 10-1/2" x 7-1/4", one-side, black and white on coated stock, illustrates 6464-125, 6464-100, 6464-150, 6464-175, and lists others. 5 10 15 20

DISTRIBUTOR'S ADVERTISING PROMOTIONS: 8-3/8" x 11", 16 pages, color covers, black, red, and yellow interior pages, cover illustration shows two boys watching 2321 FM traverse girder bridge. Issued by Distributors Advertising Promotions, Inc. Philadelphia. 7 9 12 15

ACCESSORIES CATALOGUE: 9" x 6", 20 pages, coated stock, green and black printing, four-page blue center section, pages not numbered. I. D. Smith Collection. 1 2 3 4

HOW TO OPERATE LIONEL TRAINS AND ACCESSORIES: 5-1/2" x 8-1/2", 64 pages, plus black and green wraparound cover, black ink, No. 926-54.
(A) Light green cover. 3 4 6 8
(B) Darker blue-green cover, 1954-55 Service Station Listing. 3 4 6 8

Top left: 1954 Dealer Advertising posters. *Bottom left*: 1952 Catalogue Acknowledgment. *Bottom center*: 1954 Lionel Trains for Fun and Excitement promotional sheet. *Right top and bottom*: Dealer Sales Booklets from 1952 and 1955.

64 • Greenberg's Guide to Lionel Paper and Collectibles

	G	VG	EXC	NEW

(C) Same as (B), 1955-56 Service Station Listing.
3 4 6 8

LET'S PLAN THE FINEST LIONEL LAYOUT IN TOWN: 10-7/8" x 8-1/4", 16 pages including covers. Front cover shows dad and son with Lackawanna Train Master, Seaboard NW-2, and 736 steamer; front cover and interior pages printed in black and red ink on white paper. G. Salamone Collection. **3 5 8 10**

STORE DISPLAY CATALOGUE: 12" x 9", 12 pages, white-coated stock, black and red ink. Contains "1954 Price sheet on Lionel trains" with retail prices and the statement that "Lionel products are price fixed and sold under Fair Trade Act". Diggle Collection. **NRS**

SALES PROMOTIONAL LITERATURE: 13-3/4" x 11-1/2" reprint of two articles from October 26, 1954 *New York Times* pertaining to Fair Trade laws. Special mailing to dealers included a letter dated October 26, 1954 from S. Belser, Lionel Sales Manager, requesting support for Lionel's price maintenance program. L. Connors Collection. **NRS**

CAVALCADE OF TRAINS: 8-1/8" x 5-3/4", 36 pages, private issue catalogue by Model Railroad Equipment Corp., New York; black and blue ink on glossy paper with full-color cover. Inserted in the center is the complete "mini" version of the 1954 consumer catalogue. L. Connors Collection. **5 9 12 15**

LIONEL PROMOTIONAL ARTICLE: "Sorry Junior...It's Papa Who Plays", four-page feature appearing in Winter Edition of *Exide Topics*, manufacturer of Exide-Ironclad Batteries. Cover illustrates boy with Lionel engineer's hat, and inside photo highlights Lionel's New York showroom. Included here for reference only. **NRS**

COUPON OFFER: 6" x 8", "Hello Pop! Just a Reminder...", two-page card to put at "pop's breakfast plate..", features illustrations and space for a checkmark by various Lionel sets and accessories. Black and orange ink on cream card stock. R. Osterhoff Collection.
5 10 15 20

LIONEL ADVERTISING BOOKLET: Large (10-7/8" x 15" vertical) eight-page glossy brochure outlining the ad campaign for 1954. Includes page listing newspapers carrying Lionel advertising as well as four pages illustrating the advertising in full color. Each page was printed one side only; part of the 1954 dealer's promotional kit. A. Rubin Collection. **NRS**

DEALER ADVERTISING POSTER: 22" x 9", "You're the Boss with Lionel Trains and Accessories", features boy operating 2037 locomotive. Poster printed on glossy white paper in red and black. Reader confirmation requested whether this was part of the 1954 dealer promotional kit. A. Rubin Collection.
— — — 60

DEALER ADVERTISING POSTER: 20" x 6-1/2", "Brand New 1954 Lionel Trains with Magne-Traction" featuring 2321 Lackawanna FM. Full-color drawings on white glossy paper. A. Rubin Collection. **NRS**

DEALER ADVERTISING POSTER: 20" x 6-1/2", "Brand New 1954 Lionel Trains with Magne-Traction" featuring blue/orange 6250

Top row: 1954 All Aboard (see Introduction for description), Accessories Catalogue, Distributors Advertising Promotions Catalogue, and Hello Pop folder. *Center*: 1954 Consumer Catalogue. *Bottom row*: 1954 Advance Catalogue, Mini Catalogue, and Let's Plan the Finest Lionel Layout.

Postwar Paper: 1945-1969 • 65

Top row: 1955 versions of Elliott Rowland Catalogue, versions of Advance Catalogue. *Bottom row:* 1955 Consumer Catalogue, Store Display Catalogue with merchandise assortments and dealer displays, and How to Operate Lionel Trains and Accessories.

	G	VG	EXC	NEW

Seaboard switcher; full-color drawings on white glossy paper. A. Rubin Collection. **NRS**

REFERENCE CHART: "Chart of Lionel Replacement Lamps", one page, Form No. 1291, April 1, 1954. Black ink on white paper.
— — 2 4

DEALER BROCHURE: 5-1/2" x 8-1/2", eight numbered pages, "Information for Lionel Approved Service Stations". Form 932 Revised, with Describes Service Station tools and repair requirements. R. Otten Collection. — 15 20 30

ADVERTISING MATS: Numbered mats of various sizes featuring Lionel products. Made of papier-mache. **NRS**

PRIVATE ISSUE CATALOGUE: 11" x 8-1/2" when folded, opens to four-page poster. One side green on white; opposite side black on white; issued by Woodruff Hobbies, Pittsburgh, Pennsylvania. R. Otten Collection. **NRS**

1955

ADVANCE CATALOGUE: 11-1/4" x 7-3/4", 20 pages, black and white, lightweight coated stock.
(A) Black and white cover, "Advance Catalog 1955", with single staple. 10 15 20 30
(B) Black and white cover, "Advance Catalog 1955", issued with loose pages and no staple. 10 15 20 30
(C) Orange, black, and white cover, "Advance Catalog 1955", with staples. 10 20 30 40

DEALER CATALOGUE: Showing set compositions and components, cars, track, etc. White with black and white halftones of 1955 sets on glossy paper, 27 pages printed on one side only, no cover, sheets stapled together on left-hand side, shows 27 sets. J. Zydlo and Diggle Collections. 25 35 50 60

CONSUMER CATALOGUE: 11-1/4" x 7-5/8", 44 pages, full color, coated stock, white cover with five-train set and six happy faces.
10 15 20 25

EXECUTIVE CATALOGUE: 11-3/8" x 8-5/8", 50 inside pages printed one side only on heavy glossy stock. Spiral bound, dark blue card stock cover, imprinted in gold "Lionel Trains 1955 — With Exclusive Magne Traction". R. Otten Collection. **NRS**

ELLIOTT ROWLAND CATALOGUE: Private issue catalogue, usually imprinted with store advertising.
(A) 8-3/8" x 11-1/8", yellow covers with "Lionel Trains by (Store Name)", pages 5 and 14 are yellow, pulp paper; cover illustration shows father leaning against easy chair while grandfather operates the trains and children look on. 5 7 12 15
(B) Same as (A), but color cover with blue background.
5 7 12 15
(C) Same as (A), but cover miscut, causing larger page. R. Otten Collection. **NRS**

HOW TO OPERATE LIONEL TRAINS AND ACCESSORIES: 8-1/2" x 5-1/2", 64 pages, includes Service Station listing, black ink, brown and white wraparound cover, Form 926-55.
2 3 5 7

| | G | VG | EXC | NEW |

ACCESSORY CATALOGUE: 11-1/4" x 7-3/4", 20 pages including covers, inside pages printed in black ink on white stock. This is the same as the Advance Catalogue, except for title and ink.
(A) Cover printed in black and orange. G. Salamone Collection.
                                             5   10   15   20
(B) Cover printed in black and white. L. Connors Collection.
                                             5   10   15   20

TEMPLATES: 8-1/2" x 11", one-page depiction of track, switches, and crossovers one-eighth actual size. "For Lionel O27 Layouts". Form 1061 Rev 11-55 upper left corner. Peel-off track templates (reusable if used on surface such as porcelain, linoleum, etc.) Also made available in 1977. J. Algozzini and A. Rubin Collections.
                                             2   3   4   6

BANNER: 21" x 6-1/2", "YES, WE HAVE THEM! LIONEL'S EXCITING NEW 1955 ACTION PACK ACCESSORIES", red and black on white, featuring 352 ice depot and others. L. Connors Collection.
                                            30   40   60   75

AD MAT PROMOTIONAL POSTER: 20-5/8" x 28", with coupon to order mats, printed on newsprint paper in black ink. L. Otten Collection.   NRS

STORE DISPLAY CATALOGUE: 12" x 9", eight pages, white-coated stock, black and red ink, red cover lettered "New for 1955 — Store Displays — Window Displays, etc." Lists dealer assortments at cost of $3,000, $1,200, and $600. L. Connors Collection.
                                            20   30   40   50

DEALER ORDER FORM: 18" x 11-3/4", "Lionel Trains", begins Stock No. 1525, white paper.
                                             —   —   1   2

THE GOLDEN PLAY BOOK OF TRAIN STAMPS: 8-1/4" x 10-3/4", 48 pages, glossy full-color front and back covers, black and white inside pages with line drawings. Spaces inside to paste "stamps" of railroad photographs combined with Lionel engines and rolling stock. Books with stamps intact with sheets are rare, since books typically have the stamps pasted in the spaces provided.
                                            10   15   20   30

DEALER SALES BOOKLET: 13-1/4" x 10-1/2", "And Away We Go for Record Sales in 1955", red cover illustrating Lionel Lines and steam locomotive. On the cover of the 16-page booklet was glued a playable 78 rpm record, "I'm a Lionel (Toot Toot) Engineer." Generally these records, playable on one side only, are found separate from the booklet. W. Mekalian and A. Rubin Collections. (See Chapter Ten for a separate listing of the record accompanying this booklet.)
                                                              NRS

DEALER SALES BOOKLET: 5-1/2" x 8-1/2", 32 pages, printed vertically, "Know the Answers and Sell More Lionel", light gray-black cover with man holding a 2321 Lackawanna FM, with all lettering on cover in orange. Opens like an address book with pages cut and tabs down the side. A. Rubin Collection.   20   25   35   45

DEALER SALES AID: 8-1/2" x 11", one-page sheet, on radio scripts, 60 seconds each. Part of 1955 dealer promotional pack. A. Rubin Collection.   NRS

PRICE LIST: 8-1/2" x 11", two-pages, "Canadian Price List 1955", black on white paper, identifies Canadian retail market prices.
                                             8   10   12   15

1956

ADVANCE CATALOGUE: 11" x 8", 48 pages, black and white, red cover with "Order Now!" Provides much information of dealer displays and advertising campaigns.
(A) Page 2 illustrates two outfits at left of page.   NRS
(B) Page 2 illustrates three-digit number at left of page.   NRS
(C) No outfit numbers illustrated on Page 2.
                                            25   35   50   65
(D) No outfit numbers on page 2; "714" outfit listed on page 17.
                                            25   35   50   65
(E) No outfit numbers on page 2; "714" omitted on page 17.   NRS

CONSUMER CATALOGUE: 11-1/4" x 7-5/8", 40 pages, full color, coated stock, cover illustration shows PRR and NH electrics, Lionel Lines steam locomotive, 3530, 3360, and 3927.
(A) "Remember: Lionel Train Sets Start as Low as $19.95...." in white block on back cover.
                                             7   10   15   18
(B) No lettering in white block on back cover.
                                             7   10   15   18

ACCESSORY CATALOGUE: 11" x 8", 24 pages, red and black on pulp paper.   5   10   15   20

HOW TO OPERATE LIONEL TRAINS AND ACCESSORIES:
(A) Includes Service Station listings, 8-1/2" x 5-1/4", 64 pages, black and white, red and blue wraparound cover, Form 925- 56. Graham Collection.   2   3   5   7
(B) Pale yellow and dark blue cover, drawing of dad and son playing trains, 64 pages copyrighted inside front cover of 1950, came with advertising sheet, "Send for Billboards" (25 cents) one side and send for "Romance of Model Railroading Book" on other side, copyrighted 1956, contains individual items only. C. Weber Collection.   NRS

1956 Accessory Catalogue, Consumer Catalogue, and Elliott Rowland Catalogue.

| | G | VG | EXC | NEW |

(C) Black and brown covers, 55 inside yellow pages. Booklet is stapled. **NRS**

ELLIOTT ROWLAND CATALOGUE: 8-1/4" x 11", 24 pages including covers, full-color front cover shows mom, dad, and two children looking in a store window at a Lionel layout; catalogue shows retail prices. Rowland was authorized by Lionel to print and distribute these inexpensive catalogues depicting the Lionel line.

         5   7   12   15

LIONEL MERCHANDISE ASSORTMENTS AND DISPLAYS: 11-3/4" x 8-3/8", eight pages, red and black cover, contains listing of 1956 set numbers which do not appear in either the advance or consumer catalogues. Features dealer displays and layouts. B. Stekoll Collection. **20 25 35 45**

RAISE THE CURTAIN...LET EVERYBODY SEE...LIONEL'S UNDER $20 OUTFIT FOR '56: 10-7/8" x 7-7/8", four pages, dealer promotional booklet. Four colors on white paper. L. Connors Collection. **NRS**

DEALER SALES BOOKLET: 5-1/2" x 8-1/2", 32 pages, "Know the Answers and Sell More Lionel", white cover with Lionel lion holding a 2350 New Haven, "Know the Answers" in black type and "Sell More Lionel" in orange type. Opens like an address book with pages cut and tabs down the side. J. Delgenio and A. Rubin Collections. **20 30 40 50**

DEALER SALES BROCHURE: "Quickies..to Help You Sell Lionel Trains and Accessories". Three-page brochure printed in pink, includes a radio advertising script. F. S. Davis Collection. **NRS**

OUTFIT PRICE CATALOGUE: Crude 8-1/2" x 11", eight pages, black and white dealer price list issued by Lionel in typed format. List is printed one side only with no illustrations.
(A) Pages numbered at top right. A. Rubin Collection. **NRS**
(B) Pages unnumbered. **NRS**

SERVICE STATION STICKER: Peelable sticker measures 3" in diameter, printed in red, blue, and white with inscription "Wausau" on reverse. Inscription reads "Lionel Trains — Sales, Service, Repairs" surrounding Lionel "L". A. Rubin Collection. **NRS**

TRAIN-O-RAMA PROMOTIONAL CUTOUTS: Set of 12 replicas of famous trains and scenes. Lionel entered into a partnership with National Biscuit Company's Special Products Division in placing one of these colorful models in every specially marked package of Nabisco Shredded Wheat. These three dimensional models were issued in three sections, each measuring 3-3/4" x 7- 3/8", printed one side only on card stock, and identified "T. M. Lionel Corp Spec'y Adv Serv, Inc." It is believed these were included in cereal in 1956, although a write-up of this promotion was included in a late 1957 issue of Lionel's *All Aboard* magazine. No complete sets have been observed. Parts of the set included in the R. Fetzner, G. Magner, and W. Mekalian Collections. **NRS**

AD MAT ORDER FORM: 28" x 22", black on white paper, "Free Ad Mats", and illustrating proofs for composing customized store advertising. Included in 1956 promotional kit. **NRS**

PRIVATE CATALOGUE: 8-3/8" x 11", 16-pages, black and white consumer catalogue, "Call all Engineers it's Lionel Traintime at..." (space included for store stamp). A privately-printed catalogue with discounted prices, one copy was from Paul Lauterborn's Appliance Shop, with no city given. The origin of these catalogues is unknown, and no copyright data is included in their contents. A. Rubin Collection. **NRS**

DISTRIBUTOR PRICE LIST: 8-1/2" x 11" price list issued by Akorn Distributors, black on white paper, three pages, and includes a two-page order form in similar format to Lionel's. R. Osterhoff Collection. **NRS**

PRICE LIST: 7-1/2" x 11", two pages, "Canadian Price List 1956", black and white glossy paper. **5 6 8 10**

| | G | VG | EXC | NEW |

DEALER ORDER FORM: 18" x 11-3/4", "Lionel Trains", begins Stock No. 1543, on pink paper. **— — 1 2**

PROMOTIONAL MASK: Cardboard face mask, presumably for children, featuring the Lionel Lion in full color on the front, and promotional write-ups on 2350 New Haven electric, 3360 burro crane, 465 sound dispatching station, and 3927 track cleaning car, all new items for 1956. The mask is almost circular, measuring approximately 10-1/2" in diameter, and was distributed as part of a Halloween promotion. **— — 15 25**

SERVICE REMUNERATION CHART: Form 1242 Rev. printed on full color Lionel Corporation stationery with designation "1956-57", with four-page black and white compensation charts.

         7 10 15 20

RAISE THE CURTAIN . . . LET EVERY BODY SEE: 11" x 8-1/2", dealer advertising booklet, red and black cover.

         7 10 15 20

1957

ADVANCE CATALOGUE: 11" x 8-1/4", 56 pages, red and black covers, inside printing on black and white coated stock.
(A) Regular advance issue with set numbers on all pages. Reference page 2 as a check: Set 1569-725 identified for set led by 202 Union Pacific Alco Diesel. **40 60 80 100**
(B) Catalogue contents same as (A), except that no set numbers are referenced in the catalogue. Reference page 2 as a check: no set number appears above "Lionel Diesel Freight" in large bold letters.
         50 70 90 110

CONSUMER CATALOGUE: 11-1/4" x 7-1/2", 52 pages, full color, coated stock, cover has "NEW SUPER O TRACK" and features an array of Lionel locomotives throughout.
(A) Page 51: "Layout as shown above requires two 4 x 8 plywood boards". L. Steuer, Jr. Collection. **7 9 12 15**
(B) Page 51: "Layout as shown above requires two 5 x 9 plywood boards". **5 7 10 12**

HO CATALOGUE: 10-7/8" x 7-5/8", "And Now HO By Lionel!", features engineer with lantern on front cover of four-page brochure, in full color on glossy paper.
(A) Brochure, printed four pages to fold out to 20-3/4" x 7-5/8".
         3 5 7 10
(B) Same as (A), but "Madison Hardware" and address printed in same bold black ink on bottom of front page.
         3 5 7 10
(C) Same as (A), but with some content changes on the front page, and the entire brochure folds out to 20-3/4" x 15-1/4" with printing on one side only. R. Connors Collection. **NRS**

Three Lionel Collector Trading Cards from 1957: Burlington, Western Pacific, and The General. We do not know how these cards were distributed.

COLLECTOR TRADING CARDS:
These attractive cards measure 3-1/2" x 2-3/4" and were printed in full color on the face, and include on the reverse of each card a railroad quiz game. The cards were copyrighted by Lionel and printed in the United States, as each card indicates. There are a total of 24 cards, 12 of which were reprinted in 1959 by Lionel and appear on the reverse of Lionel's *Great Locomotive Race Game*. These later reprints are not

Three Lionel Collector Quiz Cards from 1957: Western Pacific, Chicago Burlington, and The General (backs of cards shown on previous page).

	G	VG	EXC	NEW

in full color and do not include a railroad quiz game. Little is known about these cards, and reader assistance would be welcomed.

Alaskan	Norfolk & Western
Baltimore and Ohio	Northern Pacific
Boston And Maine	Pennsylvania
Burlington	Rio Grande
Canadian Pacific	Rock Island
General	Santa Fe
Great Northern	Seaboard
Illinois Central	Southern
Milwaukee	Union Pacific
M-K-T	Virginian
New Haven	Wabash
New York Central	Western Pacific

W. Mekalian, A. Rubin, and J. Trever Collections.   NRS

SALES SHEET: 19-3/4" x 14", "Vital Small Parts For Lionel Trains, Super "O" Track For Lionel Trains"; black and white. Graham Collection.   **5   7   9   12**

ACCESSORY CATALOGUE: 10" x 7-1/2", 32 pages, with "SERVICE STATION DIRECTORY" for 1957-58, red and black covers, black ink only on interior pages, pulp paper.   **4   6   8   10**

HOW TO OPERATE LIONEL TRAINS AND ACCESSORIES: 8-1/2" x 5-1/2", 64 pages plus red and black wraparound cover, black ink, pulp paper. Reader assistance is requested to determine if a 1957 Instructions booklet was issued without "1958" or "1959" on rear cover.   **NRS**

BANNER: "HO BY LIONEL THE LEADER IN MODEL RAILROADING"; 21-3/16" x 6-1/2", yellow paper printed with black and red ink. Graham Collection.   **—   —   30   35**

BANNER: "COME IN AND GET YOUR BIG NEW LIONEL CATALOGUE"; 10-1/4" x 4-1/4", red and black ink on white paper. Graham Collection.   **5   10   15   20**

DEALER PROMOTIONAL BOOKLET: "TAKE THE THROTTLE AND MAKE YOUR SALES ROLL". Features Steve Allen, Ed Sullivan, and the 2373 Canadian Pacific F-3, 12" x 18", 10 pages. G. Magner Collection.   **12   20   25   30**

PROMOTIONAL BOOKLET: 10-5/8" x 7-7/8", "LIONEL 1957 — INTRODUCING SUPER O", promotional booklet of four pages in black and white, providing descriptions on Super O track and accessories. L. Connors Collection.   **NRS**

AD MAT ORDER FORM: 33-1/2" x 22", black on white paper, "Free Ad Mats . . . the Great 1957 Lionel Campaign". Illustrates proof for making customized advertising copy.   **30   40   50   60**

DEALER SALES AID: 8-1/2" x 11", four pages, "This is What you Should Know to Sell Lionel Trains and Accessories", printed in black and white, the cover illustrates a typical sales counter — combining Lionel trains with Airex fishing equipment. Came with insert "Over and Under on a Four-by-Eight", Form 1744 with a layout schematic for a compact display. A. Rubin Collection.   **NRS**

DEALER ORDER FORM: 22-1/2" x 12", "Lionel Trains", begins Stock No. 1569, white paper.   **—   —   1   2**

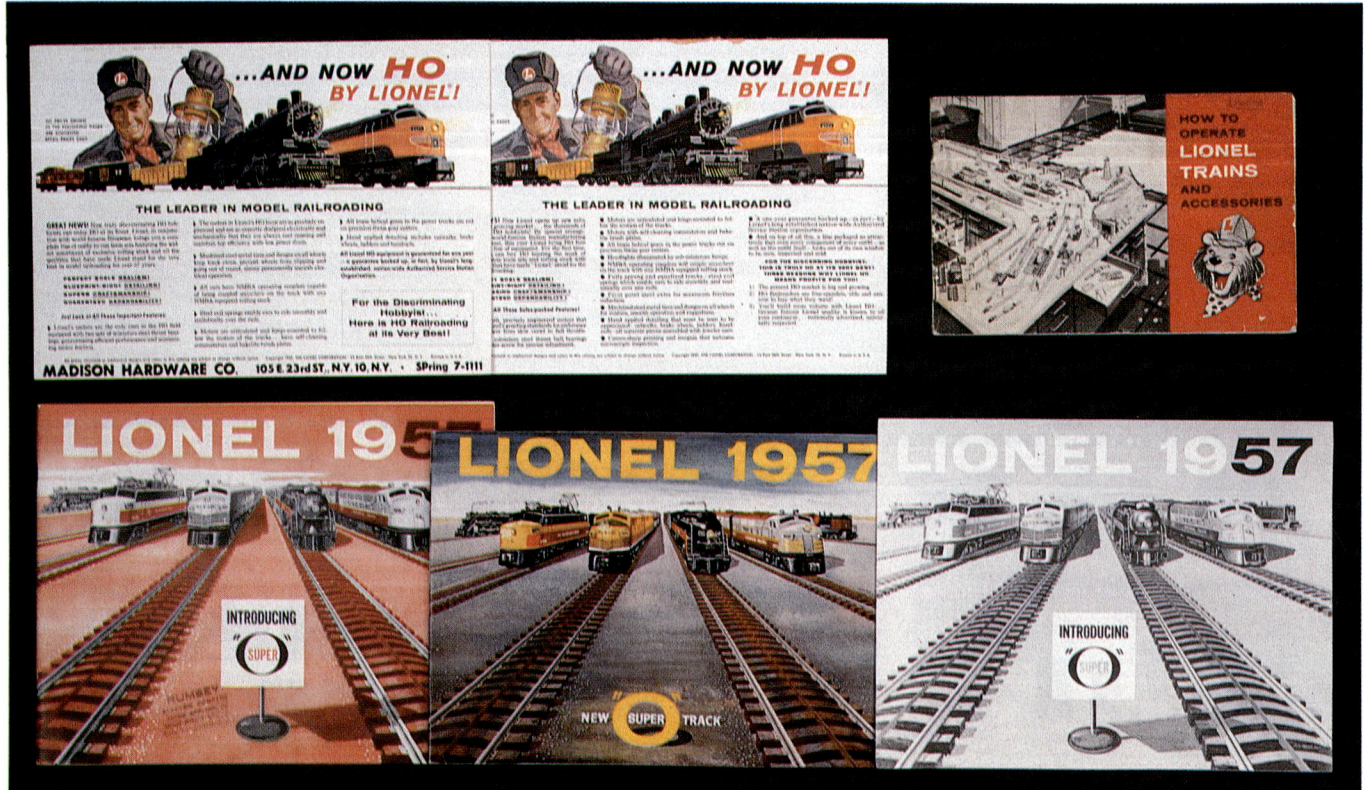

Top row: 1957 HO Catalogue "For The Discriminating Hobbyist" in a block in lower right corner, HO Catalogue without the block, and How To Operate Lionel Trains. *Bottom row:* 1957 Advance Catalogue, Consumer Catalogue, and Promotional Booklet.

	G	VG	EXC	NEW

DEALER PROMOTIONAL POSTER: 28-1/4" x 10-1/4", "Lionel Trains and Accessories", full color on pulp paper, illustrating 2351, 2373, 2379 diesels and 746 steam locomotive, all on Super O track. Graham and A. Rubin Collections. — — 35 40

DEALER POSTER: Same picture as smaller promotional poster listed above, but measures 3' x 6'. A. Rubin Collection. **NRS**

LOCOMOTIVE HALL OF FAME: Set of Lionel paper locomotives which came individually on 7-1/4" x 11-1/8" card stock pre-punched for easy removal of locomotives. Each card, folded to 3-5/8" x 7-1/4", came packed with Nabisco Shredded Wheat cereal, and although sanctioned by the Lionel Corporation, each card is copyrighted by "Spec'y. Adv. Serv., Inc.", location unknown. Cards are printed in color to correspond to the colors of the Lionel locomotives they portray. A. Rubin and R. Fetzner Collections.
(A) 520 GE electric; blue, black, and red. **NRS**
(B) 621 Jersey Central switcher; blue, black, and orange. **NRS**
(C) 736 Berkshire locomotive; blue, black, gray, and red. **NRS**
(D) 746 LTS Norfolk and Western; blue, black, gray, red, and yellow. **NRS**
(E) 1615 0-4-0 switcher; blue and black. **NRS**
(F) 2243 Santa Fe GM diesel; black, gray, red, yellow, and blue. **NRS**
(G) 2338 GP-7 Milwaukee; blue, black, and orange. **NRS**
(H) 2339 GP-7 Wabash; blue, black, gray and red. **NRS**
(I) 2351 Milwaukee Electric; red, yellow, black, gray, and blue. **NRS**
(J) 2373 Canadian Pacific GM diesel; blue, black, gray, yellow, red and brown. **NRS**
(K) 2379 Denver and Rio Grande GM diesel; yellow, black, gray and red. **NRS**

SERVICE STATION DECAL: 12" diameter, certified a Lionel approved Service Station. Printed in bright orange, blue, and white with the Lionel "L" logo in the center. A. Rubin Collection. — — 80 100

PRICE LIST: 7-1/2" x 10-1/2", Canadian Price List, "EFFECTIVE July 1, 1957", printing both sides, black print on white background, no illustration. **NRS**

PRIVATE ISSUE CATALOGUE: "LIONEL 1957", 11-3/8" x 16-5/8" tabloid-style distributor catalogue, four pages (pulp), red and black on cream background, similar format to "Ray's Bike Shop...1958". Stamped "MASTERS, NEW HYDE PARK, N.Y." **NRS**

SERVICE REMUNERATION CHART: Form 1242 Rev. printed on full-color Lionel Corporation stationery with designation "1957-58", with two pages black and white compensation charts. 7 10 15 20

DEALER PRICE LIST: 8-1/2" x 11", six-page typed format, "Lionel 1957 Outfit Component and Price List," two pages identified as Form Nos. 1688 and 1682.
(A) Original. — — 8 12
(B) M. Knoecklein Reprint, 1973. — — 2 3

1958

ADVANCE CATALOGUE: 10-7/8" x 8-1/4", 64 pages, red and black cover, NH and M & StL trains passing missile launching site,

Top row: 1958 HO Advance Catalogue, Advance Catalogue, and Private Issue Catalogue. *Bottom row:* 1958 HO Catalogue, Super O Track folder, and Consumer Catalogue.

	G	VG	EXC	NEW

black and white, HO scale section has burgundy marker with gold-stamped "HO".   10   15   22   30

HO ADVANCE CATALOGUE: 10-3/4" x 8" catalogue, eight illustrated pages, "HO by Lionel — The Leader in Model Railroading", full color including HO dealer displays.   **NRS**

CONSUMER CATALOGUE: 11-1/4" x 7-5/8", 56 pages, cover like advance catalogue but in full color on coated stock.
(A) With prices.   5   7   10   12
(B) Without prices, Canadian Edition.   10   15   20   25

ACCESSORY CATALOGUE: 11-1/8" x 8", 32 pages, with Service Station Directory, red and black cover, black ink, pulp paper. Title "Lionel 1958 Accessory Catalogue" contains individual items only. Cover picture is similar to regular catalogue, inside front cover copyrighted 1958. C. Weber Collection.   2   3   4   6

HO CATALOGUE: "HO by Lionel", features engineering with lantern and locomotives on cover in full color.
(A) 8-1/4" x 11", six-page fold-out, full color, coated stock. No. 0114 "Engine House".   2   3   4   6
(B) 8-1/2" x 11-1/2", six-page fold-out, full color, coated stock, No. 0114 "Factory with Horn".   7   9   12   15
(C) Same as (A), but included in *Railroad Model Craftsman* magazine, October 1958, as unnumbered pages 35 through 40.   3   4   6   8
(D) 8" x 11" fold-out, same as (A), published in Fall 1958 issue of *Model Trains* as unnumbered pages 19 through 24.   3   4   6   8
(E) 7-7/8" x 11" fold-out, same as (D), published in October 1958 issue of *Model Railroader* as unnumbered pages 41 through 46.   3   4   6   8

LIONEL RAILROAD MAP: 52" x 37", Accessory No. 950, published by Rand-McNally and available as a catalogue item. G. Magner Collection.
(A) Map only.   3   7   10   20
(B) Map in original mailing tube.   20   30   45   60

PRIVATE CATALOGUE: "Lionel 1958", large eight-page illustrated edition, as issued by Ray's Bike and Key Shop, Geneva, New York. Features 2018 locomotive with tender on cover, in red and black on newsprint paper. R. Otten Collection.   **NRS**

PRIVATE CATALOGUE: 8" x 10-7/16", 24 pages "LIONEL / 1958 / OUR COMPLETE LINE OF / TRAINS AND ACCESSORIES". Shows 175 Rocket Launcher, 2242 NH etc. on cover. Red and black ink on newsprint. Not copyrighted. Came with and without imprints. One sample with Taubman imprint illustrated. M. Weisblum Collection.   5   10   15   20

DEALER ORDER FORM: 22-1/2" x 12", "HO", begins Stock No. 5705, format on blue paper.   —   —   1   2

DEALER ORDER FORM: 22-1/2" x 12", "Lionel Trains", begins Stock No. 1590, pink paper, with white copy slightly smaller.   —   —   1   2

DEALER BROCHURE: 5-5/8" x 8-3/8", 40 pages, "How to sell Your Customers Lionel Trains and Accessories", illustrated with more

Top row: 1958 Dealer Advertising Poster for consumer contest, dealer display labeling packet and display stickers from early to mid-1950s. *Bottom row:* 1956 Raise the Curtain . . . Let Everybody See — a dealer advertising booklet, 1958 Promotional Sheet for Lionel's new 970 Ticket Booth, 1957 Locomotive Hall of Fame cut-out, Lionel's marketing promotional program with National Biscuit Company.

| | G | VG | EXC | NEW |

current products than prior year versions. Booklet is red, gray, and black on glossy white paper, with black illustrations and measures vertical format. **20 25 35 45**

DEALER LETTER: Single-page letter dated April 7, 1958 from Sam Belser, Lionel Sales Manager, printed on Lionel stationery with three-page attachment on highlights of the 1958 train line. I. D. Smith Collection. **NRS**

PROMOTIONAL SHEET: 8-1/2" x 11", one page, "Your Ticket to Greater Sales — Lionel's New No. 970 Ticket Booth", illustrates the ticket booth in red, green, and black. A. Rubin Collection.
— — 15 —

DEALER ADVERTISING AID: 8-1/2" x 11", one page, "60 Second Radio and TV Scripts", black on yellow paper. Part of 1958 dealer promotional pack. A. Rubin Collection. **NRS**

DEALER ADVERTISING POSTER: 22" x 9", "Hey Kids — Win Free A Lionel Train....Look for the Lucky Coupon in the New 1958 Lionel Color Book of Trains", printed one side in black and red on white glossy paper, and refers to the mysterious coupon appearing on page 29 of the 1958 consumer catalogue. From the 1958 dealer promotional pack. A. Rubin Collection. **— — 50 65**

DEALER PROMOTIONAL MATERIAL: 34" x 22-1/4", fold-out booklet containing 56 coupons plus instructions for the Lionel train contest. Lionel's 1958 consumer catalogue, page 29, contained a coupon in the bottom right-hand corner, but no instructions on why it appears. The coupon is tied to a Lionel TV advertising campaign, and viewers were required to either submit a completed coupon from page 29 of the catalogue or submit the dealer-provided coupon. In either case the coupon was to be submitted to the local television personality to be eligible to win a Lionel train set. This booklet was printed in black and white on one side only. A. Rubin Collection. **NRS**

DEALER ADVERTISING POSTER: 21-1/2" x 9', "Give Him a World of Railroading He Can Control — Lionel Trains and Accessories", printed in black and red on white glossy paper and features a boy operating a Lionel train circling the globe. One of Lionel's most creative and non-traditional posters, and part of the 1958 dealer promotional packs. A. Rubin Collection. **NRS**

SERVICE REMUNERATION CHART: Form 1242 Rev. printed on full-color Lionel Corporation stationery with no date designation, with two pages black and white compensation charts. Date confirmation requested. **7 10 15 20**

VITAL SMALL PARTS: 19-1/2" x 14", two-sided dealer poster, black and white, with reverse side caption "Super O For Lionel Trains". Request reader confirmation that this poster was included in the 1958 dealer promotional pack. A. Rubin Collection. **NRS**

HOW TO OPERATE LIONEL TRAINS AND ACCESSORIES: 8-1/2" x 5-1/2", 64 pages, plus red and black wraparound cover, black ink, inside page identifies "copyright 1957" but "1958 Edition" printed on back cover.
(A) As described above. **2 3 5 7**
(B) Similar to (A), but 1/4" white square in top right corner of cover.
5 8 10 12

CATALOGUE: 8-1/2" x 11", 24 pages, vertical format, black on white glossy paper, "Lionel O27 Gauge Train Sets", on page 1, and "Lionel HO Train Sets" on page A of four pages alpha listed through D. This appears to be an early advance edition or private issuance. Reader assistance requested. R. Otten Collection. **NRS**

PROMOTIONAL PHOTOGRAPHS: 8-1/4" x 10", black and white glossies of Lionel products, provided by Lionel's Advertising Department. Included accessories, dealer displays, and rolling stock. Price per photograph. **2 3 4 6**

PRIVATE ISSUE CATALOGUE: 8" x 10-1/4", 24 pages, "Hobbies for Fun", distributor's general catalog, includes one page in full color on Lionel HO. **6 8 12 15**

1959

ADVANCE CATALOGUE: 8-1/2" x 10-7/8", 44 pages, full-color cover, black and white fold-out inside pages, coated stock, cover lettered "Lionel 1959", illustration shows 1872 General and 44 missile launcher.
(A) Smoke from "General" on cover dark blue.
3 7 12 18
(B) Smoke from "General" on cover brown/gray.
7 14 22 30
(C) Similar format to (A), but black and white covers as well as inside pages. Printed on coated stock, and cover lettered "Lionel 1959", with illustration showing 1872 General and 44 missile launcher. This is a very scarce early edition of the advance catalogue. A. Rubin Collection. **NRS**
(D) Smoke from "General" on cover purple. **NRS**

CONSUMER CATALOGUE: 11" x 8-1/2", 56 pages, full color, coated stock, cover illustration shows 736, 1872 General, and 44 U. S. Army diesel.
(A) United States edition, catalogue includes prices.
3 5 9 12
(B) Canadian edition, catalogue does not include prices, but has inserted two one-page lists, "Lionel Trains Canadian Price List 1959", for O and HO. L. Connors Collection. **9 12 18 25**

ACCESSORY CATALOGUE: 11" x 8", 36 pages, red and black front cover with 1872 and 44 locomotives, black ink only on pulp interior pages. Schreiner Collection. **3 4 5 6**

HO CONSUMER CATALOGUE: 8" x 10-7/8", eight pages in full color on coated stock. Cover illustrates engineer with lantern and "HO by Lionel..the Leader in Model Railroading". Pages not numbered.
(A) Catalogue only. **3 4 5 6**
(B) Catalogue included in October 1959 issue of *Model Railroad Craftsman* as unnumbered pages 35 through 42.
4 5 6 8
(C) Catalogue included in October 1959 issue of *Model Trains* as unnumbered pages 31 through 38. **4 5 6 8**
(D) Catalogue included in October 1959 issue of *Model Railroader* magazine as unnumbered pages 41 through 48. A. Rubin Collection.
4 5 6 8

CARDBOARD GAME SHEET: 10-7/8" x 11-7/8", "The Great Locomotive Race", included in catalogued set 2527, a Super O set with a 44 missile launcher locomotive. Spins of a cardboard wheel move cardboard engines around the sheet. Was this sheet produced in conjunction with the movie *The Great Locomotive Chase*, which was made in 1959? Reader comments invited. P. Ambrose and J. Algozzini Collections. **30 40 50 65**

BANNER: 21-5/8" x 6-7/8", "Lionel Super O Track"; one page, black on white, illustrating Super O and conventional track. L. Connors Collection. **NRS**

DISTRIBUTORS' PROMOTIONS CATALOGUE: 11" x 8-1/2", 20 pages, "1959 Trains and Accessories", published by Distributors' Promotions, Inc., Philadelphia. Red and black cover. R. Osterhoff Collection. **— — 12 15**

WINDOW POSTER: 8-7/8" x 21-3/4", "Lionel Trains — New Outfits, Locos, Cars and Accessories" in full color. Included in 1959 dealer promotional kit. L. Connors Collection. **20 30 40 50**

WINDOW POSTER: 21-3/4" x 17-1/8", "Lionel's Track Guide and Basic Layouts", printed one side only on glossy paper in pink, yellow, black, and blue. Included in 1959 dealer promotional kit. R. Otten Collection. **15 25 35 40**

WINDOW POSTER: 22" x 9", "HO by Lionel", full color illustrating HO motor and truck. Included in 1959 dealer promotional kit. R. Otten Collection. **10 15 22 30**

	G	VG	EXC	NEW

WINDOW POSTER: 22" x 9", "HO by Lionel", full color illustrating HO engines, set. Included in 1959 promotional kit. R. Otten Collection.
10 15 25 35

AD MAT ORDER FORM: 33-7/8" x 22", "Free Ad Mats!", with coupon to order mats, and illustrating proofs for composing customized store advertisements. Black on white semi-gloss paper, includes write-ups "Here Are Some Selling Copy Ideas!" Included in 1959 dealer promotional kit. L. Connors Collection.
20 30 40 50

PROMOTIONAL LITERATURE: 19-3/4" x 14", "A Planning Guide For Setting Up Your Lionel Train Department", black on white, two-sided; "Vital Small Parts for Lionel Trains" on Side 2. Included in 1959 dealer promotional kit. R. Osterhoff Collection.
7 9 12 15

WINDOW STREAMER: 21-3/4" x 8-1/2", "Frontier Days to Space Age Trains and Accessories", full color. Most of streamer is actually 1959 commercial catalogue front and back cover, with no printing on reverse. Included in 1959 dealer promotional kit. L. Connors Collection.
15 20 30 40

PROMOTIONAL LITERATURE: 8-3/8" x 10-7/8", four pages, "What to tell Your Customers About Lionel Trains and Accessories", black ink on blue paper. Included in 1959 dealer promotional kit. L. Connors Collection.
7 9 12 15

PROMOTIONAL LITERATURE: 8-3/8" x 10-7/8", one page, "60-Second Radio and TV Copy", black on yellow paper. Included in 1959 dealer promotional kit. L. Connors Collection.
5 6 8 10

PROMOTIONAL LITERATURE: "Flash Bulletin on Lionel's Advertising Plans", 8-1/2" x 11", black and white form page brochure, appears to be aimed at distributors rather than dealers. **NRS**

WINDOW BANNER: 10-1/8" x 4-1/8", "Come In and Get Your Big New Lionel Catalogue". Included in 1959 dealer promotional kit.
(A) Black and white on all-red background. L. Connors Collection.
8 10 15 20

(B) Black and red on all-white background. L. Connors Collection.
8 10 15 20

PROMOTIONAL LITERATURE: 14" x 11-1/8", 12 pages, "Lionel is on the Move", features Lionel 1959 advertising campaign as well as illustrations of all promotional literature. Red and black on white paper. Included in 1959 dealer promotional kit. R. Osterhoff Collection.
— — 40 60

DEALER DISPLAY DECAL: 12" diameter decal in dark orange, blue and white, "Lionel Trains — Approved Service — 1959". G. Magner Collection.
40 60 80 100

PROMOTIONAL LITERATURE: 8-1/2" x 11", four pages, "How to Sell Your Customers Lionel Trains and Accessories", black on pink paper. With two-page insert on green paper, "Quickies — Capsule Selling Points to Help You Sell Lionel Trains and Accessories". If this item is from 1959, was it a part of the dealer promotional packet issued by Lionel? Reader assistance requested. A. Rubin Collection. **NRS**

PRIVATE ISSUE CATALOGUE: 8-1/4" x 10-3/4", 123 pages, "Catalog of Model Railroads", fully illustrated catalogue, one copy was issued by Hobby House, Inc. of Cleveland, Ohio, but the book was apparently available for use by many dealers. Eight pages are de-

Top row: 1959 Distributors' Promotions Catalogue, Consumer Catalogue, and letter to dealers. *Bottom row:* 1959 Promotional Flyer, Accessory Catalogue, and Advance Catalogue.

Postwar Paper: 1945–1969 • 73

	G	VG	EXC	NEW

voted to Lionel, whereas American Flyer has a listing for S Gauge! Black, red, and white cover. A. Rubin Collection.
— — 7 10

DEALER ORDER FORM: 22-1/2" x 12", "HO" begins Stock No. 5719, white, yellow, and blue form paper. — — 2 4

DEALER ORDER FORM: "22-1/2" x 11", O Trains", begins Stock No. 1609, large format, white, yellow, and blue paper.
— — 2 4

INFORMATION FOR LIONEL APPROVED SERVICE STATIONS: 5-3/8" x 8-1/2", nine pages, illustrating Lionel service tools and No. 5D test set and provides background to guidelines of being a Lionel Service Station. Designated Form 932 Revised, the booklet is black ink on white paper for inside pages, and light green card stock cover. A. Rubin Collection. NRS

LIONEL ELEVATED TRESTLE SET: 10-1/2" x 12", cardboard punch-out set designated No. 902 for the girder bridge and tunnel, not numbered for the trestle set. Contents came packed in a thick manila bag and that was probably included in certain lower-priced sets available during 1959. Black and gray ink on heavy card stock similar to earlier "paper trains". More information requested as to what products this item accompanied. — — — 40

LIONEL'S "STATION MASTER SPECIAL": Sixty-four piece cardboard railroad station came flat (unassembled) in large Manila envelope, and designated as part of outfit No. X810-NA.
— — — 60

PROMOTIONAL FLYER: 8-1/2" x 11", one page, "Lionel's New No. 92 Circuit Breaker-Controller" fully illustrated, black.
3 5 7 10

DEALER LETTER: Three-page printed letter on Lionel stationery from Alan Ginsburg, Vice President of Lionel, outlining the selling strategy for 1959. NRS

PORTER DEALER CATALOGUE: 8-1/2" x 11", 12 pages, "Porter Expands for 1959", full-color catalogue for dealer reference and includes a pull-out postal card to order copies of "The Wonders of Science" booklet plus special dealers kit, blue and multicolored glossy cover. This is a predecessor to Lionel's purchase of Porter, but identified Lionel's future products! A. Rubin Collection. NRS

WARRANTY PAYMENT SCHEDULE: Form 1905, two pages, black on light green paper, three-hole punched for Lionel Service Manual, 1959-60. — — 2 4

HOW TO OPERATE LIONEL TRAINS AND ACCESSORIES: 8-1/2" x 5-1/2", 64 pages, black and white plus red and black wraparound cover. Inside page identifies "copyright 1957", but "1959 Edition" printed on back cover.
(A) As described above. 2 3 5 7
(B) Similar to (A), but booklet has two front covers, with the staple never altered. One cover has 1/4" white rectangle at top right. R. Otten Collection. NRS

DEALER PROMOTIONAL POSTER: "Lionel Super O Track", 7" x 22" black and white printed one side only. L. Connors Collection. NRS

Top row: 1960 Contest instructions: "Instructions Sheet for Layout Contest", How to Operate Lionel Trains, and Consumer Catalogue. *Bottom row:* 1960 Accessory Catalogue, Advance Catalogue, Contest Poster, and Catalogue Poster which reads on left "Hey Kids! Big Layout Contest..."

1960

ADVANCE CATALOGUE: 8-1/2" x 11", 60 pages, color cover, black and white, red and white back cover with promotional slogan, coated stock, cover illustration shows father and son viewing twin railroad layout.
(A) "Lionel 1960" cover, dark brown heading.

	G	VG	EXC	NEW
	7	9	12	15

(B) "Lionel 1960" cover, red-orange heading. **NRS**

ADVANCE HO CATALOGUE: 8-1/2" x 11", 12 pages (unnumbered) printed in black and white, including covers, on white glossy paper stock. Cover titled "1960 — HO by Lionel", illustrated the No. D-0200 HO dealer display. A. Rubin Collection. **NRS**

CONSUMER CATALOGUE: 11" x 8-3/8", 56 pages, full color, coated stock, cover illustration shows family viewing close-up section of twin HO and O railroad layout.   3   5   9   12

ACCESSORY CATALOGUE: 8-5/8" x 11", with Service Station listing, 40 pages, color cover, black ink only on interior pages, pulp paper.   2   3   4   5

HO CATALOGUE: 8-1/2" x 10-7/8", 12 pages, full color, coated stock, cover reads, "Operating Cars — 1960's Most Exciting HO News".   2   3   4   5

HOW TO OPERATE LIONEL TRAINS AND ACCESSORIES 8-1/2" x 5-3/8", 64 pages on coated stock, heavy paper wraparound cover in red and black ink, Form 926-60.   3   4   5   7

CATALOGUE POSTER: 10-1/4" x 4-1/4", one-side, coated stock, apparently intended for store window.
(A) "Come In and Get Your Big New Lionel Catalog", red and black letters on white background.   7   10   15   20

(B) Same as (A), but black and white letters on red background.   7   10   15   20

PROMOTIONAL POSTER: 22-1/4" x 27-1/2", "Get Set for Action", folded to 11-1/8" x 7-1/8", two sides, red and black on heavy white stock. Illustrates advertising campaign for 1960. This may be a late 1959 publication.   20   40   50   60

PLEDGE POSTER: 9-1/4" x 11-3/4", black and white, green border, "We pledge to all Lionel Customers....", small tear-off section at bottom reads, "Mr. Dealer: Display this message prominently". Included in 1960 dealer promotional kit.   7   10   15   20

PROMOTIONAL POSTER: 22" x 8-1/2", one side, coated stock, "Lionel Trains and Accessories" in red letters, black 2037 train set and operating cars. Included in 1960 dealer promotional kit.   20   30   40   50

CONTEST POSTER: 22" x 8-1/2", one-side, coated stock, black ink, "Hey Kids! Big Lionel Contest..." with illustration of Lionel lion.   20   30   40   50

CONTEST INSTRUCTIONS: 11" x 8-3/8", four-page folder, color cover similar to catalogue cover, black and white interior, coated stock. Included in 1960 dealer promotional kit.   15   20   25   30

LIONEL TRACK LAYOUTS: 8-3/8" x 11", four unnumbered pages, for "O27, Super O and HO Gauges, start building yours today!"
(A) Price 10 cents on front, page 2 has "1-115" on lower right, heavy white paper, black and gray. "Address inquiries to: Lionel Service, Dept 74-E, Hoffman Place, Hillside, NJ 07205" on back page. I. D. Smith Collection.   2   3   4   5

Top row: 1960 Dealer Advertising Flyer; 1962 Dealer Promotional Brochures *(top and center)*; 1961 Promotional Literature.
Bottom left: Circa 1961, inside of Lionel Service Greeting Card; 1961 Advance Catalogue.

| | G | VG | EXC | NEW |

(B) Similar to (A), but no price, no number, coated paper stock. On bottom last three pages concerning inquires, "simply write to: Engineer Bill c/o The Lionel Corp., 15 East 26th St., New York, 10 NY." I. D. Smith Collection. **1 2 3 4**

HOW TO OPERATE LIONEL HO TRAINS: 8-1/2" x 5-1/2", 24 pages plus red and black covers. **3 4 5 6**

POSTER: "LIONEL TRAINS AND ACCESSORIES — AN INVESTMENT IN HAPPINESS:" 62" x 39", full color, features layout with family looking on, 224 and 44 diesels. Listed by Lionel as item D-206 and carried also in 1961 and 1962. R. Osterhoff Collection. **NRS**

POSTALGRAM: 17-5/8" x 11-3/4", "ON NOVEMBER 7TH...LIONEL BLASTS OFF...:". Promotional dealer flyer, black printing on yellow paper. **NRS**

BANNER: 20-3/4" x 7-1/2", "AVOID THE HOLIDAY RUSH...SPECIAL FALL CHECKUP". Full color, features Western Pacific diesel. R. Osterhoff Collection. **NRS**

WINDOW STREAMER: 22" x 8-1/2", "Come in ... see our new Lionel outfits... Ready to run! Lionel HO", black and red on white glossy paper. Included in 1960 dealer promotional kit. R. Otten Collection. **20 25 30 35**

WINDOW STREAMER: 22" x 8-1/2", "See...Get...Brand New Operating Cars — Lionel HO", black and red on white glossy paper. Included in 1960 dealer promotional kit. R. Osterhoff Collection. **7 10 15 20**

SALES TIPS: 8-1/2" x 11", four-page folder, John Bruce Medaris on cover, black and white coated stock, sales tips for dealers. Included in 1960 dealer promotional kit. R. Otten Collection. **7 10 15 20**

DEALER COUNTER DISPLAY: 10-1/8" x 14", featuring details on Lionel layout contest, features full-color illustrations of three locomotives and the Lionel lion as a fold-out on the left side. Printed on glossy heavy card stock, with stand-up easel on back. Included in 1960 dealer promotional kit. R. Connors Collection. **— — 100 130**

STORE POSTER: 20" x 14", "Vital Small Parts" and "Control and Operating Accessories for HO by Lionel", black on white paper. Included in 1960 dealer promotional kit. **5 7 9 12**

AD MAT ORDER FORM: 33-7/8" x 22", "Free! Join with Lionel in the Greatest Promotion Campaign...!", with coupon to order mats, and illustrating proofs for composing customized store advertisements. Black on white paper, includes write-up "Here are Some Selling Copy Ideas!" Included in 1960 dealer promotional kit. L. Connors Collection. **20 35 50 65**

DEALER DISPLAY DECAL: 12" diameter decal in dark orange, blue, and white, "Lionel Trains — Approved Service" and features Lionel Lion in center. At bottom a secondary (separate) 4-1/4" decal appears with "1960-1961". R. Otten and G. Magner Collections. **— — — 100**

AD MATS FOR LIONEL APPROVED SERVICE STATIONS: 17" x 8-1/2", black on dull white paper illustrating seven advertisements plus four "L" logos. Imprinted "Form 2139 6-60". **NRS**

WINDOW BANNER: 8-3/8" x 22", red and black ink in white glossy paper, printed one side only, titled "Lionel Trains and Accessories" and illustrates 2037 locomotive and tender, 6361, 6826, and other rolling stock. **NRS**

WINDOW BANNER: 9" x 22", "You're the Boss with Lionel Trains and Accessories", red and black ink on white glossy paper, features a 2037 locomotive with tender and ZW transformer. Printed single side only, part of dealer promotional pack for 1960. A. Rubin Collection. **— — 30 45**

ORDER FORM: Blank Form No. 1314B Rev. 4-60 printed in black on pink paper, came in pads with carbon; pad cover designated Form 1907. Price for single sheet. **— — — 1**

| | G | VG | EXC | NEW |

PRICE LIST: 7-1/2" x 10-1/2", "LIONEL TRAINS CANADIAN PRICE LIST 1960", printing both sides, black print on white background, no illustration. **NRS**

PROMOTIONAL PHOTOGRAPH: 8" x 10", illustrates Lionel's New York showroom, sent to dealers and used extensively in Lionel publicity. Reprints of this photograph are readily available. A. Rubin Collection. **NRS**

PARTS DEPT. ORDER FORM: Form No. 1314B Rev. black ink on pink paper, which came in pads. **— — — 1**

DEALER ORDER FORM: 22-1/2" x 12", "Lionel Trains", begins Stock No. 1609, large format, on white and pink paper. **— — — 1**

DEALER ORDER FORM: "HO Trains", begins Stock No. 5735, in white, blue, and yellow papers. **— — — 1**

PROMOTIONAL STOCK CERTIFICATE: 11" x 7-1/4", "The Lionel Rail Road Company — Common Stock". This certificate was issued to all who entered a Lionel-sponsored track layout contest. The contest rules stated that "as an honorary stockholder you will receive your very own stockholder's certificate and the right to vote for the Lionel Rail Road Company Board of Directors." A tin pin, measuring 1-1/2" in diameter, was also issued to all "stockholders." This stock was promotional only, and had no value as a negotiable instrument.
(A) Certificate as issued to the public, with signatures of President and Chairman of the Board imprinted. **— — 25 35**
(B) Certificate imprinted "Specimen" in place of signatures of President and Chairman of the Board. J. Muscanere Collection. **NRS**

WARRANTY PAYMENT SCHEDULE: Form 1905 Rev. 11-60, two pages, black on white card stock, 1960-61. **— — 2 3**

DEALER ORDER FORM: Form 1314B Rev. 4-60; pink, no products listed. **— — — 1**

PRIVATE PROMOTION: 11-3/4" x 8-1/2" brochure sent to distributors of Channel Master electronic products, folds out into full-color poster of Lionel engines and rolling stock in actual size — six feet. R. Osterhoff Collection. **NRS**

DEALER ADVERTISING FLYER: "The Biggest Action to Come Your Way . . ." red and black ink. **7 10 15 20**

1961

ADVANCE CATALOGUE: 8-1/2" x 11", 76 pages, John Medaris on cover, color cover, black ink on white-coated stock.
(A) Unnumbered, pages 2-12 contain very strong promotion for new science sets. Page 2: "command decision!"; page 3: "mission accomplished"; pages 4-5: "backed by the biggest promotion program..." B. Stekoll Collection. **15 20 25 30**
(B) Numbered, pages 2-12 contain introduction to science sets. Page 2: "Maj. Gen. John B. Medaris, U.S.A. (Ret.) authorizes release of new Lionel Science Sets"; Page 3: "CLEARED FOR IMMEDIATE RELEASE". B. Stekoll Collection. **7 9 12 15**
(C) Same as (B), but printer's proof copy. Measures 9" x 11-1/2", borders not cut, no staples. R. Otten Collection. **— — — 100**

ADVANCE CATALOGUE: 8-1/2" x 10-7/8", 12 pages, "Lionel Science Project", full color, back cover indicates "Bigger Profits — Bigger Sales". Included in 1961 Promotional Kit. **— 10 15 20**

CONSUMER CATALOGUE: 8-1/2" x 11".
(A) 56 pages, "Science Lines" layout and science sets on cover, red and black covers, inside black ink only, white pulp paper, "Honorary Stockholder" on rear cover. **4 6 8 10**
(B) 72 pages, "Lionel Porter Science Lines", layout and science sets on cover, full-color coated stock with "Lionel '61" in orange-brown color. HO raceways on rear cover. **4 6 8 10**
(C) Same as (B), but "Lionel '61" on cover in red-orange. HO raceways on rear cover. **5 9 12 15**

	G	VG	EXC	NEW

(D) 72 pages, HO raceways on rear cover, but Canadian edition. No prices published in catalogues, but does include a separate four-page flyer "Canadian Price List 1961" and "HO Canadian Price List 1961". Price with lists. L. Connors Collection. — — 30 35

(E) Same as (B), "Lionel '61" on cover in orange. 4 6 8 10

VITAL SMALL PARTS FOR LIONEL TRAINS: 8-1/2" x 11", sales sheet, folded, unfolds to 17" x 11", printed one side, black ink on heavy paper, lockons, Super O track parts, O and O27 track parts, etc. Form No. 2524, 11-61, "Printed in U. S. of America", lower left. Smith Collection. 5 7 9 12

POSTER: LIONEL SCIENCE CENTER: 39-5/8" x 62", full-color mural, depicting six different series, Inventor, Electronic Engineering, Plastic Engineering, and Weather Stations. Lithograph printed. R. Osterhoff Collection. **NRS**

DEALER WINDOW STREAMER: 10" x 13-1/2", two-page fold-over designed to hang over wire. "New From Lionel — Sheriff and Outlaw Car". Red and black on yellow rag paper. Included in 1961 dealer promotion kit. 15 20 25 30

DEALER WINDOW STREAMER: 10" x 13-1/2", two-page fold-over designed to hang over wire. "New From Lionel — Minuteman Missile Launching Car". Red and black on yellow rag paper. Included in 1961 dealer promotion kit. 15 20 25 30

DEALER WINDOW STREAMER: 10" x 13-1/2", two-page fold-over designed to hang over wire. "New From Lionel — Satellite Launching Car". Red and black on yellow rag paper. Included in 1961 dealer promotion kit. 9 14 20 25

DEALER WINDOW STREAMER: 10" x 13-1/2", two-page fold-over designed to hang over wire. "New From Lionel — Electronic Engineering Sets". Red and black on yellow rag paper. Included in 1961 dealer promotion kit. 9 14 20 25

DEALER WINDOW STREAMER: 10" x 13-1/2", two-page fold-over designed to hang over wire. "New From Lionel — Plastic Engineering Sets". Red and black on yellow rag paper. Included in 1961 dealer promotion kit. 9 14 20 25

DEALER WINDOW STREAMER: 10" x 13-1/2", two-page fold-over designed to hang over wire. "New From Lionel — Weather Stations". Red and black on yellow rag paper. Included in 1961 dealer promotion kit. 9 14 20 25

DEALER WINDOW POSTER: 21-1/2" x 9", "Come in...See Lionel Trains and New 1961 Operating Accessories!" Black and red

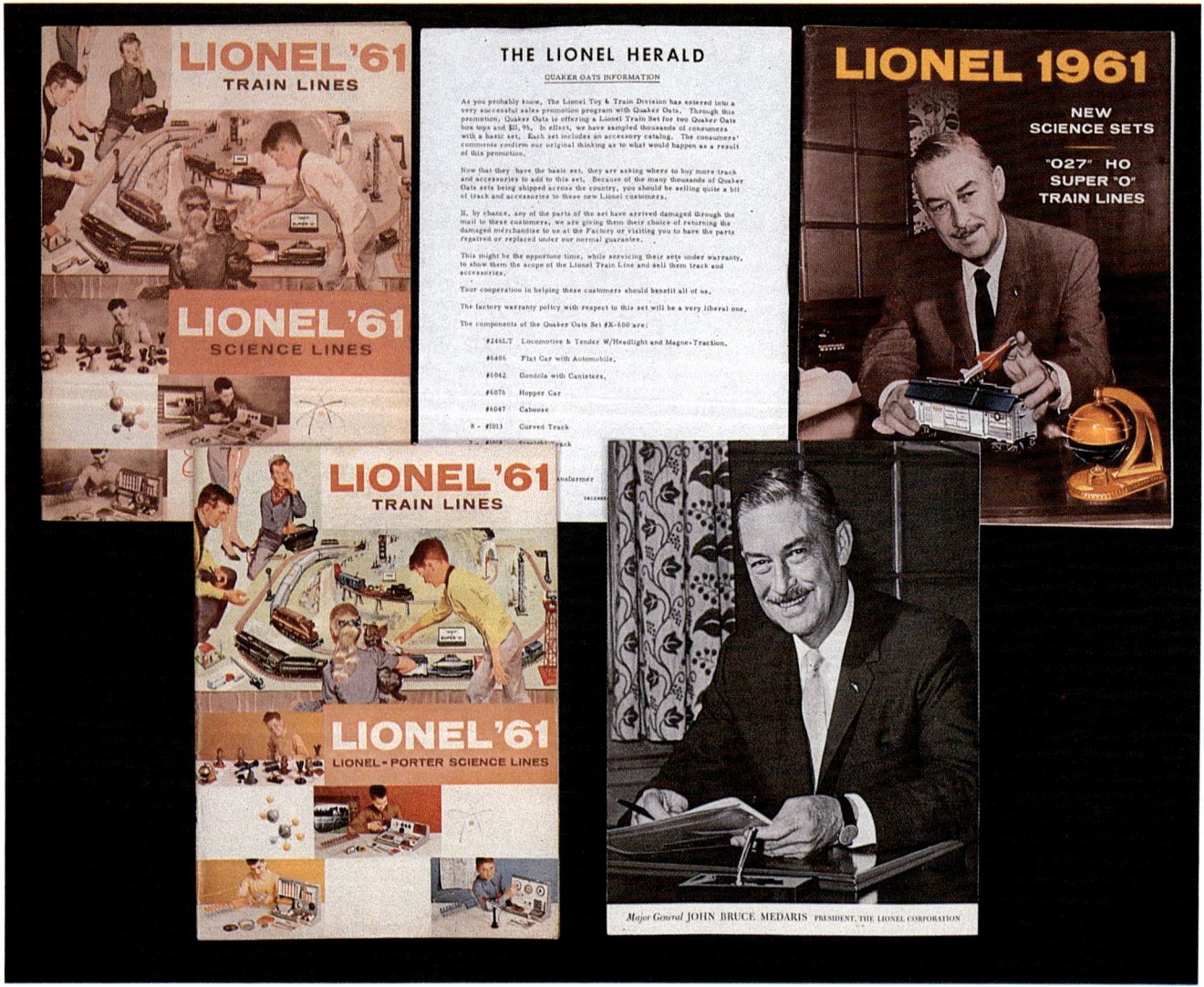

Top row: 1961 Consumer Catalogue (E), The Lionel Herald for Service Stations, and the Advance Catalogue. *Bottom row:* 1961 Color Consumer Catalogue (A), Dealer Sales Tips — Major General Medaris on cover.

	G	VG	EXC	NEW

on yellow rag paper. Included in 1961 dealer promotion kit. L. Connors Collection. — **15 22 30 40**

DEALER WINDOW POSTER: 21-1/2" x 9", "HO By Lionel — The Leader in Model Railroading". Black and red on yellow rag paper. Included in 1961 dealer promotion kit. L. Connors Collection.
15 22 28 35

DEALER WINDOW POSTER: 21-1/2" x 9", "See Lionel's Famous Inventors Series". Black and red on yellow rag paper. Included in 1961 dealer promotion kit. R. Osterhoff Collection.
15 22 28 35

SCIENCE SETS PROMPT CARDS: 7-1/4" x 7-1/4", set of four cards illustrating Lionel sets, printed black on white card stock, two pages with "Attention Dealer" on reverse side. Included in 1961 dealer promotion kit.
(A) "Lionel's Plastics Engineering Sets". L. Connors Collection. **NRS**
(B) "Lionel's Famous Inventors Sets". L. Connors Collection. **NRS**
(C) "Lionel's Electronics Engineering Sets". L. Connors Collection. **NRS**
(D) "Lionel's Weather Stations". L. Connors Collection. **NRS**

LIONEL-PORTER SCIENCECRAFT CATALOGUE: 8-1/2" x 11". 12 pages, red and black on dull paper, imprinted on front cover "The Porter Chemical Company, Hagerstown, Maryland". Included with these catalogues was a "Special Advance Bulletin for all Lionel Approved Service Stations" for pre-ordering Porter merchandise and also included a two-page order blank. Mailed to dealers November 1961. I. D. Smith Collection. — — **15 20**

CONTROL AND OPERATING ACCESSORIES FOR HO BY LIONEL: Sales sheet, same as "Vital Small Parts" sheet, and similarly printed one side only. Included in 1961 dealer promotion kit. Lists No. 928 maintenance kit at $1.95.
7 9 12 15

AD MAT ORDER FORM: 33-5/8" x 22", "Get Your Free Lionel Train Mats — Featuring New and Dramatic Merchandise in 1961", with coupon to order mats, and illustrating proofs for composing customized store advertisements. Black on white paper, includes write-up "Here are Some Selling Copy Ideas!" Included in 1961 dealer promotion kit. R. Otten Collection. — — **50 60**

LIONEL TRACK LAYOUTS: 8-3/8" x 11", four pages, "For O27, Super O and HO Gauges, Start building yours today!", pages not numbered.
(A) As described above with "10c" on face. Pulp paper.
2 3 4 5
(B) As described above, without "10c" on face. Glossy paper.
1 2 3 4

PROMOTIONAL LITERATURE: 8-3/8" x 10-7/8", one-page "Mr. Dealer...Let Lionel's Colorful Banners Work for you this Christmas." Black ink on white paper. Illustrates all six yellow banners available in 1961. Included in 1961 dealer promotion kits. R. Otten Collection.
NRS

PROMOTIONAL LITERATURE: 8-3/8" x 10-7/8", four pages, "Selling Aids to Help You Increase Your Volume and Profits with Lionel Trains and Accessories", black ink on white glossy paper. Included in 1961 dealer promotion kit. **7 10 15 20**

Top row: 1961 Lionel ScienceCraft catalogue, 1962 Lionel "Track Layouts", 1962 Promotional Literature. *Bottom row:* 1964 Tri-ang dealer brochure, 1964 Advertising Flyer for Engineer's Hat, 1964 Promotional Brochure, and 1966 Internal Memo Form.

| | G | VG | EXC | NEW |

PROMOTIONAL LITERATURE: 8-3/8" x 10-3/4", 12-pages, "Please stand by for the Greatest Sales Program Ever!" Features television advertising campaign. Separate mailing from other dealer literature for 1961, mailed in a special imprinted envelope, "You're in the TV Picture this Fall". Black and red ink on white glossy paper. L. Connors Collection. **NRS**

DEALER DISPLAY DECAL: 12" diameter decal in dark orange, blue and white, "Lionel Trains — Approved Service" and features Lionel lion in center. At bottom a secondary (separate) 4-1/4" decal appears with "1960-1961". R. Osterhoff Collection. **NRS**

SALES PROMOTION PACK: 9-3/4" x 12-1/2", blue folder containing press information of March 10, 1961 on the Lionel Science Series. Contents include biographical sketch of General Medaris, press releases on Science Series, artist rendering of Point-of-Sale Lionel Science Center, and "Lionel Science Project" color catalogue. Also contains set of nine 8" x 10" black and white glossies of Science Sets, with captions. R. Osterhoff Collection. **NRS**

TRI-ANG SCALEXTRIC CATALOGUE: 16" x 19", "Second Edition", two fold-out pages printed in black and blue on white paper. This catalogue was prepared prior to Lionel acquiring Scalextric, and no mention of Lionel is made in the contents; however, these catalogues were distributed by Lionel. — — 6 8

ADVENTURES WITH CHEMISTRY: 5" x 8", 230 pages, manual for use with Master Chemcraft chemistry sets, by Harold M. Porter. Original copyright 1951, softback, blue and black cover. A. Rubin Collection. — — — 20

LIONEL PORTER ATOMIC ENERGY: 5" x 8", 34 pages with colored cover and black and white inside pages. Manual for use with Lionel Chemcraft chemistry sets, by Harold M. and Jermain D. Porter. Original copyright 1955. A. Rubin Collection. **NRS**

LIONEL'S COMPLETE SCIENCE SERIES: 3" x 5-5/8" when folded, 14-page brochure, 3" x 5-5/8", printed in orange and black on a white glossy paper. Illustrating the entire series, this promotional brochure was packed with certain Science Series sets. — — — 2

PARTS ORDER FORM: Form No. 2418 9-61, pink paper, and begins with No. 0530-10. — — — 1

ORDER FORM: Form No. 2418 8-61 for HO parts, one-page, black on thin pink paper. — — — 1

DEALER ORDER FORM: Begins Stock No. 1123, white and pink paper. — — — 1

DEALER ORDER FORM: Begins Stock No. 5750, white, yellow, and blue papers. — — — 1

DEALER ORDER FORM: Non-train merchandise, begins Stock No. 3100 of Inventor Series, white, yellow, and blue papers. — — — 1

DEALER ORDER FORM: Orange-colored paper with an example of two form numbers on double-sided sheet. One side lists the item as Form 1909 Rev. 11-61 and the other side lists the reference as Form 1314 Rev. 4-60. — — — 2

PARTS ORDER FORM: Form 2469 9-61, pink paper, begins with product code TK-1. — — — 1

LIONEL INTERNAL MEMO: 5-3/8" x 3-1/4" Form 24, revised 6/61, internal use document, blank for writing notes between departments. Black printing on white paper. W. Mekalian Collection. — — — 1

WARRANTY PAYMENT SCHEDULE: Form 1905 Rev. 10-61, two pages black on white card stock, 1961-62. — — 2 3

CUSTOMER QUESTIONNAIRE: Form 1938, double reply postal card with feedback survey on satisfaction with Lionel's repair service. Responses were encoded by state. **NRS**

PROMOTIONAL FLYER: 8-1/2" x 11", two pages, "Lionel D.C. Power Units for All HO Trains", illustrates No. 0100 power pack and No. 0150 rectifier. Date confirmation requested. — — 7 10

SEASON'S GREETINGS: 11" x 5", printed Christmas Card, "From Your Lionel Service Department", with all employee signatures printed. Printed in olive green and red on Manila heavy stock. **NRS**

PARTS ORDER FORM: Form No. 1314 Rev., single-sheet blank form on pink paper. — — — 1

DEALER SALES TIPS: 8-1/2" x 11", four pages, Major General Medaris on cover, "Know Your Product . . . You'll Set It Faster and Easier," black ink. 2 3 5 7

1962

ADVANCE CATALOGUE: 8-1/2" x 11", 64 pages, "Lionel Trains and Accessories — The Leader in Model RR 1962", four-color cover, black and white inside, includes displays and HO.
(A) First Edition Pre-Toy Fair bright blue cover, back page "Three Powerful New Lionel Lines". 10 15 20 25
(B) Second Edition; dull blue cover, back page "Four Powerful New Lionel Lines". 9 12 17 20

CONSUMER CATALOGUE: 8-1/2" x 11", 100 pages, cover lettered "Lionel 1962". Features in full color Lionel's complete line of trains and science products. 3 6 8 10

ACCESSORY CATALOGUE: 8-3/8" x 10-7/8", 62 pages, full-color cover, first two and last two pages are coated stock, rest is black ink on pulp paper. M. Ocilka Collection. **NRS**

ACCESSORY CATALOGUE: 8-3/8" x 10-7/8", 40 pages, red and black cover, black ink on interior, pulp paper. 2 3 4 6

DEALER CATALOGUE: 8-3/8" x 11", non-train catalogue features Lionel-Spear record players, engineer and inventor sets, Scalextric model racing, and other Lionel products. Multicolored dealer reference catalogue.
(A) "Lionel 1962" at top of cover, thin textured paper. A222 listed on page 55. A. Rubin Collection. **NRS**
(B) No "Lionel 1962" at top of cover, thicker glossy paper. No A222 listed on page 55. A. Rubin Collection. **NRS**

LIONEL-SPEAR-TRI-ANG ADVANCE CATALOGUE: 8-3/8" x 11", fill color, coated stock, top cover illustration shows science lab, bottom illustration shows phonographs, rear cover features "Scalextric" racing. 1 2 4 6

LIONEL-SPEAR CATALOGUE: 8-3/8" x 11", full color, coated stock, cover lettered "Lionel-Spear '62".
(A) 56-page edition. 3 5 7 10
(B) 12-page edition. 3 5 7 10

LIONEL-PORTER SCIENCECRAFT CATALOGUE: 8-1/2" x 11", eight pages, red and black dull paper. Imprinted "The Lionel Corporation, Hagerstown, Maryland" on covers. — — 15 20

LIONEL PHONOGRAPH AND TAPE RECORDER PARTS AND SERVICE GUIDE: 8-1/2" x 11", further details needed. Magner Collection. **NRS**

DEALER WINDOW STREAMER: 10" x 13-1/2", two-page fold-over designed to hang over wire. "New From Lionel — Sheriff and Outlaw Car". Red and black on yellow rag paper. Included in 1962 dealer promotion kit. 9 14 20 25

DEALER WINDOW STREAMER: 10" x 13-1/2", two-page fold-over designed to hang over wire. "New From Lionel — Minuteman Missile Launching Car". Red and black on yellow rag paper. Included in 1962 dealer promotion kit. L. Connors Collection. 9 14 20 25

Top row: 1962 Advance Catalogue (B), Advance Catalogue (A); Lionel-Spear-Tri-ang Advance Catalogue; and the Accessory Catalogue. *Bottom row:* 1962 Consumer Catalogue, Lionel-Spear Catalogue; and The Lionel Herald May-June issue.

	G	VG	EXC	NEW

DEALER WINDOW STREAMER: 10" x 13-1/2", two-page foldover designed to hang over wire. "New From Lionel — Satellite Launching Car". Red and black on yellow rag paper. Included in 1962 dealer promotion kit. L. Connors Collection.
          9   14   20   25

DEALER WINDOW POSTER: 21-1/2" x 9", "HO By Lionel — The Leader in Model Railroading". Black and red on yellow rag paper. Included in 1962 dealer promotion kit. L. Connors Collection.
          15   22   28   35

CONTROL AND OPERATING ACCESSORIES FOR HO BY LIONEL: 20" x 14", sales sheet, printed one side only, black on white paper, lists No. 928 maintenance kit at $2.50. Included in 1962 dealer promotion kit.
          5   7   9   12

AD MAT ORDER FORM: 34" x 22", "Free! Lionel Ad Mats — Lionel Trains — Science — Phonographs — Scalextric", with accompanying coupon to order mats, and illustrating proofs for composing customized store advertisements. Black on white paper, but unlike prior years is a cheaper rag content and quite fragile. No write-up accompanies the proofs. Included in 1962 dealer promotional kit. R. Otten Collection.
          —   —   50   60

LIONEL TRACK LAYOUTS: 8-3/8" x 11", four unnumbered pages. "For O27, Super O, and HO Gauges, start building yours today!" Included in 1962 dealer promotion kit. Glossy paper.
          2   3   4   5

PROMOTIONAL LITERATURE: 8-3/8" x 10-7/8", four pages, "Selling Aids to Help You Increase Your Volume and Profits with Lionel Trains and Accessories", black on white glossy paper. Included in 1962 dealer promotion kit.
          7   10   15   20

PROMOTIONAL LITERATURE: 8-1/2" x 11", four pages, "Planning Guide for Setting Up Your Lionel Trains and Accessory Department", black and white with illustrations. Included in 1962 dealer promotion kit. L. Connors Collection.
          7   10   15   20

PROMOTIONAL LITERATURE: 8-1/2" x 11", four pages, "What to Tell Your Customers", black ink on blue paper. Part of 1962 dealer promotional kit.
          7   9   12   15

PROMOTIONAL LITERATURE: 8-1/2" x 11" sheet "60-Second Radio and TV Copy". Part of 1962 dealer promotional kit.
          4   6   8   10

ADVERTISING PROOF SHEETS: 11" x 17", black ink on white high gloss paper, complete set of ad mats for all products. Printed one side only.
(A) "O" and "O27" trains, eight pages.   —   —   50   60
(B) "HO" trains, six pages.   —   —   —   25
(C) Lionel-Tri-ang Scalextric, two pages. —   —   —   25
(D) Lionel-Spear Line, two pages.   —   —   —   10
(E) Lionel's New Line of Science Kits, seven pages.
                                          —   —   —   25

SALES PROMOTION PACK: 9-1/2" x 12-5/8" Manila folder with four different Lionel "L" logos on cover and containing two advance catalogues of trains and science products, plus the following:

	G	VG	EXC	NEW

(a) Remarks at 3/9/62 press conference by General J. Medaris.
(b) Eight black and white glossy photographs with captions.
(c) Labstock catalogue.
(d) Store display folder.
(e) Five press release articles on new Lionel products for 1962. Unlike the later-issued science catalogue, the catalogue contained in this kit is the pre-Toy Fair edition with no date on the front cover. R. Osterhoff Collection. **NRS**

TRI-ANG SCALEXTRIC CATALOGUE: 16" x 19", "Second Editions", two fold-out pages printed in black and blue on white paper. This catalogue was prepared prior to Lionel acquiring Scalextric, and no mention of Lionel is made in the contents; however, these catalogues were distributed by Lionel. L. Connors Collection. **NRS**

TRI-ANG SCALEXTRIC INSTRUCTION MANUAL: 5-1/2" x 4", 34 pages, "Third Edition", black and blue on white paper. This booklet was prepared prior to Lionel acquiring Scalextric, and no mention of Lionel was made in the contents; however, these catalogues were distributed to all Lionel authorized Service Stations.
(A) Dark blue and black. **NRS**
(B) Light blue and black. **NRS**

PROMOTIONAL BROCHURE: 5-3/4" x 5-1/4", "Announcing Colgate's Easy-to-Enter Lionel Train Contest", four-page contest brochure with rules, printed in full color on thin white paper. **NRS**

LIONEL PHONOGRAPHS: 9" x 5-7/8" fold-out brochure illustrating all models of Lionel phonographs. Listed as Form 44630-21, this brochure was printed on white glossy paper in black and off-red colors. L. Connors Collection. **NRS**

DEALER ORDER FORM: Scalextric by Lionel-Tri-ang begins Stock No. GP1 in white, blue, and yellow papers.
— — — 1

DEALER ORDER FORM: "HO" begins Stock No. 14003, in white, blue, and yellow papers. — — — 1

DEALER ORDER FORM: Begins Stock No. 1100l in large format, white, blue and yellow papers. — — — 1

DEALER PROMOTIONAL SHEET: 8-1/2" X 11", one page, Form No. 2594 2-62 D-5 announces availability of parts for newly-acquired Lionel Scalextric products. Form is red on white paper, 8-1/2" x 11".
— — 3 4

PARTS ORDER FORM: Begins with 259E-1, form 2756A 9/62, two pages on blue paper. — — — 1

PARTS ORDER FORM: Begins with 2559-2, form 2633 3-62, blue paper. — — — 1

PARTS ORDER FORM: Begins with 1655M-1, blue paper.
— — — 1

PARTS ORDER FORM: Begins with 64-64, pink paper.
— — — 1

PARTS ORDER FORM: Blank form on orange paper, Form 1314A.
— — — 1

PARTS ORDER FORM: Blank form on pink paper, Form 1314B.
— — — 1

PARTS ORDER FORM: Form 1314F, 16 pages, begins with I-92, pink paper. — — — 5

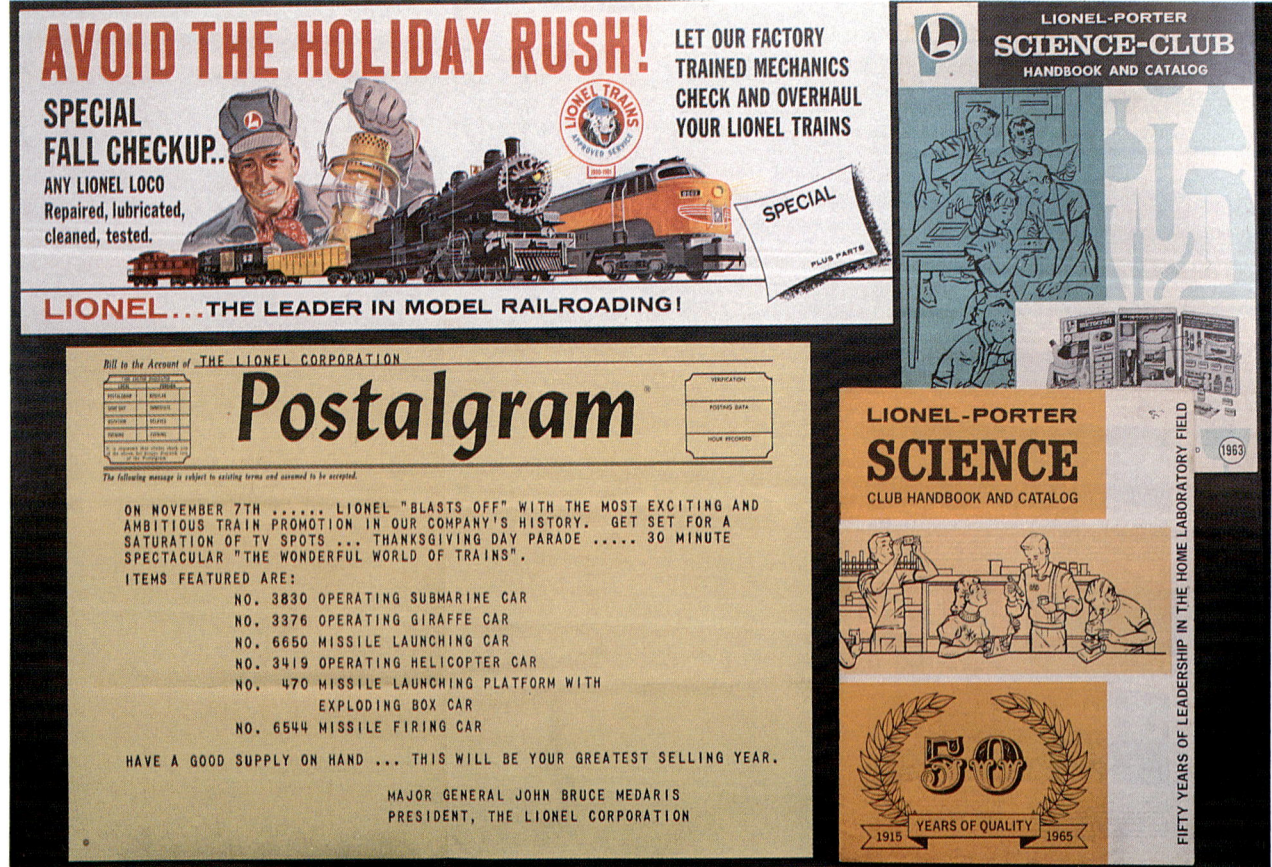

Top row: 1960 Avoid The Holiday Rush window banner, and the Lionel-Porter Science Club Handbook and Catalogue.
Bottom row: The Postalgram announces the "most exciting and ambitious promotion in our Company's history" and the Lionel-Porter Science Club Handbook and Catalogue which notes "Fifty years of leadership in the home laboratory field".

| | G | VG | EXC | NEW |

ORDER BLANK: Forms 2591, 2592, 2593, 2605 2-62 D-5, all for ordering Scalextric products, unusual that one continuous order form has different form numbers assigned to each page. Price for all pages.
— — 3 4

SCALEXTRIC SERVICE POLICY: Two pages, Form 2632 3-62 D-5, black on white card stock. — — 1 2

SERVICE STATION FLYER: One page, black and white sheet advertising HO train sets "Vagabond" and "Zephyr". Form 2679 6-62 D-5. — — 7 10

TRACK LAYOUT BOOKLET: 8-1/2" x 5-1/2", 24 pages, "Rudleys Track Layouts for Lionel Super O", blue ink on white paper. This was probably a private issue booklet, published by Rudley's Lionel Train Headquarters, Pennsauken, New Jersey, and not officially sanctioned by Lionel. D. DiDio, Jr. Collection. **NRS**

WARRANTY PAYMENT SCHEDULE: Two-page flyer lists fees paid to dealers for warranty work. Form 1905 Rev. 8-62 D-5.
(A) Black ink on white card stock. 2 4 6 8
(B) Brown ink on white card stock. 3 5 8 12

SPEAR WARRANTY PROGRAM: Two-page flyer, black on white card stock, form 2680 6-62 D-5 provides information for dealers on how to process phonograph warranty claims.
— — — 4

STROBOSCOPE DISC: 7-1/2" x 8-3/8" printed card stock circular test pattern composed of dots to test phonograph speed. Printed in black on white glossy card stock, designated Form 2742 8-62 D-5; accompanied by one-page instruction sheet, form 2750 9-52 D-5. Price for both forms. 4 6 8 10

DEALER ORDER BLANK: 8-1/2" x 11", single page, special form "Sell Lionel Assortments and Displays and Earn an Extra Bonus", begins with assortment and display No. 1812, and came in three different colored pages. W. Mekalian Collection. **NRS**

WARRANTY SHEET: 8-1/2" x 11", one page, Form 2749 9-62 D-5, explaining warranty information for the adult line of Lionel phonographs. — — 1 2

DEALER PROMOTIONAL SHEET: "Lionel Dealer Merchandise Assortments" 8-1/2" x 11", one page, black on glossy white paper, included science, phonographs and raceway dealer assortments, generally came with "Planning Guide for Setting Up Your Lionel Trains and Accessory Department". R. Osterhoff Collection.
2 5 7 10

LAYOUT GUIDE: 8-1/2" x 11", four pages, "Lionel Track Layouts", black ink, fold-out brochure, printed on dull white paper, variety with "Price 10¢" on front page. 1 2 3 5

ATOMIC SUB BASE: Eleven pieces of prefolded, scored and tabbed cardboard, 28" x 28" when assembled. Came as part of outfit No. 19201, and was packed in flat brown paper bag. Super structure has "U.S. Navy / Atomic Submarine Base / Railroad Loading Platform" on wall. R. LaFashia Collection. **NRS**

PRODUCT BROCHURE: 4-5/16" x 7-1/8", seven pages total, "LIONEL 1962....COMPLETE SCIENCE SERIES", pulp fold-out pamphlet, illustrations both sides, yellow and gray on cream background. Form 3107-48. **NRS**

1963

ADVANCE CATALOGUE: 8-1/2" x 11", 80 pages, "Lionel 1963 Trains and Accessories", yellow, black, and white cover, interior black and white, includes trains, science labs, phonographs, and motor racing.
(A) Dark yellow cover, D-466 Operating Display Net Cost blank, unnumbered page between HO1 and HO2 completely blank, no holes punched on inside pages. I. D. Smith and J. Zydlo Collections.
40 65 80 100
(B) Light yellow cover, D-466 Operating Display Net Cost $180.00, unnumbered page between HO1 and HO2 contains seven-line inscription, binder holes punched on inside pages, but not cover. R. Osterhoff Collection. 40 65 80 100

CONSUMER CATALOGUE: 8-3/8" x 10-7/8", 56 pages, color cover, red and black interior coated stock. Cover prominently declares Lionel now as the "Pioneer in Model Racing".
1 2 4 6

ACCESSORY CATALOGUE: 8-3/8" x 10-7/8", 40 pages, with Service Station listing, blue and black cover, interior black and white pulp paper. 2 3 4 5

SCIENCE CATALOGUE: 8-3/8" x 10-7/8", 32 pages, red and black two-tone pulp paper, cover lettered "Lionel 1963 Science Catalog".
2 3 4 5

LIONEL-PORTER SCIENCE CLUB HANDBOOK AND CATALOGUE: 8-1/2" x 11", combination science product catalogue and order forms; "1963" clearly identified on cover. Includes membership in the Chemcraft Science Club. Reader assistance is requested in knowing how many issues were produced.
(A) Red and black printing throughout. **NRS**
(B) Blue and black printing throughout. **NRS**

INSTRUCTION BOOKLET: 8-1/2" x 5-1/2", 62 inside pages, black on gray cover, printed in black ink on yellow paper. This edition has two staples on the front surface, and is loose-leaf. It is believed this particular copy was a prototype for the consumer edition. A. Rubin Collection. **NRS**

APPOINTMENT BOOK: 2-3/4" x 5", inscribed "1963 Lionel Toy Fair", bright red cover, inside printed "In 1963 it's Lionel First with the Finest". R. Osterhoff Collection. **NRS**

1963 Lionel Toy Fair Appointment Book.

PROMOTIONAL FLYER: 10-7/8" x 8-1/2", two pages, "Make Your Lionel Railroad Grow!!!", Form 2870 6/63, black and white, highlights No. 2002 and 2003 Lionel track "Make-Up" kits. A. Rubin Collection. **NRS**

WARRANTY REGISTRATION CARD: 5-1/2" x 8-1/2", two-sided card to complete under the terms of the Lionel train guarantee, orange and blue on cream card stock. Identified by 1-63 in corner.
— — 1 2

PARTS ORDER FORM: Blank Form No. 2924 11/63 D-5, with space for ordering 56 parts. W. Mekalian Collection.
— — — 1

1963 Science Catalogue, Consumer Catalogue, and Accessory Catalogue.

	G	VG	EXC	NEW

DISPLAY PROMOTIONAL SHEET: 11" x 17", one page, poster-type notice to dealers and jobbers advertising the motor raceway display rack D471. Black on white paper, designated Form No. D471-9 4/63.   **7 9 12 18**

WARRANTY PROGRAM: 8-1/2" x 11", four pages, fold-out brochure printed in black on green paper, Form 1905 Rev. 4/63 D-5. Includes warranty information for 1963-64 on trains and other Lionel products.   **2 3 4 5**

DISPLAY PROMOTIONAL SHEET: 8-1/2" x 11", one page, announcement of D-465 motor racing operating display. Black on white, designated Form No. 2857 4.63 D-11.   **2 4 7 12**

ORDER FORM: One page, Form 2858 4/63 D-5, blank form, black on thin pink paper.   **— — — 1**

DISPLAY PROMOTIONAL SHEET: 8-1/2" x 11", one page, "Make Your Railroad Grow" Form 2869 6/63, black on white advertises No. 2001 Lionel track make up kit.   **1 2 4 6**

DISPLAY PROMOTIONAL SHEET: 8-1/2" x 11", two pages, "Make Your Railroad Grow" form 2870 6/63, black on white advertises Nos. 2202 and 2003 Lionel Track Make Up Kits.   **1 2 4 6**

SERVICE STATION DECAL: 4-1/2" x 2-1/2", add-on decal for larger previously-issued Service Station decal. Decal only includes "1963" in red with a border. R. Otten Collection.   **— — 15 20**

ORDER FORM: Blank Form No. 2924 11/63, printed in black on blue paper, came in pads with carbon; pad cover designed Form 1907. Price for single sheet.   **— — — 1**

ORDER FORM: Completed Form No. 2924 11/63 D-5, three pages, black on thin pink paper, begins with Part No. RW-24.   **— — 2 3**

1964
ADVANCE CATALOGUE: Was a special catalogue issued for the Toy Fair? Reader assistance requested.   **NRS**

CONSUMER CATALOGUE: 8-3/8" x 10-7/8", 24 pages, black and blue-green, features dreaming boy superimposed over freight set on cover.
(A) Pulp paper, page 13 lists 6402 flatcar at $2.50.

	G	VG	EXC	NEW
	1	2	4	5

(B) Same as (A), but 6402 is incorrectly listed at $3.95.
   1 2 4 5
(C) Same as (A), but coated stock.   **1 2 5 7**
(D) Same as (B), but coated stock.   **1 2 5 7**

LIONEL RACEWAYS CATALOGUE: 8-1/2" x 11", 12 pages, green and black-coated stock, cover lettered "Lionel Raceways and Accessories for 1964". W. Mekalian Collection.   **4 6 8 10**

HELIOS 21: 8-1/2" x 11", four pages, remote-control spacecraft, red and black with black and white photos, cover lettered "Hey! Hey Helios 21 is Here"; Advance for dealers.   **4 6 8 10**

PROJECT X CATALOGUE: 22-7/8" x 11", tri-fold, red and black with silver, Lyter-N-Air remote-control space ships; Advance for dealers.   **4 6 8 10**

LIONEL "U-DRIVE" BOAT: 8-1/2" x 11", two pages. This versatile boat can be used in a backyard, local pond, or small lake. B. Stekoll Collection.   **3 4 5 7**

LIONEL COMBINES SIGHT WITH SOUND: 8-1/2" x 11", four- pages, Phono-Vision, two-color printing, front cover shows boy and girl with record player with slide projector lens on right side and image shown on inside of record player case. B. Stekoll Collection.   **3 4 5 7**

PROMOTIONAL BROCHURE: 3-1/2" x 8-3/8", 12 pages, "Your Lionel Guide to Fun, Action, and Excitement", fold-out brochure, two actual pages feature entire Lionel line of trains, science, phonographs, etc. Black ink on white paper with gold front and back covers. A. Rubin Collection.   **NRS**

ORDER FORM: Form 2962, 17" x 11" large format, begins with No. 50 gang car. W. Mekalian Collection.   **— — — 2**

PARTS LIST: Form 3041 D-74, 11 pages, pink paper begins with part No. I-92.   **— — — 1**

PARTS ORDER FORM: Form 3060A 10/64 on blue paper for Helios 21.   **— — — 1**

PARTS ORDER FORM: Form 3060B 10/64 on blue paper for Helios 21.   **— — — 1**

Top row: 1964 Consumer Catalogue, Lionel Combines Sight with Sound, and Lionel-Spear Catalogue, Lionel-Porter Science Sets Catalogue. *Bottom row:* Helios 21, Lionel Raceways Catalogue, Project X Catalogue, and the Lionel U-Drive Boat.

	G	VG	EXC	NEW
PARTS ORDER FORM: Form 3060B 10/64 on blue paper for Helios 21.	—	—	—	1
PARTS ORDER FORM: One page, "Special Pre-Season Parts Sale", Form 3051 8/64 D-74, yellow.	—	—	—	2
ADVERTISING FLYER: 8-1/2" x 11", one page, "Lionel Engineer Hats Are Available!!!!" advertising flyer, blue on white paper.	—	—	—	15
GREETING CARD: 8-1/2" x 5-1/4", "Season's Greetings", heavy cream paper stock greetings from Lionel Service Dept.				NRS
SPECIAL DEALER NOTICE: One page, "To all…Service Stations" notice regarding Sears Raceway Sets, on pink paper.				NRS
SERVICE STATION FLYER: One page, Form 3060C 10/64, flyer on yellow paper.	—	—	—	3
ADVERTISING FLYER: 8-1/2" x 11", two pages, "Lionel Movie-Jector", red and black on white paper, directed to dealers and distributors.				NRS
SCHEMATIC DIAGRAM: For Service use, Form 3060D 10/64 "Helios 21", one page on white paper.	—	—	—	3
RACING FLAGS: One page, full color, Form 5150-35 8/64, "Track Flags for Use with Your Lionel Motor Racing Equipment".	1	2	3	4
TRI-ANG DEALER BROCHURE: 8-1/2" x 11", Scaletric road racing, red and black ink.				NRS
LIONEL-SPEAR: 8-1/2" x 11", four pages, phonographs and accessories, orange and black ink. M. Weisblum Collection.	3	5	7	9
LIONEL-PORTER SCIENCE SETS: 8-1/2" x 11", eight pages, "CHEMCRAFT, MICROCRAFT …", orange and black ink. M. Weisblum Collection.	3	5	7	9

1965

ADVANCE CATALOGUE: 8-1/2" x 10-7/8", 40 pages, multicolored cover with a drawn locomotive, automobile, rocket, and microscope. Page 12 illustrates No. 239 locomotive in erroneous 2-6-4 wheel configuration, and "Mark 2" listed on page 38. A. Rubin Collection. **NRS**

CONSUMER CATALOGUE: 8-1/2" x 10-7/8", 40 pages, multi-colored cover with drawn locomotive, automobile, rocket, and microscope. Page 12 illustrates No. 239 locomotive in correct 2-4-2 configuration, and "Mark II" corrected on page 38.
(A) Pulp paper; work caboose as page 6 is listed as 6130 and flatcar is listed as 6402 on page 14. 1 2 4 5
(B) Coated stock; otherwise same as (A). 1 2 5 7
(C) Same as (A), but work caboose listed as 6119 on page 6 and flatcar is listed as 6401 on page 14. 1 2 4 5
(D) Same as (C), but coated stock. 1 2 5 7

HOW TO OPERATE LIONEL TRAINS: 8-1/2" x 11", 32 pages, black and white pages with yellow wraparound cover, uncoated paper. Identified as Form 4080 9/65. 5 7 9 12

HOW TO SELL LIONEL TRAINS AND ACCESSORIES: 5-3/4" x 8-1/2", 40 pages including covers, dealer promotion booklet. Front cover is orange with white border and black sans-serif lettering; rear cover is white with Lionel logo at bottom. Pages are tabbed for easy

	G	VG	EXC	NEW

use. Contents give specific selling points for Lionel features such as Magnetraction, smoke, etc. J. Algozzini Collection.

| | 5 | 10 | 15 | 20 |

POSTER: "LIONEL / A LIFETIME INVESTMENT IN HAPPINESS", white background, black lettering, red and blue arrows in oval form. R. Sabby Collection. **NRS**

SALES MANUAL: Second Half Distributor Program. 37 pages marked "Personal and Confidential" on face. Loose-leaf for internal Lionel distribution to sales management, and not made available to Lionel dealers. Contents include product descriptions, credit arrangements with distributors, and complete details on a contest which ran from July 5, 1965 to September 30, 1965. The first prize for the contest was a 1966 Cadillac and second prize a 1966 Ford Mustang. The sales contest was organized on an award point basis, with Lionel-Porter merchandise worth ten points per product, and train sets being awarded five points each. The documentation indicates that significant efforts were made to sell Lionel merchandise through large drug store chains, catalogue houses such as J. C. Penney, and major trading stamp plans such as S & H. R. Osterhoff Collection. **NRS**

LIONEL-PORTER SCIENCE '65: 8-1/2" x 11", 12 unnumbered pages, full color, features Lionel microscopes, chemistry sets, and other non-train products. Back cover highlights "50 years of Chemcraft". A. Rubin Collection. — — 35 50

LIONEL-PORTER SCIENCE CLUB HANDBOOK AND CATALOGUE: 24-page fully illustrated booklet highlighting "fifty years of leadership in the home laboratory field." The booklet is printed black and yellow ink on white paper, with no reference to trains. An interesting note appears on the back cover, "...during the past year over 50,000 young scientists enrolled in the Lionel-Porter Science Club and received their Membership Cards..." A. Rubin Collection. **NRS**

DEALER PROMOTIONAL BOOKLET: 8-1/2" x 11", 12 pages, "To Help You Sell", illustrated with dealer display and layout photographs. Black and red ink, white heavy bond paper. **NRS**

DEALER PROMOTIONAL BROCHURE: Two pages, "Lionel Levels with the Trade", black and white ink on glossy paper featuring a photograph of Arthur Godfrey, described as "America's Number One Salesman". A. Rubin Collection. **NRS**

PROMOTIONAL BROCHURE: 9-1/2" x 5-1/4", one page, "Stock Car Race" No. 16508, line drawings in blue, red, and black ink. **NRS**

DEALER PROMOTIONAL MANUAL: 8-1/2" x 11", two pages, titled "Co-operative Advertising and Promotion Manual". This form could hardly be considered a manual as titled. Printed on white paper.
— — — 7

DISTRIBUTORSHIP APPLICATION: 8-1/2" x 11", two pages, "Application for Distributorship for Products", Form 4001 1/65 D-13, printed on white paper. — — 12 15

SERVICE STATION BROCHURE: 8-1/2" x 11", seven pages, "Information for Lionel Approved Service Stations", illustrated booklet outlining such things as equipment required, tools available, how to order, plus a two-color illustration of the No 5F Universal Test Set. Printed on white paper, listed as Form 932 rev. 3/65. Original issuance 1960. — — 20 25

WARRANTY PROGRAM: 8-1/2" x 11", four pages, fold-out brochure Form 4042 3/65 D-74, covers 1965-66, printed in black on white paper. 2 3 4 5

Top row: 1965 Consumer Catalogue, How to Operate Lionel Trains, Dealer Promotional Manual, How to Sell Lionel Trains and Accessories. *Bottom row:* Four Lionel Promotional Advertisements.

| | G | VG | EXC | NEW |

STROBOSCOPE: 8-1/2" x 11", one page, similar to 1962 version, circular dot form printed on a semi-gloss card stock, and designated Form 4049 D20 4/65. Accompanied by one-page instruction form, spirit duplicated. **2 4 6 8**

DEALER PROMOTIONAL BROCHURE: 8-1/2" x 11", eight pages, "This toy doesn't kill. . .", black and white on glossy paper, describes 1965 advertising campaign. R. Otten Collection. **NRS**

DEALER PROMOTIONAL BROCHURE: 8-1/2" x 11", 16 pages, "An extremely timely proposition . . .", black ink on glossy paper, describes 1965 advertising campaign.
(A) Original as described above. **NRS**
(B) 1978 reproduction by Greenberg Publishing Company, and identified as reprint on back cover. **1 2 3 4**

TRAVEL ITINERARY REPORT: 4-1/2" x 8-1/2", one page, black and white.
(A) Form 4000 1/65 D-13 printed at bottom.
— — — **2**
(B) No form number printed at bottom. — — — **1**

1966

ADVANCE CATALOGUE: 9-7/8" x 8-1/2", 40 pages, full-color front and back cover, but unlike the consumer edition, front color is deep blue rather than purple. Page 2 printed "Advance Catalog" and all inside pages are black and white.
(A) Coated paper. L. Connors Collection. — — **110 150**
(B) Pulp Paper Stock. D. Siehl Collection. **NRS**

CONSUMER CATALOGUE: 10-7/8" x 8-3/8", 40 pages, full-color coated stock, cover illustration shows father and son watching trains rush by.
(A) Set illustrations on pages 8 and 10. **1 2 3 4**
(B) No set illustrations on page 8 and 10. **10 20 30 35**

WELCOME TO THE WONDERFUL WORLD OF LIONEL: 8-1/2" x 21-3/4", trains, race-ways, phonographs, science sets, brochure, folded to 3-1/2" x 8-1/2", No. 1-117.
(A) Black and white with dark orange and blue trim.
2 3 4 5
(B) Black and white with pink and blue trim.
— — **8 10**

LIONEL TRAIN & ACCESSORY MANUAL: Operating and Wiring Manual for O27 and Super O, $1.00, 36-page illustrated booklet No. 4080, $1.25 to cover cost of postage and handling charge. Shown on page 17 of 1966 catalogue. **3 4 6 8**

ADVERTISING PROMOTIONAL FOLDER: 9-3/8" x 12-1/4", black on heavy white glossy paper with cover heading "There is nothing so powerful as an idea whose time has come". Folder contains the following items:

(A) "The Hot Ones", black and white brochure details highlights of advertising campaign, eight pages. — — **7 9**
(B) Two one-page inserts on Batman and Walt Disney advertising.
— — **9 11**
(C) "To Help You Sell", 12-page brochure on merchandise and displays. **7 9 12 15**
(D) 1966 color consumer catalogue. (See previous listing.)
1 2 3 4
(E) Lionel Mat and Repro Catalogue, 23-page black and white glossy booklet illustrating all Lionel products, to be used for advertising purposes. — — **15 20**
(F) Outer folder only. — — **7 9**

RENEWAL APPLICATION: One-page "Renewal Application and Amended Policy for 1966-1967", Form 4174 2/66, printed on white paper, cover letter only. — — **12 15**

SERVICE STATION APPLICATION: 8-1/2" x 11", two pages, "Application for Appointment as an Approved Service Station", Form 977 Rev. 3/66, printed on white paper. — — **12 15**

DEALER ILLUSTRATION: 8-1/2" x 11", one page, raceway set No. 17693 promotional layout illustration, blue/black on white paper.
NRS

LIONEL SALESMAN PITCH BOOK: 61 pages, red vinyl-bound loose-leaf with clear plastic sleeves, to include product description with 8" x 10" Lionel Sales Dept. black and white glossy photographs. Fully illustrated. R. Osterhoff Collection. **NRS**

LAYOUT DRAWING: 11" x 18", original custom line drawing of Lionel promotional layout for dealer display use. Black on white heavy card stock. R. Osterhoff Collection. **NRS**
(A) As above, but engineering draft copy. — — — **50**
(B) Original color photograph of constructed display, of which the display itself was believed to have been destroyed. See article at end of 1966 listing. **NRS**

WARRANTY PROGRAM: 8-1/2" x 11", four pages, fold-out brochure form 4186 2/66, covers period 1966-1967, printed in black on white paper. **2 3 4 5**

ORDER FORM: Two separate pages, Form 4209A 4/66, black on thin white paper, begins Part No. 100-5. — — **1 2**

ORDER FORM: One page, Form 4210 4/66, black ink on thin white paper for ordering No. 69 motorized unit only.
— — **1 2**

DEALER PROMO SHEET: One page, "Service Station Exclusive — Standard (1/32) Raceway Set". Form No. 4255 7/66, offers set 16508 at a special one-time price to dealers. Black ink on white paper.
— — — **6**

SURVEY ORDER BLANK: 8-1/2" x 11", one page, Form 4227 5/66, black ink on white thin paper. — — **1 2**

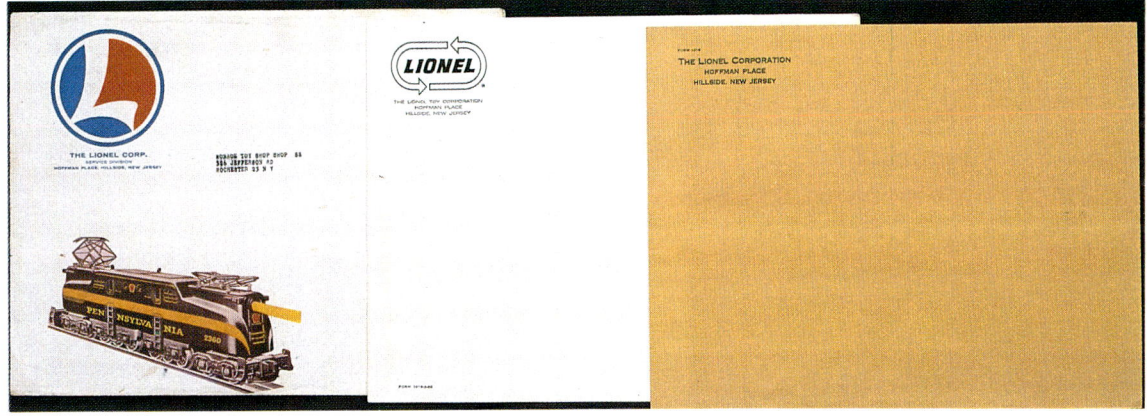

1961, and two 1966 catalogue mailing envelopes.

	G	VG	EXC	NEW

SURPLUS INVENTORY FORM: 8-1/2" x 11", one page, Form 4228 5/66, black ink on white thin paper. — — 1 2

ORDER FORM: One page, Form 4236 6/66, begins Part No. 478-1, black ink on thin white paper. — — — 1

ORDER FORM: Two pages, Form 4237 6/66, phonograph parts, begins 47601-100, black ink on thin white paper. — — 1 2

ORDER FORM: One page, Form 4240 6/66, for ordering No. 3252-34 barometer, black ink on thin white paper. — — — 1

ORDER FORM: One page, Form 4273 8/66, black ink on thin pink paper, begins with Part No. 53-301. — — — 1

SALES PROMOTIONAL BOOKLET: 20 pages, "Toy Fair Meeting", February 25, 26, 28, 1966. Spirit-duplicated with Form 4187 2/66; 4189 2/66; 4190 2/66 product order blanks inserted. Loose-leaf spiral-bound with two-color Lionel cover. **NRS**

PROMOTIONAL FLYER: 8-1/2" x 11", one page, blue/black flyer illustrating set No. 17693, "Alpine Loop-the-Loop" raceway. Believed sent to distributors only. **NRS**

PROMOTIONAL FLYER: 7" x 21-1/2", one page, two-color promotional poster, "Loop-the-Loop", features raceway set No. 17140. **NRS**

DEALER PROMOTIONAL SHEET: 8-1/2" x 11", "Presenting a new feature-packed train set from Lionel—the leader!" Certificate format in green and black features set No. 19500. — — — 8

DEALER ORDER FORM: Form 4187 2/66, begins with set No. 14240 and includes HO and non-train products, on white paper. — — — 1

DEALER ORDER FORM: 14-1/2" x 11", Form 4189 2/66, begins with set No. 11520 and includes trains only. White paper. — — — 1

DEALER ORDER FORM: 8-1/2" x 11", Form 4190 2/66, begins with chemistry set No. 21410. White paper. W. Mekalian Collection. — — — 1

DEALER ORDER FORM: 8-1/2" x 11", Form 4191 1/66, begins with record player No. 41140. White paper. W. Mekalian Collection. — — — 1

SERVICE STATION DECAL: 4-1/2" x 2", update to larger circular illustrated decal, includes "1966-1967" only with blue outline. — — — 20

LIONEL WARRANTY PROGRAM: 8-1/2" x 11", four-page brochure outlining dealer warranty policies and payments, Form 4186 2/66, includes trains, phonographs, and raceway repairs. — — — 4

DEALER WIRING DIAGRAM: 8-1/2" x 5-1/2", Form 44320-12 3/66, "Wiring Diagram for Transistorized Phonographs". — — — 3

DEALER WIRING DIAGRAM: 8-1/2" x 11", one page, Form 4194 3/66, "Phonograph Electronic Amplifier", on white paper. — — — 4

THE GOLDEN BOOK OF TRAIN STAMPS: 8-1/4" x 10-3/4", 48 pages, black and white narrative with line drawings as well as space for adhesive train stamps. Revised edition of 1955 Golden Book, with the only changes being the front and back covers. Features full-color monorail on front cover. R. Osterhoff Collection. — — 15 20

OPERATING MANUAL: 8-1/2" x 11", 31 pages, "Lionel train and Accessory Operating and Wiring Manual". Form 4080, orange and black cover, black and white inside pages. 3 4 6 9

DEALER PROMO PHOTOGRAPHS: 8" x 10" glossy black and white photographs distributed by Lionel's Advertising Department for publicity purposes. These photos were provided for most of Lionel's 1966 product line.
(A) Train and dealer display photographs. — — 3 5
(B) Science and phonograph photographs. — — 1 2
(C) Spirit-duplicated description of products, 8-1/2" x 11" one page. — — 1 2

SALES NEWSLETTER: "The Lionel Line — Confidential and important news for the Lionel Selling Organization Only". An internal company publication, blue spirit-duplicated and printed on Form 4231, featuring the Lionel lion and "Best wishes for better sales from Engineer Bill". Six known issues published from July through December 1966. **NRS**

RAILROAD CLUB LETTER: 8-1/2" x 11", one page, blue spirit-duplicated letter to "Dear Lionel Railroader". The letter states: "It is with great regret that, although the Lionel Railroad Company still exists, its activities have been greatly curtailed... we realize that the Lionel Railroad Company has been most utilitarian in giving young Americans an opportunity to know how American corporations exist..." **NRS**

LIONEL STATIONERY: 8-1/2" x 11", one page, "Lionel Corporation" imprinted at bottom. — — 1 2

LIONEL STATIONERY: 8-1/2" x 11", one page, Lionel colored insignia at top left. — — 1 2

INTERNAL MEMO FORM: 8-1/2" x 11", one page, internal use, Form 4181 2/66 "District Sales Manager's Correspondence". — — 1 2

INTERNAL MEMO FORM: 8-1/2" x 11", one page, form 392 "Inter-Office Communication — Lionel Corporation" imprinted at top. — — 2 3

WELCOME TO THE WONDERFUL WORLD OF LIONEL: 3-5/8" x 8-1/2", folder with 12 panels on two sides; orange and black ink on side 1, blue and black ink on side 2. M. Weisblum Collection. 3 5 7 9

A PROTOTYPE DEALER DISPLAY?

When one talks of prototype, immediately engines or accessories come to mind. But prototypes exist of many other Lionel items, including paper. At least one example is attributed to a 1960s dealer display. For many years Lionel manufactured most of its dealer display layouts, for stores and Service Stations who invested in valuable floor space to sell more Lionel trains. Although most layouts were constructed in New Jersey, Lionel often contracted for store displays west of the Mississippi River. Subcontracting of display construction also took place when Lionel's own factory was backlogged in building these displays.

One such prototype display was designed and built by John Brigham of Dallas, Texas for Lionel. The attractive display was constructed for the American Furniture Company of Albuquerque, New Mexico in 1966. It was customary for Lionel to provide much of the material, and this particular layout provided for operations of Lionel Super O, O and HO Gauges, as well as a model racing car layout. Although the actual layout no longer exists, the paper documents the existence of the display. To create the layout, a 17" x 10-3/4" line drawing was made.

The drawing, although crudely executed with a track configuration that was virtually impossible to construct, nevertheless allowed a concept to be converted to final form, with modifications such as the addition of an HO track, and routing the race car around the tunnel rather than through portals as displayed on the original drawing.

From the original line drawing, negative and positive engineering-type prints were produced, four of which survive. In addition, the final paper collectible from this display is a photograph in full color of the actual display itself. Unfortunately for dealer display specialists, this photograph is the only surviving piece representing the final display.

1967

CONSUMER CATALOGUE: No consumer catalogue was issued; the 1966 catalogue was considered in use during 1967. **NRS**

LIONEL LIQUIDATION AUCTION: 11" x 17", 23 pages, red and black on white paper, "5-day Auction August 7th-11th, 1967 Machinery and Equipment Used to Manufacture the Products of The Lionel Toy Corporation, Hillside, New Jersey". Auction catalogue issued by Samuel L. Winternitz & Co., Chicago, contains a wealth of photographs, primarily of tooling but also of the Lionel factory floor. No Trains included. **30 45 60 75**

PORTER-SPEAR '67: 8-1/2" x 11", 12 pages, dealer catalogue, illustrated in color, multicolored cover and contents advertise chemistry and biology sets, microscopes, and phonographs. Although Lionel is no longer mentioned in this catalogue, Porter-Spear retained a similar five-digit numbering system and the products are identical to those previously sold by Lionel. Catalogue includes a "1967 Confidential Price Schedule" consisting of two thermofaxed pages. A. Rubin Collection. **NRS**

1968

ADVANCE PRODUCT SHEET: 11" x 8-1/2", two-sided, blue on white-coated stock, shows 11600 Hagerstown set on one side with "Lionel 68", track and accessories on the other with "The Lionel Toy Corporation — Hagerstown, Maryland 21740".

	G	VG	EXC	NEW
(A) Original.	3	4	6	8
(B) Reproduction by Greenberg Publishing Company.	—	—	1	2
(C) Reproduction by Train Collectors Association.	—	—	1	2

CONSUMER CATALOGUE: 8-1/2" x 11", eight pages, folds out to 34" x 11", full-color coated stock, features man and boy viewing steam locomotive. **1 2 3 5**

PORTER-SPEAR 1968: Dealer catalogue, 24 pages illustrated in color, red and white cover format. Catalogue also includes "1968 Confidential Price Schedule" printed black ink on pink paper, two pages. This catalogue is actually from The Porter-Spear Company, Hagerstown, Maryland and although no mention is made of Lionel, the products and numbering system appear to be the same as 1960s Lionel. This is a late paper item. A. Rubin Collection. **NRS**

WARRANTY REPAIR FORM: Form SE-38 with designation "This is a No Charge Memo for Service on Lionel Products".

	G	VG	EXC	NEW
(A) Three-part blue, white, and yellow paper.	—	—	—	7
(B) Blue paper.	—	—	—	2

Top row: 1969 Consumer Catalogue, 1966 Welcome to the Wonderful World of Lionel, and the 1968 Advance Product Sheet for Hagerstown set. *Bottom row:* 1967 Liquidation Auction; 1968 Consumer Catalogue, 1966 Consumer Catalogue, and brown 1969 Advance Catalogue..

1966-67 Authorized Service Station window decal.

	G	VG	EXC	NEW

ORDER FORM: Six pages, phonograph order form, unnumbered and not dated, black on thin white paper, begins with Part No. 41010-18.   —   —   —   4

1969

ADVANCE CATALOGUE: 8-1/2" x 11", eight pages, with cover featuring a 2331 FM and steam locomotive. Brown and white coated stock, pages not numbered.   5   10   15   20

CONSUMER CATALOGUE: 8-1/2" x 11", eight pages, with cover featuring a 2331 FM and steam locomotive.
(A) Full-color coated stock, tan cover background.
  1   2   3   5

	G	VG	EXC	NEW

(B) Similar to (A), but greenish-tan cover background.
  1   2   3   5

OPERATING BROCHURE: 5-1/2" x 8-1/2", 16 pages, black and white, "How to Operate the Train", with "1969" on inside page.
  2   3   4   5

YEAR NOT IDENTIFIED

(Reader assistance in positively identifying the years for following listings would be most welcomed.)

DEALER BROCHURE: 16-3/8" x 11", "Desirable Types of Track Layouts for Lionel Counters", blue on white paper, features four layouts. It is believed this form was issued in 1946. W. Mekalian Collection.   NRS

CHANGE OF ADDRESS NOTICE: 8-1/2" x 3-1/2", Form 900, white paper, indicating Lionel Service Dept. address changed to Hillside, New Jersey.   NRS

REGRETS ENVELOPE: Small 5" x 3" envelope specially folded to contain a quarter as a refund because "we cannot complete the special offer as advertised because we have exhausted our supplies of catalogues, records, and billboards." Probably early 1950s, with accompanying outer envelope mailer.   NRS

BOX LABEL: 9" x 4", orange and blue on white glossy paper, designed for placement on set boxes of late 1940s and early 1950s era. No printing on label.   2   4   6   8

ORDER FORM: 7-3/4" x 10", four pages, Lionel-Porter form, black on white paper, for ordering chemical, biological, microcraft, and other Lionel non-train supplies.   —   —   —   2

LIONEL TOOL PROMOTION SHEET: Two pages, Form 1533 printed in black ink on blue paper, illustrating Service Station hand tools, from later 1950s since ST-311 wheel puller is also included. Similar to tool pages included in Service Manual, however no mention of the manual nor page designation is included. R. Osterhoff Collection.   NRS

Chapter Four
MODERN ERA: 1970-1990

It is not certain who first coined the term "modern era," but one fact is known. The phrase has been adopted to accommodate the many Lionel organizational titles after 1969: MPC, Fundimensions, Kenner Parker Toys, and Lionel Trains, Inc. None of these organizations accurately describe Lionel in the 1970s and 1980s. From the struggles of organization and ownership, the Lionel name has again survived as a winner.

The 1970 catalogues came in many formats, ranging from a poster in 1970 to more traditional booklets. The marketing theme of Fundimensions in 1981 was "Grow With Us," yet few understood the message since the 1981 train catalogue was reduced to a size that had not been used since the 1920s. Was the Lionel emphasis on marketing declining? Would Lionel history repeat itself, and bring the magical train manufacturing to extinction?

As we enter the 1990s, the Lionel name appears to be stronger than ever. We no longer hear mention of "the" catalogue. Now it is "Book One" and "Book Two," produced by Lionel Trains, Inc. The printed color is crisp. The marketing effort is world class. The products are innovative and fun, with not only smoking locomotives but smoking buildings as well, and layout panoramas imaged live on television screens.

The ups and downs of Lionel are vividly depicted in the paper of the prewar and postwar eras. The listings that follow continue the ride on Lionel's roller coaster. As this book is written, there is a difference. Perhaps it was fitting that for 1990, Lionel Trains, Inc. has chosen as a slogan — "90 Years of Magic" for its marketing campaign. For paper, the magic has returned.

Note: Lionel published some of its catalogues, brochures, and flyers in the year before the date that appears on the piece. In our listings, we have located these pieces under the year they were issued rather than the year stated on the piece. For example, the 1990 Consumer Catalogue Book One was actually released in late 1989, therefore it is listed under the 1989 heading.

1970

TOY FAIR CATALOGUE: 8-1/2" x 11", eight pages, including covers. Front cover illustrates red, white, and blue banner with white stars; black steam engine on red banner "1903-1970", red "There is a NEW LIONEL" and black-printed text, and red "LIONEL" in modern typeface. Back cover: pictures of Lionel accessories and white "ACCESSORIES" on red banner.   **5   10   15   20**

CONSUMER CATALOGUE: 8-1/2" x 11", eight-page folder / poster. Front cover illustrates same banner as Toy Fair catalogue, but white "A LIFETIME OF RAILROADING" replaces star motif; shows Wabash Cannonball and Yard Boss sets found on page 3 of earler edition; red "BONUS...OPEN UP TO A 22" x 34" POSTER"; $1.00 price in upper right-hand corner. Rear cover has picture of layout found in 1957 Lionel catalogue, black print, pictures of Lionel features. Folder opens to reveal poster in brown, red, and gold tones with red and black "A LIFETIME OF RAILROADING" in Old West script; tintype pictures of old railroad scenes and personalities surround modern diorama of trains going every which way.
2   3   5   7

"Bonus" poster from the 1970 Consumer Catalogue.

| | G | VG | EXC | NEW |

DESIGN AND DISPLAY IDEA BOOK: 20 pages including covers. Earliest version of track layout book; 1970 only. Front cover has white background; black and white banner similar to that on early consumer catalogue; locomotive and "1903-1970" banner, black "LIONEL / brings / LIFE / to / LIFETIME RAILROADING / in / Design & Display Ideas". Rear cover: white background, centered "LIONEL" and MPC logo in black with black-printed address. No copyright date on inside front cover. G. Salamone and R. LaVoie Collections.
4   6   8   10

DEALER FLYER: One page printed on one side. Black and white print: "LIONEL TRAIN DISPLAYS". Content gives details of two ready-made dealer display boards, Number 3000, and Number 3001. These displays were available FOB from Hillside, New Jersey. G. Salamone and G. Halverson Collections.
2   3   5   7

DEALER AD MATS: 8-1/2" x 11", one page, black on white glossy paper, advertises Pacemaker and Diesel Express sets, "Lionel Ad Mats" in block letters at top.
3   4   6   8

SERVICE STATION GUIDEBOOK: 8-1/2" x 11", five pages, "Information & Procedures for Lionel Approved Service Stations" Form No. 932 Revised 3/70, black ink on white paper. B. Munn Collection.
9   15   20   25

DEALER PROMOTIONAL KIT: 9" x 12" folder issued for the 1970 Toy Fair; black, red, blue, and yellow on white card stock with caption "Now Appearing at Stores Everywhere — The MPC Explosion".

Folder contains over 30 non-train flyers, printed one side in full color on glossy white paper. A. Rubin Collection.   **NRS**

TRAIN AND ACCESSORY MANUAL: Form 4080, 32 pages, fully illustrated and printed in black and white. The front cover has the often-used locomotive and star scrollwork with "1903-1970", and a price of $1.50 is also printed in the bottom right corner. A. Rubin Collection.
—   —   7   10

CONSUMER BROCHURE: Four pages, "Lionel Accessories", black ink and white, with caption "Build with Lionel ... For a Lifetime of Railroading" with layouts on back page. A. Rubin Collection.
—   —   2   3

1971

TOY FAIR CATALOGUE: 8-1/2" x 11", twelve pages including covers, glossy black front cover; with red-orange or orange "LIONEL", yellow "1971", pictures of Lionel catalogues; cover opens out to fold-out introducing electronic Sound of Steam with Silver Star set. No price on cover, back cover has "LIONEL" underlined.
(A) "LIONEL" on cover in bright orange.   7   9   12   15
(B) "LIONEL" on cover in red orange.   4   5   8   10

CONSUMER CATALOGUE: 8-1/2" x 11", twelve pages including covers, glossy black front cover; with red "LIONEL", yellow "1971", pictures of Lionel catalogues; cover opens out to fold-out introducing

Top row: 1970 Toy Fair Catalogue; Consumer Catalogue; Train and Accessory Manual. *Bottom row:* 1971 Toy Fair Catalogue with extra panel cover; Consumer Catalogue with possible printing error.

Modern Era Paper: 1970-1990 • 91

G   VG   EXC NEW

electronic Sound of Steam with Silver Star set. Price of 50 cents on cover.
(A) Listing of components for set 1184 includes "Foam Model Buildings".   2   3   6   8
(B) Reference to foam packaging deleted from set 1184.
           2   3   4   6
(C) Color sections of cover are done in monochrome pink-red instead of full color. This is a probable printing error due to omission of the blue and green components of the color separations used to print in full color. R. LaVoie Collection.   **NRS**

CONSUMER CATALOGUE: Canadian distribution.
(A) 8-1/2" x 11", eight pages including covers. Front cover has black background, yellow "PARKER BROTHERS / INTRODUCES THE / LIONEL / O27 TRAIN LINE / FOR 1971". Rear cover has Parker Brothers logo and Canadian address.   4   6   8   10
(B) 8-1/2" x 11", twelve pages including covers. Same general contents as (A), but four additional smaller pages inside refer to Lionel stores in Canada. G. Halverson Collection.   4   6   8   10

TRACK LAYOUT BOOK: Second version; 24 pages including covers. Front cover: light brown background; red "LIONEL" at upper right, dark blue "TRACK / LAYOUT / BOOK" at upper right; line sketches of diesel engine, steam engine, water tower, and layout in dark brown.
(A) Has blue "50 cents" at lower right of front cover with MPC and General Mills logos on back cover. This was used from 1971 through 1972. T. Wagner Collection.   3   5   8   10
(B) No "50 cents" on front cover, has Fundimensions logo in place of the MPC and General Mills logos. This version was used for 1973-1974. T. Wagner Collection.   2   3   5   7

TRAIN AND ACCESSORY MANUAL: First version; 30 pages including covers. Front cover: white background; red "LIONEL" along top border, black "TRAIN AND ACCESSORY MANUAL" at top, multicolored outline drawings of locomotive, rolling stock, and accessories on remainder of cover. Rear cover: white background; red "LIONEL" at bottom center, dark blue-printed company address.
(A) Has $1.50 price on front cover with MPC and General Mills logos on back cover. This version was used for 1971-1972. T. Wagner Collection.   5   7   9   12
(B) No price on front cover, has Fundimensions logo in place of the MPC and General Mills logos. This version was used for 1973-1974. T. Wagner Collection.   4   6   8   10

PROMOTIONAL COUPON: 4-1/4" x 2-3/4", 10 cents coupon, inscribed "Lionel instruction sheet recommends Playnts" poster paints, issued by General Mills. Red and black on white paper.
           —   1   2   3

ACCESSORIES BROCHURE: 8-1/2" x 11", four-page, black and white folder. "LIONEL ACCESSORIES" at top of first page. Shows all items available in 1971. Rear page has mail order prices for ordering direct from Lionel. This was included in all 1971 train sets. T. Wagner Collection.   1   2   3   5

DEALER FLYER: 8-1/2" x 11" sheet, two pages, printed in blue and red ink on white glossy paper. "NEW ACCESSORIES FROM / LIONEL / FOR JANUARY / FEBRUARY SHIPMENT" on first page. Has "A LIFETIME OF RAILROADING" banner in top left corner. Front features 8030 Illinois Central GP-9 plus rolling stock. T. Wagner Collection.   **NRS**

ADVERTISING PROOF BROCHURE: 11" x 25-1/2" sheet folded into thirds to form an 8-1/2" x 11" sheet. Features the entire 1971 train line printed in black on a glossy white sheet. This was used for dealer advertising. T. Wagner Collection.   **NRS**

CONSUMER INFORMATION PACKET: Canadian distribution through Parker Brothers. White envelope with track running around border; black and red "WITH / LIONEL / TRAINS / YOU GET

G   VG   EXC NEW

/ DAD FOR / CHRISTMAS". Contents of envelope includes small 5-1/2" x 8-1/2" version of 1971 Canadian consumer catalogue, containing special Canadian sets, 12 pages; letter to consumers dated 11/2/71 and signed by M. J. Buder; $1.00 refund coupon for 5030 Lionel track expander set; and four-page paint-by-number railroad plaque offer. G. Salamone and G. Halverson Collections.   5   10   15   20

DEALER FLYER: One page printed on one side. Dark tan background, "LIONEL STOKES UP / YOUR 1971 SALES"; contains details of radio and television advertising campaign.
           2   3   5   7

PRICE LIST: 8-1/2" x 11", one page, black and white, "Effective — Mar. 1, 1971"; printed on one side only.   **NRS**

1972

TOY FAIR CATALOGUE: 8-1/2" x 11", sixteen pages including covers. Front cover has red "LIONEL", gold "1972", irregularly-sized rectangles containing pictures of Lionel rolling stock and accessories. No price on cover.   4   6   8   10

CONSUMER CATALOGUE: 8-1/2" x 11", sixteen pages including covers. Front cover has red "LIONEL", gold "1972"; irregularly-sized rectangles containing pictures of Lionel rolling stock and accessories, 50 cents price upper right.
(A) Glossy paper, heavy-coated stock.   2   3   4   5
(B) Glossy lesser-grade paper, thinner coated stock.
           4   6   8   10

CONSUMER CATALOGUE: 8-1/2" x 11", Canadian edition; eight pages including covers, color contents, dated 1972-73 on cover with Concord, Ontario address of Parker Brothers.
           4   5   8   10

ACCESSORIES BROCHURE: 8-1/2" x 11", four-page, black- and-white printed folder. "LIONEL ACCESSORIES" at top of first page; pictures and descriptions continue through rest of page. Inside two pages have pictures and descriptions of locomotives and rolling stock. Rear page has track pictures and descriptions and an order checklist with current prices. Often included with 1972 catalogued and uncatalogued sets.   1   2   3   5

DEALER BROCHURE: 8-1/2" x 11", four-page black- and white- printed folder. "LIONEL / ELECTRIC TRAIN SETS / AND ACCESSORIES / FOR 1972" on front page; eight train sets on pages 2 and 3.
           3   4   6   8

DEALER FLYER: 8-1/2" x 11", one sheet printed on one side, green with black printing, "JOHNNY CASH TEAMS UP AGAIN / WITH LIONEL IN 1972". Details of television and radio advertising campaign.   2   3   5   7

TRAIN DISPLAY FLYER: 8-1/2" x 11", one sheet, black and white printed one side. Illustrates display sets 3004 and 3005.
           2   3   5   7

REFUND COUPON: 3-5/6" x 9-1/8" vertical; $1.00 refund for purchase of Lionel Track Expander Set. Green and black on white paper.
           2   3   4   5

DEALER BROCHURE: 8-1/2" x 11", four pages, black and white with caption "New Engines / New Cars / and / Revolutionary / New Track System". Features B & O F-3 on cover. A. Rubin Collection.
           1   2   3   5

OPERATING INSTRUCTIONS: Dual language (French and English), 6" x 9", 16 pages with Canadian product codes listed. A. Rubin Collection.   —   —   —   5

DEALER FLYER: Single page printed in full color on white glossy paper with caption "T-1273 — SILVER STAR — SOUND OF STEAM", in English and French. Canadian dealer flyer found in 1972-73 Canadian catalogue.   **NRS**

	G	VG	EXC	NEW

FREE TRACK / PROMOTION: One-page flyer printed in blue and red ink on white glossy paper. Details an offer to dealers when four dozen 9200 series cars are ordered, a case of 200 pieces of straight track is included free. T. Wagner Collection. **NRS**

ADVERTISING PROOF BROCHURE: 11" x 17" single-page sheet folded in half to form an 8-1/2" x 11" sheet. Shows entire 1972 train line printed in black on white glossy paper. This was used for dealer advertising. T. Wagner Collection. **NRS**

DEALER FLYER: Four separate flyers, single page printed in full color and numbered T-1172, T-1173, T-1174, and T-1280. Printed in English and French for Canadian market. T. Wagner Collection. **NRS**

DEALER POSTER: Full color poster with slogan "GET 4 PIECES / OF TRACK FREE / WHEN YOU BUY / ONE OF THESE / BOX CARS!" Additional information requested. **NRS**

1973

ADVANCE CATALOGUE: 8-1/2" x 11", sixteen pages including covers. Front cover has black and white picture of grandfather, father, son, and dog looking at Blue Streak Freight racing around oval track; red "LIONEL / 1973". Differs from regular catalogue as follows: mock-up passenger cars shown in Milwaukee Special set; regular catalogue has prototypes. The 8360 Long Island GP-20 shown in light gray and dark gray; regular catalogue shows engine as all charcoal gray. Accessory pictures are rearranged from advance catalogue to consumer catalogue. **4 5 8 10**

CONSUMER CATALOGUE: 8-1/2" x 11", same as advance catalogue, but front cover and contents are in full color rather than in black and white. "LIONEL" on rear cover is at lower left instead of lower right. **1 2 3 4**

DEALER FLYER: 8-1/2" x 11", one sheet printed on both sides. One side has red "BILLBOARD REEFER CAR SERIES!!!" at top, artists' drawings of six reefer cars, red "LIONEL" at lower right, and light blue square with white lettering at lower left explaining coupon promotion. Other side has red "NEW FROM LIONEL... / OPERATING / U.S. MAIL / CAR!!!" at upper left; artists' drawings of 9301 red, white, and blue mail car (curiously, numbered 3428 as was older Lionel car) and red "LIONEL" at lower left. **3 4 6 8**

DEALER FLYER: 8-1/2" X 11", "NEW ENGINES / NEW CARS / AND REVOLUTIONARY NEW TRACK SYSTEM", black ink on white glossy paper. **3 4 6 8**

SEARS CONSUMER BUYING GUIDE: provides details on three Lionel sets. **3 4 6 8**

ACCESSORY BOOKLET: 5-1/4" x 7-1/4", eight-page booklet, usually packed with service station listings and warranty cards in enve-

Top row: 1971 Toy Fair Catalogue (A) with orange "Lionel"; Canadian Consumer Catalogue; 1972 Consumer Catalogue. *Bottom row:* Canadian Consumer Catalogue; 1973 Advance Catalogue; rear cover of 1972 Accessories Brochure.

	G	VG	EXC	NEW

lope included with sets. Front cover has light blue background, black "How to build / a great railroad / Lionel accessories." Page 2 states "Lionel's 1973 Engine..." — — 1 2

ADVERTISING PROOF BROCHURE: Three consecutive foldouts, 8-1/2" x 11" black on white glossy pages used for dealer advertising. Top right begins Santa Fe Freight. 7 9 12 15

DEALER FLYER: 8-1/2" x 11", one sheet printed on one side; black and red "NEW ACTION-PACKED ACCESSORIES FROM / LIONEL", shows 9302 searchlight car, 9123 automobile carrier, and 2260 bumper. 1 2 3 5

TRAIN DISPLAY FLYER: 8-1/2" x 11", one sheet printed on one side. Black and white print; illustrates display sets 3006 and 3007. 2 3 5 7

ADVERTISING FLYER: 8-1/2" x 11", one sheet printed on one side. Tan background with blue lettering and background; gives details of television, mail, magazine, and other advertising campaigns, but makes no mention of radio. 4 5 7 9

SERVICE STATION POSTER: "Authorized Lionel Service Center", 10" x 6", with Fundimensions and address identified at bottom. Red and dark blue colors on a clear, peelable background. B. Munn Collection. NRS

1974

CONSUMER CATALOGUE: 8-1/2" x 11", twenty pages including covers. Front cover: white background; red "LIONEL", blue "O27" and "1974", pictures of father and family playing with trains, pictures of locomotives and rolling stock. This is the first catalogue in Lionel history to show a girl playing with trains on the front cover. Rear cover: plain white, red "LIONEL" in lower left corner. — 1 2 3

CONSUMER HO CATALOGUE: 8-3/8" x 11", eight pages including cover, vertical format in full color, "LIONEL HO — 1974" on front.
(A) Deep blue cover, "The Great Northern" colored border on page 4 is in light blue, as normally issued to the public. 1 2 3 5
(B) Deep blue and purple cover, "The Great Northern" colored border on page 4 is in violet color. R. Osterhoff Collection. NRS

DEALER BROCHURE: 8-1/2" x 11", four pages; front page has red "LIONEL" at lower right and pictures of rolling stock and accessories in square pattern. Inside pages describe Spirit of '76 series. Rear page describes 8463 Chessie GP-20 and three O scale building kits.
(A) As described above. 1 2 3 5
(B) Same as (A) but with "COMPLIMENTARY COPY / NOT FOR SALE" in lower left corner of front cover. T. Wagner Collection. NRS

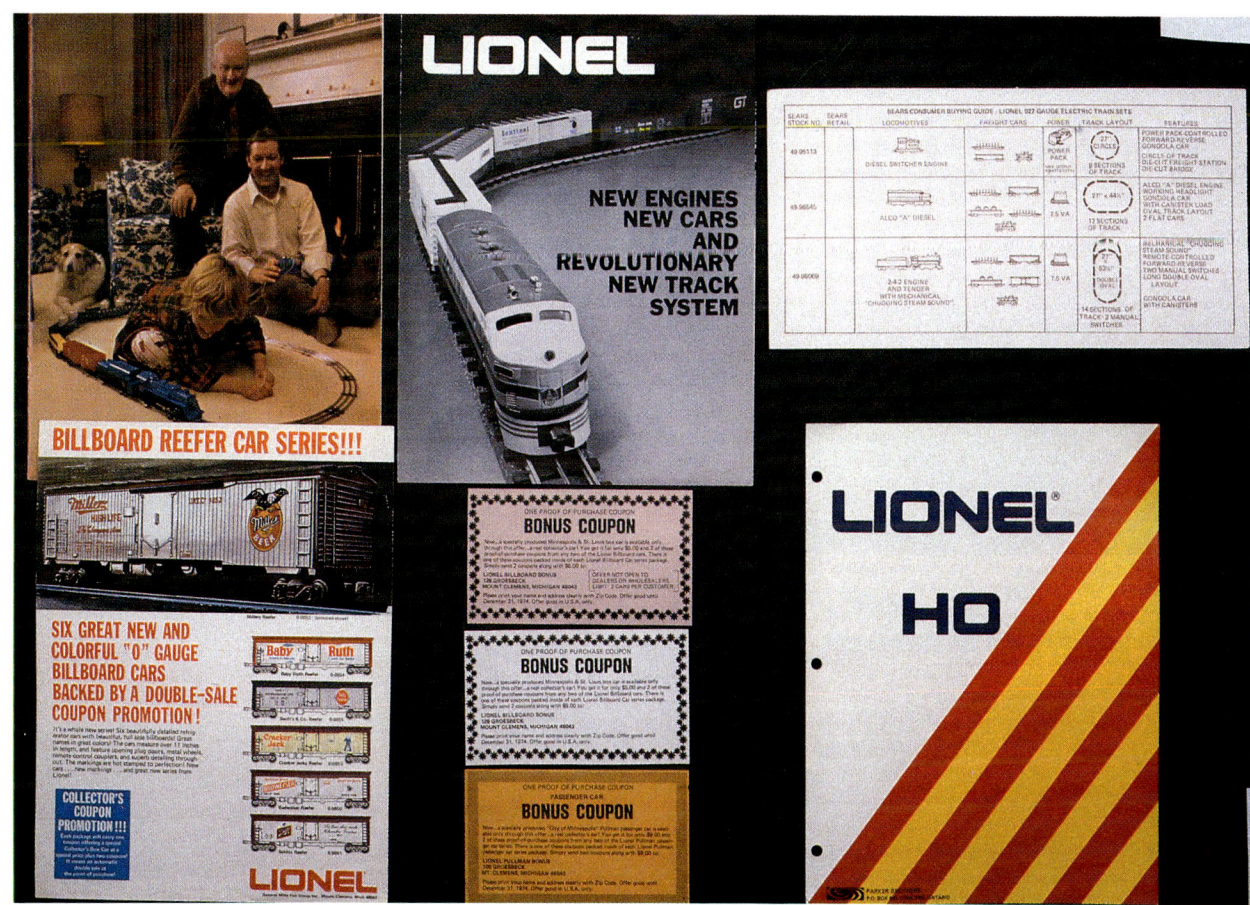

Top row: 1973 Consumer Catalogues; Dealer Flyer; Sears Consumer Buying Guide. *Bottom row:* 1973 Dealer Flyer; Billboard Reefer; 1974 Consumer Coupons; 1975 HO Catalogue; Canadian edition.

| | G | VG | EXC | NEW |

DEALER BROCHURE: Four pages; black and white "PROFIT BONUS SPECIAL". Fall deal for 1974 includes 9757 Central of Georgia boxcar and baggage cars for Pennsylvania and Milwaukee sets. **1 2 3 5**

PROMOTIONAL CARTOON: 8-1/2" x 15-1/2" full color cartoon advertisement entitled "DAD'S BIG SURPRISE". This was issued with the "Profit Bonus Special" dealer package. T. Wagner Collection. **NRS**

POSTCARD: 3" x 9" postcard with full color picture of the COKE train set. Back has caption "LIONEL "O" GAUGE TRAIN SET" along with box for postage stamp. Confirmation of authenticity requested. T. Wagner Collection. **NRS**

DEALER FLYER: Two-page flyer printed in full color. One side features 7604 through 7607 Spirit of '76 cars; other side has 9506 and 9510 Illuminated Baggage Passenger Combo cars. T. Wagner Collection. **1 2 3 5**

BUMPER STICKER: 2-1/2" x 12" sticker with "LIONEL" in bright orange lettering on a white background. Confirmation of date requested. T. Wagner Collection. **NRS**

CONSUMER COUPON: 5-3/8" x 3-1/8", black ink on white or pink paper, one side printed, irregular asterisk border, "BONUS COUPON" in bold type atop coupon. Special offer: 9742 Minneapolis & St. Louis boxcar for $5.00 and two of these coupons, which were included in specially marked covered hopper or refrigerator rolling stock boxes. Similar coupons were issued for the 9719 New Haven double-door boxcar and the 9511 Milwaukee "Minneapolis" passenger car, but the coupons for the 9719 were actually part of the Type II boxes for hopper and refrigerator cars.

(A) Black print on white paper. T. Wagner Collection. **NRS**
(B) Black print on pink paper with added notation "OFFER NOT OPEN TO / DEALERS OR WHOLESALERS / LIMIT:2 CARS PER CUSTOMER." T. Wagner Collection. **NRS**

CONSUMER COUPON: 5-3/8" 3-1/8", black ink on goldenrod paper, one side printed, dot matrix black border, "BONUS COUPON" in bold type atop coupon. Special offer: a special Milwaukee Road City of Minneapolis Pullman car for $9.00 with two of these coupons from specially marked passenger car boxes. The coupon for the 9719 New Haven boxcar was printed right on the box, but purchasers were reluctant to cut the boxes, so Fundimensions went to separate coupons. See entry above. **NRS**

DEALER FLYER: 8-1/2" x 11", one sheet printed on both sides. One side shows three Milwaukee Road passenger cars; other side shows 9858, 9859, and 9860 reefers and 9128 Heinz pickle car.
1 2 3 5

TCA PROMOTIONAL BROCHURE: "The TCA Bicentennial Special", 8-1/2" square full-color brochure, four pages full-color, with ordering instructions. **3 4 5 6**

Top row: 1974 Consumer Catalogue; Consumer HO Catalogue; 1974 Dealer Flyer – illuminated passenger cars (Milwaukee Road) on one side, reefers (9858, 9859, 9860, etc) on the other side. *Bottom row:* 1975 Dealer Flyer; Lionel Goes To Pre-School; 1974 Accessory Booklet; 1975 Consumer Catalogue.

Modern Era Paper: 1970-1990 • 95

	G	VG	EXC	NEW

ACCESSORY BOOKLET: 5-1/4" x 7-1/4", eight pages including covers. Front cover has blue background with train set on trestle and another set on siding 1 2 3 4

1975

CONSUMER CATALOGUE: 8-1/2" x 11", 24 pages including covers. Front cover has white background; irregular rectangular pictures of trains, catalogue covers, and accessories from all periods of Lionel history; "LIONEL "O" 1975" in red at bottom; large circular 75th Anniversary logo in silver, red, black, and white; $1.00 price on front.
(A) Yellow light coming from tender of 8506 switcher engine on page 14. Although there is a price on front, the edition is also considered a Toy Fair edition. 2 3 5 7
(B) Red light coming from tender of 8506 switcher, printed additions to text of second and third pages and to description of set 1585.
 2 3 4 5

CONSUMER HO CATALOGUE: 8-1/2" x 11", 12 pages including covers. Front cover has white background, American Freedom Train photos, circular Lionel 75th Anniversary logo, blue "LIONEL HO / 1975". First two pages show details of American Freedom Train in both five-unit diesel and seven-unit steam sets. Previous year's sets continued; separate sale rolling stock and accessories added.
 1 2 3 4

HO CATALOGUE: 8-1/2" x 11", Canadian edition in full color, features a numbering system different from the United States, in that all items begin with a "T" prefix, followed by five digits. Issued by Parker Brothers of Canada. Cover features bright red and yellow stripes with no illustrations. NRS

ANNIVERSARY BOOK "ON THE RIGHT TRACK": 5-1/4" x 7-1/2", 49 pages, "The History of Lionel Trains". Part number 2961. Hardcover book. Cover: dark blue, gold rectangle, gold-stamped lettering; black, red, silver, and blue circular 75th Anniversary logo sticker on cover. Book contains text of history and numerous black and white photographs from all periods. Came in white cardboard container with and without "HISTORY / BOOK 6-2961" printed in black on white label. 2 4 6 8

TRACK LAYOUT BOOK: Third version; 24 pages including covers. Front cover has same colors and design as second version in 1971, except "TRACK / LAYOUT / BOOK" at upper right is light blue and at lower right is different. Rear cover similar to 1971 version, except MPC and General Mills logos are eliminated. Contents similar to previous editions, but additions and rearrangements have been made. This version was continued to 1985.
(A) "O27/75¢" on cover. 2 3 5 7
(B) "O27" only on cover. 2 3 5 7

TRAIN AND ACCESSORY MANUAL: Third version; 34 pages including covers. Front cover: light blue background; red "LIONEL" along top border, dark blue "O / O27" at top right, dark blue "TRAIN AND ACCESSORY MANUAL" vertically along right side of cover, dark blue drawing of left half of steam engine front at left side of cover.

Top row: 1975 Anniversary Book "On The Right Track"; Accessory Booklet; Dealer Brochure – four pages with Liberty Special set, 8551 etc. *Bottom row:* Dealer Brochure – four pages with drawbridge, bumper etc.; 1975 Dealer Flyer – baggage cars, Hi Cube cars, etc.; 1975 Dealer Flyer – Grain Elevator.

	G	VG	EXC	NEW

Rear cover: light blue background; red "LIONEL" at bottom center, dark blue-printed company address and part number "6-2953". This version was continued through 1985 with only pricing changes.
(A) "O / O27" and "$1.50" in upper left corner of front cover. T. Wagner Collection.   2   3   4   6
(B) "O / O27" only in upper left corner. T. Wagner Collection.   2   3   4   6

DEALER BROCHURE: 8-1/2" x 11", four pages. Front page has ochre background, red "LIONEL" at lower right and line drawings of EP-5 locomotive and rolling stock in black. Inside pages describe Liberty Special set, 8551 Pennsylvania EP-5 locomotive, and 8568 Preamble Express F-3 A unit locomotive. Rear page describes three Pennsylvania passenger cars.   —   1   2   3

DEALER BROCHURE: Fall 1975, 8-1/2" x 11", four pages. Front page has white background and red, black, silver, and white 75th Anniversary logo at lower left, irregular square pattern of pictures, black and red lettering. Inside pages describe drawbridge, lighted bumpers, three billboard hoppers, and coaling station kit; rear pages describe tunnel, three Spirit of '76 boxcars, and 8573 Union Pacific U36B dummy unit with electronic horn.   —   —   1   2

DEALER FLYER: Two pages, "LIONEL INTRODUCES AN HO INDUSTRY FIRST—THE U-18-B DIESEL"; back side features HO building kits. A. Rubin Collection.   1   2   3   5

DEALER FLYER: Late 1975, one page printed on both sides. One side describes Pennsylvania, Milwaukee, and B & O full baggage cars, hi-cube boxcars and Uncle Sam boxcar; other side describes 8576 Penn Central GP-7 locomotive, three Spirit of '76 cars, three covered hoppers, and three SP-type lighted cabooses.   1   2   3   5

DEALER FLYER: 8-1/2" x 11", one sheet with both sides printed, "LIONEL T.V. / Accessory Center Program", blue and black printing; Number 1561. This program was aimed at hobby shops which weren't Lionel service stations.   1   2   3   4

DEALER FLYER: 8-1/2" x 11", one sheet with both sides printed, "LIONEL T.V. / Accessory Center Program", red and black printing; Number 1565. This program was aimed at mass merchandisers.   1   2   3   4

RETAIL ADVERTISING KIT: Came in white one-pocket folder printed in black and gray with Lionel 75th Anniversary logo; contains 15 single-sided sheets printed in black and white with ready-made dealer advertising pages. Directions for use printed on inside of folder cover.   12   20   25   35

SOUVENIR COVERS: Pair of cacheted envelopes issued by the Midwest Railway Historical Society for the 75th Anniversary of Lionel trains. One cover is postmarked Christmas, Michigan and the other New York, New York, with both dated December 25, 1975. Red and black cachet illustrates Lionel Standard Gauge.   —   —   —   20

PROMOTIONAL STICKER: "LIONEL — 75th ANNIVERSARY" logo circular paper adhesive-backed sticker in black and gold.
(A) Diameter of 1-1/4".   —   —   1   2

Top row: 1974 Dealer Brochure with square pictures of equipment, inside is the Spirit of '76 series; Dealer Flyer – HO Industry First U-18-B, Consumer HO Catalogue. *Bottom row:* 1975 Dealer Flyer; HO Daylight; Retail Advertising Kit; Thunderball Freight advertising from Retail Advertising Kit.

	G	VG	EXC	NEW
(B) Diameter of 5".	—	—	2	4

DEALER FLYER: 8-1/2" x 11", two pages, "LIONEL GOES TO PRE-SCHOOL", full-color promotional flyer, advertises Happy Huff 'n' Puff on one side and Gravel Gus on the other.

	1	2	3	4

DEALER FLYER: 8-1/2" x 11", one page, "NOW...LIONEL GOES TO PRE-SCHOOL." Full-color promotional flyer, advertises Happy Huff 'n' Puff on one side only. Believed to have been issued at the 1975 Toy Fair. T. Wagner Collection.

	3	5	8	10

DEALER FLYER: 8-1/2" x 11", four-page folder, "Lionel is tripling advertising", black on white glossy paper describes Lionel's 1975 advertising campaign.

	2	3	5	7

PROMOTIONAL STICKER: "Lionel — 75th Anniversary" logo, circular red and black on a clear, peelable background. Sticker is 6-1/8" diameter but mounted on a 6-1/2" x 6-1/2" sheet of paper. B. Munn Collection. **NRS**

1946 CATALOGUE REPRINT: 16 pages, Lionel consumer catalogue, reproduced by Lionel, and so designated in the lower left-hand corner on page 2, "Reproduced by Lionel of Fundimensions ... copyright 1975". The catalogue reproduced was actually missing the front and back covers, and was the *Liberty Magazine* version. The 20-page version was reproduced by Greenberg Publishing Company. A. Rubin Collection. — — — 10

1937 CATALOGUE REPRODUCTION: Lionel consumer catalogue, reproduction by Lionel, and so designated in the lower left-hand corner on page 2, "Reproduced by Lionel of Fundimensions ... copyright 1975." The original catalogue from which the reproduction was made was well worn since numerous creases and tears appear on the reproduced version. A. Rubin Collection. — — — 15

DEALER FLYER: Eight pages, black cover with "Fundimensions" and colored arrows pointing to four product lines, including trains. Back cover features Lionel SP Daylight HO set and designation that "Lionel means business in HO..." A. Rubin Collection.

	2	3	5	7

DEALER FLYER: Two pages, features Lionel HO diesels beginning with the Soo Line 5-5520 on one side, and on the reverse page features the introduction of the Penn Central GP-7, 6-8576. A. Rubin Collection.

	1	2	3	4

PRICE LIST: 8-1/2" x 13-7/8", two pages, black on white paper, with three columns for consumer ordering, plus a section on "Exciting O27 Track Layout Ideas". A. Rubin Collection. — — — 1

PRICE LIST: Dated 4-1-75, two pages black and white, one page an order form, page 2 "Exciting Track Layout Ideas". A. Rubin Collection. — — — 2

Top Row: 1974 Dealer Flyer with Spirit of 76...State Cars; 1976 Consumer HO Catalogue; 1976 Dealer Flyer –"Fundimensions Means New Dimension in ...." *Bottom row:* Dealer Flyer – Johnny Cash / Ridin' The Rails... Television Special; 1974 TCA Promotional Brochure; 1976 Consumer Catalogue.

1976

	G	VG	EXC	NEW

CONSUMER CATALOGUE: 8-1/2" x 11", 24 pages including covers. Front cover has white upper strip across cover with red "LIONEL" and black "O / O27 1976"; five strips run across rest of cover depicting Lionel locomotives and rolling stock; $1.00 price on front.
— 1 2 3

CONSUMER HO CATALOGUE: 8-1/2" x 11", 12 pages including covers. Front cover has white background, black outline photo of SP Daylight GS-4 4-8-4 Northern steam engine, locomotive and accessory photos and red typeface "LIONEL HO 1976". Catalogue describes new Burlington 181 and Chessie Golden Arrow sets, two new GS-4 steam locomotives.
— 1 2 3

ACCESSORY BOOKLET: 5-1/4" x 7-1/4", 12 pages including covers. Front cover: white background, medium blue lettering "HOW TO BUILD A / RAILROAD EMPIRE" at upper right, red "LIONEL" at upper right, black "FOR "O" & "O27" GAUGE RAILROADERS" at upper left, picture of large layout on rest of page.
(A) White paper stock. — — 1 2
(B) Off-white paper stock. — — 1 2

DEALER BROCHURE: 8-1/2" x 11", four pages. Front page has medium and light brown background, page describes Rico Station and 8558 Milwaukee EP-5 electric locomotive. Inside pages describe Virginian locomotive and rolling stock and Tobacco Road boxcars.
1 2 3 4

DEALER BROCHURE: 8-1/2" x 11", "THE PROFIT BONUS SPECIAL".
2 3 4 6

DEALER BROCHURE: 8-1/2" x 11", four pages. Front cover pictures Johnny Cash and Southern 2-8-2 Mikado steam locomotive 4501 in black and white; lettered "LIONEL TRAINS: / LIONEL MEANS MORE CASH IN '76". G. Salamone and G. Halverson Collections.
2 3 4 6

DEALER BROCHURE: 8-1/2" x 11", four pages. Front page black and white background; red "LIONEL MEANS MORE CASH / IN '76...AND '77 TOO!", photo of side of Johnny Cash boxcar at station with miniature cartons, black print at lower left. Inside pages describe new rolling stock and list carton assortments for dealers. Mailed to dealers in October 1976. G. Halverson and R. LaVoie Collections.
2 3 5 6

DEALER BROCHURE: 8-1/2" x 11", four pages. Front page has lettering "LIONEL: ENGINES AND CABOOSES, NEW BOXCARS AND HI-CUBES, NEW SOMETHING SPECIAL". Front page shows first three Soda Pop Road boxcars 7800, 7801, and 7802; pages 3 and 4 show three new engines and matching cabooses and three hi-cube boxcars; back page shows Johnny Cash boxcar.
1 2 3 4

Top row: 1976 Dealer Brochure featuring the Rico Station and 8558 Milwaukee Electric; 1976 Dealer Poster – New Lionel Trains Are In; 1976 Dealer Flyer – Presidential Campaign Cars. *Bottom row:* Dealer Brochure – The Profit Bonus Special; Dealer Brochure – "Lionel Means More Cash in '76...And '77 Too!"

Modern Era Paper: 1970-1990 • 99

	G	VG	EXC	NEW

DEALER FLYER: Two pages, full color flyer. One side advertises the Lionel Southern Pacific HO GS-4, other side has the American Freedom train HO GS-4. T. Wagner Collection.

	1	2	3	5

DEALER FLYER: 8-1/2" x 11", "Spirit of '76", shows 7601, 7607, 7604, 7606.   1   2   3   5

DEALER FLYER: 8-1/2" x 11", "fundimensions / MEANS NEW / DIMENENSIONS / OF MODEL KITS".   1   2   3   5

TRACK TEMPLATE SHEET: "Templates for Lionel "O27" Layouts"; one page sheet with track diagrams printed in black on an adhesive sheet. Form 1061, rev. 11-55. This is unchanged from the postwar era. T. Wagner Collection.   1   2   3   5

DEALER POSTER: Poster measures 12" x 16"; heavy paper printed in four colors on one side, "LIONEL ACCESSORIES / TO EXPAND YOUR LAYOUT" at top and bottom, pictures of accessories inside light brown border; six full-color photos of action accessories inside border; black typeface.   7   9   12   15

DEALER POSTER: 8-3/8" x 16-1/2", white border, dark gray-brown background, large gold lettering "NEW / LIONEL / TRAINS / ARE IN", sepia-style photo of Reading 2100T-1 4-8-4 Northern-type steam locomotive on lower half of poster.
(A) As described above.   7   10   15   20
(B) Brown on white paper only.   7   10   15   20

DEALER FLYER: 8-1/2" x 11", one page, printed on one side. White background; red, white, and blue bunting at left and right upper corners, red and blue old-fashioned "PRESIDENTIAL / CAMPAIGN CARS" lettering at top, three special observation cars, red "LIONEL" at lower right corner.   —   1   2   3

DEALER FLYER: 8-1/2" x 11", one page, printed on one side. White background; gold "GRAIN / ELEVATOR" and black "O GAUGE KIT" at upper right, pictures of 2796 grain elevator, red "LIONEL" at lower left.   2   3   4   5

DEALER FLYER: 8-1/2" x 11", one page, printed on one side. Black and white print, "IT'S / LIONEL / TRAIN / TIME!". Details 1076 Lionel electric clock for dealers.   2   3   4   5

DEALER COUNTER POSTER: Yellow 12" x 13" poster board which folds into a counter stand-up display. "Pop-up" head of Johnny Cash and black typescript: "Johnny Cash Says / If Your Boy Is Under 10 / Buy Him The Big Lionel... / The Big Train For Small Hands". R. LaVoie and A. Rubin Collections.   5   10   15   20

ADVERTISING KIT: 8-1/2" x 11", thirteen pages, printed on one side only, cut-out advertisement pages for preparing ad copy. Included black on white glossy folder "LIONEL MEANS MORE CASH IN 1976". Identified as Form AK-76-100.   NRS

PROMOTIONAL LETTER: 8-1/2" x 11", single page, black on white paper, letter from Bill Johnson, "Chief Engineer", inviting

Top row: 1976 Dealer Flyer – black cover with boxed GG1 illustration; 1977 Iron-on Transfer Sheet which came as premium with Cocoa-Puff cereal; Dealer Brochure – "... Powerful, New, Limited Edition, Dual Motor Engines ..."
Bottom Row: 1977 Dealer Brochure – New Engines And Porthole Cabooses; 1977 Dealer Brochure – Lionel Big-Train Accessory Center; Trains n' Truckin Engineer's Manual.

	G	VG	EXC	NEW

recipient "to join the Lionel Railroader Club. It's brand new ... established October 1, 1976 with Johnny Cash as its first member." **NRS**

INTERNAL USE FORM: 8-1/2" x 11", lined note paper, with Lionel Service logo and "Lionel Service Seminar" at top. B. Munn Collection. — — — 3

WARRANTY SCHEDULE: "Warranty Payment Schedule for Lionel Train Products". Form CS-8 (Rev. 7-76). 8-1/2" x 11", eight pages, black and white. B. Munn Collection. 2 4 6 8

DEALER POSTER: 6" x 36", inscribed "Lionel Big-Train Accessory Center" in red, black, and yellow. Printed on thick card stock and folded twice. A. Rubin Collection. **NRS**

DEALER POSTER: 9" x 21", black on yellow card stock, "Johnny Cash's TV Special Ridin' the Rails — Brought to you by Lionel". Part of dealer's promotional package. A. Rubin Collection. **NRS**

DEALER FLYER: 8-1/2" x 11", two pages, black on tan card stock paper, reprinting what critics said when they reviewed Johnny Cash's "Ridin' the Rails" TV special. A. Rubin Collection. **NRS**

DEALER FLYER: 8-1/2" x 11", four pages, with inside fold-out, cover in black with boxed illustration of GG-1, plus four other Lionel products. Inside pages feature Disney set. Printed in full color on high gloss paper, identified with Form L-11-76- 2.

(A) Cover printed in dark black. A. Rubin Collection. — — 2 5

(B) Cover printed in flat black. A. Rubin Collection. **NRS**

DEALER POSTER: 8-3/4" x 12", with 2-1/2" fold-over shelf lip, "Lionel Workin' on the Railroad Train Sets" advertising flyer, in full color on white glossy card stock. A. Rubin Collection. **NRS**

DEALER SIGN: "Lionel Service — Authorized Lionel Service Station" window sign, printed in red and black on silver peelable sticker paper. Measures 6" x 12" at largest points. A. Rubin Collection. **NRS**

PRICELIST: 8-1/2" x 15" dealer order form for "Cash Bonus" Accessory specials, including newspaper allowance instructions. Form dated 9-10-76. A. Rubin Collection. — — — 2

DEALER POSTER: 14" x 52", includes photograph of Johnny Cash with inscription "Johnny Cash says, If your boy is under 10, buy him the big Lionel ... the big train for small hands". Print is in black and red on white non-glossy paper. This appears to be unusual advertising for the 1970s, and the question is whether Lionel thought to issue similar advertising for the female market! A. Rubin Collection. **NRS**

DEALER POSTER: 18" x 24", printed one side in black and red on white glossy paper, featuring a railroad crossing signal and the caption "Lionel Train Center". A. Rubin Collection. **NRS**

Top row: 1976 Dealer Poster – "Lionel Accessories To Expand Your Layout"; 1977 Advertising Kit – "Lionel Means More Cash in '76". *Bottom row:* Dealer Brochure - "New Engines & Cabooses" with soda pop cars, 1977 Consumer Catalogue, 1977 Consumer HO Catalogue.

1977

	G	VG	EXC	NEW

CONSUMER CATALOGUE: 8-1/2" x 11", twenty-four pages, including covers. Front cover has white background; red "LIONEL" and black "O / O27" at top, black "1977" at bottom, sixteen square pictures of individual children and adults playing with various Lionel locomotives and rolling stock. This catalogue cover was the first to show a black child playing with Lionel trains.   1   2   3   4

CONSUMER HO CATALOGUE: 8-1/2" x 11", twelve pages including covers. Front cover: grayish-white background, overhead photo of two locomotives, red "LIONEL HO / 1977" typeface. New Great American Railroads sets, Western Pacific GS-4 Northern, hi-cube boxcars. Identified as Form L 1/77-1 on back cover.
    1   2   3   4

DEALER BROCHURE: Four pages. Front page has lettering "LIONEL BIG TRAIN / ACCESSORY CENTERS". Includes 7803 Trains 'N Truckin' boxcar as special dealer bonus car.
    2   3   4   5

DEALER FLYER: 8-1/2" x 11", "NEW ENGINES & CABOOSES / NEW BOX CARS & HI CUBES...".   2   3   4   6

CEREAL BOX LABEL: 2" x 6", offer to join (in 1977) the Lionel Railroader Club. Printed in full color with locomotive. **NRS**

DEALER FLYER: 8-1/2" x 11", one page, printed on two sides. One side describes three new GP-series locomotives and matching N5C cabooses. Other side describes additions to Soda Pop series and Disney series, black "BIG TRAINS FOR SMALL HANDS" and red "LIONEL" at lower left.   1   2   3   4

DEALER FLYER: 8-1/2" x 11", one page, printed on one side. "LIONEL 1977 SERVICE STATION SPECIAL SET..." at top; drawings of Baltimore and Ohio Budd commuter rail diesel cars.
    1   2   3   4

DEALER POSTER: 18" x 24", printed one side in full color on white glossy paper, featuring a man and boy playing with a Trains 'n' Truckin' set, with the caption "Johnny Cash Introduces Trains 'n Truckin' — The Big Trains and Trucks for Small Hands". One of the best designed postwar Lionel advertising posters. A. Rubin Collection. **NRS**

INSTRUCTION MANUAL: 8-1/2" x 11", "LIONEL Trains n' Truckin' ENGINEERS'S MANUAL", black ink on uncoated paper.
    1   2   3   4

IRON-ON TRANSFER SHEET: Small sheet, 4-1/4" x 7", with stylized drawing in red, black, blue, gold, and white with legend "KEEP ON TRACKIN" and "LIONEL" in red. Made by Mach III, Inc. These four iron-ons were available as premiums in Cocoa-Puffs cereal from General Mills. T. Wagner comment. Date confirmation requested.
(A) Drawing features locomotive. R. LaVoie Collection.
    —   —   —   5

Top row: 1978 Consumer Catalogue; 1977 Dealer Flyer – 1977 Service Station Special Set; Lionel Workin' On The Railroad Engineer's Manual. *Bottom row:* 1978 Dealer Flyer – "New Power For Your Lionel Line - New SD18"; 1978 Dealer Flyer – Minneapolis & St. Louis Service Station Set, Dealer Brochure – Lionel Add-cessories Center, Expand Your Profits...

	G	VG	EXC	NEW
(B) Drawing features caboose.	—	—	—	5
(C) Drawing features "Sandy Andy".	—	—	—	7

(D) Drawing features locomotive with a human face wearing an engineer's hat in place of a boiler front. T. Wagner Collection.
— — — 7

IRON-ON TRANSFER SHEET: 6" x 9", single sheet, featuring stylized locomotive drawing in multicolors with legend "KEEP ON TRACKIN". **NRS**

WARRANTY SCHEDULE: "Warranty Payment Schedule for Lionel Train Products For 1977-78". Form CS-8 (Rev. 7-77). 8-1/2" x 11", eight pages black and white. B. Munn Collection.
2 4 6 8

ADVERTISING KIT: Eleven single 8-1/2" x 11" glossy sheets, one-sided with "AK77" page numbers, providing ad copy for dealer advertising. **NRS**

RACING MANUAL 8-1/2" x 11", 16-page manual, Form 73-3715-250 also features assembly instructions. Black on white dull paper.
1 2 3 4

DEALER BROCHURE: 8-1/2" x 11", single page, full color on glossy paper featuring the Burlington 181 set (5-2682).
2 3 4 5

CARDBOARD HEADERCARD: "LIONEL BIG-TRAIN / ACCESSORY / CENTER" printed in black and orange on white posterboard. Came with 1977 Trains-n-Truckin' box car accessory center. T. Wagner Collection. **NRS**

DEALER BROCHURE: 8-1/2" x 11", two pages, "Cash-In on LIONEL Big Train / Complete Display / Layout". Labeled 2-77, printed in blue and red on white paper.
2 3 4 5

CATALOGUE DISPLAY: Cardboard container for displaying catalogues, with an easel for countertop use. "For O27, Big-Train / Railroaders" printed in black on bright orange background, 8-5/6" x 6-1/2" front only. Packed with full cases of 1977 consumer catalogues. B. Munn Collection. **NRS**

CONSUMER CATALOGUE: "Power Passers — Total Control Racing System", 12-page catalogue in full color, 8-1/2" x 11", features two racing cars on cover.
2 3 4 6

DEALER BROCHURE: Four-page brochure in full color, 8-1/2" x 11", "LIONEL / announces / POWERFUL, NEW, / LIMITED EDITION, / DUAL MOTOR ENGINES / and / ANTIQUE ROLLING STOCK / FOR THE GENERAL". Illustrates GG-1, F-3's and General cars on cover.
2 3 4 6

SET STORY BOARD: Original art drawing of proposed train sets Lionel was considering for issuance. These were drawn for concept only for discussion among Lionel's Marketing Dept., but these boards give a clear idea of some of those sets that didn't make it to production. Date confirmation on these boards is requested.
(A) "James Bond's 007" set, featured Alco and 44 postwar mobile missile launcher with a set of reissued and presumably redesigned space cars. Measures 15" x 20", in full color. **NRS**
(B) "Apollo Limited" set, featured U36B diesel with reissue of postwar space rolling stock. Measures 15" x 20", in full color. **NRS**
(C) "Paul Bunyan Logger" set, low priced engine with log cars and plastic crane. Measures 15" x 20", in full color. **NRS**
(D) "The Golden Spike" set, "General" type steam locomotives mounted on display board with inscription "Driving the Golden Spike", with attached plastic gold spike. Measures 20" x 15", in full color. **NRS**

1978

TOY FAIR CATALOGUE: 8-1/2" x 11", 24 pages, including covers. Front cover has light maroon background; silver "LIONEL" at center,

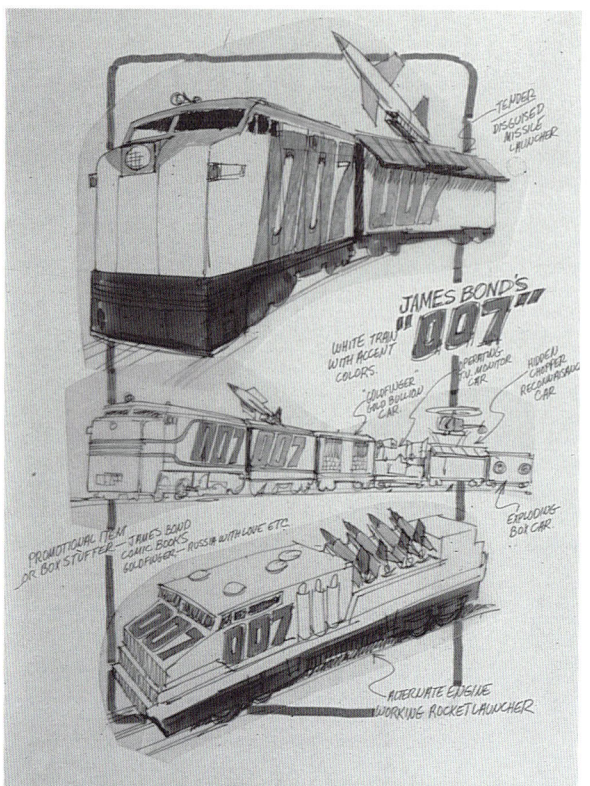

The original art drawing to the planned "James Bond's 007" set. This set, as well as several other exciting "concept" sets, never made it to production.

white "Big Scale Trains and Accessories" at center, white "for 1978" at lower right. No price on cover.
2 4 6 8

CONSUMER CATALOGUE: 8-1/2" x 11", 24 pages, including covers. Front cover has maroon background; silver "LIONEL" at center, white "Big Scale Trains and Accessories" at center, white "for 1978" at lower right. Price of $1.00 on cover.
1 2 3 4

DEALER BROCHURE: "LIONEL / ADD-CESSORIES CENTER", Four pages; bright orange front cover with black outline locomotive front end and orange and black typescript on white background. Inside pages give details of dealer accessory packages and photo of 9672 Mickey Mouse 50th Anniversary hi-cube boxcar. Rear cover shows accessory centers setup. Each center had 15" x 26" header card duplicating the brochure cover. R. LaVoie and A. Rubin Collections.
2 4 6 8

CARDBOARD HEADERCARD: "LIONEL / ADD-CESSORIES CENTER", 15" X 26", printed in black, orange, and yellow on white poster-board. Came with 1978 Add-cessories center. T. Wagner Collection. **NRS**

ADVERTISING PROOF FLYER: One page flyer printed in black on white glossy paper. Features the 1978 Add-cessories center. Used for dealer advertising. T. Wagner Collection. **NRS**

DEALER FLYER: 11" x 8-1/2" (oblong), single page, printed on one side. "LIONEL 1978 SERVICE STATION SPECIAL, SET #6-1868", red stripe along top, pictures and descriptions of Minneapolis & St. Louis Service Station.
— 1 2 3

DEALER FLYER: 8-1/2" x 11", single page, printed on both sides. One side has lettering, "NEW POWER FOR YOUR LIONEL LINE" and pictures of 8872 Santa Fe SD-18, 9274 Santa Fe bay window caboose, and operating cars 9310, 9311, and 9312. The other side

Modern Era Paper: 1970-1990 • 103

	G	VG	EXC	NEW

shows the 9669, 9670, and 9671 Disney hi-cube boxcars and the 9090 rolling stock assortment. G. Halverson Collection.
— 1 2 3

DEALER CATALOGUE: Spring 1979 Collector Center, late 1978. 8-1/2" x 11", 8 pages, including covers. Front cover has dark and light blue background; red "LIONEL" at upper left, white "COMMAND PERFORMANCE / SPRING 1979" lettering at upper left, pictures of new rolling stock and locomotives on rest of cover.
2 3 4 5

LIONEL WORKIN' ON THE RAILROAD ENGINEER'S MANUAL: 8-1/2" x 11", 20 pages, color covers, black and white contents. Identified as Form 70-1862-250 on front and back covers, and includes Lionel Railroader Club application. 2 4 6 8

ADVERTISING KIT: 8-1/2" x 11" glossy white folder, "1978 Retail Advertising Kit" for Power Passers. Kit includes racing manuals and ad mats in black and white. R. Otten Collection. **NRS**

ADVERTISING KIT: 8-1/2" x 11" glossy folder containing ad mats for the 1978 Train Line. Further information requested. **NRS**

DEALER CATALOGUE: Power Passers "Year 2 Brings Ideas..." 8-1/2" x 11", 12 unnumbered pages, full color, with Lionel logo in bottom right corner of front cover. 2 4 6 8

SERVICE STATION PRICE LIST: 13-1/4" x 11-3/4", single page, yellow paper, Form CS-10 (Rev. 3-78). — 1 2 3

"The Golden Spike" was one of Lionel's "concept" sets that never was produced. This original Set Story Board measures 20" x 15" and is a beautiful full-color rendition.

Top row: 1979 Consumer Catalogue; Advance Catalogue, late 1988; Dealer Catalogue – Command Performance, Spring 1979. *Bottom row:* Dealer Flyer – 1979 Lionel Super Center, 1979 Dealer Brochure – Collector's Accessory Center, 1980 Toy Fair Catalogue.

	G	VG	EXC	NEW

CONSUMER CATALOGUE: "Power Passers — ROAD RACING / SETS AND / ACde folder pages describe Lionel's current advertising campaign. A. Rubin Collection.
(A) As described above. **NRS**
(B) Four-page dealer folder only, no catalogue insert and no staple holes. **NRS**

1978 Continued

DEALER FLYER: 8-1/2" x 11", four pages, full color on white glossy paper, "LIONEL'S BEEN WORKIN' ON YOUR RAILROAD" explaining details of an after-Christmas sales promotion for consumers. A. Rubin Collection.   **2   3   6   8**

DEALER POSTER: Large 20" x 31", printed one side on glossy white paper, "Lionel" logo in red in top right corner and "Workin' on the Railroad" dominating lower half. Set by same name portrayed in artist drawing. A. Rubin Collection.   **NRS**

PROMOTIONAL WRITEUP: December 1979 issue of *Production Engineering* features an illustrated five-page feature on Lionel, "Bring Back Those Old-Time Lionel Trains". The issue cover also features a Lionel train set, and the article is written from a tooling perspective. Listed here for reference only. A. Rubin and B. Munn Collections.   **—   —   —   10**

1980

TOY FAIR CATALOGUE: 8-1/2" x 11", 28 pages. Front cover has deep maroon background; light blue "LIONEL / ELECTRIC TRAINS / 1980" at bottom. No price on cover.   **4   6   8   10**

TOY FAIR FOLDER: Lettered "take a closer look" with interior pockets containing Craftsmaster Hobby and Craft Line, Family Fun Line and Scale Models Line.   **NRS**

CONSUMER CATALOGUE: Twenty-eight pages including covers, 8-1/2" x 11". Front cover: deep maroon background; light blue "LIONEL / ELECTRIC TRAINS / 1980" at bottom; light blue "take a closer look..." at top, blue-edged pictures of rolling stock spell stylized "FUN" across page; $1.00 price on front cover. This was the first Lionel catalogue to be divided into Traditional and Collector sections.   **1   2   3   4**

DEALER BROCHURE: 8-1/2" x 11", four pages. Front page has maroon background; white "LIONEL" at upper right, large white "FALL 1980 / COLLECTORS / CENTER" at lower center, picture of three F-3 B units on rest of page.   **1   2   3   4**

DEALER CATALOGUE: Eight pages including covers, 8-1/2" x 11". Front cover has maroon background; light blue borders, white "Fundimensions / presents / a sneak preview of a great / 1981 / Lionel

Top row: 1980 Toy Fair Folder – Take A Closer Look; part of Dealer Kit – Fundimensions Advertising Materials; Toy Fair Catalogue. *Bottom row:* 1980 Dealer Price List; 1979 Dealer Brochure – Lionel Spring 1980 Collector Series; Dealer Brochure – Fall 1980 Collectors Center.

Line". Picture of Norfolk and Western J Class steam locomotive front end on page. **2 3 4 5**

DEALER FLYER: "LIONEL / MODEL RAILROADER / STARTER CENTER". One page printed on one side; white background, red and white typeface. Details accessory center including layout starter packs, track, and rolling stock assortments. Included in 1980 Dealer Kit; see next entry. **1 2 3 4**

DEALER KIT: Fundimensions Toys, Crafts & Hobbies, 1980: White two-pocket folder with the following contents: Toy Fair versions of 1980 Lionel Electric Trains, Craft Master Hobby And Craft Kits, Fundimensions Family Fun Line, and MPC Scale Models; folder containing "1980 / FUNDIMENSIONS / ADVERTISING MATERIALS", had eight one-sided sheets of prepared dealer ads; dealer flyer, "Model Railroader Starter Center", order blanks for all catalogues. R. LaVoie and A. Rubin Collections. **20 30 35 40**

RETAIL ADVERTISING KIT: "1980 / FUNDIMENSIONS / ADVERTISING / MATERIALS" on a one-pocket folder which is identical to the front cover of the consumer catalogue with the exception of the lettering. Contains eight one-sided glossy ad mats. T. Wagner Collection. **NRS**

DEALER PRICE LIST: "Premium Recommendations", five-page duplicated pricelist of all products, reproduced on Fundimensions color stationary. **NRS**

DEALER PRICE LIST: "1980 Toy Fair" dated 2-1-80, 15- 3/4" x 12-3/8", brown on white paper, two sides. **— — 1 2**

ORDER FORM: "Authorized Lionel Service Station Parts Order Form", Form F-103-11/80. **— — 1 2**

1981

TOY FAIR CATALOGUE: "FUNDIMENSIONS — GROW WITH US — 1981" on cover. 8-1/2" x 11", ninety-eight pages, product catalogue, pages 65-89 devoted to trains. **15 20 30 35**

CONSUMER CATALOGUE: Thirty-two pages including covers, 5-1/2" x 7" small booklet. Front cover: brown background; white "GROW WITH US" at top (ironic in view of catalogue's reduced size!), white-edged dark brown rectangle with woodcut of old-time dockside steam engine, white "LIONEL / ELECTRIC TRAINS" below rectangle and white "1981" in lower right corner. Rear cover: brown background; small red and blue "F" and "FUNDIMENSIONS" at lower left. This catalogue prompted howls of protest from collectors, especially coming on the heels of the attractive 1980 catalogue and 1981 advance brochure. Many copies are blurred and difficult to read.
(A) As described above. **— — 1 2**
(B) Same as (A), except for printer's error on inside of back cover (page 31). Black printed track layout is missing in this version. Very scarce. T. Wagner Collection. **NRS**

CONSUMER BROCHURE: "LIONEL / 1981 FALL COLLECTOR CENTER". Four pages. Front cover has red typeface and large photo of 8162 Ontario Northland SD-18 diesel. Rear cover describes collector center carton contents. **1 2 3 5**

Top row: 1981 Dealer Brochure – Model Railroader Starter Center; 1983 Sales Brochure – The Classic Hudson. *Bottom row:* 1981 Consumer Brochure – 1981 Fall Collector Center; 1980 Dealer Catalogue – Fundimensions Presents A Sneak Preview; Consumer Catalogue – Grow With Us in 5-1/2" x 7" format; Toy Fair Catalogue – Fundimensions Grow With Us.

Top row: 1982 Toy Fair Catalogue – Models, Crafts, Hobbies & Trains; Dealer Flyer – Get Aboard For the Nibco Express; Dealer Flyer with Santa Claus and Nibco Faucets train set. *Bottom row:* 1982 Consumer Catalogue – Collector Series; Consumer Catalogue – Traditional Series; Dealer Brochure – 1982 Fall Collector Center.

	G	VG	EXC	NEW
CONSUMER BROCHURE: Six pages including fold-out. Front page has dark and medium maroon background; white "LIONEL SPRING '82 / COLLECTOR CENTER", pictures of fronts of three new locomotives at lower center.	1	2	3	5
DEALER FLYER: One sheet printed on both sides. Lettered "LIONEL TRAINING CENTER"; shows details of packages including common accessories, track, and manuals.	3	4	5	6
DEALER BROCHURE: 8-1/2" x 11", "MODEL RAILROADER STARTER CENTER".	2	3	4	5
PRESS KIT: Press releases and 8" x 10" glossy photos of 1981 product line contained in glossy folder. Primarily non-train oriented, as it covers the entire Fundimensions line.				NRS
AD MAT: "Be the first kid on your block to own a Lionel. Again."; one page full color, 10-1/2" x 13-1/2", on white glossy paper.				NRS
ORDER FORM: Two large 17" x 12-3/8" pages, inscribed "1981 Toy Fair", brown print on four different colored papers, identified by Rev. 2-1-81. A. Rubin Collection.	1	2	3	4
PROMOTIONAL PHOTOGRAPHS: 7" x 5" horizontal format, issued by Lionel's Advertising Department to promote the L.A.S.E.R. train set. Two different in full color. A. Rubin Collection.				NRS

1982

	G	VG	EXC	NEW
TOY FAIR CATALOGUE: "MODELS, CRAFTS, HOBBIES & TRAINS, 1982", 9-1/4" x 11" total spiral-bound Fundimensions product catalogue. One hundred thirty-four pages, with Lionel Traditional and Collector Series catalogues included; heavy card-stock covers and dividers.	12	20	25	30
CONSUMER CATALOGUE, TRADITIONAL SERIES: This is the first year Fundimensions issued two separate catalogues for Traditional and Collector series. Twenty pages including covers, 8-1/2" x 11". Front cover has dark and light maroon background; row of Traditional locomotives and rolling stock across page, red "LIONEL" at bottom, white line across page, "TRADITIONAL SERIES, 1982" below line at bottom.	1	2	3	4
CONSUMER CATALOGUE, COLLECTOR SERIES: Twelve pages including covers, 8-1/2" x 11". Front cover is same format as Traditional Series catalogue, but locomotives from Collector series items.	—	1	2	3
DEALER FLYER: 8-1/2" x 11", single page printed on one side. Dark and medium maroon background; photo of Santa Claus at upper left, white lettering describing special Nibco Faucets train set offer at upper right, picture of Nibco NW-2 switcher locomotive and cars, white lettering. R. LaVoie Collection.	2	3	4	5

	G	VG	EXC	NEW

DEALER FLYER: 8-1/2" x 11", single page printed on one side. Yellow background; broad white over and underscored stripe at top containing black "GET ABOARD / FOR THE NIBCO EXPRESS" and green "BOX CAR" lettering, black-printed typescript, picture of 7520 Nibco boxcar, green coupon with white "LIONEL" at lower right. R. LaVoie Collection. **2 3 4 5**

DEALER BROCHURE: 8-1/2" x 11", four pages. Front page has dark maroon and black background; red "LIONEL" at bottom center, white stripe, white "1982 FALL COLLECTOR CENTER" below stripe at bottom, picture of 8215 Nickel Plate Road 2-8-4 steam locomotive at top. **— 1 2 3**

AD MAT: One page glossy ad mat in black and white comparing the size of a Lionel 6P-20 to a Fairbanks Morse Trainmaster to the new SD-40. T. Wagner Collection. **NRS**

DEALER BROCHURE: Eight pages including covers, 8-1/2" x 11". Front cover has dark and light maroon background; red "LIONEL" at top center, light blue stripe across top, white "1983 COLLECTOR PREVIEW" below stripe, picture of front of 8307 Southern Pacific GS-4 Daylight steam engine on rest of cover. **— 1 2 3**

PRESS KIT: 9" x 12", black booklet. Contains 8" x 10" black and white photos of Lionel, MPC, and Craftmaster items and explanations for them. A great amount of dealer information in this booklet. D. Johns comment. **NRS**

SHAREHOLDER LETTER: Three-page letter to Lionel Corporation stockholders indicating the filing of Chapter 11 bankruptcy, dated May 12, 1982. **NRS**

PRICE LIST: "1982 Toy Fair". Dated 2/82, four-part, two-page form, 16" x 10". **— 1 2 3**

1983

CONSUMER CATALOGUE, TRADITIONAL SERIES: Twenty pages including covers, 8-1/2" x 11". Front cover has silver background; black-edged red "LIONEL" at top, black "TRADITIONAL SERIES, 1983" at top, 25 black-engraved pictures of traditional rolling stock and locomotives in small squares, red and blue "F" and "FUNDIMENSIONS" in black small square at lower right, "THE ONE-STOP HOBBY SHOP" in small black print at lower right. **1 2 3 4**

CONSUMER CATALOGUE, COLLECTOR SERIES: Sixteen pages including covers, 8-1/2" x 11". Front cover is same format as Traditional catalogue, except black engravings are of collector items. **1 2 3 4**

Lionel has frequently published brochures in the year before the cover date. *Top row:* 1981 Consumer Brochure – Spring 1982 Collector Center; 1983 Consumer Folder with grandfather, father, son, and uncle; 1982 Dealer Brochure – 1983 Collector Preview. *Bottom row:* 1983 Consumer Catalogue – Collector Series; 1983 Consumer Catalogue – Traditional Series; 1983 Consumer Folder – Traditional Series Train Sets.

	G	VG	EXC	NEW

CONSUMER FOLDER: One page, both sides printed. Folds out to an 8-1/2" x 11" sheet, includes engines, layouts, rolling stock, accessories, and track plans; photo of grandfather, father, son, and uncle. This item usually found in set boxes. Form 70-1355-252.
— — 1 2

DEALER BROCHURE: 8-1/2" x 11", four pages. Front page is black, dark brown, and light brown background; red "LIONEL" and white "1983 Fall Collector Center" across top, white stripe, large photograph of front of 8380 Lionel Lines SD-28 diesel locomotive.
— 1 2 3

DEALER FOLDER: 8-1/2" x 11", eight pages, including two fold-outs. Front page has dark and medium maroon background; red and white "LIONEL / HIGHBALLS / INTO / 1984!" at top center, picture of 8406 Scale Hudson steam locomotive in 3/4 view.
— — 1 2

CONSUMER FLYER: "LIONEL / TRADITIONAL SERIES / TRAIN SETS". One page printed on one side, red and black typeface. Details of five catalogued Traditional series sets for 1983.
— — 1 2

BUMPER STICKER: 2-7/8" x 14-3/8", "LIONEL — MORE THAN A TOY — A TRADITION SINCE 1900". Orange and black on white adhesive background. Locomotive in white illustrated at right. Date confirmation requested.

(A) Manila paper backing. — — 6 8
(B) Blue paper backing. — — 6 8

NOTICE OF COURT HEARING: Court notice relating to Lionel's bankruptcy filing.
(A) Dated June 20, 1983, four pages, Approval of Disclosure Statement. **NRS**
(B) Dated June 15, 1983, four pages, Sale of Dale Electronics Common Stock. **NRS**

PROMO BROCHURE: Full-color flyer mailed by American Express, 3-1/2" x 5-1/2", folds out to two larger pages, advertising for mail order "The Fast Freight Flyer" from Lionel. Includes free membership in Lionel Railroader Club. **NRS**

AD MAT: Full-color, one-page printed on white glossy paper, 5-3/8" x 16-3/8", "There's no substitute for good, solid training". Features 8213 locomotive and set. **NRS**

SHELF LINER: 3-1/2" x 24-1/4" card stock with adhesive backing, black on orange with "LIONEL / MORE THAN A TOY / A TRADITION / SINCE 1900". — — 12 15

PRICE RAIL TAG: 4" x 3" with "tail" to fit into price rail, with Lionel logo, diesel, and "MORE THAN A TOY..." phrase. **NRS**

DEALER PROMOTIONAL PACK: From 1983 Toy Fair, 9" x 11" folder printed in silver with heading "The One Stop Hobby Shop".

Top row: 1983 Dealer Brochure – 1983 Fall Collector Center; 1984 Press Kit; 1984 Press Kit news release. *Bottom row:* 1983 Dealer Folder – Lionel Highballs into 1984; 1984 Consumer Catalogue – Collector Series; 1984 Consumer Catalogue – Traditional Series.

Modern Era Paper: 1970-1990 • 109

	G	VG	EXC	NEW

Folder contains five train and non-train catalogues issued for 1983. A. Rubin Collection. — — 25 35

SALES BROCHURE: 10-1/2" x 8-1/4", four-section fold-out. Lettered "THE CLASSIC HUDSON". Contains American Express offer, Joshua Lionel Cowen engine, and display case. This is not Fundimensions-issued paper, but deserves mention here because of its products. **NRS**

1984

CONSUMER CATALOGUE, TRADITIONAL SERIES: Twenty pages including covers, 8-1/2" x 11". Front cover has dark and light maroon background, white "LIONEL TRADITIONAL SERIES 1984" across top, picture of Traditional locomotive stopping at station.
                                                                   1 2 3 4

CONSUMER CATALOGUE, COLLECTOR SERIES: Sixteen pages including covers, 8-1/2" x 11". Front cover has light maroon background; "LIONEL COLLECTOR SERIES 1984" across top, picture of three Collector locomotives crossing trestle bridges atop one another. **1 2 3 4**

PRESS KIT: 9" x 12" folder containing news releases, fact sheets, descriptions, and numerous 8" x 10" photos of Lionel, Craft Master, and MPC products. Front cover of folder is white with red, white, and blue Fundimensions lettering and logo. — — — 30

1985

CONSUMER CATALOGUE, TRADITIONAL SERIES: Twenty pages including covers, 8-1/2" x 11". Front cover has medium brown background; large yellow "GOOD / AS / GOLD! / 1985" at top and center, large gold "LIONEL" at center, white "TRADITIONAL SERIES / ELECTRIC TRAINS" at bottom. **1 2 3 4**

CONSUMER CATALOGUE, COLLECTOR SERIES: Twelve pages including covers, 8-1/2" x 11". Front cover has dark brown background; same "GOOD / AS / GOLD! / 1985" and "LIONEL" as Traditional catalogue, yellow "85TH ANNIVERSARY COLLECTOR SERIES" across lower center, rectangular picture of 85th Anniversary boxcar with white border. **1 2 3 4**

PRESS KIT: 9" x 12" folder titled "Fundimensions" containing news releases, fact sheets, descriptions, and numerous 8" x 10" glossy photos of Lionel products. No catalogues included.
                                                         — — — 30

NOTICE OF COURT HEARING: Court notice relating to Lionel's bankruptcy filing.
(A) Dated September 19, 1985, seven pages. **NRS**
(B) Dated May 23, 1985, three pages, Notice of Proposed Settlement. **NRS**

Top Row: 1985 Consumer Catalogue – Collector Series; 1986 Consumer Brochure – Direct from Lionel.
Bottom row: 1985 Consumer Catalogue – Traditional Series; 1986 Consumer Catalogue – Collector Series; 1986 Consumer Catalogue – Traditional Series.

	G	VG	EXC	NEW

DISCLOSURE STATEMENT: Complete public documentation of the bankruptcy filing, dated May 8, 1985. Approximately 400 pages, 8-1/2" x 11", black on white paper, primarily financially-oriented.
NRS

1986

CONSUMER CATALOGUE, TRADITIONAL SERIES: Sixteen pages including covers, 8-1/2" x 11". This and its accompanying Collector series catalogue are the only catalogues issued under Kenner-Parker management. Front cover has sky blue background, 726-type Berkshire steam locomotive in light and dark blue; red, white, and blue new Lionel logo and typeface; "TRADITIONAL / SERIES ELECTRIC TRAINS" in black. An 8516 NYC switcher locomotive is paired erroneously with an 8616 tender on page 13, but is consistent on all editions. — 1 2 3

CONSUMER CATALOGUE, COLLECTOR SERIES: Except for product contents, essentially similar to Traditional series, except orange color replaces blue on front cover; 16 pages including covers, 8-1/2" x 11". — 1 2 3

CONSUMER BROCHURE: "INTRODUCING A CLASSIC / DIRECT FROM LIONEL". 8-1/2" x 11", four pages. Front cover portrays Modern Era 773-type Hudson, lettered for Boston and Albany. Inside pages depict engine, seven Standard O series cars and details concerning direct mail order. Back page has order form; expiration date September 1, 1986. This brochure was mailed directly to members of major train collecting organizations, and is generally found folded. Lionel's bypassing of its normal distribution network was an unusual step which created considerable controversy between the firm and its dealers.   1 2 3 4

DEALER FLYER: One page printed on one side only, 8-1/2" x 11". Illustrates 1986 Santa Fe Service Station Set against light blue background with red, white, and blue Lionel logo and typeface.
— — 1 2

CONSUMER BROCHURE: "Lionel / Stocking Stuffers"; 8-1/2" x 11", four pages. Front cover has white script typeface, green background, photo and mirror image of 1986 Christmas boxcar. Inside pages detail six special end-of-year cars, including Chessie Steam Special and Chicago and Alton diner cars.
— 1 2 3

DEALER FLYER: 1 page glossy color sheet showing all 1986 sets, including service station set. T. Wagner Collection.
— — 1 2

6-2985 THE LIONEL TRAIN BOOK: Operating, construction, and maintenance manual and guide; 131 pages excluding covers, eight-page color photo insert, numerous black and white photos: Robert Schleicher, author, John W. Brady, editor; Fritz von Tagen, photographer. Twenty chapters in five sections: "LIONEL

Top row: 1986 Dealer Flyer – 1986 Santa Fe Service Station Set; Consumer Brochure – Lionel Stocking Stuffers; Press Kit. *Bottom row:* 1986 News From Lionel from Press Kit; 1986 Dealer Brochure – 1987 Spring Preview; 1987 Consumer Catalogue.

Top row: 1987 Dealer Flyer – The Southern Freight Runner; 1987 Consumer Brochure – Side Tracks; 1987 Consumer Brochure – Happy Lionel Holidays! *Bottom row:* 1987 McDonald's Contest Literature; inside pages from Lionel 1987 Large Scale Consumer Folder.

	G	VG	EXC	NEW

"TRAINS", "ACTION", "THE BASICS", "BUILDING A LAYOUT", and "MAINTENANCE." Front cover is black with Lionel logo and typescript, white lettering and white-edged rectangular color layout photo. Rear cover shows photo of new 12701 operating diesel fueling station.

	5	7	10	12

DEALER BROCHURE: 1987 Spring Preview, eight pages including covers, 8-1/2" x 11". Front cover: dark, light blue, and purple background, red and blue Lionel logo and lettering edged in white, white "1987 SPRING PREVIEW!", large end-on photo of Conrail SD-40 in background and silhouette of Wabash steamer at bottom.

	—	1	2	3

PRESS KIT: 9" x 12" glossy folder titled "Lionel" in then-new logo, containing news releases, fact sheets, descriptions and numerous 8" x 10" glossy photos of Lionel products. No catalogues included.

	—	—	—	25

PROMO FLYER: 8-1/2" x 11", "The Lionel Story", one page, brown on parchment-like paper.   — — — 2

SERVICE STATION IDENTIFICATION: Circular 8" diameter peelable sign, "Authorized Lionel Service Station" in red, blue, and black on a white adhesive background.   **NRS**

SHELF LINER: 3" x 22", Lionel logo repeated twice with "BIG, RUGGED TRAINS, A TRADITION Since 1900". Red and blue on black background.   **NRS**

PROMOTIONAL CONTEST: Flyer "Amvets — All Aboard" mass mailing campaign to the general public designed to raise funds for the national Amvets organization. One of the contest prizes was a Lionel Cannonball Express set, which was illustrated in color in the promotional flyer.   **NRS**

1987

CONSUMER CATALOGUE: Combined Traditional and Collector series; 40 pages including covers, 8-1/2" x 11". Black front cover, new "LIONEL" logo and typeface, pictures of new 18401 handcars, 18300 bronze Pennsylvania GG-1, and 18001 Rock Island Northern 4-8-4 steam engine. Rear cover is black with new Lionel logo and typeface, white type "Photography by Fritz von Tagen". This catalogue, the first issued under the new Lionel Trains, Inc. management, shows a large number and variety of new items, including new colors for many older accessories. The Traditional series has been greatly expanded. A new five-digit numbering system has been introduced. Catalogue opens with an "Open Letter" from Richard P. Kughn, new owner and Chairman of Lionel Trains, Inc.   — 1 2 3

CONSUMER BROCHURE: "Happy / LIONEL / Holidays"; four pages, 8-1/2" x 11". Continues special year-end package strategy begun in previous year. Front cover has black background, Christmas ornaments on top, white typescript, shadowed picture of new 18002 773-type Hudson, the third of the modern era series, in gunmetal gray with spoked drivers.   — — 1 2

DEALER FLYER: "THE SOUTHERN / FREIGHT RUNNER". One page printed one side only, 11" x 8-1/2" (oblong). Green border,

| | G | VG | EXC | NEW |

white background, illustrates set 11704, the 1987 Service Station set, with 18802 Southern twin-motored GP-9 and five freight cars.

— — 1 2

CONSUMER BROCHURE: "SIDE TRACKS / FROM / LIONEL"; four pages, 8-1/2" x 11", and separate plain-paper order sheet. Front cover has dark gray "SIDE TRACKS" on black background along left side of page; rest of cover shows new line of Lionel souvenir and keepsake items, as do inside pages and back cover. Merchandise ranges from flashlights to coasters to travel alarm clocks. Early in 1987, Lionel, Inc. sent letters to distribution network requesting a halt to unauthorized use of the Lionel trademark and logos.

— 1 2 3

RIGHTS AGREEMENT: Agreement dated February 12, 1987 between The First Jersey National Bank and Lionel Corporation, outlining in detail the rights to purchase common stock in the event of a company takeover. This 88-page document was issued, upon request only, to Lionel stockholders of record on February 12, 1987, as additional data to support a previously-issued "Summary of Rights to Purchase Common Stock". The agreement as issued by Lionel was photocopied. **NRS**

PRESS KIT: Two-pocket glossy white folder with red, white, and blue Lionel logo and typescript on front cover. Contents include five press releases on light brown paper, total 10 pages, with red, white, and blue "NEWS / FROM LIONEL / FOR IMMEDIATE RELEASE / FOR FURTHER INFORMATION, CONTACT:" also has one sheet, "Interesting Facts About Lionel", one sheet, "Lionel Trains, Inc. Fact Sheet", and nine 8" x 10" black and white photos of 1987 product line with tape-attached sheets detailing photo captions.

10 15 20 25

LARGE SCALE CONSUMER FOLDER: Six pages in horizontal fold-out format, 11" x 8-1/2" (oblong). Front cover has black background, light gray rectangle with perspective photo of Large Scale locomotive coming down two-rail track. Black "A / NEW TRAIN'S / COMING / DOWN THE TRACK, red and blue Lionel lettering and logo edged in white, white "Because no childhood should be / without a train". Contents show Gold Rush Special set and separate sale Large Scale items.

— — 1 2

CONSUMER BROCHURE: "SPRING 1988"; 16 pages including covers, 8-1/2" x 11". Front cover has deep to light maroon background, photos of Rock Island Northern, mail pickup set, and Southern Fairbanks-Morse, red, black, and blue Lionel lettering and logo edged in white. Contents feature Great Northern Fallen Flags set, Chessie unit train, and (most noteworthy) two American Flyer Hudson steamers which will not be produced due to excessive production costs.

— — — 2

DEALER FLYER: "LIONEL / ELECTRIC TRAIN SETS ... COMPLETE AND READY TO RUN". One page, 8-1/2" x 11", full color, features six sets.

— — 1 2

Top row: 1987 Consumer Catalogue, Spring 1988; 1988 Press Kit; 1988 Consumer Catalogue. *Bottom row:* 1988 Consumer folder – The Hiawatha; 1988 Consumer Folder – Double Crossing; 1988 Large Scale Consumer Catalogue.

From left to right: 1981 Fundimensions mailing envelope, 1988 Lionel mailing envelope and 1988 Lionel Railroader Club envelope.

                             G   VG EXC NEW

CONTEST BROCHURE: "Greetings 1987", 5-3/8" x 8-3/8", mailed by Chrysler Motors to customers, announcing the MOPAR/LIONEL "On Track Sweepstakes" to win the Mopar Express set. Not issued by Lionel but included here for reference only.   **NRS**

PROMOTIONAL LITERATURE: Winter 1987 issue of *Spectator*, publication of Chrysler-Plymouth. Includes feature on Lionel, "Back on Track", and is included here for reference.   **NRS**

CONTEST DISPLAY: Cardboard display publicizing Chrysler Motors Mopar Express Sweepstakes. Display board measures 10" x 21" with part of train set illustrated, "On Track Sweepstakes" at top, with space to write in the winning number. Also came with square foot cardboard box to deposit contest coupons. We list here rather in "Displays" chapter since it was totally cardboard and not issued by Lionel.   **NRS**

6-5800 BUMPER STICKER: 14" x 3" in black, red, and blue with caption "Lionel — MADE IN AMERICA".   1   2   3   4

6-5810 POSTER: 21" x 27" featuring a sleeping boy and legend "MORE THAN A TOY — A TRADITION". For consumer sale.
                                                   5   7   10   12

6-5811 POSTER: 34" x 20", features Nickel Plate Special and titled "BIG RUGGED TRAINS, SINCE 1900". For consumer sale.
                                                   5   7   10   12

6-5812 POSTER: 34" x 20", features the Rail Blazer set and titled "NO CHILDHOOD SHOULD BE WITHOUT A TRAIN". For consumer sale.   5   7   10   12

POCKET CALENDAR: 3-1/2" x 6" gold-edged calendar inserted into an imitation leather jacket inscribed "1987 — Lionel Trains, Inc." with address. Provided to VIP guests attending the 1987 Toy Fair.   **NRS**

McDONALD'S CONTEST LITERATURE: During a short period in early 1987, the McDonald Corporation ran a "Monopoly" contest at most of the franchised and company fast food outlets nationwide. Customers who obtained stickers of all four Monopoly railroads won a Lionel Nickel Plate Special set, which was illustrated in color in the contest brochure. Reference to Lionel was also made on thousands of paper placemats provided to customers. The giveaway stickers of the B & O, Reading, and Pennsylvania were readily obtainable; however, the Shortline sticker designated a winner; contest rules indicated 1,100 winners were projected. **NRS**

                             G   VG EXC NEW

1988

CONSUMER CATALOGUE: Forty pages including covers, 8-1/2" x 11". Front cover has dark to light blue background, square photos of overhead signal bridge, Santa Fe Alco RS-3 switcher and Lackawanna 4-8-4 Northern steamer; red, black, and blue Lionel lettering and logo edged in white, white lettering. Last two pages detail RailScope locomotives and Double Crossing board game.
(A) As described above.   —   —   1   2
(B) Printer's error. Page sequence is 4, 9, 10, 11, 12, 9, 10, 11, etc., duplicate page inserted.   —   —   —   6

LARGE SCALE CONSUMER CATALOGUE: Sixteen pages including covers, 8-1/2" x 11". Front cover in light gray background, circular Lionel Large Scale gold, red, and black logo, white lettering, three new Large Scale locomotives.   —   —   1   2

CONSUMER FOLDER: RailScope. 8" x 10" size, four pages. Front cover has photo of interior of EMD diesel cab and windshield; diesel is approaching signal and tunnel. Inside pages show phantom view of RailScope GP-9, television, and text.   —   —   1   2

CONSUMER FOLDER: Double crossing train board game. 8-1/2" x 11", four pages. Front cover in medium blue background, orange border, white lettering, circular Double Crossing gold, white, and red-brown logo with black and brown "Snidely Whiplash" mustachioed figure.   —   —   1   2

CONSUMER FOLDER: The Hiawatha passenger set; 8-1/2" x 11", four pages. Front cover has white background, green rectangle, wing-and-"L" logo at top, front-end view of Hiawatha steam locomotive. Inside pages give photos and details of set.
                                           —   —   1   2

CONSUMER FOLDER: Lionel Classics, four-page, full-color, 8-1/2" x 11". Front cover: mirror-image photo of 390E Standard Gauge locomotive against light and dark gray background, red, white, silver, black, and blue Lionel Classics wing logo, white lettering.
                                           —   —   1   2

DEALER FLYER: The Dry Gulch Special Service Station set. 8-1/2" x 11", single sheet, printed on one side. White and light gray background, red, white, and blue Lionel lettering and logo, black descriptive lettering, photos of General-style locomotive and three matching passenger cars.   —   —   1   2

DEALER FLYER: Christmas year-end special; single sheet printed on one side. Photos of Pennsylvania and Milwaukee Road diner cars and 1988 Christmas boxcar.   —   —   1   2

CONSUMER FLYER: Lionel Classics Spring 1989 package; legal size, four pages. Photos detail, among other items, the revival of the 440 Standard Gauge signal bridge. — — 1 2

PRESS KIT: Folder containing fact sheets, press releases, and descriptions of new Lionel equipment for 1988, along with numerous 8" x 10" photos. Front cover of folder features Lionel lettering and logo, Lionel Classics logo, Double Crossing, Rail Scope, and Large Scale emblems. 10 15 22 27

AD MAT SHEETS: Set of four advertising proof copies, each 8" x 11", printed one side on glossy white paper. Ads include "You hear it in the long, low whistle…"; "Help him follow in your tracks…"; "Together, you'll build more than a railroad…", all in full color, and in black and white "Visionary" ad for RailScope. **NRS**

DEALER FLYER: 8-1/2" x 14", one page, full color, "Lionel O27 Gauge Electric Train Sets" and "Lionel Large Scale Electric Train Sets". — — 1 2

CONTEST BROCHURE: "Season's Greetings" from Chrysler Motors, 5-1/2" x 8-1/4", six-page brochure provides information on the 1988 Mopar Express Sweepstakes, including full-page illustration of the set. **NRS**

NOTE PAD: "LIONEL—Toys to Grow Up With, Not Out Of", black on white, with Lionel logo on top. **NRS**

CONTEST DISPLAY: Cardboard display publicizing Chrysler Motors Mopar Express Sweepstakes. Display board measures 12" x 18-1/2" with easel, slot to deposit entry forms, and insert with "On Track" entry forms. Card illustrates in full color the Mopar Express. **NRS**

CONSUMER CATALOGUE: "1989 Pre-Toy Fair Edition", 8-1/2" x 11", 20 pages in full color; front page features 8203 diesel engine with Lionel logo at top left. While this is the first 1989 catalogue, it was actually released in late 1988. — — 1 2

CONSUMER BROCHURE: "1989 Lionel Classics Pre-Toy Fair Edition", 8-1/2" x 11", four pages in full color; front cover features 384E Steam locomotive and cars. — — 1 2

McDONALD'S CONTEST LITERATURE: A repeat of the 1987 promotion with similar paper items (see 1987 listing). Again the Nickel Plate Special was a prize in the "All New 1988" version. **NRS**

NOTE PAD: "Lionel — Champions For Success". Gray on white paper, Lionel logo and five circular tracks in form of Olympic symbol. Used internally at sales promotional meeting. **NRS**

1989

CONSUMER CATALOGUE: "Toy Fair Edition 1989", 8-1/2" x 11", 28 pages in full color. Cover features new Pennsylvania 0-6-0 as inlay photo against actual railroad yards. — 1 2 3

CONSUMER CATALOGUE: "LIONEL LARGE SCALE — TOY FAIR EDITION 1989", 8-1/2" x 11", 20 pages in full color. Cover

Top row: 1988 Consumer Folder – Lionel Classics; 1988 Consumer Folder – RailScope. *Bottom row:* 1988 Dealer Flyer – Christmas year-end special with 1988 Christmas boxcar, Dealer Flyer – Dry Gulch Special Service Station set, Consumer Folder – Lionel Classics with signal bridge and trolleys.

Modern Era Paper: 1970-1990 • 115

Top row: 1988 Consumer Catalogue – 1989 Pre-Toy Fair Edition with 8203 on cover; 1988 Press Kit; 1989 Consumer Catalogue – Toy Fair Edition 1989. *Bottom row:* 1989 Consumer Catalogue – Lionel Large Scale Toy Fair Edition; 1989 Dealer Brochure – Lionel Classics Toy Fair Edition; 1989 Dealer Brochure – Holiday Collection 1989.

	G	VG	EXC	NEW
features inlay photo of 5107 Great Northern locomotive against an actual railroad photograph.	—	1	2	3

AD MAT SHEETS: Set of advertising proof copies, printed on one side on glossy white paper.
(A) 16-3/8" x 5-3/8", "The best reason for a Lionel train may be gone before you know it", features 8617 locomotive. **NRS**
(B) 16-3/8" x 5-3/8", "Sometimes the way to get close is to let something come between you", features 785 locomotive. **NRS**
(C) 8-3/8" x 11", "Lionel has a vision of what lies ahead", features Loco Scope. **NRS**
(D) 8-3/8" x 11", "For once in your life, Double Crossing pays off", features game. **NRS**
(E) 8-3/8" x 11", "Lionel Trains — Sands of Time", illustrates 30-second TV commercial. **NRS**
(F) 9-1/2" x 11", two-sided RailScope advertising, with free battery holder kit, used during the second half of 1989. **NRS**

DEALER BROCHURE: 8-1/2" x 11", "LIONEL CLASSICS TOY FAIR EDITION" 1989, features reissued 381E on cover. Four pages in full color. — — 1 2

DEALER BROCHURE: 8-1/2" x 11", "1989 Advertising Schedule", four pages, black and red on white card stock; identifies Lionel's plans for advertising. — — 4 5

PRESS KIT: Folder similar to 1988 contains fact sheets, press releases, and descriptions of new products for 1989, with 25 8" x 10" glossy photographs. 10 15 22 27

CONSUMER BROCHURE: "Side Tracks 1989-90", 8-1/2"x 11", four pages in full color, describing keepsake products offered by Lionel. Often came with a one-page black and white order form. — — 1 2

6-5823 BUMPER STICKER: "Lionel — The Legend Lives On", 11-1/2" x 3", printed on silk-screened vinyl. Available for consumer purchase. — — 2 3

6-5824 NOTE PAD: 3" x 5" pads in sheets of 100; illustrates Lionel "L" with insignia "Official Lionel Enthusiast". Price per pad. — — — 3

DEALER BROCHURE: 8-1/2" x 11", one page in full color, "Desert King"; Fall 1989 Service Station Special advertisement with illustration of Rio Grande set. — — — 2

DEALER BROCHURE: 8-1/2" x 11", one page in full color, "The Old Glory" Series, illustrating three new reefers. — — 1 2

DEALER BROCHURE: 8-1/2" x 11", four-page folder, "Holiday Collection 1989", illustrates 1945 and 1989 locomotive on cover.
(A) Full-color throughout. — — 1 2
(B) Black and white throughout, perhaps privately issued. — — — 1

DEALER BROCHURE: Four-page color folder, two pages 5-1/2" x 11" and two pages 8-1/2" x 11", advertising availability of Revolvers race cars in spring of 1990. — — 1 2

GREETING CARD: 4-3/4" x 6-1/4" white card, features embossed Christmas tree on cover with three boxes; inside is printed greetings with three Lionel boxes in orange and blue. **NRS**

RAILSCOPE VIDEO CONTEST NOTICE: Two-sided cardboard A-frame, 8-1/2" x 6-3/4" each side when assembled, announcing the contest to "Show Off Your Train Layout". One side blue letters against a red background; other side red letters against a blue background. **NRS**

ENTRY FORM: To enter the RailScope Video Contest; 8-1/2" x 14" blue on white paper with complete instructions and entry blank. **NRS**

NOTE PAD: "90 Years of Magic". Light red on white paper, featuring magician and Lionel 90th anniversary logo. Used internally at sales promotional meetings. **NRS**

1990

CONSUMER CATALOGUE: "LIONEL BOOK ONE 1990". Issued late 1989, 8-1/2" x 11", 20 pages in full color, describes new 1990 line. New 90th anniversary logo, "90 YEARS OF QUALITY", featured on cover. — 1 2 3

CONSUMER CATALOGUE: "BOOK TWO 1990". Issued early 1990, 8-1/2" x 11", 36 pages in full color, front page features new 90th anniversary logo with new Scale Hudson HI-700E superimposed in background. "90 YEARS OF QUALITY". Contents describe new 1990 line. **NRS**

CONSUMER CATALOGUE: "Lionel Large Scale", 16 pages, 8-1/2" x 11", in full color. Cover features inlaid Conrail diesel and 5110 steam engine with "L" and 90th anniversary logos in color**NRS**

DEALER BROCHURE: "1990 Advertising Schedule", 8-1/2" x 11" six-page fold-out on heavy glossy paper stock. Cover features new Scale Hudson locomotive and tender and contents describe Lionel's advertising plans. **NRS**

DEALER BROCHURE: "REVOLVERS...YOUR WAIT IS OVER!", 8-1/2" x 11"; eight unnumbered pages describing new die-cast car line, with one page devoted to television advertising. **NRS**

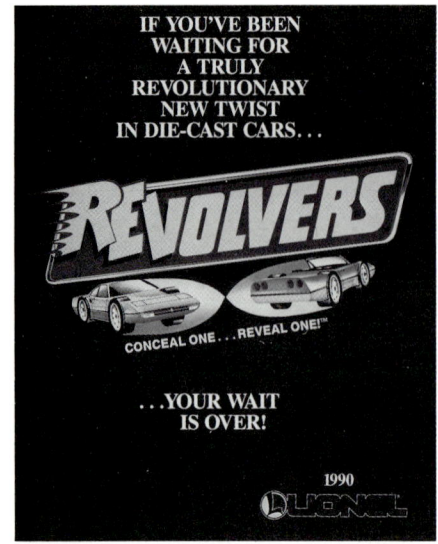

1990 Dealer Brochure – Revolvers.

DEALER BROCHURE: "Stocking Stuffers", 8-1/2" x 11", six-page fold-out in full color, features Lionel Classics on cover, and describes holiday cars and other new products scheduled for late 1990 release. **NRS**

INSIGNIA LABEL: Peelable "90 Years of Quality 1900-1990" logo for 1990 in black, white, red, and blue on 3" square clear adhesive backing. Distributed at 1990 Toy Fair. **NRS**

PRESS KIT: 9" x 12" glossy folder contains fact sheets, press releases, and 8" x 10" glossy photos of 1990 product line. **NRS**

1990 Consumer Catalogue – Book One issued in late 1989.

1990 Consumer Catalogue – Book Two issued at Toy Fair in February 1990.

1990 Consumer Catalogue – Lionel Large Scale Electric Trains and Accessories book issued at Toy Fair in February 1990.

Chapter Five
SERVICE STATION PAPER

Over a period of many years, extending from the prewar era to present day, the Lionel Service Department irregularly issued bulletins to approved service stations. These bulletins contained information of a mundane nature, such as straightforward price listings for parts, to some rather fascinating data on hints for repairing trains. This chapter is an initial effort to chronologically list all known bulletins, and undoubtedly many more issues will surface in the future. Reader assistance is requested in adding service bulletins not listed below. It is also important to note that titles for the bulletins changed periodically over the years; the titles given below are as they appear on observed bulletins. The titles of all bulletins are listed as Lionel produced them; i.e. if a bulletin was issued with a "No." designation, that is part of the title; if issued with a "#", that too is listed in the title. This inconsistency is how Lionel issued its bulletins.

                                                            G   VG   EXC   NEW

SERVICE STATION BULLETINS

NOTICE TO ALL SERVICE STATIONS: Dated November 1, 1938. This apparently is the initial attempt of Lionel in providing service bulletins, and a comment is made to the extent that "other Service Bulletins will follow at regular intervals". **NRS**

LIONEL SERVICE BULLETIN: No. SB-101, November 1938. Nine pages on electro-magnetic couplers, plus six-page repair estimates matrix. **NRS**

LIONEL SERVICE BULLETIN: No. SB-102, January 1939. Ten pages, deals with Lionel remote-control whistles. This Bulletin contains perhaps the best documented exploded drawings of the prewar era and contains a wealth of information on prewar whistle components. **NRS**

LIONEL SERVICE BULLETIN: No. SB-103, January 1939. Eleven pages, with the first page unnumbered, describing and illustrating the Lionel coupler gauge. (See Chapter Eight on Tools for a more detailed description.) The ten numbered pages provide additional information on the Lionel remote-control whistle, however pages appear to be identical to the SB-102 with one exception: Pages 1 and 2 of SB-103 are in reverse order from the previous SB-102 Bulletin, which places Table 1 in the proper order. Nevertheless, this was a major expense for Lionel in correcting a seemingly insignificant error, if, in fact, it was an error at all. **NRS**

                                                            G   VG   EXC   NEW

SERVICE STATION BULLETIN: No. 40-1, September 16, 1940. Features "Tools Most Commonly Required by Service Stations Engaged in Repairing Lionel Equipment". Format, unlike the previous SB bulletins, is crudely typewritten, and interestingly enough the list of recommended tools contains neither Lionel's own test set, nor the SE-1 coupler gauge set, both of which were just announced as being available in the previous bulletins! **NRS**

LIONEL SERVICE BULLETIN: No. SB-104, October 1940. Five pages, provides details on the Nos. 65, 66, 67, and 166 whistle controllers, including line drawings and circuit diagrams. This appears to be the final bulletin in the attractively-produced SB series, perhaps brought about by Lionel's increased readiness to be a part of the coming military production effort. **NRS**

BULLETIN FOR LIONEL APPROVED SERVICE STATIONS: No. 40-1 Copy and reader assistance requested. **NRS**

BULLETIN FOR LIONEL APPROVED SERVICE STATIONS: No. 40-2, October 17, 1940. One page, contains general information on 1940 switching locomotives and tenders. **NRS**

BULLETIN FOR LIONEL APPROVED SERVICE STATIONS: No. 40-3, November 4, 1940. One page, contains list prices of multivolt transformers. **NRS**

BULLETIN FOR LIONEL APPROVED SERVICE STATIONS: No. 40-4, November 4, 1940. Two pages, contains price list of tenders when sold separately. **NRS**

BULLETIN FOR LIONEL APPROVED SERVICE STATIONS: No. 40-5, November 26, 1940. One page, contains illustrated instructions for rewiring No. 022 switches. Illustrates "right" and "wrong" way to wire. **NRS**

BULLETIN FOR LIONEL APPROVED SERVICE STATIONS: No. 41-1. Copy and reader assistance requested. **NRS**

BULLETIN FOR LIONEL APPROVED SERVICE STATIONS: No. 41-2, February 4, 1941. One page, notice of price changes on replacement parts for 50 and 55 Lionel airplanes. This Bulletin provides the first insight into Lionel's war effort, since the 50 aluminum plane arm availability was being delayed "due to the heavy demand for aluminum created by the National Defense Program". **NRS**

BULLETIN FOR LIONEL APPROVED SERVICE STATIONS: No. 41-3, February 4, 1941. One page, notice of price changes on replacement parts for Lionel 022 and 711 switches. **NRS**

BULLETIN FOR LIONEL APPROVED SERVICE STATIONS: No. 42-1. Copy and reader assistance requested. **NRS**

| | G | VG | EXC | NEW |

BULLETIN FOR LIONEL APPROVED SERVICE STATIONS: No. 42-2, June 1, 1942. One page, retraction of price increase announced in Bulletin No. 42-1. **NRS**

TO ALL SERVICE STATIONS: Undated bulletin requesting use of provided order forms, reference No. 758. A. Rubin Collection. **NRS**

TO ALL SERVICE STATIONS: No date, reference No. 770. One page, refers to a better smoke unit developed by the Lionel engineering department. A. Rubin Collection. **NRS**

NOTICE TO ALL SERVICE STATIONS: Undated (late 1940s). One page, reference No. 785, bulletin reminding dealers to file for order shortage claims within 30 days. A. Rubin Collection. **NRS**

NOTICE TO ALL SERVICE STATIONS: Same as listing above, but reference No. 785 Rev. Printed on Hillside, New Jersey stationery rather than Irvington, New Jersey, and inscription "Use Pink Order Forms Only" added. R. Osterhoff Collection. **NRS**

NOTICE TO ALL SERVICE STATIONS: Undated (late 1940s). One page, reference No. 789 bulletin, reminding use of no charge invoice pads, signed by W. Melillo of the Service Station Division. This particular notice was issued on both multicolored (Santa Fe-type) as well as plainer "The Lionel Corporation" stationery. **NRS**

T. C. TRUCK BULLETIN: Undated, but believed to be issued early 1946. Bulletins Nos. 1 through 7 provide special instructions for the repair of Lionel postwar O/O27 Gauge trucks and couplers. I. D. Smith Collection. **NRS**

(NO TITLE): Bulletin dated June 15, 1949. One page, reference No. 918, regards a revised Time Schedule Chart for warranty repairs. A. Rubin Collection. **NRS**

TO ALL SERVICE STATIONS: Bulletin dated July 1, 1949. One page, reference No. 920, offering a 40-percent discount on certain items. A. Rubin Collection. **NRS**

NOTICE TO ALL SERVICE STATIONS: Dated June 15, 1949. One page, reference No. 921, lists quantities in which certain products will be packed. A. Rubin Collection.

— — 17 —

(NO TITLE): "Sale of Trucks" bulletin, dated August 10, 1949. One page, reference No. 937. A. Rubin Collection. **NRS**

(NO TITLE): "2026 Locomotive" bulletin, dated September 21, 1949. One page, reference No. 950, refers to truck and lamp plate assembly. A. Rubin Collection. **NRS**

NOTICE TO ALL SERVICE STATIONS: Dated September 22, 1949. One page, no reference number, refers to no charge invoice pads. A. Rubin Collection. **NRS**

(NO TITLE): Undated, Form 1009. One page, refers to Remuneration reports on warranty merchandise and defective parts. **NRS**

SPECIAL BULLETIN: Dated December 29, 1950. One page, reference No. 1069, refers to 1120 and 6110 Scout locomotives stopping on the track even when the power is on. **NRS**

TO ALL SERVICE STATIONS: Dated March 1, 1951. One page, reference No. 1086, refers to parts back order status. **NRS**

(NO TITLE): February 28, 1951. One page, reference No. 1087, refers to price changes to go into effect immediately. **NRS**

SPECIAL SERVICE BULLETIN: November 5, 1954. One-page bulletin, three holes punched, Form 1503 on colored Lionel stationery. Subject matter addresses problem of 711-54 lamp cover becoming distorted due to the heat from the bulb. **NRS**

LIONEL SERVICE INFORMATION: One-page bulletin, three holes punched for insertion into the Service Manual, Form 1522, dated December 1954, "Operation of 'O27' Remote Control Switches". Blue paper. A. Rubin Collection. **NRS**

| | G | VG | EXC | NEW |

TO ALL LIONEL APPROVED SERVICE STATIONS: December 30, 1954. One page, reference Form No. 1523, clarifies the Lionel Service Policy. A. Rubin Collection. **NRS**

(NO TITLE): September 1955. One page, reference No. 1567, indicates limited quantities of motors, trucks, and reversing units are available. **NRS**

SPECIAL BULLETIN TO SERVICE STATIONS: September 15, 1956. One page, addresses problem of certain Service Stations refusing to perform warranty repairs. I. D. Smith Collection. **NRS**

TO ALL AUTHORIZED LIONEL SERVICE STATIONS: Dated October 16, 1957. One page, identifies availability of HO parts, Form 1736. **NRS**

SPECIAL BULLETIN TO SERVICE STATIONS: Undated (issued March 1958). One page, reference No. 1569, regards replacement parts, on colored Lionel stationery. A. Rubin Collection. **NRS**

TO ALL AUTHORIZED LIONEL SERVICE STATIONS: January 22, 1958. One page, reference Form No. 1759, refers to service and replacement parts for Lionel "HO" equipment. A. Rubin Collection. **NRS**

LIONEL SERVICE DEPARTMENT BULLETIN: No. 1. Copy and reader assistance requested. **NRS**

LIONEL SERVICE DEPARTMENT BULLETIN: No. 2. Copy and reader assistance requested. **NRS**

LIONEL SERVICE DEPARTMENT BULLETIN: No. 3, May 25, 1959. One page, regards availability of obsolete parts. **NRS**

LIONEL SERVICE DEPARTMENT BULLETIN: No. 4. June 5, 1959. One page, "important announcement regarding service and warranty changes", accompanied by letter from A. Kagan, Lionel Director of Services, providing background of policy change. **NRS**

LIONEL SERVICE DEPARTMENT BULLETIN: No. 5, July 22, 1959. Two pages, black on yellow paper, refers to a newly-issued Parts Book as well as a revised warranty payment schedule. A. Rubin Collection. **NRS**

LIONEL SERVICE DEPARTMENT BULLETIN: No. 6, October 19, 1959. Four pages, black on yellow paper, refers to availability of new ad mats as well as the fact "a small quantity of the No. 1862 'General' locomotive was made with side rod screws which had #2-64 threads," later replaced with 3-48 screws. A. Rubin Collection. **NRS**

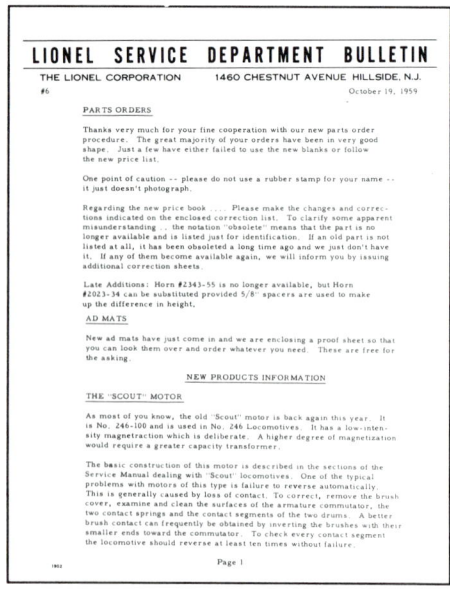

Page 1 of the Lionel Service Department Bulletin #6 dated October 19, 1959.

| | G | VG | EXC | NEW |

LIONEL SERVICE DEPARTMENT BULLETIN: No. 7, November 10, 1959. One page, black on yellow paper, plus numerous attachments. A. Rubin Collection. — — 17 —

LIONEL SERVICE DEPARTMENT BULLETIN: No. 8, December 14, 1959. Two pages, black on yellow paper, with article on how to test rectifiers on a 5D tester. A. Rubin Collection. — — 17 —

LIONEL SERVICE DEPARTMENT BULLETIN: No. 9, January 7, 1960. One page, black on yellow paper, with information on HO parts. A. Rubin Collection. — — 17 —

LIONEL SERVICE DEPARTMENT BULLETIN: No. 10, February 24, 1960. Two pages, black on yellow paper, no attachments. — — 17 —

LIONEL SERVICE DEPARTMENT BULLETIN: No. 11, June 17, 1960. Two pages, black on yellow paper, with parts lists attached. Interesting statement includes on page 1 of Bulletin: "You have probably noted from our advance catalog that Lionel has not listed too many new items for 1960. The reason for this is that the energies and time of our Engineering Department have been concentrated on improving the items we have." A. Rubin Collection. — — 17 —

LIONEL SERVICE DEPARTMENT BULLETIN: No. 12, July 25, 1960. One page, black on yellow paper, "Special Parts Promotion". — — 17 —

LIONEL SERVICE DEPARTMENT BULLETIN: No. 13, September 13, 1960. Two pages, plus "Repair Tags" attachment, all black on yellow paper. — — 15 —

LIONEL SERVICE DEPARTMENT BULLETIN: No. 14, November 28, 1960. Three pages, black on yellow paper, no attachments. — — 15 —

LIONEL SERVICE DEPARTMENT BULLETIN: No. 15, February 1, 1961. Four pages, plus "Lionel Service Station Questionnaire" attachment. Black on yellow paper. — — 15 —

LIONEL SERVICE DEPARTMENT BULLETIN: No. 16, April 3, 1961. One page, black on yellow paper, "1961-1962 Service Station" decal also enclosed. — — 15 —

LIONEL SERVICE DEPARTMENT BULLETIN: No. 17, June 1, 1961. Three pages, black on yellow paper, with parts sale attachments. Includes interesting article on stockroom error in which special industrial relay drums were mixed with regular E-unit drums, of which the former could not be used in locomotives. — — 15 —

LIONEL SERVICE DEPARTMENT BULLETIN: No. 18, June 1961. Two pages, plus several attachments, includes a "Name That Bulletin" contest, parts sales, and brochures on visiting New York City. Also included with this bulletin is a four-page brochure, "The Lionel Parts Story", printed black on white paper, and a 17-1/2" x 11-5/8" one-page announcement "The Lionel Corporation Announces with Pride the Acquisition of the Porter Chemical Company". This sheet, printed black, gray, and red on white glossy paper, may also have been used for sales promotional purposes. Bulletin printed black on yellow paper. **NRS**

LIONEL SERVICE DEPARTMENT BULLETIN: No. 19, August 1961. Four pages, plus attachments, includes a letter from General Medaris dated August 9, 1961, thanking the Service Stations for their fine service. Bulletin printed black on yellow paper. R. Osterhoff Collection. **NRS**

LIONEL SERVICE DEPARTMENT BULLETIN: No. 20, October 1961. Four pages, black on yellow paper, no attachments. R. Osterhoff Collection. **NRS**

SPECIAL ADVANCE BULLETIN: Single page, red ink on white paper, bulletin was mailed November 1961 to all Lionel-approved Service Stations advertising the availability of the Lionel-Porter science hobby merchandiser display cabinet; this display was available free with a science stock purchase. This special bulletin was mailed with the 1961 Sciencecraft catalogue and is therefore frequently missing as a catalogue insert. **NRS**

THE LIONEL HERALD: November 1961. This represents the first issue of the retitled Service Bulletin. It is interesting to note the winner of the "Name That Bulletin 'Contest'" was Harry Maurer of Ronks, Pennsylvania who submitted "The Lionel Order Board", and oddly enough, that title is not used on the bulletin! The front page of the "Herald" is printed black on white paper with various railroad emblems in full color on both sides running vertically. The remainder of the paper was printed black on dull white stock. Eight pages plus numerous attachments, including a four-page brochure, "The Lionel Service Story", written and printed in the same format as the "Parts Story" previously issued. **NRS**

THE LIONEL HERALD: December 1961. Full-color page 1 features "The Great Locomotive Chase" with 24-page brochure attached, compliments of Louisville & Nashville Railroad. This brochure is issued in two versions, glossy white and dull white papers, both red and black ink. The "Herald" consists of six pages, with several important attachments:

(A) Two-page leaflet on Lionel No. 5F universal test set with red and black illustration, plus Form 2522 order sheet for test set.
(B) Form 2526 "United Parcel Service" data card.
(C) "The Jiffy Bag Story".
(D) "Control and Operating Accessories for HO by Lionel", one page, 17" x 11" sheet, with "(Form) 2523 11-61" in bottom left corner.
(E) "Vital Small Parts for Lionel Trains", one page, 17" x 11" sheet, with "(Form) 2524 11-61" in bottom left corner. R. Osterhoff Collection. **NRS**

THE LIONEL HERALD: January 1962. Four pages, plus attachments. **NRS**

THE LIONEL HERALD: February-March 1962. Four pages, plus attachments. Imprinted on this issue is "Form 2598 2-62 D-5". **NRS**

THE LIONEL HERALD: April 1962. Seven pages, plus attachments. The front page is again full color with the railroad emblems, and contains a story "The Santa Fe Coyote Special" with illustration of locomotive 1010 on page 2. **NRS**

THE LIONEL HERALD: May-June 1962. Eight pages, plus attachments. Page 1 in full color features "Yellowhead Pass", lore from the Canadian National Railroad. One important attachment is listed as "Form 2679 6-62 D-5", a one-page illustrated leaflet, "Lionel Service Station Exclusives! Two Fast Moving HO Outfits with Built-in High Volume Sales", printed on glossy paper. **NRS**

MERRY CHRISTMAS MR. LIONEL DEALER: Two-page bulletin printed on two-color Lionel letterhead and sent by Jacques Zuccaire, Lionel Advertising Manager. Bulletin plus order blank details Christmas advertising campaign, but was sent to dealers July 2, 1962. **NRS**

THE LIONEL HERALD: September 1962. Full-color front page with article "Rock Island Had its Troubles with the James Boys — But Good". Further information on this issue requested. **NRS**

THE LIONEL HERALD: October 1962. Six pages, plus attachments. Attachments relate primarily to warranty information, and also include a 1963 date decal. **NRS**

THE LIONEL HERALD: December 1962. Five pages, plus attachments. Page 1 in full color features "Whistler's Father", a railroad story of the Baltimore and Ohio Railroad. Important attachments include the Tri-ang Scalextric Instruction Manual, "Lionel Phonographs" brochure, plus numerous pages on servicing Lionel phonographs. R. Osterhoff Collection. **NRS**

THE LIONEL HERALD: February 1963. Two pages, page 1 in full color with railroad emblems, with a story on John Brown's raid

The Lionel Herald December 1962 cover letter

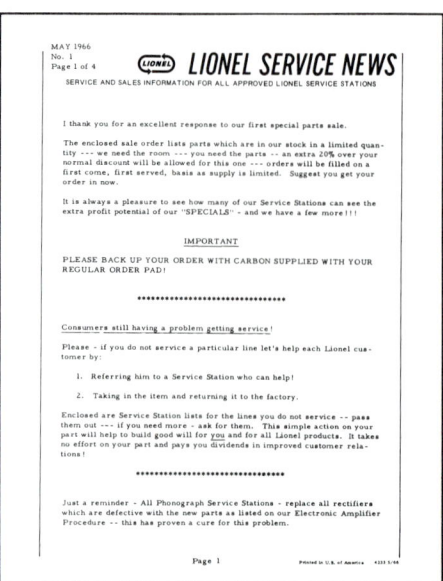

Page 1 of 4 of the Lionel Service News dated May 1966.

                                                                                  G   VG EXC NEW

on Harper's Ferry, October 17, 1859. Lionel acknowledges the B & O Railroad's contribution to the Herald. **NRS**

THE LIONEL HERALD: (Undated.) One page, with booklet attached, "The Illinois Central Railroad and the Civil War", which in turn was a reprint from the book *Main Line of Mid-America — The Story of the Illinois Central*, by Carlton J. Corliss. **NRS**

THE LIONEL HERALD: (Undated.) One page, with booklet attached, "Union Pacific Railroad — A Brief History". **NRS**

IMPORTANT TO ALL SERVICE STATIONS: Assigned Form No. 2859 4/63 D-5, single-page bulletin on the subject of Lionel phonographs. **NRS**

TO ALL OUR LIONEL APPROVED SERVICE STATIONS: 1964. One-page flyer, black on pink paper, provides supplementary information to Service Stations regarding Raceway Sets sold through Sears, plus other general service data. **NRS**

TO ALL LIONEL APPROVED SERVICE STATIONS: Late 1965 (not dated). Two pages, begins by refering to enclosed mailing to help perform duties of Lionel Approved Service Station. I. D. Smith Collection. **NRS**

TO ALL LIONEL APPROVED SERVICE STATIONS: Early 1966 (not dated). Two pages, refers to recent New York Toy Show and enclosure of new 1966 catalogue. **NRS**

LIONEL SERVICE INFORMATION: (Undated.) One page, refers to 480-1 magnetic coupler truck, symptoms of service problems, and method of correction. I. D. Smith Collection. **NRS**

LIONEL SERVICE NEWS: No. 1, May 1966. Five pages, includes surplus inventory and Service Station questionnaire. Listed as Form 4233 5/66. **NRS**

LIONEL SERVICE NEWS: No. 2, June 1966. Five pages, includes survey to determine "which tender should be sold with the 773 loco, the 2426W?" **NRS**

LIONEL SERVICE NEWS: No. 3, July 1966. Ten pages, Lionel Engineering Dept. announces that 1966 started with a goal of "Best Quality"; also includes listing of Service Stations with surplus parts. **NRS**

LIONEL SERVICE NEWS: No. 4, August 1966. Four pages, features Lionel's national advertising campaign, and newsletter has attached full-color Batman / Superman comics ads for Lionel. **NRS**

                                                                                   G   VG EXC NEW

LIONEL SERVICE NEWS: No. 5, September 1966. Eight pages, urges dealers to place their orders early because "we have seen train sales show an excellent increase recently, after some years of disappointment". **NRS**

LIONEL SERVICE NEWS: No. 6, October 1966. Two pages, highlights the current TV and print promotions for the holidays. Apparently this was the last Service Bulletin until the post-1969 era began. **NRS**

SERVICE STATION BULLETIN: Unnumbered, June 7, 1971. One page, "Service Information", refering to #2328-173 collector assembly. **NRS**

SERVICE STATION BULLETIN: Unnumbered, July 1971. Two pages, "To All Service Stations", indicates availability of ST-350 Arbor Press with tools. This bulletin, like many postwar and even into the 1980s, bore the signature of Leonard Dean, Lionel's parts and service spokesman for many years. **NRS**

SERVICE STATION BULLETIN: Unnumbered, July 1971. Two pages, "Lionel Approved Service Stations", with attached Survey #5. **NRS**

SERVICE STATION BULLETIN: Unnumbered, July 1971. Three pages, "To All Service Stations", with enclosed parts sheets. **NRS**

SERVICE STATION BULLETIN: Unnumbered, September 1971. Two pages, "To All Service Stations", indicates separate ST-350 tools will not be available. **NRS**

SERVICE STATION BULLETIN: Unnumbered, January 1972. Three pages, "To All Service Stations — Special!", indicating limited availability of certain items from the 1971 catalogue. **NRS**

SERVICE STATION BULLETIN: Unnumbered, January 1972. One page, "To All Service Stations", emphasizing Service Stations must honor warranty repairs. **NRS**

SERVICE STATION BULLETIN: Unnumbered, May 1972. Two pages, "Lionel Service Station Exclusive", announcing availability of Service Station Set #6-1250. **NRS**

SERVICE STATION BULLETIN: Unnumbered, May 1972. One page, indicates availability of ST-384 track pliers. **NRS**

TO ALL SERVICE STATIONS: Dated October 29, 1973. One page reminding Service Stations of their warranty responsibilities. Letter from L. E. Kennie. **NRS**

	G	VG	EXC	NEW

SERVICE STATION BULLETIN: Unnumbered, 1976. One page, indicates a short supply of gold-lettered tender bodies. **NRS**

SERVICE STATION BULLETIN: Unnumbered, Summer 1976 (?). One page, refers to tender 8206. **NRS**

SERVICE STATION BULLETIN: Unnumbered, undated. One page, refers to uncoupler button missing in certain sets. **NRS**

SERVICE BULLETIN: No. 1, unnumbered and undated. Refers to "Workin' on the Railroad" parts kit, and would therefore be from circa 1978. **NRS**

SERVICE BULLETIN: No. 2, unnumbered and undated. Two pages, mentions that bulletins will now be issued monthly to replace seminars that Lionel had been conducting. **NRS**

(NO TITLE): Undated, but 1978. One-page letter indicating that effective January 1, 1979 there will be a new sales policy. **NRS**

1978 SERVICE STATION SPECIAL: Undated, but 1978. One-page notice indicating 1978 Service Station set orders will be confirmed in writing. **NRS**

(NO TITLE): Dated January 19, 1979. One-page letter clarifying sales policy changes previously communicated. **NRS**

SERVICE BULLETIN: No. 3 (?), fall 1979. It is believed that this is number 3, since Lionel, perhaps inadvertently, did not complete a number, and called this a Special Bulletin on bulletin letterhead. This one-page flyer did reference that additional Service Manual pages were enclosed. **NRS**

SERVICE BULLETIN: No. 4, September 1979. Two pages, includes lengthy write-up on repairing 9550-50 trucks. **NRS**

SERVICE BULLETIN: No. 5, December 1979. Two pages, highlights Spring 1980 Collector Series. **NRS**

SPECIAL BULLETIN: Unnumbered, January 1980. One page, includes a new binder for the Service Manual, among other enclosures. **NRS**

SERVICE BULLETIN: No. 6, February 1980. One page, refers to availability of 1980 catalogue, and that sample catalogues will be distributed to dealers in March. **NRS**

SERVICE BULLETIN: No. 7, April 1980. Two pages, features explanation of warranty replacement procedures. **NRS**

SERVICE BULLETIN: No. 8, June 1980. One page, includes write-up on types of wheels Lionel carries in stock. **NRS**

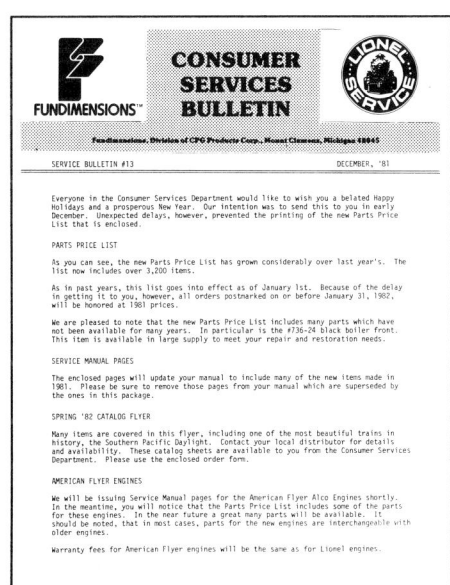

Consumer Service Bulletin No. 13 dated December 1981.

	G	VG	EXC	NEW

SERVICE BULLETIN: No. 9, September 1980. One page, includes attachment of latest back-in-stock parts list. **NRS**

SERVICE BULLETIN: No. 10, November 1980. Two pages, refers to new Parts Price List effective January 1, 1981, which is enclosed. **NRS**

SERVICE BULLETIN: No. 11, February 1981. Two pages, refers to a preliminary copy of the 1981 Fundimensions catalogue which is enclosed. **NRS**

SERVICE BULLETIN: No. 12, July 1981. Two pages, provides hints on speeding up the parts ordering process. **NRS**

SERVICE BULLETIN: No. 13, December 1981. Two pages, refers to availability of Spring 1982 flyer introducing the Southern Pacific Daylight. **NRS**

SERVICE BULLETIN: No. 14, Spring 1982. Two pages, mostly describes changes to 1982 parts prices. **NRS**

SERVICE BULLETIN: No. 15, Summer 1982. One page, refers to changes to Parts Price List dated 12/81. **NRS**

SERVICE BULLETIN: No. 16, Fall 1982. One page, announces availability of Lionel playing cards. **NRS**

(NO TITLE): September 13, 1982. Three pages, letter from Dan Johns, correcting two items on the September Parts Sale order form, and announcing a special September parts sale. It is not known why a bulletin number was not assigned to this communication, since it definitely continued similar information as previous bulletins. **NRS**

SERVICE BULLETIN: No. 17, October 1982. Two pages, includes an instruction sheet on how to add traction weights to the Quicksilver and GP-7 locomotives. **NRS**

SERVICE BULLETIN: No. 18, November 1982. One page, refers to Lionel's new DC-motored American Flyer Alco. **NRS**

SERVICE BULLETIN: No. 19, December 1982. One page, wishes everyone a happy holiday. **NRS**

(NO TITLE): Dated March 11, 1983. One-page letter announcing Lionel is moving production operations to San Diego, California. **NRS**

SERVICE BULLETIN: No. 20, Spring 1983. Two pages, begins with reference to enclosing copies of 1983 catalogue. **NRS**

SERVICE BULLETIN: No. 21, June 1983. Two pages, announces special sale of Lionel playing cards and the Lionel antique mirror. **NRS**

SERVICE BULLETIN: No. 22, September 1983. One page, refers to availability of Spring 1984 flyer for the reintroduction of the Scale Hudson. **NRS**

SERVICE BULLETIN: No. 23, December 1983. One page, two sentences wishing happy holidays. **NRS**

SERVICE BULLETIN: No. 24, March 1984. Two pages, includes order form for a special Lionel sign, 35-1/2" x 29-1/2" and done in relief. **NRS**

(NO TITLE): Dated June 19, 1984. One-page letter announcing three- to four-week shutdown of Parts Department. **NRS**

(NO TITLE): Dated August 21, 1984. One-page letter announcing that the Service Department move is now complete. **NRS**

SERVICE BULLETIN: No. 25, Summer 1984. One page, announces Service Department will be moving to new Mount Clemens location. **NRS**

SERVICE BULLETIN: No. 26, December 1984. One page, request made of Service Stations if there is any interest in having available such merchandise as tools, belt buckles, mugs, and other items. **NRS**

SERVICE BULLETIN: No. 27, March 1985. One page, indicates Lionel was "disappointed in the response to our survey on Service Tools and Promotional Material". **NRS**

G VG EXC NEW

CONSUMER SERVICES BULLETIN: Unnumbered, undated but on same stationery as previous bulletins. One page, begins with a note: "Our next Service Bulletin will be printed on new letterhead that does not include the Fundimensions logo". Yet the next two Bulletins carried the same logo. This bulletin also refers to orders for parts at 1985 prices, good through January 1, 1986. **NRS**

SERVICE BULLETIN: No. 27, December 1985. One page, emphasizes that "Lionel is not being sold". **NRS**

SERVICE BULLETIN: No. 28, February 1986. One page, indicates enclosure of the 1986 Lionel catalogues. **NRS**

(NO TITLE): Undated, but sent May 1986. One-page letter with attached order form for 1986 Service Station Special catalogue sheets. **NRS**

(NO TITLE): Dated May 6, 1986. One-page letter announcing that Lionel Trains, Inc. will offer scale Hudson directly to consumers. **NRS**

(NO TITLE): Undated, but 1986. One-page letter announcing Santa Fe Service Station Special for 1986. **NRS**

SERVICE BULLETIN: No. 29, June 1986 (but not dated). One page, addresses problem of unavailability of parts. **NRS**

SPECIAL SERVICE BULLETIN: October 1986 (but not dated). One page, announces changes in factory services to dealers, including computerized parts ordering, processing, and billing. **NRS**

SERVICE BULLETIN: No. 30, December 1986. One page, comments on Lionel Trains, Inc.'s first year of operation, and that warranty reimbursement rates will increase. **NRS**

SERVICE BULLETIN: No. 31, January 1987. One page, with Lionel Service Manual supplement attached. **NRS**

SERVICE BULLETIN UPDATE: Unnumbered, February 1987. One page, corrects Service drawing D-60. **NRS**

SERVICE BULLETIN: No. 32, February 1987. One page, refers to the fact that 1987 Lionel catalogues are enclosed. **NRS**

(NO TITLE): Undated, but 1987. One-page letter announcing 1987 Service Station Special. **NRS**

(NO TITLE): (Undated.) One-page letter announcing the formation of the Lionel Classics Service Center. **NRS**

(NO TITLE): Unnumbered, September 1987. Letter, includes a Service Station survey. **NRS**

(NO TITLE): Unnumbered, October 1987. One-page, letter indicates the enclosing of a copy of "our latest special catalogue" (for 1988). **NRS**

(NO TITLE): Unnumbered, April 1988 (but undated). Letter, announces the formation of the Lionel Classics Service Center. **NRS**

(NO TITLE): Unnumbered, April 1988 (but undated). Letter, encloses instructions to repair couplers that have trouble staying closed. **NRS**

(NO TITLE): May 1988. One-page letter announcing Dry Gulch Service Station Special, as well as reintroduction of Lionel Wheel Puller. **NRS**

(NO TITLE): Unnumbered, May 1988 (but undated). Letter, emphasizes the Lionel Classics Tinplate price list is intended for the use of consumers as well as Service Stations. **NRS**

(NO TITLE): Unnumbered, May 1988 (but undated). Letter, refers to the fact that Lionel will be reintroducing the Lionel wheel puller and also includes Service Manual supplement No. 11. **NRS**

(NO TITLE): December 1988. One-page letter with four-page 1989 Service Station Survey and Rail Scope instruction sheet. The survey asked interesting questions on type of Service Station products desired. **NRS**

(NO TITLE): February 1989. One-page letter with samples of 1989 catalogues. **NRS**

G VG EXC NEW

(NO TITLE): May 1989. One-page letter announcing 1989 Desert King Service Station Special. Attached were catalogue sheets, a policy statement, and parts definition list. **NRS**

(NO TITLE): July 1989. One-page short notice providing Service Stations with chance to purchase certain parts at a discount. **NRS**

(NO TITLE): November 1989. One-page letter with attached Parts Price List effective January 1, 1990. **NRS**

LIONEL SERVICE AND PARTS MANUALS

One of Lionel's greatest assets was its ability not only to produce a quality product, but to provide technical support for its products in the form of documentation. The most significant category of Lionel paper is, of course, the catalogue. However, there was a wealth of information provided to authorized Lionel Service Stations, primarily beginning in the mid-to-late 1930s, and extending well through the postwar years, into the 1960s.

The postwar Lionel Service Manual is a masterpiece of engineering documentation, containing an abundance of exploded line drawings, comprehensive parts listings, and suggestions for repairs. Unfortunately, Lionel's prewar documentation is quite limited. Although advanced compared to its competitors, by contemporary standards the prewar documentation is weak. This author has not observed detailed prewar Lionel exploded line drawings for distribution to its Service Stations, although such a manual is rumored to exist. Lionel did issue several service bulletins covering whistlers and couplers. These are covered under Bulletins in this book. Although it is possible to produce a prewar manual today using advanced technology such as Engineering Work Stations with CAD/CAM computer software, the development cost would be prohibitive given the small size of the collector market.

Prior to World War II, Lionel published *Replacement Parts for Lionel Trains and Accessories* in several different versions. The most useful documentation, however, comes with the advent of the postwar Lionel era. The earliest known postwar Service Manual pages are dated August 1947, and describe the 671 locomotive. Lionel did issue several service bulletins in 1945 for its new trucks. Many Service Manual updates were issued to Service Stations accompanied by Service Bulletins and sales promotional literature. As products were improved, manual pages were also revised. Since many products have Service Manual pages for as many as ten years or more, no attempt is made to provide comprehensive dating for specific manuals, although certain assumptions can be made for the issuance of major manual changes. Over the years, binder composition and color changed, and the pages alternated between white and green-tinted paper stock. Complete and original Lionel Service Manuals are extremely rare, and excellent reproductions are currently available. The Greenberg four-volume reproduction is likely more complete than any originals because so many volumes were cross-collated to produce it.

	G	VG	EXC	NEW

REPLACEMENT PARTS FOR LIONEL ELECTRIC TRAINS AND ACCESSORIES: Undated, but from early 1930s. 12-3/8" x 9-1/8", ten unnumbered pages, dark green on white glossy paper. A. Rubin Collection. **NRS**

REPLACEMENT PARTS FOR LIONEL ELECTRIC TRAINS: 1933. 6" x 9" booklet, 15 numbered black and white pages, includes replacement parts listing and service information. Identified on back cover with R.P.B.-S.M.-10-33.
(A) "NOTICE — When ordering trimmings. . ." rubber-stamped on front cover. **NRS**
(B) Same as (A); no rubber stamp. **NRS**
(C) Same as (B); 1974 Reproduction by Max Knoecklein.
— — 3 4

REPLACEMENT PARTS FOR LIONEL TRAINS: 9" x 6", 32 pages including covers, black ink on white paper, rear cover lower right corner:"FORM NO...5M-11-35". Original. Weisblum Collection. **NRS**

REPLACEMENT PARTS FOR LIONEL TRAINS AND ACCESSORIES: 8-3/8" x 10- 3/4" manual, 54 pages, fine grade paper stock, with paper front and back covers fastened with two wire staples. This manual does not contain a form number nor is there a dating, however it is of prewar origin and frequent mention is made of parts applicable to products prior to 1937 and those applicable to 1937 products specifically. The cover is printed in black on off-white paper, and no copyright notice is given. R. Osterhoff Collection.
15 25 35 50

REPLACEMENT PARTS FOR LIONEL TRAINS AND ACCESSORIES: Manual issued November 1939. 90 pages, 8-1/2" x 11", no illustrations. Brown card stock cover, black ink on white paper, often designated with "Form No. 334C". Each chapter is separated by imprinted colored dividers with tabs and imprinted "Form No. 334B". Binding is with a Wilson-Jones tin, two-hole strip binder. R. Otten Collection. 25 50 75 100

REPLACEMENT PARTS FOR LIONEL TRAINS AND ACCESSORIES: Manual issued November 1939, Revised May 1941. 8-1/2" x 11". no illustrations. Cover, contents, and binding are similar to November 1939 edition with some changes in products and parts.
(A) Original. R. Otten Collection. 25 50 75 100
(B) Reproduction by Greenberg Publishing Company, 1977. Designated a reprint on cover page only; inside pages appear very similar to that of the original. — — 8 10
(C) Reproduced by Greenberg Publishing Company as part of *Greenberg's Prewar Lionel Parts and Instruction Sheets*.
— — 35 40

INSTRUCTION MANUAL FOR NO. 5B TEST SET: 1940. 8-1/2" x 11" manual, 20 numbered, illustrated, and typed pages, with Form 5B-45 identification. Provides details on proper use of Service Station Test Set. **NRS**

DEALER'S AND AUTHORIZED SERVICE STATION ORDER LIST: Date unknown, but circa 1939-40. 8-1/2" x 11", three pages, spirit-duplicated and stapled, begins with 1668E-16 armature.
NRS

LIONEL TRAINS PARTS CATALOG: Blue binder only with orange lettering and "* The Lionel Corporation — New York, New York *" on cover and "Lionel Trains" on spine. Binder contains eleven 3/4" spiral rings, and manufactured by Shyers Bookbinding Co., Newark, New Jersey, at least precluding the Zip Code. More information on this binder with probable contents requested. **NRS**

ELECTRONIC CONTROL SERVICE MANUAL: 8-1/2" wide x 11" high, 15 pages illustrated, three-hole drilled loose-leaf format. The front and back covers are tan, with white inside pages. The Table of Contents is printed on the cover, and the contents are remarkably similar to that included in the Lionel Service Manual. Although this Manual is not dated, it is believed to be a forerunner to the Service Manual itself. R. Osterhoff Collection. **NRS**

TEMPORARY REPLACEMENT PARTS LIST OF CURRENT TRAINS AND ACCESSORIES: Designated Form 775 and dated September 1, 1948. Contains 36 numbered pages, loose-leaf bound from top, and printed on spirit-duplicated pages. The front and back covers are of a heavier stock, and front cover, although typewriter prepared, was printed in black ink. A. Rubin Collection. **NRS**

LIONEL SERVICE MANUAL: Original postwar first edition, Table of Contents dated October 1, 1948. Black ink on white 8-1/2" x 11" pages, one side only, and housed in a black thick card stock Wilson-Jones three-ring binder. The binder front has "Service Manual and Replacement Parts Catalog for Lionel Trains and Accessories" imprinted in orange, as well as "Lionel" imprinted on the side binder spine. Coverage is limited, for example — only ten locomotives are included, representative of the current product line, and no prewar items are now part of the manual. R. Osterhoff Collection. **NRS**

REPLACEMENT PARTS LIST: September 1954 edition, vertical format, 8-1/2" x 11" white paper, 143 numbered pages with Table of Contents. **NRS**

LIONEL SERVICE MANUAL: Original postwar second edition, Table of Contents dated January 1, 1956. Black ink on light green 8-1/2" x 11" pages, two-sided. It is difficult to determine an exact date for the so-called second edition, but it is interesting that January 1, 1956 Table of Contents clearly indicates it is "replacing Table of Contents Issued September 1949 — a span of over six years!" There were a number of manual improvements from 1949-1962. However, an accelerated number of Manual updates were published from 1957 to 1962: 1) the Manual was expanded to two volumes, 2) A new binder was made available, this version in blue vinyl with orange lettering identical to the first edition, and 3) the binder size was increased from 1-1/2" ring to 2" ring to provide for expansion.
(A) Original. R. Osterhoff Collection. 125 175 300 400
(B) Reprint by Greenberg Publishing Co., 1984, released in four volumes and edited by I. D. Smith. Very comprehensive and includes all key service instructions from both the first and second postwar editions. — — — 100

NUMERICAL LIST OF LIONEL REPLACEMENT PARTS: List effective August 1, 1959, printed with a horizontal format, black ink on white paper with 77 numbered pages. This listing was also updated in March 1960 with several additional pages under the title "Additions, Changes and Corrections for Lionel Replacement Parts List". R. Osterhoff Collection. **NRS**

NUMERICAL LIST OF LIONEL REPLACEMENT PARTS FOR HO EQUIPMENT: List effective July 1, 1960, printed horizontally, black on white paper with a light blue cover. This listing covers HO products only, manufactured by Lionel through 1960, and includes updated pages through December 1960. A. Rubin Collection. **NRS**

INSTRUCTION MANUAL FOR NO. 5F TEST SET: 1961. 8-1/2" x 11" manual, 12 numbered, illustrated and black and white printed pages, with "Form 5F-38" imprinted on back cover. Provides details on proper use of Lionel's last Service Station Test Set.
(A) Cover in black on white paper. **NRS**
(B) Cover in black on green paper. **NRS**

NUMERICAL PARTS LIST: 1968. 7" x 8-1/2", "The Lionel Toy Corporation" in color on cover, printed on heavy glossy paper, two holes drilled. A total of 155 numbered pages with no illustrations nor narrative, printed both sides of paper. R. Otten Collection.
— — 12 16

NUMERICAL PARTS LIST: 1970. 7" x 8-1/2", "Lionel Lifetime Railroading" in color on cover, printed on heavy glossy paper, two holes drilled. A total of 119 numbered pages with no illustrations nor narrative, printed one side of paper. R. Otten Collection.
5 10 15 20

	G	VG	EXC	NEW

REPLACEMENT PARTS CATALOG FOR LIONEL: 1970. 8-1/2" x 11", blue printing on glossy white cover with "1.50" price designation on cover. Few schematic diagrams are included but no product illustrations. A. Rubin Collection.
— — — 15

REPLACEMENT PARTS CATALOG FOR LIONEL: 1972, 8-1/2" x 11", approximately 40 pages in a 1" binder with posts, green printing on a glossy white cover. Inside pages list parts plus several exploded drawings. — — 15 20

LIONEL SERVICE MANUAL: Original Third Edition, completely redesigned from the previous formats, and dated October 1977. The manual consists primarily of price listings, however there are many excellent exploded views of locomotives, rolling stock, and accessories for trains produced since General Mills began manufacturing certain items since 1970. It is also ironic that one price list contained in the manual, dated 1983, now contains American Flyer S Gauge under the banner of "Lionel Service". The manual is housed in a well-designed two-volume red binder with white printing. The initial binder has a title "Parts Manual" with a designation "Lionel of Fundimensions, A Division of the General Mills Fun Group, Inc.", whereas the second volume is designated "Volume II" and bears the designation "Lionel c 1979 Fundimensions, Division of CPG Products Corp." All inside pages are white with yellow card stock dividers. It should also be noted that the loose-leaf version was designed to be for Service Stations only; in the Manual introduction, it states "A bound edition of this manual will be released at a later date for sale to customers. This bound version will have the same information as the loose-leaf, but revisions will not be included. A new bound version will be printed each year and will only be available as a full manual."
— — 60 75

SERVICE PARTS PRICE LIST: 1981. 8-1/2" x 11", 16 bound black and white pages, designated "1982", but with date on cover of December 1981. Price of $1.00 included on cover. **NRS**

LIONEL SERVICE MANUAL: 1986 edition (Fourth Edition), published by Greenberg Publishing Company. This edition is printed in black ink on 70 lb. offset paper with over-sized holes designed for a standard 8-1/2" x 11" binder. The contents of the Third Edition were reprinted but accompanied by a new and much more elaborate index. A new page numbering system was developed. A newly designed heavy duty "D" ring loose-leaf binder is supplied. Extra binders are available. Supplements 9, 10, 11, 12, 13, and 14 have been issued for this manual. The manual is available to the general public.
— — — 45

APPROVED SERVICE STATIONS

1939-40: 6" wide x 9-1/2" high, four pages coated white stock, Form No. 331, 10-39. — 5 7 10

1946-47: 7" wide x 8-1/2" high, six-page fold-out, Form No. 331.
(A) White coated stock. — — 2 3
(B) White pulp stock. — — 2 3

1947-48: 7" wide x 8-3/4" high, white, folds out to 8-3/4" high x 22-1/2" wide, coated stock. No date on cover. **NRS**

1948-49: 7-1/2" wide x 8-3/4" high, white, folds out to 8-3/4" high x 22-1/2" wide, coated stock. — — 2 3

1949-50: 5-1/2" wide x 8-1/2" high, 12 pages coated white stock, Form 935-50M (8-49). — — 2 3

1950-51: ("August 1" above "1950" and "July 31" above "1951", front cover), 5-3/8" wide x 8-1/2" high, white, 12 numbered pages, except front and rear, coated stock, Form 927-51-TT. Smith Collection.
— 1 2 3

1951-52: 5-1/2" wide x 8-1/2" high, 12 pages coated white stock, Form 927-51. — — 2 3

1952-53: 5-3/8" wide x 8-1/2" high, 12 pages, white-coated stock, numbered, Form 927-51-TT. — 1 2 3

1952-53: 8-1/2" wide x 5-1/2" high, 12 numbered pages (except inside front cover); white-coated stock, Form 927-52-TT.
— 1 2 3

1953-54: 8-3/8" wide x 5-1/2" high, 12 pages, white-coated stock, numbered pages, except inside front cover and rear not numbered, Form 927-53-TT. Smith Collection.
(A) Heavy paper stock, Form 927-53. — 1 2 3
(B) Tissue-like paper stock, Form 927 Rev. 8-1-53.
— 1 2 3

1954-55: 8-3/8" wide x 5-1/2" high, 12 pages, white-coated stock, numbered pages, except inside front cover and rear not numbered.
(A) Form 927 Rev. 1-11-54. — — 2 3
(B) Form 927 Revised 4-19-54. — — 2 3
(C) Form 927 Revised 8-30-54. — — 2 3

1955-56: 8-1/2" wide x 5-1/2" high, 12 pages, white-coated stock, numbered pages, except inside front cover and rear not numbered.
(A) Form 927 Revised-2-28-55. — — 2 3
(B) Form 927 Revised 9-1-55. — — 2 3

1956-57: 8-1/2" wide x 5-1/2" high, 12 pages, white-coated stock, numbered pages, except inside front cover and rear not numbered, Form 927 Revised 7-30-56. — — 2 3

1958-59: 3-3/8" wide x 8" high, 12-page fold-out, pulp paper. No form number. — — 3 4

1959-60: 8-1/2" x 11" high, four pages on white glossy paper. Form No. 1893 5-59. — — 3 4

1960-61: Form unknown. Reader assistance requested. **NRS**

1961-62: Form unknown. Reader assistance requested. **NRS**

1962-63: 8-1/2" wide x 5-1/2" high, pages white-coated, four pages, pages not numbered, no form number. — — 2 3

1963-64: 8-1/2" wide x 5-1/2" high, pages white-coated, four pages, pages not numbered, no form number. — — 2 3

1964-65: 8-1/2" wide x 5-1/2" high, pages white-coated, four pages, pages not numbered, no form number. — — 2 3

1965-66: LIONEL APPROVED SERVICE STATIONS, 8-9/16" wide x 11" high, four pages, not numbered, (926-65 lower right page 1), white paper, black ink. — — 2 3

1966-67: LIONEL RACEWAY APPROVED STATIONS, 8-9/16" wide x 11" high, four pages, uncoated, black ink on yellow paper, not numbered, Form No. 5100-166. — — 2 3

1966-67: LIONEL PHONOGRAPH APPROVED STATIONS, 8-9/16" wide x 11" high, four pages, not numbered, no form number, green paper, black ink. — — 2 3

1966-67: LIONEL TRAIN APPROVED STATIONS, 8-9/16" wide x 11" high, four pages, not numbered, no form number, white paper.
— — 2 3

1968-69: LIONEL TRAIN APPROVED STATIONS, 8-9/16" wide x 11" high, four pages, not numbered, white paper, Form No. 926-68 rear lower left corner. — — 2 3

1969-70: LIONEL TRAIN APPROVED STATIONS, 8-1/2" wide x 13-7/8" high, four pages, not numbered, white paper.
— — 2 3

1971-72: 9-1/4" wide x 16" high, two pages, not numbered, no form number. — — 2 3

1976-77: 6-7/8" wide x 24" high, two pages, not numbered, no form number. — — 2 3

Chapter Six
INSTRUCTION SHEETS FOR LIONEL TRAINS: 1901-1969

One of the most challenging tasks of Lionel train collecting, perhaps second only to identifying 6464 boxcar varieties, is sorting through and identifying the myriad of instruction sheets issued by Lionel over the years. There are well in excess of six hundred different major instruction sheets, and over 1,350 total sheets including date varieties. And these figures apply only to prewar and postwar Lionel — not modern era (1970-90), although in time efforts will be made to provide a similar listing. It is doubtful if this count will ever be totally accurate, since new varieties are surfacing constantly. Come to think of it, analyzing instruction sheets is more of a challenge than taking on the 6464 task!

Packed with any reasonably complex mechanical or electrical toy is a set of instructions in some format. Lionel products are no exception, and Lionel provided these instructions often containing very fine details, and almost never missed the opportunity to include a page of advertising even on these otherwise utilitarian instructions. Instruction sheets were not dated in the early decades of Lionel history, and it was not until 1934 that Lionel formalized its instruction sheets and assigned a form number and dated the sheet with a month and year. The form number generally coincided with the number of the primary product, however the second set of digits, playing a role similar to that of a part number, did not follow a consistent or logical format.

Why did Lionel reuse an instruction sheet? Let us look at two examples to better understand why Lionel modified a sheet. For example, there are three known versions of 623-17 which applies to diesel switcher models 623 and 624. The first is dated September 1952, the second June 1953, and the third March 1954. These versions can be described as follows:

9-52 Page 3, 14 volt lamp identified as No. 151-51; Fig. 4 motor illustration "DO NOT OIL" in caps.

6-53 Page 3, 14 volt lamp identified as L363 (old number 151- 51); Fig. 4 motor illustration "DO NOT OIL" in caps.

3-54 Page 3, 14 volt lamp identified as L363 (old number 151- 51); Fig. 4 motor illustration "Do Not Oil" in caps and lower case letters.

Perhaps the printing plate type was damaged, requiring resetting the lettering (a redrawn Figure 4 illustration), however, no other content changes have been noted between the second and third instruction sheets.

An interesting study can be made of the rather common instruction sheet 022-60 which accompanied Lionel's O Gauge remote-control switches. For almost thirty years 022-60 was published, but significant changes in content occurred among the different versions. These changes included 1) the addition of a fixed voltage plug illustration, 2) the addition of illustrations on wiring the 151 semaphore and other accessories in conjunction with the switch, 3) illustration changes to update new transformer availability, and 4) the inclusion of different advertising, including

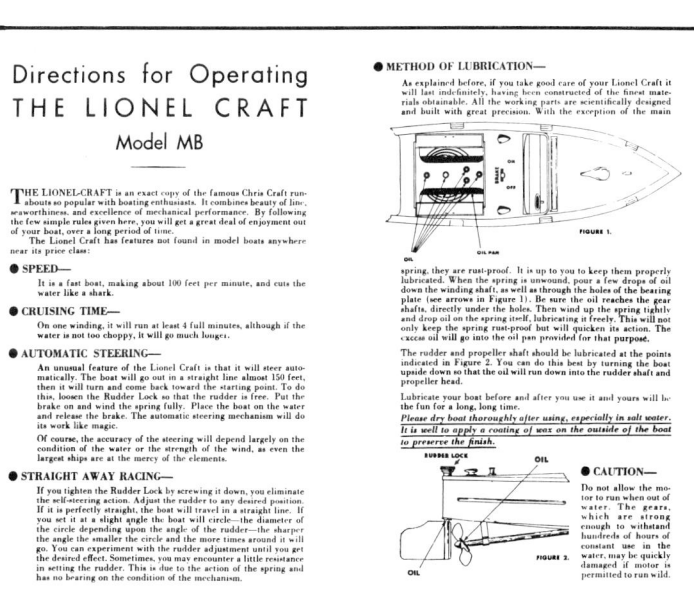

Prewar instruction sheet showing the rare Lionel boat model MB.

Postwar instruction sheet showing the Lionel operating mail car, the postman will toss the mail sack to the side of the track.

that for *Model Builder* magazine, the Bantam classic book *Model Railroading*, as well as the promotional booklets *Track Layouts* and *Romance of Model Railroading*. With thirty editions of this instruction sheet alone being issued, specializing in collecting switch instruction sheets can be an exhaustive study.

Instruction sheets can be readily distinguished by date, and in some instances, by lack of a date. However, there are other noteworthy differences: sheet color (most are printed black on white paper, but sheets do appear in blue, yellow, blue-green, green, pink, and buff); sheet size (the same instruction sheet can appear in distinctly different sizes); and advertising. Just as a boxcar collector searches for common cars in uncommon colors, an instruction sheet collector may be interested in sheet varieties. The sheet formats varied. There were three basic sheet sizes: small — 4" x 4" squares; large — a 6-7/8" x 9-3/8" vertical format for prewar; and medium — 6-1/8" x 9-3/8"

vertical format for postwar issuances. Forms range from a single sheet to six pages folded for the remote-control O Gauge switches noted above. Usually the sheets were issued one at a time with the item which they supported. However, there is at least one exception. Alan Rubin has a "Manual of Lionel Instructions", a 7-3/8" x 9-3/4" loose-leaf booklet in orange color and dated 1940, containing thirty different contemporary instruction sheets. Each instruction sheet is dated 1940, and includes dates as late as October 1940. The booklet's origin is unknown, however it provides another chapter in the instruction sheet story and may help us better understand the "paper" that Lionel prolifically published.

Inevitably, we come to the topic of value. To assign a value to each instruction sheet would be guesswork in many cases, as a market for instruction sheets did not exist until recently. However, guidelines can be established, and values can be divided into three categories, **common**, **scarce**, and **rare**. Each category requires further explanation.

COMMON: This class of instruction sheets is often found in small piles at train shows. Prices for common sheets range from 10c to $1, depending on condition. Examples of common sheets include, but are not limited to:
* Steam locomotives of the 1940s (eg. 671)
* Common small locomotives
* Common operating cars (eg. 3472 milk car, 3451 dump car)
* Common accessories (eg. 154 highway flasher, 145 Gateman, 252 crossing gate)
* Most switches, contactors, and other track items
* Transformers up to Model V
* Most controllers

SCARCE: Occasionally some scarce sheets are found in piles at train shows, but these good finds have become less frequent. A rule of thumb in determining sheet scarcity is — if the actual train item is scarce, the instruction sheet that accompanied that item is also scarce. Scarce simply means the sheet is not often seen, but certainly not impossible to locate. Like a scarce cosmetic part, one might expect to pay between $1 and $7 for a given item, and includes examples such as:
* Smaller motorized units (e.g. snowplow, trolley, etc.)
* 2000 series diesel locomotives
* Most operating cars
* Most accessories
* Models V through ZW transformers
* Better train outfits
* Layouts

RARE: It is difficult to define a "rare" instruction sheet in that there is no correlation in price/value between a rare locomotive designation, for instance, and a rare instruction sheet. Rather, the term is used only to indicate that the item is not often found, but certainly many were produced by Lionel. For instance, for purposes of this classification, a collector probably would see many more actual 773 locomotives than the actual instruction sheets for these locomotives. Yet there is no comparison in value between the two. Generally speaking a "rare" instruction sheet may bring $10 or more, but instruction sheets have even been observed being offered (or sold) well beyond a $25-$50 range. The listing in this category can be more definitive than the others, and would include the following:
* GG-1 diesel locomotives
* Scale Hudson locomotives and scale cars
* Rarer accessories (e.g. bascule bridge)
* All OO instructions
* Prewar remote-control airplane
* Dealer displays

The listing that follows is based on an enormous compilation made by Mike Ocilka with later additions by R. Hutchinson, B. Hunn, and other contributors. It provides a straightforward listing including the form number that accompanies each Lionel product, a brief product description, and the date(s) imprinted on the respective instruction sheets. Certain sheets were issued without dates, in which case an "N.D." designation is provided. This is an area where we will need continuing reader assistance, and ask that even the minor additions and/or corrections to this listing be reported for future editions. Future updates will provide studies of sheet sizes and colors, and it is also expected that a listing from 1970 to date will be added.

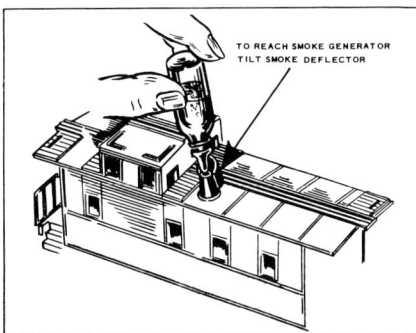

Postwar instruction sheet showing how to operate the 6557 smoking caboose.

Item #	Form #	Item Description	Date(s)

LOCOMOTIVES AND DIESEL ENGINES

Item #	Form #	Item Description	Date(s)
4U	no form	Bild-A-Loco No. 4U, 9-1/4" x 15" Bild-A-Loco No. 1	N.D.
9U	no form	Bild-A-Loco No. 4U and No. 1 Bild-A-Motor, 9-1/4" x 15"	N.D.
41	41-56	diesel switcher	8-55, 8-56, 6-57
42	42-8	diesel switcher	6-57
44/45	44-7	mobile missile launchers	9-59, 7-60
50	50-94	gang car	8-54, 10-54, 1-56, 7-57, 8-58, 9-60
51	51-56	Navy yard switcher	6-56
52	52-43	fire car	9-58, 10-58
53	53-18	snowplow	7-57, 6-58
54	54-60	ballast tamper	10-58
55	55-76	Tie-jector car	10-57
56	56-10	mining locomotive	8-58
57	57-10	A.E.C. diesel switcher	9-59
58	58-28	rotary snowplow	11-59
59	59-7	Minuteman switcher	6-62
60	60-103	trolley	8-55, 2-56
65	65-36	motorized handcar	10-62, 4-65
68	68-81	executive inspection car	10-58
69	69-14	maintenance car	8-60
—	no form	Bild-A-Loco No. 9U and 9E Bild-A-Motor	N.D.
201, 1663	201-10	steam switcher with magic electrol	9-40, 3-41
202	202-59	Alco	9-57
203, 1662	1662-11	steam switcher	6-41
205, 204	205-55	Alco	9-57, 4-58
208	208-11	Alco	5-58
211	211-6	Alco	4-62
211	211-151	Alco	6-64
212	212-59	Alco	3-58
212	212-64	Alco	4-65, 6-66
216	216-55	Alco	5-58
217	217-17	Alco	5-58, 5-59
218	218-11	Alco	4-59, 7-60
220	220-11	Alco	8-59
225	225-6	Alco	3-60
227, 228, 701	227-107	steam switcher, scale	11-39, 5-40
229	229-7	Alco	3-62
230	230-6	Alco	8-61
232, 233	232-14	steam switcher, electrol	6-40
233	233-11	steam locomotive	8-61
235	235-6	steam locomotive	8-61
236	236-11	steam locomotive	8-61
237, 238	237-11	steam locomotive	3-63, 1-65, 6-66, 4-65
239	239-18	steam locomotive	7-65
243	243-6	steam locomotive	2-60
244	244-4	steam locomotive	1-60
245	245-7	steam locomotive (246)	9-59
246	246-7	steam locomotive (246)	5-59, 3-60, 6-61
247	247-11	steam locomotive (246)	5-59
249	249-8	steam locomotive (246)	1-58, 9-58
250	250-8	steam locomotive (246)	3-57

Item #	Form #	Item Description	Date(s)
400	400-29	Budd RDC	5-56, 6-56
404	404-8	Budd RDC	5-57
600	600-28	NW-2 switcher	1-55, 7-55, 9-55
601	601-19	NW-2 switcher	4-56
602	602-19	NW-2 switcher	5-57
611	611-	NW-2 switcher	5-57
613	613-8	NW-2 switcher	5-58
614	614-6	NW-2 switcher	8-59
616	616-9	NW-2 switcher	6-61
622, 6220	622-147	NW-2 switcher	1-50
623	623-17	NW-2 switcher	1-55
623, 624	623-17	NW-2 switcher	9-52, 6-53, 3-54
626 (626, 627, 628, 629)	626-15	44 tonner	4-56, 6-56
634	634-22	NW-2 switcher	6-65, 6-66
646, 665	2035-13	steam locomotive	1-57, 7-58
646, 665, 685	2035-13	steam locomotive	8-50, 9-50, 1-54, 2-54, 6-54, 2-55, 5-66
671, 2020	671S-2	how to install heater-type smoke generators	11-47
671, 703, 726, 2020	671-135	steam locomotive	6-46
671, 2025, 2020, 675, 726	671-210	steam locomotive	3-47, 6-47 (blue and white), 1-48
671, 2025, 2020, 675, 726, 2026	671-210	steam locomotive	1-48, 12-48
675	926-25	steam locomotive	
671-210		See "2025, 2020, 675, 671, 726"	N.D.
	671-210	steam locomotive	1-48
671	671-210	steam-type locomotives	2-52
671	2035-13	steam locomotive	2-52
681	2035-13	steam locomotive	2-50, 4-50, 5-50, 7-50, 2-51, 8-50, 9-50, 7-51

Item #	Form #	Item Description	Date(s)
681, 736	681-27	steam locomotive	1-53, 5-53
682, 736	682-16	steam locomotive	4-54, 6-54, 5-55, 12-55, 11-61, 6-65
696	696	maintenance of smoke locomotives	3-48
700, 700EW	700E-285	steam locomotive Scale Hudson	10-37, 8-38, 10-40, N.D.
700KW	700K-7	instructions for assembling No. 700KW Hudson-type 4-6-4	7-38, 10-40
726	726S-4	steam locomotive smoke information	11-47
746	746-71	steam locomotive	10-57
751E	751-10M	streamline train	10-34, 11-34
763E	763E-285	steam locomotive, semi-scale Hudson	10-37, 11-38
773	773-132	steam locomotive, semi-scale Hudson	11-50, 8-64
1100	N/A	Mickey Mouse handcar	N.D.
1110	1110-16	steam locomotive, Scout	8-49
1120	1120-21	steam locomotive, Scout	6-50
1615	1615-90	steam locomotive, switcher	6-55
1664, 1666, 1668, 1688	1067E-1	steam locomotive	6-39, 8-40 (blue)
1664E, 1666E, 1668E, 1688E	1067E-100	steam locomotive	8-38
1668E	1067E-60	steam locomotive	8-37 (blue), 11-37
1681E	1062-4	steam locomotive	4-35
1688E, 1689E, 1700E, 1700	1067E-1	steam locomotive	8-36 (yellow)
1862	1800-10	steam locomotive, General	10-59
1862	1862-88	steam locomotive, General	10-59
1872	1872-71	steam locomotive, General	11-59
2016	2016-6	steam locomotive	4-55, 8-55
2018	2018-5	steam locomotive	3-56
2018	2018-11	steam locomotive	5-56, 1-57, 3-59
2023	2023-77	Alco	8-50, 9-50
2025	2025-5	steam locomotive	5-51, 10-51, 2-52
2025, 2020, 675, 671, 726, 2026	2026-61	steam locomotive	3-49, 3-51, 5-51, 10-51
2026	2026-73	steam locomotive	6-53, 6-54
2028	2028-5	GP-7	7-55
2029	2029-5	steam locomotive	5-64, 5-65
2032, 2033	2032-21	Alco	6-52, 4-53, 5-53
2035	2035-13	locomotive	2-50, 4-50, 5-50, 7-50, 8-50, 9-50, 7-51, 1-54, 2-54, 6-55, 1-57
2034	1266	steam locomotive	11-52
2034	1394	steam locomotive	11-53
2036	2036-21	steam locomotive	3-50
2037, 646, 665	2035-13	steam locomotive	6-53, 1-54, 2-55, 2-56
2037	2037-14	steam locomotive	4-57, 2-58
2037	2037-500	Girls Train Set	1-57, 9-57
2037, 637	2037-16	steam locomotive	3-59
2037, 2046, 2055, 685	2035-13	steam locomotive	6-53
2037, 2046, 2055, 685, 665	2035-13	steam locomotive	1-54
2046, 2055, 685	2035-13	steam locomotive	4-53
2056	2056-11	steam locomotive	6-52
2243	2243-4	F3 diesel	7-55, 6-56, 8-56, 5-57, 6-58
2245	2245-45	F3 diesel	6-54
2321	2321-85	FM Trainmaster	9-54, 6-55, 4-57
2322	2322-10	FM Trainmaster	6-65, 5-66
2328	2328-6	GP-7	7-55, 3-56, 4-57
2329	2329-17	E33 rectifier	7-58
2330	2330-63	GG-1	10-50
2332	2332-277	GG-1	12-47, 8-48, 7-49
2333	2333-146	F3 diesel	4-49
2337	2337-9	GP-7	6-58
2340	2340-12	GG-1	4-55
2343, 2344	2343-15	F3 diesel	4-50, 3-51, 4-52
2343, 2344	2343-160	F3 diesel	1-53
2346	2346-5	GP-9	6-65
2348	2348-14	GP-9	6-58, 8-59
2350	2350-14	EP 5 rectifier	7-56
2350, 2351	2351-14	EP 5 rectifier	4-57
2352	2352-12	EP 5 rectifier	9-59
2353	2353-53	F3 diesel	4-53, 6-53, 9-54
2360	2360-12	GG-1	3-56 (blue and white), 8-61
2365	2365-11	GP-7	6-62
2367, 2368	2367-18	F3 diesel	7-55, 7-56
2373	2373-12	F3 diesel	6-57, 6-58, 6-64
3360	3360-91	Burro crane	8-56
N/A 403, 1165, 6110	2403B-11	steam switcher and tenders	6-46, 8-48, 11-49
	6110-11	steam locomotive, Scout	8-49, 7-50, 12-50 (blue)

ROLLING STOCK

Item #	Form #	Item Description	Date(s)
219, 810	810-57	derrick car	5-36, 9-37, 11-37, 5-37
219, 810, 2810	810-57	derrick car	3-39, 9-39, 10-40
714K	714K-16	scale boxcar kit assembly	12-40
715K	715K-11	scale tank car kit assembly	12-40
716K	716K-14	scale hopper car kit assembly	12-40
717K	717K-17	scale caboose kit assembly	12-40
3309	3309-5	turbo missile car	7-62 (buff and white)
3330, 3830	3330-107	Commando submarine	8-60
3349	3349-8	turbo missile car	7-62
3356	3356-78	horse car set	9-56, 5-57, 9-64
3356	3356-112	horse car adjustment note	10-66
3357	3357-8	cop and hobo car	9-62
3359	3359-79	twin bin dump car	9-55, 12-55
3361	3361-29	lumber car	9-55, 2-56, 3-56, 6-57, 6-58
3362	3362-15	helium tank unloading car	6-61
3364	3364-10	log unloading car	4-65, N.D.
3366	3366-33	operating circus car set	5-59
3366, 3356	3366-33	operating circus and horse cars	5-59
3370	3370-17	sheriff & outlaw car	6-61
3376	3376-117	giraffe car	6-60, 1-61
3409	3409-10	helicopter launching car	5-61
3410	3410-5	helicopter launching car	6-61
3410, 3419	3419-43	helicopter launching car	9-59, 10-59
3419	3419-51	helicopter launching car	6-60, 3-61
3413	3413-8	Mercury capsule launcher	9-62
3424	3424-95	brakeman car	8-56
3428	3428-23	post office car	8-59
3434	3434-21	poultry car	8-59
3435	3435-33	aquarium car	8-59
3444	3444-33	animated gondola	5-57 (yellow), 5-59
3451	3451-27	operating log dumper	5-46, 5-47, 2-48, 4-48
3454, 3854	3454-47	merchandise car	5-46 (blue), 5-47
3459	3459-28	dumping ore car	5-46, 7-46
3459, 3451, 3559	3451-27	operating dump cars	5-47, 2-48, 4-48
3461, 3469	3461-11	operating dump cars	2-49 (blue and white), 11-49, 2-50, 3-50, 4-50, 9-50, 10-51, 2-52, 2-53, 1-54
3462	3462-67	automatic milk car	1-48, N.D.
3464	3464-28	operating boxcar	3-49 (blue and black), 1-50, 5-50, 9-50, 4-51, 10-51
3470	3470-8	aerial target launch car	8-62
3472	3472-11	automatic milk car	2-49, 11-49, 6-50, 10-50, 11-51, 2-52, 4-53
3474, 3484	3474-14	operating boxcar	5-52, 6-53, 2-56, 5-57, 8-57
3482	3482-36	automatic milk car	4-54, 6-54
3509	3509-5	satellite launching car	8-61, 4-62
3509	3509-7	flight instructions	8-61
3510	3510-5	satellite launching car	4-62
3512	3512-60	fire and ladder car	9-59
3519	3519-7	satellite launching car	8-61
3520	3520-33	searchlight car rotating	5-52, 2-53, 6-53
3530	3530-45	generator car set	11-56
3535	3535-11	operating security car	6-61
3540	3540-38	operating radar car	9-59
3559	3559-4	coal dump car	1-46, 5-46
3562	3562-54	barrel car unloading ramp	6-54, 8-54, 8-55, 4-56, 5-57

Item #	Form #	Item Description	Date(s)
3619	3619-8	recon. copter launch car	9-62
3619	3619-102	recon. copter launch car	3-63
3620	3620-14	searchlight car rotate/on/off	4-54, 4-55
3650	3650-38	searchlight extension car	7-56, 2-57, 7-57
N/A	1629	cable reel notice for 3650	N.D. (yellow or white)
3651, 3811	3651-33	operating log dump cars	8-39, 10-39, 8-40, 9-40, 3-41
3652	3652-45	remote-control gondola car	8-39, 10-39, 8-40, 3-41
3659, 3859	3659-29	operating ore dump cars	5-39, 7-40, 3-41
3659, 3859	3659-43	operating ore dump cars	9-38, 5-39, 7-40, 3-41
3656	3656-43	stock car outfit	9-49, 11-49, 9-50, 3-51, 5-51, 2-52, 5-52, 1-53, 5-54, 2-55
3662	3662-81	automatic milk car	4-55, 12-55, 2-57, 6-58, 9-64, 6-65
3665	3665-23	Minuteman missile launcher	6-61
3666	3666-20	operating Marine cannon car	8-64
3814	3814-56	merchandise unloading boxcar	10-39, 10-40
3927	3927-44	track cleaning car	8-56, 5-57 (blue and black), 8-58
3927	3927-46	cleaning fluid notice	N.D.
6361	6361-16	timber transport car	N.D.
6413	6413-8	Mercury capsule car	6-62
6448	6448-14	exploding target car	3-61
6470	6470-17	exploding boxcar	8-59 (blue and black)
6480	6480-5	exploding boxcar	4-61
6500	6500-3	Beachcraft Bonanza flat	5-62
6501	6501-14	jet motorboat car flat	7-62 (dark yellow, light yellow and white)
6512	6512-19	cherry picker car	8-62
6520	6520-23	searchlight car	5-49, 5-50
6544	6544-12	missile firing car	6-60
6557	6557-18	smoking caboose	8-58
6560	6560-26	crane car (cord replacement)	6-66
6630	6630-6	missile launcher	4-61
6650	6650-92	IRBM missile launching car	8-59, N.D.
6651	6651-10	USMC cannon car	8-64
6660	6660-58	boom derrick car	6-58
6670	6670-5	boom derrick car	4-59
6800	6800-62	airplane car flat	11-57, 2-59
6805	6805-22	radioactive waste disposal	8-58
6812	6812-22	maintenance car	8-59
6817	6817-130	A/C motor scraper	11-59
6827	6827-113	excavator load car	4-65, N.D.
6828	6828-149	crane load car	N.D.
N/A	none	P & H story	N.D.

ACCESSORIES

Item #	Form #	Item Description	Date(s)
23	23-10	illuminated lockon	5-52
26	26-18	bumper	11-48, 8-49, 4-50
30	30-11	water tower	1-47, 8-48, 5-49
38	38-62	water tower pumping	6-46
43, 44	43LF	boats	2-34, 3-35
44	44-8	operating the Lionel craft	3-37
N/A	MB	the new Lionel craft	2-34
45	45-50	Gateman	1-36
45, 045	45-50	Gateman	11-35, 10-36
45, 045	45-045	Gateman	1-36
45N	47-51	Gateman	1-42
45N	45N-1	Gateman	3-37
45N	45N-2	Gateman	10-45, 2-40
46, 47	47-51	crossing gate	10-40, 10-41, 4-41, 1-42
47	47-51	crossing gate	8-37
48W	48W-13	whistling station	9-37, 11-37, 5-38, 4-39, 4-41
65	65-35	Lionel whistle	5-36
69N	69N	warning signal	3-27
69N	69N-1	warning signal	4-38
69, 069	69-069	warning signal	5-34
75	75-15	teardrop lamps	11-61
76	76-30	warning bell and shack	8-39, 2-40
76	76-10	boulevard lamp	9-65
77N	77N-8	crossing gate	3-36, 9-37
77, 077	77-077-5M	crossing gate	5-34
78, 078	no form	auto. train control signal	N.D.
79	no form	crossing signal	N.D.
79, 83, 87	83-23	crossing signal	3-37, 3-39, 5-40
80	80-080	semaphore	N.D.
80N	80N	semaphore	3-37
80N	80N-3.X	semaphore	11-38
80N	80N-1	semaphore	9-40
80, 080	no form	semaphore	N.D.
82N	82N-1	automatic semaphore	11-38, 3-41
82N	82N-8-2	automatic semaphore	8-36
82N	82N	automatic semaphore	1-37
82, 082	82-082	automatic semaphore	5-34, 3-35
96	96-10	coal elevator, hand	11-38, 3-40
97	97-60	coal elevator, operating	11-38, 3-39, 3-41, 1-42, 1-46, 3-48, 8-49
98	98-9	elevated coal bunker	6-39
98	no form	coal tipple (transformer hook-up instructions)	N.D.
99, 099	no form	color light train control	N.D.
99N	99-27	color light train control	5-36, 1-37, 11-37
99N	99N-1	color light train control	11-38
110	110-21	trestle set	9-55, 1-56 (yellow), 1-56 (white)
110	110-30	trestle set	1-58
110, 111	110-30	trestle set	1-58, 2-59, 5-59, 1-60, 3-61
114	114-32	newsstand	8-57 (yellow)
115	115-2	passenger station	3-37, 3-38, 3-39, 10-40, 3-46, 4-48, 8-48, 3-49, 3-50
115, 116, 117	115-2	passenger station	5-36
115, 132	115-2	passenger station	3-49, 3-50
115, 132, 137	115-2	passenger station	3-46
118	118-14	newsstand with whistle	8-57 (yellow or white)
125	125-12	whistle station (shed)	8-50, 4-53
128	128-80	animated newsstand	10-57
132	132-55	passenger station w/control	1-51, 3-54
132	132-80	passenger station	1-51
133	133-7	illuminated station	5-57 (yellow), 5-61
138	138-29	water tower	6-53, 3-56
140	140-59	banjo signal	8-54
145C	145-40	contactor	10-51
148	148-13	dwarf signal	10-57
152	152-40	crossing gate	9-40, 2-41, 10-45
153	153-30	block signal	8-40, 10-45
153	153-45	block signal	4-46, 12-46
154	154-20	highway flasher	6-40, 3-41, 11-41, 10-45, 3-46, 12-46, 2-48 (blue), 2-49, 7-49, 2-50, 5-53, 4-56, 2-57 (yellow), 8-59, 4-61, 4-65
155	155-44	ringing signal	9-55
159	159-4	block control contact set	9-40, 3-41
161	161-32	mail pickup set	9-61
164	164-65	lumber (shed) loader	9-40, 3-41, 1-46, 11-46 (blue), 4-48, 7-49
165	165-80	magnetic crane	10-40, 3-41, 8-41
175	175-69	rocket launcher tower	10-58, 6-59
182	182-35	gantry crane	7-46
192	192-39	railroad control tower	10-59
193	193-24	flashing water tower	6-53
195	195-25	floodlight tower	9-57, 10-57, 9-59, 2-62, 3-65
197	197-31	rotating radar antenna	9-57, 6-58
199	199-14	microwave relay tower	10-58
253	253-43	block signal	10-56, 3-57 (yellow)
257	257-20	freight station with horn	8-56 (yellow and white)
260	260-11	bumper	8-51, 3-53 (black and blue), 2-56 (yellow, white and white), 5-57 (yellow and white)
260	260-14	bumper	2-58, 3-59, 5-62
262	262-11	highway crossing gate	8-62, 3-65
264	264-28	forklift	7-57 (yellow), 8-58
N/A	1733	cleaning 264 truck notice	9-57
282	282-99	portal gantry crane	10-54, 2-55, 7-55
299	299-14	code transmitter set	9-61
313	313-44	bascule bridge	8-47
313	313-94	bascule bridge	10-40

Item #	Form #	Item Description	Date(s)
313	313-95	bascule bridge	12-40, 4-41, 1-42, 7-46
313	313-144	bascule bridge	4-48
321	321-8	trestle bridge	9-58, 2-59
332	322-16	arch under bridge	9-59
332	332-16	arch under bridge	5-66
334	334-86	dispatch board	9-57
342	342-46	culvert pipe loader set	9-56, 4-57 (yellow)
345	345-78	culvert unloader	10-57
346	346-21	manual culvert unloader	8-64, 6-66
347	347-10	cannon firing range set	8-64
350	350-88	transfer table	11-57
352	352-44	icing station	10-55, 9-55
356	356-42	freight station	10-52, 11-52, 6-53, 6-57
362	362-96	barrel loader	10-52, 4-54, 4-55, 4-53
364	364-85	lumber loader	10-48, 1-49, 7-49, 4-50, 10-53, 2-55
365	365-10	dispatching station	3-58
375	375-76	turntable	10-62
375	375-77	turntable	N.D.
394	394-30	rotary beacon	8-49, 5-50, 9-50, 2-52
395	395-37	floodlight tower	8-49, 7-53 (blue and white)
397	397-49	coal loader	12-48
397	397-64	coal loader	2-49, 11-49, 8-52, 4-53, 5-55, N.D.
410	410-19	blinking billboard	6-56
413	413-11	countdown control panel	9-62
415	415-124	diesel fueling station	9-55
419	419-24	heliport	7-62
437	no form	switch signal tower	N.D.
438	no form	signal tower	N.D.
440, 0440	440N-2	signal bridge	11-48
440, 0440	no form	signal bridge	N.D.
440N	440N-2	signal bridge	5-38, 4-41, 9-41, 11-48
445	445-55	switch tower	1-53
448	448-6	missile firing range	8-61
450	450-42	signal bridge	10-52, 4-53, 3-54, 4-55, 12-55, 2-57
452	452-14	gantry signal	4-61
455	455-81	oil derrick	8-50, 2-51, 5-51
455	no form	electric range	N.D.
456	456-93	coal ramp set	10-50, 11-50, 3-51, 5-52, 11-52, 6-53, 8-53
460	460-70	truck transporter	10-55
462	462-26	derrick platform set	10-61
464	464-57	lumber mill	11-56
465	465-19	dispatch station	11-56
470	470-5	missile launching platform	9-59
494	494-38	rotary beacon	4-54, 8-54, 2-55, 6-55, 12-55, 9-56, 3-57 (yellow), 8-58, 6-59, 5-66
497	497-90	coaling station	4-50, 12-53
840	no form	power station	N.D.
920	920-22	scenic display set	11-57
943	943-11	exploding bunker	9-59
953	953-10	figure set	3-59
963	963-10	frontier set	3-59
970	no form	ticket office	N.D.
980	no form	ranch set	N.D.
985	985-10	freight area set	N.D.
1045	1045-15	automatic watchman	9-38, 2-39, 1-42, 8-47

TRACK, TRACK ITEMS, CONTROLLERS

Item #	Form #	Item Description	Date(s)
011, 223	223-13	O & Standard R.C. switches	3-36, 1-37
011	223-13	O & Standard R.C. switches	1-34, 3-35, 9-35, 11-36, 1-37, N.D.
022	022-60	O Gauge R.C. switches	9-38, 11-38, 5-39, 9-39, 7-40, 3-41, 6-41, 9-45, 1-46, 4-47, 3-48, 7-48, 3-49, 6-50, 9-50, 1-51, 6-51, 10-51, 2-52, 2-53, 5-53, 1-54, 1-55, 4-55, 2-56, 3-57, 8-57, 5-58, 6-59, 8-59, 6-66
022	022-60X	corrected wiring diagram	N.D.
N/A	1312	correction diagram	4-53
N/A	1322	correction diagram	4-53
022A	022A-21	O Gauge R.C. switches	N.D.
37	none	Super O uncoupling unit	N.D.
38	38-94	Super O acc. adapter track	11-57, 6-58 (yellow-orange)
39	39-2	how to assemble Super O track	9-57, 10-57, 15-58, 5-59
39	39-7	instructions for Super O track	5-59, 5-61, 2-62, 6-85
042	042-15	hand-controlled switches	12-47, 11-49, 2-51 (large and small)
042	042-37	hand-controlled switches	4-52, 5-53, 2-56, 6-59
042, 721	721-17	hand-operated switches	5-40, 1-46
112	112-160	R.C. switches for Super O	11-57, 2-58, 10-59, 4-65
142	142-157	manual switches for Super O	12-57, 10-59, 6-61
145	145-40	contactor	6-50, 9-50, 4-51, 10-51, 5-52, 6-53
—	145-51	contactor	1-54, 2-55
—	145-56	contactor	1-55, 5-55, 1-56, 2-57, 2-58, 2-55, 1-57, 7-59, 4-65
153C	153C-18	contactor	12-45, 3-46, 4-46, 11-46, 8-47
	153C-22	contactor	3-48, 7-48, 4-49 (blue and white), 6-49, 10-49, 2-50, 5-52
—	153C-23	contactor	1-51, 8-53, 2-54, 4-55, 6-57
—	452-15	contactor	4-61
223	223-13	Standard Gauge R.C. switches	1-34, 3-35, 3-36, 1-37, 4-40, 3-41
480-25	480-23	conversion couplers	1-50, 5-52, 6-54, 4-55, 8-56, 10-56, 4-65
480-32	480-23	conversion couplers	9-60
711, 731	711-83	distant control switches O72	12-35, 10-36, 7-37, 1-38, 8-38
721	721-17	hand-operated switch	7-37
1008	1721	"cam-trol" uncoupling unit notice	N.D.
RCS, 1019	RCS-8	R.C. uncoupler & unload tracks	9-38, 2-39, 7-39, 1-40, 9-40, 2-41, 11-45, 10-46, N.D.
1022	1022-38	O27 hand-controlled switches	3-41, 9-55, 2-56, 1-57 (yellow), 1-59, 3-66
1045C	1045-15	contactor	6-49
1121	1121-42	O27 R.C. switches	8-37, 11-37, 4-40, 9-40, 1-42, 1-46, 8-47, 8-49, 6-50, 3-51, 5-51
1122	1122-141	O27 R.C. switches	9-52, 10-52, 6-53
1122	1122-229	O27 R.C. switches	6-54, 11-54, 2-55, 2-56, 2-58, 8-58, 1-59, 6-57
1122	1122-253	O27 R.C. switches	9-55
1122E	1122-259	O27 R.C. switches	6-56, 1-60
—	1522	O27 R.C. switches	12-54
2001	2869	track make-up kit (O27)	6-63
2002, 2003	2870	track make-up kit (O27)	6-63
6019, UCS	6019-16	R.C. unload & uncoupler tracks	4-48, 1-49, 4-49, 7-49, 11-49, 1-50, 2-50, 4-50, 5-50, 9-50, 2-51, 3-51, 10-51, 3-52, 5-52, 8-52, 3-53, 6-53, 9-53, 1-54, 5-54, 11-54, 1-55, 12-55, 4-56, 1-57, 8-58, 6-65
6149	6149-17	R.C. track (O27)	3-65, 6-65
OSS, OCS	OCS-16	insulated track sections (O)	11-50
—	022-503	intermixing O and Super O	6-65
LTC	23-10	illuminated lockon	12-50, 5-52, 2-53, 5-53, 3-54, 4-55, 2-56, 3-59
—	no form	electro-magnetic couplers w/shields	N.D.

TRANSFORMERS

Item #	Form #	Item Description	Date(s)
1011X	1011X-13	25W 25 cycle	8-49
1015	1015-61	45W	2-60
1032, 1033	1032M, 1232 1033-68	75/90W 115/125/250V	5-48, 1-49

Instructions Sheets: 1901-1969 • 131

Item #	Form #	Item Description	Date(s)
1032M, 1033, 1232			
	1033-68	40W	5-48, 1-50 (blue and white), 4-50, 6-50, 9-50, 1-51, 3-52, 5-52, 1-53, 6-53, 1-54, 11-54, 7-55, 12-55
1034	1034-21	75W	5-48, 9-49, 1-52, 1-52
1041, 1241	1041-52	60W; 115v/200/250V	7-40, 3-41, 1-42, 1-46
1042, 1241	1042-10	75W; 115v/220V	7-46, 9-46, 2-47
1044, 1244	1044-59	90W/75W	3-56, 4-57, 5-58, 6-59, 3-65, 6-66
A	A-10	90W	4-47, 2-48
A	1.B	90W	2-34
B	B-285	75W	5-36, 12-36, 6-38, 10-38, 4-40
H	H-4	75W; 110 to 120V 24 to 40 cycles	7-38, 11-38
J	J-23	90 to 200V 40 to 123 cycle	5-38
K	K110-79	150W	2-37, 5-38
K	K110	150W 5-50	
KW	20-97	190W	9-50, 6-51, 10-51, 6-53, 6-54, 3-55, 1-57, 6-58, 7-59
LW	22-86	125W	5-55, 12-55, 1-57, 1-58, 6-59, 6-60, 3-65
Q	Q-24	75W	9-39, 4-40, 3-41, 4-41, 1-42, 1-46
R	R-72	100W	9-39, 11-39, 4-40, 3-41, 1-42, 1-46, 4-46, 9-46
R	R-72	110W overprinted	9-46
R	R-42	110W	6-47, 9-50
R	SE-13	two-train operation w/Type R	1-46
RW	RW-43	110W	2-48, 12-48, 2-50, 5-50, 9-50, 5-51, 5-52, 6-53
RX	RX-31	110W	2-51, 8-51
S, S220	S-47	Sears 80W 25 cycle	8-47, 11-47
SR	SR-4	75W	9-39, 2-40
SW	25-36	130W	4-66
T	none	(booklet) 100W	N.D. (blue)
T	T-148	100W	5-36, 12-36, 10-38, 11-38, 5-38
TW	21-80	175W	9-53, 8-54, 3-55, 12-55, 5-57, 5-58, 6-59
V	V-80	150W	8-40
V, Z	V-166	150/250W	5-47
VW, ZW	ZW-134	150/250W	7-48, 2-49
W	W-44	75W	3-38, 5-39, 9-39, 2-40
Z	Z-80	250W	8-40, 9-45
ZW	ZW-134	275W	7-48, 1-50, 5-50, 1-51, 3-51, 5-51, 10-51, 5-52, 1-53, 1-54, 4-54, 4-55, 4-56, 1-57, 5-57, 7-58, 8-59
ZW	ZW-251	275W	1-61
ZW220	ZW-227	275W/220V	5-57

TRAIN OUTFITS

Item #	Form #	Item Description	Date(s)
—	111-18	father-son twin railroads	6-60
—	122-10	train outfit	5-62
—	126-10	incl. 3419, 3665	5-62
—	126-10	train outfit	5-62
—	502-10	train outfit	5-55, 3-56
—	610-2	for 248 uncat. set	7-58
—	704-10	train outfit	6-58, 6-59
—	1067E	operating Lionel O27 trains	11-37, 8-38, 6-39
—	1067E	Lionel junior electric trains	8-36
—	1105-10	train outfit	8-59
—	1109-10	train outfit	3-60
—	1110-11	train outfit (Scout)	5-51
—	1110-16	train outfit (Scout)	8-49
—	1123-10	train outfit	3-61
—	1125-10	train outfit	4-61
1465	1465-10	train outfit	4-52
1465	1465-11	train outfit	8-52
1500	1500-10	train outfit	3-53, 3-54
—	1501S	train outfit	8-53
1569	1569-11	train outfit	6-57
1569	1569-13	train outfit	9-57, 3-58
—	1581-11	train outfit	8-57
1595	1595-10	train outfit	6-58
1609	1609-4	train outfit	4-59
1611	1611-10	train outfit	8-59
1612	1612-10	train outfit	10-59

Item #	Form #	Item Description	Date(s)
1613S	1613-10	train outfit	5-59
1627	1627-2	train outfit	1-60
1642	1642-10	train outfit	6-61
1646	1646-10	train outfit	6-61 (blue-green)
1648	1648-10	train outfit	5-61
1649	1649-10	train outfit	6-61
5719	5719-15	train outfit	8-59
—	5719-15	HO train outfit	3-59
5732	5732-10	train outfit	8-59
5750	5750-10	train outfit	5-61
—	5809-10	train outfit	6-61
—	9670-10	train outfit	6-61
—	9656-10	train outfit	8-62
11385	11385-10	train outfit	6-63
11430	11430-10	train outfit	6-64
11450	11450-10	train outfit	6-64, 6-65
11460	11460-10	train outfit	4-65
11530	11530-10	train outfit	6-65
11600	11600	train outfit	2-68
12700	12700-10	train outfit	8-64
19142	19142-10	train outfit	8-62 (green)
19230	19230-10	train outfit	6-63
19394	19394-10	train outfit	8-64
19442	19442-10	train outfit	4-65
—	no form	Lionel junior electric trains	N.D.

CONTROLLERS

Item #	Form #	Item Description	Date(s)
—	8X-91	prewar circuit breaker	10-37
—	91-6M	prewar circuit breaker	11-34
—	91-20	prewar circuit breaker	2-37, 10-38, 3-39
—	none	rheostat	N.D.
—	I.F. 95	rheostat	1-35
—	form 95	rheostat	3-37
—	95-3	rheostat	5-36, 5-39, 1-42
65	65-35	whistle controller	8-35
66, 67	66-2	whistle controller	6-36, 8-37, N.D.
80	2085	reversing controller	3-60
81	none	rheostat	N.D.
91	none	prewar circuit breaker	N.D.
91	91-37	postwar circuit breaker	10-57, 11-59
92	92-22	circuit breaker-controller	11-59
01, 02	1807	transformer/circuit breaker	0-59
95	95-27M	rheostat	3-34
107, 170	107-170	DC current reducers	4-34
166	166-4	whistle controller	9-38
166	166-80	whistle controller	8-41
167	167-29	whistle controller	8-39, 4-42, 1-46
167C	167-55	whistle controller	4-47, 9-47, 2-50, 6-53, 8-54
171, 172	171-2	DC to AC inverters	11-36, 9-37, 8-39
480-25	480-23	conversion couplers	1-50, 5-52, 12-52, 4-53, 6-54, 4-55, 4-56, 8-56, 10-56, 3-57
480-32	480-23	conversion couplers	9-60

LIONEL HO

Item #	Form #	Item Description	Date(s)
0039	0039-61	track cleaning car	10-61 (blue)
0056	0056-23	Husky diesel switch locomotive	9-60 (blue), 9-59 (blue)
0100	0100-53	power pack	10-57, 5-60
0101	0101-72	power pack	9-58, 8-59, 6-61
0102	0102-20	power pack	10-58
—	0909-62	aligning HO track	9-62
0103	0103-17	power pack	4-61 (blue)
0104	0104-57	power pack	10-61
0110	0110-19	trestle set	8-59
0140	0140-35	banjo signal	7-62
0145	0145-35	automatic gateman	10-59
0197	0197-28	radar antenna	9-58, 9-59
0300	0300-7	operating cars	6-60
0319	0319-22	operating helicopter car	8-60
0333	0333-12	operating satellite car	7-61
0337	0337-120	giraffe car	8-61
0349	none	turbo missile car	N.D.
0357	0357-33	cop & hobo car	9-62

Item #	Form #	Item Description	Date(s)
0365	0365-32	Minuteman missile car	9-62
0366	0366-44	unloading milk car	9-61 (blue)
0370	0370-29	sheriff and outlaw car	9-62
0390C	0390-51	controller for HO	N.D.
0470	0470-5	missile launching platform	7-60
0494	0494-28	rotating aircraft beacon	11-59
0535	0535-34	diesel locomotive	10-62
0545	0545-8	GE 44 tonner	8-61
0561	0561-16	rotary snowplow	10-59
0565	0565-83	Alco diesel	8-59, 9-59, 3-61
0568	0568-5	Alco diesel	8-62
0569	0569-5	Alco diesel	4-63
0594	0594-51	GP-9	7-65
0602	0602-65	steam switcher	9-60
0605	0605-6	steam switcher	10-59
0625	0625-83	steam locomotive	11-59
0626	0626-20	steam locomotive	11-59
0635	0635-48	steam locomotive	10-61
0636	0636-20	steam locomotive	6-63
0642	0642-40	steam locomotive	6-62
0643	0643-20	steam switcher	6-63
0647	0647-36	steam locomotive	5-66
0712	0712-26	passenger car	10-61
0847	0847-23	exploding target car	6-60
0850	0850-19	missile launching car	N.D.
0879	0879-10	wrecker crane	12-58
0922	0922-11	remote-control switches	4-59
0922	0922-25	remote-control switches	3-61 (blue)
0961	0961-7	illuminated bumper	9-61
390C	390-51	HO controller	N.D.
—	407-10	HO train outfit	5-62
5732	5732	HO train outfit	N.D.
5750	5750-10	HO train outfit	5-61
5754	5754-10	HO train outfit	6-61, 10-62
—	2523	control and operating accessory for HO	N.D.
5700	5700-7	simple HO layouts	9-57
5700	5700-8	HO trains	9-57
5700	5700-60	HO instruction booklet	N.D.

LIONEL OO GAUGE

Item #	Form #	Item Description	Date(s)
0046K	0046K-4-1.1X	hopper car kit	5-39
0047K	0047K-4-1.1X	caboose kit	5-39
0072	0072-72-2.2X	R.C. switches (three-rail)	12-39
001E	001E-290-3.5	set up and operating instructions	11-38
001E	001E-290-VLX	set up and operating instructions for three-rail track	6-40
003	003-39-XEX	set up and operating instructions for two-rail track	10-39, 6-40

MISCELLANEOUS

Item #	Form #	Item Description	Date(s)
ST-350	1298	riveting set	3-53 (blue)
ST-350	ST350-24	riveting set	N.D. (pink)
50	50-81	remote-control airplane	10-36
55	55-2	remote-control airplane	6-37
570	570-32	Linex stereo camera	11-53
—	671-2	smoke pellet notice	11-47
861	861-52	Helios 21 space ship	9-64
—	926-3	lubrication notice	4-40, 11-45 (red ink)
—	926-15	lubrication notice	10-46
—	926-25	lubrication notice	N.D.
—	926-26	lubrication notice	4-50, 2-51
—	927-14	how to clean and lubricate	1954
—	928-13	lubrication notice	8-60 (pink)

Item #	Form #	Item Description	Date(s)
—	1123-40	maintaining efficient pulling power	2-61 (blue), 2-62 (white and blue)
—	1267	notice (362 voltage)	11-52
—	1268	lamp replacement notice	12-52
—	1465-11	lubrication notice	8-52 (card stock)
—	1574	battery replacement in GPs	10-55
—	1629	cable end notice	N.D.
—	1927	wheel lubrication	N.D.
—	2872	racing car set clips instructions	5-63
—	5159-22	how to clean & lubricate	3-65
—	5457-27	flag tag relay racing kit	7-64
6100	6100-10	HO Raceway game	7-61
—	17030-5	Raceway 99	6-63
—	17155-10	speedway	8-63
—	17215-10	Pikes Peak auto relay set	8-64
—	17215-15	Pikes Peak auto relay set	11-64
44000	44000-88	four-speed elec. phonograph	4-62
44050	44050-41	four-speed elec. phonograph "Talking Teddy"	5-62
44516	44516-26	four-speed transistorized phonograph (Sears models 679 & 680)	9-65
—	no form	method of assembling and attaching lamp & socket	N.D.
—	no form	directions for assembling Lionel Bild-A-Loco	N.D.
—	no form	directions for assembling Lionel Bild-A-Loco	N.D.
—	no form	diagram for wiring access to Lionel display No. 10	N.D.
—	100X	lubrication notice	2-39
—	ECU-50	electronic set	N.D.
—	1-66	Scout tender electrically ground replacement truck	6-64

SHOWROOM DISPLAYS AND LAYOUTS

Item #	Form #	Item Description	Date(s)
—	2094	special track layout instructions	6-60
—	1802-10	special track layout instructions	8-64
—	1802A	special layout instructions	N.D.
—	1802B	special layout instructions	6-59
—	1841	5' x 9' Lionel O27 showroom display for two-train operation	3-59
D-192	D-192-25	assembly of Super O display	7-57
D-224	D-224-31	assembly of Super O display	6-58
D-292	D-292-30	Lionel 8' x 8' Super O display	8-60
—	1751	template for Super O layout	12-57
—	1854	template for Super O layouts	12-58
—	no form	method of assembling and attaching lamp and socket	N.D.
—	no form	directions for assembling Lionel Bild-A-Loco	N.D.
—	no form	directions for assembling Lionel Bild-A-Loco	N.D.
—	no form	diagram for wiring access to Lionel display No. 10	N.D.
—	1749	panorama display	11-57
—	2228	template for Super O layout	11-60
—	1823	display layout	N.D.
D-288	no form	Lionel lion display	N.D.
D-133	D133-B	assembly of dealer display	N.D.
—	1651	two-train operation instructions	N.D.
—	1841	O27 two-train operation	11-58
D-132	no form	view and wiring diagram	N.D.
D-162	D162-10	view and wiring diagram	4-56
—	1946	template for Super O layout	12-59
—	1943	template for Super O layout	12-59
—	2227	template for Super O layout	11-60
—	1942	template for Super O layout	12-59

Chapter Seven
BILLBOARDS

Next to the consumer catalogue, Lionel's miniature billboards are perhaps the most recognized items of Lionel paper ever produced. Millions of these clever advertisements were issued for well over a half century, and even today Lionel Trains, Inc. sees a value in continuing the tradition. It is believed a study of Lionel paper would not be complete without including these miniature works of art.

This listing is the first to incorporate prewar, postwar, and modern era into a story of America's advertising evolution. We begin by sharing new information on the few billboards produced for the prewar era. The postwar section included represents some additions to the outstanding work accomplished by I. D. Smith and Don Corrigan, which appeared in *Greenberg's Guide to Lionel Trains, Volume II*, First Edition. The modern era is the third update of billboards produced by Lionel since 1970.

In the past, prices were not assigned to billboards, although this material frequently appears on the market. Perhaps some day all items will be priced, but we will leave that list for a future project. Included instead are a few general guidelines which may be useful to the collector.

PREWAR

The forerunner of Lionel's promotional layout billboards is a set of Standard Gauge billboards that were offered by Lionel free for two months, from late 1932 until February 10, 1933. This set, each billboard of which was printed on heavy card stock, measures 6-1/4" from the base to the top of "Great Outdoor Adv. Co." The width of the sign itself (not including the foliage at the bottom) is 9-1/3". There is an exception to these sizes. Several boards have been observed as measuring just less than 6" tall, and are distinctly shorter than the other boards in their respective sets.

This limited offer was extended to those who enrolled — for 50 cents annually — in the Lionel Engineers Club. There has been confirmed two separate sets of four billboards, but it is not known if both were sent in response to Lionel's promotion offer.

Set 1 — Lifebuoy Soap, Black Jack Gum, Ipana Tooth Paste, and Vitalis Hair Oil. Battley and Osterhoff Collections.

Set 2 — Shredded Wheat, Uneeda Bakers (National Biscuit Company), Sunkist, and Coca Cola. A. Rubin Collection.

Prewar billboards were issued individually and did not come in attached sheets. The value for each set of four ranges from $50 to $150, depending on condition.

Prewar Lifebuoy and Black Jack Gum billboards.

Two unusual prewar billboards, Ipana tooth paste and Vitalis.

POSTWAR

The following writeup originally appeared as written by I. D. Smith, with major contributions from the research of Don Corrigan. Updated information has also been included by the author. Mr. Corrigan's original research was published in the Spring 1980 issue of the Train Collector's Quarterly, and it should be noted he was aided in his research by J. E. Felber, Jim Gates, Bill Mekalian, George Shewmake, Don Simonini, and Joe Snuggs.

In his original study, I. D. Smith listed the page number of the catalogues where the No. 310 Billboard is listed, the number of plastic frames, and the number of billboards or posters noted in the catalogue as a set for that year. Following this, if there were possible billboards shown in the catalogue, listed were those pages on which they appear. Obvious advertisements on particular sets or train features printed inside the green billboard frame picture were not included.

Many single billboards are available for an average of 25 cents each. Collectors however prefer to obtain complete, intact sheets by year, similar in format to those illustrated in this chapter. Prices for complete sheets of billboards vary by year, and average from $10 in the early 1960s to over $20 in the early postwar years of billboard issuance. Unique billboards or those previously believed not manufactured can of course bring a substantial figure that only the buyer and seller can agree on. This aspect of collecting nevertheless remains fairly inexpensive but

challenging — and a great insight into Americana spanning many decades of history.

Beginning in 1949, Lionel offered a billboard assortment, the No. 310. The assortment consisted of an uncut sheet of eight different billboards. In 1950 the billboard assortment usually consisted of five green unpainted plastic frames with an uncut sheet of different billboards. In 1950 ten different billboards were offered. Later this was reduced to eight, six, and in the later years to three different billboards.

The billboards made through 1956 include the words "Standard" in white letters with black background. Thereafter "Standard" was dropped from the sign. Many different billboard advertisements were offered. It appears that there were partial annual changes in the billboards as shown each year in the Lionel catalogues starting in the 1950s. In later years, changes in billboards show up on other catalogue pages. The dating of these billboards has been based on the Lionel catalogues and uncut dated billboard sheets.

Mr. Corrigan states that "a complete billboard collection consists of 15 sheets containing 104 boards, 73 of which are different. This includes two almost duplicate sheets, one for 1951-52 and one for 1953." It may be that our readers have reliable source information that will contradict or supplement these billboard dates, and readers' comments are welcomed. It is very important to note the date that appears on uncut billboard sheets which will aid in establishing and verifying other billboard set dates as well as those that were never made.

In describing these signs, the exact words and spelling including upper and lower case letters are noted as they appear on the sign. Additional words have been added to aid in the proper identification.

Mr. Corrigan also provides the following comments from his research efforts: "Item numbers 9, 21, 38, 40, 68, 86, 87, and 90 were never produced, at least for the consumer market. These generally were pre-production mock-ups, used for their Lionel catalogues and the showroom and dealer layouts; some probably were never made. The number produced may never be known, given the transient nature of these layouts. I have never actually seen one but have several photos in which boards like these appear.

"Item 80 was produced in HO, and it was made to be used with the 6100 race set. Item 89 was never produced. As for the Lionel Porter and Spear phonograph boards, I am certain they were never made."

This listing does not include any of the small-sized HO or raceway game Lionel billboards. Many of those were reduced sizes of the No. 310 billboards.

Editor's Note: Items referred by an asterisk (*) in the Postwar listing indicate comments by Don Corrigan.

1949

Although not catalogued, the billboards for 1949 were available through a special catalogue offer, the ads for which appeared in various magazines. The 1949 catalogue offer included the billboards, the consumer catalogue, a sound effects record, and a train layout planning book for "Pop." The billboard ads included Ford, Lionel

These two uncut Lionel Billboards are from 1949 *(left)* and 1950 *(right)*. D. Corrigan Collection and photograph.

Construction Sets, Kleenex, Nash, Baby Ruth, Wrigley's Spearmint, Kellogg's, and Heinz Soup, identical to one in the 1951 sheet.*
The following billboards have been observed:
1: LIONEL Construction Kits (shows boy with wrecker truck built from kit), Std.
2: DROF (FORD mirror imaged) (shows man, boy, and dog looking through window with **DROF** on window), Std.
3: FRESH Kellogg's CORN FLAKES (shows box of Corn Flakes on right, bowl with bananas on left), Std.
4: He'll only chase a Nash (shows black dog on right, two girls on left), Std.
5: Your nose knows, your best buy in tissues! (shows box of Kleenex Tissues on right; girl pointing to her nose on left), Std.
6: Compare . . . and you'll know they're better; Heinz Soups (bowl of tomato soup with can of Heinz Tomato Soup), Std.
7: Enjoy Chewing Wrigley's SPEARMINT GUM (with light green background) (man with hat placing piece of gum to his mouth), Std.
8: Slice and Serve, Baby Ruth (candy bar shown partly in wrapper with slices falling into dish), **Another CURTISS Candy**, Std.

1950

This was the first year the billboards were catalogued. Ads included those for Ford, Wrigley's, Silver Springs, Nash, Plymouth, Baby Ruth, DuPont Anti-Freeze, and Northern Tissue. They came in a sheet of eight, two wide by four deep.* Billboards appeared on page 41 of the 1950 Consumer Catalogue (five frames, eight billboards).
9: AMERICA'S BIG THREE: GRAND CANYON, NIAGARA FALLS, SILVER SPRINGS (American flag design in red, white, and blue), Std.

8: Slice and Serve, Baby Ruth (candy bar shown partly in wrapper with slices falling into dish), **Another CURTISS Candy**, Std.
10: Get a DUPONT ANTI-FREEZE, ZEREX, ZERONE $3.50-1.25, Std.
7: Enjoy Chewing Wrigley's SPEARMINT GUM (with light green background) (man with hat placing piece of gum to his mouth), Std. This billboard previously appeared in 1949 as number 7.
11: Wow! FORD V-8 (bear with tree), Std.
12: GREAT CARS SINCE 1902 NEW Nash . . . RAMBLER (ad shows old car and current model), Std.
13: YOUR PLYMOUTH DEALER INVITES YOU TO DRIVE THE NEW PLYMOUTH 1950 (blue car, red background), Std.
14: Snowy-Soft made with "FLUFF" NORTHERN TISSUE (ad shows dog and boy on red sled), Std.
Catalogued, but not manufactured:
LIONEL MAGNE-TRACTION GIVES YOU MORE SPEED, MORE PULL, MORE CLIMB, MORE CONTROL (1950 red and silver Santa Fe with part of second diesel unit, blond-haired boy).

1951

Lionel expanded the sheet to ten billboards this year. Plymouth, Wrigley's, Hallicrafters, Heinz Soups, Frigidaire, Baby Ruth, Atlantic Gas, Silver Springs, General Tires, and DuPont Anti-Freeze were illustrated. The DuPont prices changed this year.* Billboards appeared on page 31 of the 1951 Consumer Catalogue (five frames, 10 billboards).
8: Slice and Serve, Baby Ruth (candy bar shown partly in wrapper with slices falling into dish), **Another CURTISS Candy**, Std.
9: AMERICA'S BIG THREE: GRAND CANYON, NIAGARA FALLS, SILVER SPRINGS (American flag design in red, white, and blue), Std.

These two uncut Lionel Billboards are from 1951 *(left)* and 1952 *(right)*. D. Corrigan Collection and photograph.

15: Get a DUPONT ANTI-FREEZE, ZEREX, ZERONE $3.75-1.50, Std.
16: Level best on the roughest roads, NEW PLYMOUTH (green Plymouth; man, woman, and dog in car), Std.
6: Compare . . . and you'll know they're better; Heinz Soups (bowl of tomato soup with can of Heinz Tomato Soup), Std.
17: Made for once-a-week shopping. The new FRIGIDAIRE, SEE YOUR FRIGIDAIRE DEALER (open refrigerator in center of yellow background), Std.
18: Safe Traveling, THE GENERAL TIRE, SEE YOUR GENERAL TIRE DEALER (shows tire on right, squaw and papoose on left), Std.
19: I'm a television cameraman . . . and in my home we have Hallicrafters. (shows TV on right, man on left), Std.
20: Enjoy Wrigley's Spearmint Gum daily-chewing aids teeth, breath, digestion (shows pack of gum lower right of billboard), Std.
21: Keeps your car on the go ATLANTIC (shows waterway with city in background, red and white Atlantic sign), Std. This billboard does not appear in the 1951 catalogue but is part of the uncut 1951 sheet from the D. Corrigan Collection.
Catalogued, but not manufactured:
WOW! ITS A "LIONEL" (shows blond-haired boy on floor with steam engine, dog, part of passenger car, automatic gateman).

1952

Ten billboards were again offered this year. The sheet at first was printed as being for 1951, but it was later changed to 1952. Products included were Plymouth, Wrigley's, Sunsweet Prunes, Heinz Beans, Frigidaire, Baby Ruth, DuPont Anti-Freeze, Sunoco High-Test, Silver Springs, and General Tires.* Billboards appeared on page 33 of the 1952 Consumer Catalogue (five frames, 10 billboards).
22: HEINZ OVEN-BAKED BEANS (shows blond-haired boy holding a plate of beans on left and can on right), Std.
23: You mean you haven't seen FLORIDA'S SILVER SPRINGS! (shows baby's face on left), Std.
24: WRIGLEY'S SPEARMINT for real chewing enjoyment (shows pack of gum), Std.
25: SUNSWEET good to feel good! (lady in two-piece white sunsuit on beach; box of Sunsweet Prunes on right), Std.
26: HIGH-TEST at regular gas price BLUE SUNOCO ANTI-KNOCK PERFORMANCE! (shows man on left winking, red arrow Sunoco sign), Std.
8: Slice and Serve, Baby Ruth (candy bar shown partly in wrapper with slices falling into dish), **Another CURTISS Candy,** Std.
27: Shelves roll out . . . All the way! CYCLA-MATIC FRIGIDAIRE Automatic Defrosting! SEE YOUR FRIGIDAIRE

These two uncut Lionel Billboards are from 1953 *(left)* and 1954 *(right)*. D. Corrigan Collection and photograph.

DEALER (shows refrigerator on left and closer view of roll-out shelves on right), Std.
29: Straight to the Point . . . TOP QUALITY, SEE YOUR GENERAL TIRE DEALER, THE GENERAL TIRE (shows tire on right, dog on left), Std.
30: VOTE FOR VALUE Plymouth (shows red X by word Plymouth, Plymouth car on right side of billboard), Std.
15: Get a DUPONT ANTI-FREEZE, ZEREX, ZERONE $3.75-1.50, Std.

1953

The sheet was reduced to eight billboards again, the start of a continued reduction throughout the remaining years. Plymouth, Wrigley's, Coca-Cola, Heinz, Frigidaire, DuPont Anti-Freeze, Sunoco, and Silver Springs were made. There are three different versions of this billboard. One version has "Outside Trim..." printing on the left border of the sheet with a poster for Heinz Ketchup. A second has Heinz Beans rather than Heinz Ketchup but without "Outside Trim..." printing on the left border of the sheet. The third version has Heinz Beans with "Outside Trim..." Billboards appeared on page 33 of the 1953 Consumer Catalogue (five frames, eight billboards); also see page 21.
31: Travel refreshed. DRINK Coca-Cola IN BOTTLES (shows train engineer drinking a bottle of Coca-Cola, portion of steam locomotive to right), Std.
32: NO SHIFTING! NEW PLYMOUTH HY-DRIVE (shows new Plymouth blue convertible), Std.
15: Get a DUPONT ANTI-FREEZE, ZEREX, ZERONE $3.75-1.50, Std.
33: WRIGLEY'S SPEARMINT CHEWING GUM (shows earth in background with infinite packs of gum coming from earth. Planet Saturn also shows in background), Std.

34: Save at Sunoco, Tires and Batteries (shows Kelly tire on left, Sunoco battery center, SUNOCO yellow sign with red arrow pointing to the left), Std.
35: Relax now! at FLORIDA'S SILVER SPRINGS (shows lady in two-piece red swimsuit on beach), Std.
36: Cycle-matic FRIGIDAIRE Food Freezer-Refrigerator YEARS AHEAD (shows open refrigerator on left), Std.
22: HEINZ OVEN-BAKED BEANS (shows blond-haired boy holding a plate of beans on left and can on right), Std. This billboard does not appear in the 1953 catalogue, but Weaver Collection ties this billboard to 1953.
37: RED MAGIC, HEINZ Ketchup (shows bottle of Heinz Tomato Ketchup, a hamburger with pickles on a plate), Std. This billboard does not appear in the 1953 catalogue, but is part of a 1953 uncut sheet from the D. Corrigan Collection.
Catalogued, but not manufactured:
LIONEL "O" GAUGE plus LIONEL MAGNE-TRACTION, MORE PULL, MORE SPEED, MORE POWER.

1954

A sheet of eight billboards was offered this year. Products advertised were Lipton Tea, Wrigley's, New Departure Safety Brakes, Campbell's Soups, Sunoco, Fram Filters, Breck Shampoos, and DuPont Anti-Freeze. Again changed were the DuPont prices. Zerex was priced at $2.95 and Zerone at $1.50.*
The Distributor's Advertising Promotions Catalogue, page 14, shows eight billboards.
These billboards were shown in the Accessories Catalogue, page 8, with five frames and eight billboards. Billboards also appeared in the Consumer Catalogue, page 40 (five frames, eight billboards).
38: Change now for LONG Mileage (shows service station man on right holding in his hand on left side of billboard a can of Sunoco Dynalube Motor Oil), Std.

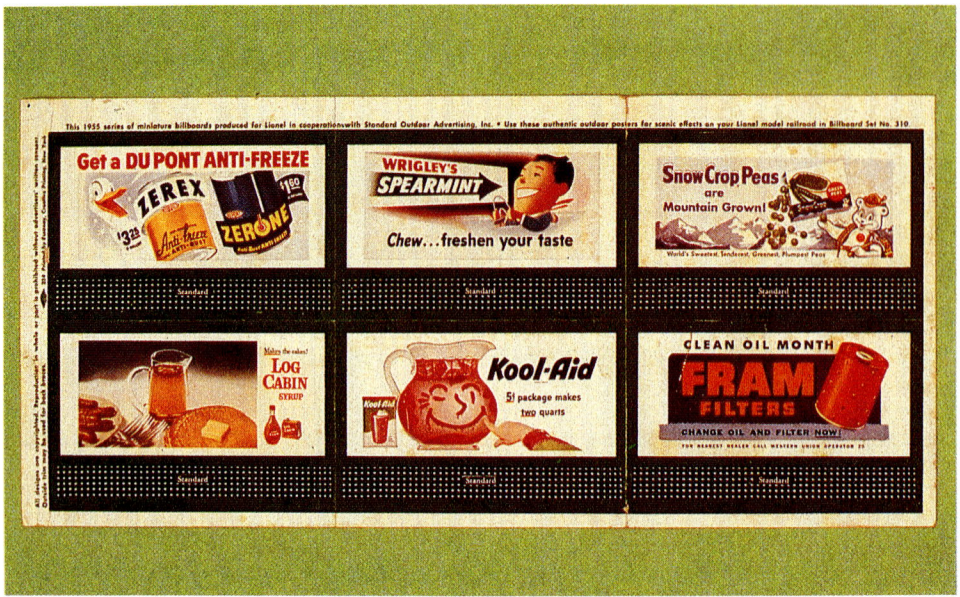

This uncut sheet of Lionel Billboards cover both 1955 and 1956. D. Corrigan Collection and photograph.

39: GET a DUPONT ANTI-FREEZE ZEREX-ZERONE $2.95/$1.50, Std.
40: BRECK Beautiful Hair THREE BRECK SHAMPOOS (shows woman and hair trademark in center and bottles of shampoo on left side), Std.
41: NEW DEPARTURE, Safety Brake, STEER WITH YOUR HANDS STOP WITH YOUR FEET (shows brake on right, boy riding red bike on left), Std.
42: It's Still Clean FRAM — OIL — AIR — FUEL — WATER FILTERS (shows service man looking at clean oil on oil dip stick, filter on right, yellow background), Std.
43: Campbell's SOUPS MMM, GOOD! (shows can of Campbell's Tomato Soup on right, Campbell's chef on left, yellow background), Std.
44: WRIGLEY'S SPEARMINT GUM (man holding a car steering wheel. On bottom:) **Chew — freshen your taste**, Std.
45: Coolest drink under the sun LIPTON ICED TEA (shows tall glass of iced tea on left, man sitting on grass holding glass of iced tea and leaning against push lawn mower; box of Lipton Tea pictured in lower right corner), Std.

1955

The sheet was reduced to six this year. Ads for Wrigley's, Snow Crop Peas, Log Cabin Syrup, Kool-Aid, Fram Filters, and DuPont Anti-Freeze were made. The DuPont prices changed for a last time, with prices for Zerex and Zerone now at $3.25 and $1.60 respectively.* Billboards appeared on page 38 of 1955 Consumer Catalogue (five frames, eight billboards) with additional illustrations on page 19. There were only six produced.
46: SNOW CROP PEAS are Mountain Grown (shows package of frozen peas with peas spilling out left end; bear on right), Std.
47: Makes the Cakes! LOG CABIN SYRUP (shows picture of sausage, forks, pitcher of syrup, pancakes with butter; bottle and tin of syrup lower right), Std.
48: FRAM FILTERS (shows red filter on right) **CLEAN OIL MONTH CHANGE OIL AND FILTER NOW!**, Std.
49: Get a DUPONT ANTI-FREEZE ZEREX-ZERONE (catalogue illustration does NOT show prices. However, actual billboard shows $3.25/$1.60), Std.
44: WRIGLEY'S SPEARMINT GUM (man holding a car steering wheel. On bottom:) **Chew — freshen your taste**, Std.
50: Kool-Aid, .05 package makes two quarts (shows package of Kool-Aid lower left. Pitcher of Kool-Aid with happy face being drawn by finger), Std.
Catalogued, but not manufactured:
Only LIONEL has MAGNE-TRACTION, MORE SPEED — MORE POWER — MORE CLIMB (shows boy on left), Std.
LOG CABIN SYRUP (shows bottle and famous "Log Cabin Tin" of Syrup).

1956

Lionel did not produce a new sheet for this year, with the catalogue showing the 1955 billboards. It is assumed the 1955 sheet was offered both years.* Billboards appeared on page 34 of the 1956 Consumer Catalogue (five frames, six posters) with references also on pages 13 and 23.
46: SNOW CROP PEAS are Mountain Grown (shows package of frozen peas with peas spilling out left end; bear on right), Std.
47: Makes the Cakes! LOG CABIN SYRUP (shows picture of sausage, forks, pitcher of syrup, pancakes with butter; bottle and tin of syrup lower right), Std.
48: FRAM FILTERS (shows red filter on right) **CLEAN OIL MONTH CHANGE OIL AND FILTER NOW!**, Std.
49: Get a DUPONT ANTI-FREEZE ZEREX-ZERONE (catalogue illustration does NOT show prices. However, actual billboard shows $3.25/$1.60), Std.
44: WRIGLEY'S SPEARMINT GUM (man holding a car steering wheel. On bottom:) **Chew — freshen your taste**, Std.
50: Kool-Aid, .05 package makes two quarts (shows package of Kool-Aid lower left. Pitcher of Kool-Aid with happy face being drawn by finger), Std.

1957

The design of the billboards was altered this year, the most noticeable difference being the elimination of the "Standard" logo. Ads included Airex, Nabisco Shredded Wheat, Wrigley's, the Navy, and Lionel Trains. For this year only, the five rows of squares along the bottom of the billboards were pale yellow instead of white.* The billboards

These four uncut Lionel Billboards *(left to right)* are from 1957, 1958, 1960, and 1961. The 1961 billboard was used in 1964 and again in 1965. D. Corrigan Collection and photograph.

appeared on page 48 of the 1957 Consumer Catalogue (five frames, five posters); also see pages 4, 5, 8, 15, 24, 32.
51: NAVY, Graduates choose your field (shows young man with diploma on left and five Navy insignia over NAVY).
52: WRIGLEY'S SPEARMINT CHEWING GUM, pure, wholesome, inexpensive (shows man with hat reaching way out with right arm showing pack of gum).
53: NABISCO, the original SHREDDED WHEAT (shows boy holding box of Shredded Wheat).
54: AIREX - REELS - RODS - LINE - LURES (fisherman in center).
55: LIONEL TRAINS (red letters) **with MAGNE-TRACTION** (shows lion with engineer's cap on left on page 48).

1958

Five billboards were again offered, with ads for the Navy, Airex, Juicy Fruit, PurOlator, and Chevrolet being made.* Billboards appeared on page 39 of the 1958 Consumer Catalogue (five frames, five posters); also see pages 21, 37, 38, 40.
56: Train and gain new nuclear NAVY (shows nuclear sub, two white-hatted sailors, officer, and missile).
57: TWICE AS POPULAR CHEVROLET OK USED CARS AND TRUCKS (shows three smiling faces).
58: "Change-um oil filter . . . car run heap better". PurOlator (shows American Indian driving car).

59: WRIGLEY'S JUICY FRUIT CHEWING GUM / DIFFERENT, DELICIOUS (shows pack of Juicy Fruit gum in yellow wrapper; leaf with picture of a woman's face superimposed on leaf).
60: AIREX - REELS - RODS - LINES - LURES (shows man on right in stream fishing near rocks about to net hooked fish).

1959

This is a year in which no new ads were produced, as far as we know.* We assume this was a full repetition of the 1958 posters. Billboards appeared in the 1959 Advance Catalogue, page 25 (five frames, five billboards); also see page 31.

1960

Five billboards were produced. Products shown were Underwood, the Navy, Cities Service, Airex, and a bulls-eye Target range.* Billboards appeared in the 1960 Advance Catalogue, page 32 (five frames, five posters); also see pages 42, 45.
61: GOOD TRAINING FOR GETTING AHEAD, Underwood PORTABLE TYPEWRITERS (shows portable typewriter on right side, boy with first prize cup on left).
62: SPACE AGE TRAINING NAVY (shows Planet Earth in background with Navy jet in center and red rocket).
60: AIREX - REELS - RODS - LINES - LURES (on right-hand shows man in stream fishing near rocks about to net hooked fish).
64: TARGET RANGE (red, white, blue target; yellow background).

63: EAGER BEAVER SERVICE all the way (shows gasoline pump on left and Cities Service emblem on right, beaver reading road map center left).
The listing for 1960 would not be complete without a reference to a train set issued as part of a contest sponsored by Channel Master. A promotional flyer announcing the contest clearly illustrates a Channel Master layout with six billboards comprising the standard 1960 set, and the sixth was a custom board advertising Channel Master electronic products.

1961

This was the last year five different billboards were offered. Ads for the Navy, Cities Service, Swift's Premium Franks, and the Lionel Science Series were made along with a Target Range billboard.* Billboards appeared on page 58 of the 1961 Consumer Catalogue (five frames, five posters); also see pages 23, 29, 30, 31, 39.
64: TARGET RANGE (red, white, blue target; yellow background).
66: BIG GALLON, BIG Mileage Performance (shows a gas pump as the "I" in BIG. Cities Service emblem upper right).
67: Hot Diggety! Swift's Premium FRANKS (shows a frank on fork, cheese on frank).
65: NAVY Diploma — Stay in school (shows American flag on staff in center).
68: SEE THE NEW LIONEL SCIENCE SERIES (ad shows atom model at bottom center).
Catalogued, but not manufactured:
FINISH LINE (shows black and white checkered flag with two cars racing).

1962

Only three billboards were printed and how anyone can spread these among five frames is a mystery. Pictured were ads for Cities Service, the Navy, and Van Camp's Pork and Beans.* Billboards appeared on page 50 of the 1962 Consumer Catalogue (five frames, five posters); billboards pictured are the same as shown in the 1961 Advance Catalogue (items 10, 13, 22, 24, 25).

This uncut billboard sheet shows the three billboards offered in 1962. D. Corrigan Collection and photograph.

70: AMERICA'S FIRST, FINEST, FAVORITE (shows can of Van Camp's Pork and Beans on left; ladle of beans on right).
69: Get close to America by car! BIG GALLON, Quality alone makes it BIG! (shows City Service emblem on right, part of car center bottom; Big Gallon in red).
65: NAVY Diploma — Stay in school (shows American flag on staff in center).

1963

On page 33 of the Lionel Consumer Catalogue of this year appeared an illustration of the 1961 billboards, with the first two changed to promote Lionel Porter and Spear phonographs. No one I know has ever seen examples of these, and I believe they do not exist.* Billboards appeared on page 33 of the 1963 Consumer Catalogue (five frames, five posters); also see pages 18, 19.
Catalogued, but not manufactured:
LIONEL PORTER (shows Microcraft Student Microscope).
LIONEL Spear (shows Mickey Mouse phonograph).

1964-65

The catalogues for these years shows the 1961 sheet continuously.*
1964 Billboards appeared on page 14 (five frames, five posters). Billboards shown are the same as shown in the 1961 Catalogue and the 1962 Trains and Accessories Catalogue.
1965 Page 15 (set of billboards with five frames). Billboards shown are the same as shown in the 1961 Catalogue and the 1962 Trains and Accessories Catalogue.

1966-68

Lionel produced a five-billboard sheet during these years. The border was radically changed from the forest green of previous years to a purple. Two ads for U. S. Savings Bonds (identical), two ads for Education (also identical), and an ad for Dodge. Blister Pack No. B310 is the above described 1966-68 billboard set; the blister pack may have different-colored arrow design.* Reader comments requested.
Blister Pack B310, Billboard set of five plastic frames. Top frame shows poster "Buy U.S. Savings Bonds" (shows package of savings bonds, Series E, color light purple), Lionel with red and blue arrow design on pack like 1966 catalogue. Weaver Collection.
73: Education is for the birds (the birds who want to get ahead) To get a good job get a good education (Light purple, two copies).
71: Get a Dodge. (Cartoon-horse with collar, light purple, Weaver Collection.)
72: Buy U.S. Savings Bonds (shows package of savings bonds, Series E, color light purple. Two copies.)

1966 Page 15 (set of billboards with five frames). Billboards shown are the same as shown in 1961 Consumer Catalogue.
1967: Lionel did not issue a Consumer Catalogue.
1968: (Inside of back page) (Set of billboards with five frames.) Billboards shown are the same as shown in 1961 Consumer Catalogue.
1969: No billboards listed in Consumer Catalogue.
The following billboard has been dated as post-1970 Lionel production: **Curtis Baby Ruth** (red letters on large Baby Ruth candy bar — background white. No green billboard outline.)

Postwar Billboard Observations

By Don Corrigan*, with updates by the Author.

• **HO Billboards:** As far as can be determined, Lionel made only two sheets of HO billboards as part of a No. 0310 billboard set. The first sheet was produced in 1960 and the illustrations were identical to the O Gauge sheet for that year. The second sheet was made the

This uncut billboard sheet shows the five billboards offered in 1966-68. D. Corrigan Collection and photograph.

Lionel 1960 *(left)* and 1961 *(right)* HO Billboards D. Corrigan Collection and photograph.

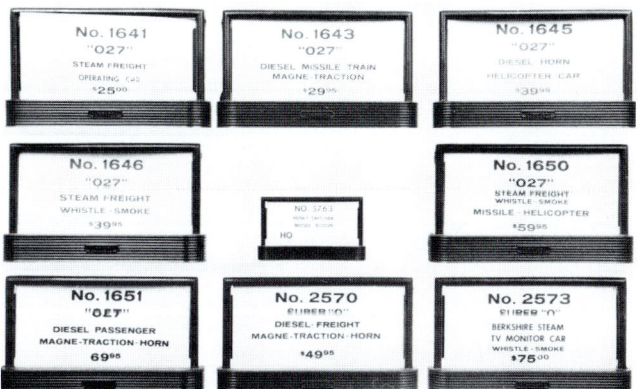

These billboards advertise 1961 train sets.

next year and was identical to the 1961 O Gauge sheet with the following exceptions: instead of a "Target Range" board, Lionel substituted a "Finish Line" board to be used with the HO raceway sets. Also, the Lionel Science Series board was printed without the white molecular diagram which appeared below the word "Series" on the O Gauge version.

Except as noted above, the illustrations on these sheets are identical to the O Gauge boards, but the HO sheets did not have the green borders, just the illustrations on a die-cut white card. The uncut sheets are 9-1/2" long and 2-11/16" wide.

In addition to the regular Lionel production billboards, a crop of decidedly different billboards have appeared. The size and format of these boards are identical to the Lionel boards, but these cannot be placed among the others. In fact, most were not made by Lionel at all.

• **Silver Springs:** During the 1950s, Lionel made up lists of Lionel train set owners which it then gave to Florida's Silver Springs Amusement Park. Silver Springs printed up their own billboards, then sent them out in groups of three or more to the people on Lionel's list. The exact number, variety, and years these boards were made is unknown, since the management of Silver Springs does not have any records of them. Because of all this, the final counts of these boards will probably never be known.

The Silver Springs billboards came in at least two styles, the difference being the color of the border. All of them had the logo "Outdoor Adv." instead of "Standard" in the bottom border. Group A has the traditional green border that Lionel used on their boards. While the "Tommy Bartlett" board is unique, the "Relay Now!" board is exactly like the one in Lionel's 1953 sheet, the difference being the "Outdoor Adv." logo. A third board has an ad for the Glass-Bottom Boat Ride. (**Note:** With the duplication of Lionel's "Relax Now!", the possibility

Two Lionel billboards advertising Silver Springs in Florida.

exists of Silver Springs duplicating the other two billboards made by Lionel.)

Group B is quite different from any other because the border is sky blue rather than green. This is the only group that I have seen with this color.

Other Lionel Billboards: In 1961, Lionel manufactured a set of billboards advertising some of the 1961 train sets. Lionel published other billboards whose year of issue and method of distribution is unknown:

(A) **LIONEL REAL RAILROAD REMOTE CONTROL KNUCKLE COUPLERS**
(B) **LIONEL MAGNE-TRACTION MORE CLIMB, SPEED AND PULL**
(C) **LIONEL LOCOS PUFF CLEAN WHITE SMOKE**

These two billboards (date unknown) advertise both Lionel knuckle couplers *(left)* and Magne-Traction *(right)*. D. Corrigan Collection and photograph.

• **Mystery Boards:** Two billboards that have been observed are absolute mysteries. The ads are for Narragansett Beer and Fisher's Golden Roll Creamery Butter. The 'Gansett board is different in that the ad is printed on a separate sheet of paper, which is glued to the cardboard billboard. There may be three possible explanations: It is either 1) a pre-production mock-up, 2) a special run printed by or for the 'Gansett Brewery to distribute for themselves, or 3) a homemade board. The third alternative could be ruled out, since the ad is the perfect size, layout, and format for the billboard.

The Fisher's Butter billboard is unusual in that it has the "Outdoor Adv." logo rather than the "Standard". This is the only non-Silver Springs board I have seen like this.

All of these non-Lionel billboards are, needless to say, very hard to come by.

MODERN ERA

The following is the third listing of billboards produced by Lionel since 1970. Unless otherwise stated, dates reflect catalogue period for a particular billboard. Unlike postwar boards, it is not possible to list modern era by year only. We welcome additions to this listing, including descriptions of the color and lettering schemes for some of the billboards. Average price ranges for modern era sets are generally below $10. The examples listed are from the collections of I. D. Smith, G. Halverson, S. Hutchings, J. Sawruk, and R. LaVoie.

1: BUY U. S. SAVINGS BONDS, 1970-71, stack of $50 bonds wrapped in red, white, and blue flag wrapper on white background.
2: EDUCATION IS FOR THE BIRDS (The Birds Who Want To Get Ahead), 1970-71, uncatalogued; blue and red lettering on plain white background.
3: GET A DODGE, 1970-71, uncatalogued; cartoon figure of mule in brown tones, blue lettering on white background.
4: SHERATON HOTELS, 1970-71, blue and red rectangles; black lettering and black Sheraton logo.
5: BETTY CROCKER, 1970, blue script lettering on white background.
6: CHEERIOS, 1970, blue General Mills "G" and red lettering on white background.
7: LIONEL MPC, 1970-71, red "LIONEL" in modern typeface; red and blue lettering; red and blue MPC logo on white background.
8: AUTOLITE, 1970-71, uncatalogued; "Autolite Small Engine Spark Plugs For Work Or Play," red, black, and maroon lettering, green and blue rectangles with lawn mower and motorcycle.
9: PLAY-DOH, 1970-71, uncatalogued; "America's Favorite" in blue; child pulls can of Play-Doh on red wagon.
10: FOAM VILLAGE FOR LIONEL BY MYCO, 1971, uncatalogued; conveyor belt carries housing structures out of factory, black "Imagineering for Packaging & Material Handling Systems", yellow background with black conveyor and green building with black "My-T-Veyor" lettering and logo; very hard to find.
11: LIONEL, 1972-86, picture of Santa Fe F-3 locomotive in red, silver, black, and yellow; "LIONEL" in modern red typeface.
12: FAMOUS PARKER GAMES, 1971-76, dark orange background, black lettering and black Parker Brothers "swirl" logo.
13: CRAFT MASTER, 1971-84, blue square at left with black and white Craft Master logo and white lettering, light brown portrait of mountain range at right.
14: MPC MODEL KITS, 1971-84, dark blue and white MPC logo, red lettering, cars, rocket, and train on yellow and white background.
15: KENNER TOYS, 1972-76, yellow and red cartoon bird at right, white lettering on blue background.
16: SCHLITZ BEER, 1977-84, beer can and white lettering on red background.
17: BABY RUTH, 1977-84, picture of candy bar wrapper, red lettering on white background.

Three Lionel double-sided billboards, numbers 25A-25B, 24A-24B, and 23A-23B.

18: NIBCO WASHERLESS FAUCETS, 1982, uncatalogued; black Nibco logo, red lettering, and picture of faucet on white background.
19: RIDE THE NIBCO EXPRESS, 1982, uncatalogued; black and white lettering and script on dark red background.
20: TAPPAN IS COOKING, white lettering on black background, "LIONEL" with red, silver, and yellow Santa Fe set, came with 7908 Tappan car as part of special promotional set; hard to find. S. Hutchings and J. Sawruk Collections.
21: T C A CONVENTION billboard; description needed.
22: T C A CONVENTION billboard; description needed.
23A-23B: 1987-90, double-sided 12707 Billboard. Side A: "Buy U. S. Savings Bonds" in black to left of American flag on white background. Side B: Red "Adopt-A-Pet" and white "Support Your Local Humane Society" on blue background with picture of puppy and kitten.
24A-24B: 1987-90, double-sided billboard with 12707 frames. Side A: Large white "BUCKLE UP!" and black "For Safety's Sake" above black seat belt on medium green background. Side B: Red "Keep America Beautiful" atop dark, medium, and light blue and gray stylized mountain pass with white background.
25A-25B: 1987-90, double-sided billboard with 12707 frames. Side A: Black "READ...AND KNOW THE WORLD!" with multicolored balloon, airplane, Oriental child, locomotive, windmill, etc. on white background. Side B: Black "Take The Train" below large red, white, and blue "AMERICAN FLYER LINES" shield logo on white background.
26. WELCOME TO LIONELVILLE, 1990. One of two alternating messages on 12761 Animated Billboard accessory. Overall measurements 8" x 4-7/8".
27. LIONELVILLE . . . the home of JOCKO SPORTING GOODS, CO., 1990. One of two alternating messages on 12761 Animated Billboard accessory. Overall measurements 8" x 4-7/8".

Seven Lionel modern era billboards. *Top row:* Billboard numbers 7, 15, 4, and 9. *Bottom row:* Billboards numbers 13, 14, and 11.

Chapter Eight
SERVICE STATION TOOLS

"Tools" is one Lionel product line that cannot be found in its consumer or dealer catalogues. Dealers did not carry tools for sale to the public, nor were these products advertised through the media by the Lionel Corporation. Lionel tools are products intended for one purpose: to allow Authorized Lionel Service Stations to repair Lionel products in an efficient and safe manner. With few exceptions, tools were available exclusively to these Service Stations direct from the Lionel Parts Department. Lionel itself served only as a supplier, for these tools in most instances were manufactured under contract by outside suppliers to Lionel. The noted exceptions to that rule include Lionel's own manufacture, for instance, of test sets and rivet press tool blocks.

Lionel Service Station tools represent one of the most fascinating aspects of serious Lionel collecting, and by understanding this exclusive distribution arrangement, one can conclude why tool collecting today can also be one of the most challenging. Lionel tools are sought after for one of two reasons: their collectability as being representative of the Lionel brand name, and the fact many collectors and current Service Station owners use them in the repair of trains even today. Use of such tools as test sets and hand tools present little risk, however breaking the lip off a wheel puller — a common occurrence as the metal ages — renders the tool useless, and its value similarly reduced.

Three categories of tools pertain to Lionel: 1) Test Sets, 2) Riveting Press Sets, and 3) Hand Tools. While narrative comments are provided for each of these major categories, all tools known to the author are included in a numerically sequenced listing. A visit to any train show will quickly demonstrate why it is difficult to establish a consistent market value on tools. Unlike many locomotives and rolling stock sometimes produced in the many thousands of units, tools had extremely limited availability from Lionel, and in addition many would not have a distinct "railroading" recognition, such that old, worn tools would have over the years been relegated to the junk pile. As more and more collectors are seeking these evasive tools and willing to pay collector premiums, market values on certain items are gradually being established. It is believed much of this market activity takes place privately between collectors rather than during established train shows, judging by the few times that tools remain on tables at larger shows such as the semi-annual York Train Collectors Association meet or the annual conventions of the TCA, TTOS, or Lionel Collectors Club of America. Input from our readers on tool varieties, as well as assistance on market trends, would be sincerely welcomed.

The Tools That Almost Were!

Before we provide in detail a commentary and listing of tools known or believed to exist, there are two tools conceived by the Lionel Corporation that we know do not exist. One, as verified with a former Lionel management employee, was in the discussion stage; the other was actually patented, but for an unknown reason was not produced. Rodney Haggard, Lionel's Sales Manager for the Southwest District, recalled that in the mid-1960s Lionel investigated the feasibility of a form of an otoscope. The otoscope was in use in the optometry market, for examining the internal ear. Why, then, would Lionel be interested in such an instrument? The answer is quite logical. Comments from Service Station owners indicated it was cumbersome to inspect the condition of the smoking locomotive heating element. Inspection often required disassembly of the locomotive — a time-consuming function — to inspect these elements. Lionel planned to develop a tool to look into the locomotive smoke chamber and thereby easily examine the heating element. The concept appeared sound, but the product did not go beyond the conceptual stage.

The other tool (or more appropriate, tools) conceived but not manufactured by or for Lionel had more far-reaching implications. A patent was applied for on August 30, 1951 by Joseph L. Bonanno, originally Lionel's Chief Engineer and later Treasurer, and was granted May 18, 1954. The initial patent application paragraphs are key:

"The present invention relates to magnetizable hand tools and more particularly to hand tools suitable for use either magnetized or non-magnetized.

"The present invention contemplates hand tools such as wrenches and screwdrivers having work engaging tips or ends adapted to cooperate with the magnetizable work piece, such as a screw, a nut or a bolt head, and provided with a permanent magnet which can be brought into position to magnetize the tip so that it then acts as a keeper, or shifted to another position, where upon the magnetized tip loses its magnetism, and the permanent magnet is retained there. It is thus possible to use the screwdriver, wrench or similar article as an ordinary non-magnetized tool or as a magnetized tool, as desired."

The shank of the proposed tool was of a non-magnetic tubular material, allowing for a magnetic object to flow through the tube, magnetizing the tip for the work intended, or as alternative tips on both sides, since a combination wrench/screwdriver configuration was also proposed.

Bonanno's documented tool was ingenious, and certainly most appropriate to the repair of toy trains. In repairing toy trains small screws are removed and reinserted. These screws often fall either into the many tiny spaces of the locomotive or to the floor. It is unfortunate this tool was not marketed, perhaps only because it was a product, like many Lionel introduced, ahead of its time. And today magnetic tools are a standard of the trade!

Lionel Service Station Test Sets

Lionel intuitively recognized that placing a priority on catering to the needs of its authorized Service Stations added to sales. This policy is evident in merchandising displays, and other sales incentives made available to hobby shops, department stores, and other retail outlets carrying the Lionel brand, many stores of which included a Service Station. One of the most unusual products offered to Service Stations to assist in the repair of model railroading merchandise was the test set. This was a self-contained metal box which included a basic AC transformer as well as the necessary meters and other components to properly test virtually every electrical product available from Lionel. As the trains evolved over the years, test set design also changed, reflecting more advanced circuitry and changes in track gauges.

The initial testing equipment produced by Lionel was the No. 5 test set, first released in the mid-to-late 1930s. The set, although somewhat crude in its engineering design, was credibly state-of-the-art for its time. The set was able to test Lionel O, O27, and Standard Gauges atop a well-designed five-rail tester. It was well-constructed, and even the rails were the solid scale T-rail rather than the mass-produced and less expensive tinplate rails. The No. 5 test set had dimensions of 24" long x 8" wide (variable at an angle) x 9-1/2" high, was designed with an attractive black metal-faced control board, and could test locomotives, rolling stock, transformers, accessories, and controllers. The earliest documented reference to this unit appears in the Introduction to the "Lionel Service Bulletin," dated November 1938: "Properly equipped Service Stations should carry a complete replacement parts stock. A handy tool kit, testing equipment such as THE LIONEL TEST SET, and other standardized service tools and instructions are indispensable."

There is little doubt the No. 5 test set as a collectible is highly desirable, and though it appears to be a production item rather than of prototype origin, few appear to have survived.

A number of similarities exist between the No. 5, the upgraded 5A, and the final prewar version, the 5B, first released in the early 1940s. There were some notable differences, however. The 5B was offered in configurations of 110-120 volts or a modified version at 220 volts. The tester, in addition to being able to test O, O27, and Standard Gauges, could now test OO Gauge equipment atop a redesigned eight-rail test track. The 5B model was similar in dimension and basic testing capabilities as its predecessors, with one addition: one common usage, for which a "test station" was included on the face, was a light bulb tester! The Instruction Manual for the 5B tester was 19 pages, also in a rather crude format; nevertheless the equipment itself, like Lionel's primary railroad product line, was a clear, quality-oriented product of the prewar Lionel era, and an ideal repair source in a compact area that occupied less than 200 square inches of workbench space.

Like its predecessors, few 5B test sets exist today. However, for those inclined to build their own test set, the 5B unit can well serve as a model. While the exterior controls portray a significantly functional layout, the inside of a 5B set reveals a number of common Lionel hardware items, including a 167 whistle controller, an RCS Controller, transformer, and common rheostat.

Before leaving the discussion of prewar era test sets, one so-called tool distributed by Lionel deserves comment. While it is not a test set, per se, the one function the SE-1 coupler gauge board was designed to perform overlapped that of the 5B test unit.

A close observation of the 5B unit indicates that to each side of the eight-rail track is a built-in, sponge-padded bumper with a rectangular piece of black metal. On the metal is designated "TS" and "TT", which stood for the two standard heights of electric couplers on Lionel O and O27 Gauge cars and tenders. According to the 5B instructions, the "TS" size is generally used on all O Gauge equipment and the "TT" on the small cars used in the O27 outfits and frequently in the lower-priced O Gauge line. The instructions go on to point out that "the necessity of lining up the coupler points is to insure that cars of the same type couple and uncouple with one another freely. The car to be checked is placed on the track and the point of the coupler hook lined up with the proper gauge. A simple hand-tool operation is the only adjustment required."

These same instructions can well apply to the elusive SE-1, a tool described in the 1939 and 1941 editions of *Replacement Parts for Lionel Trains and Accessories*. Under the "Miscellaneous" section, the SE-1 is described as a coupler gauge board, selling for $2.50 net. Close examination of this tool lends intrigue to its simplicity. A single 14-1/2" piece of tinplate track is mounted to a stained and varnished piece of wood measuring 18" long x 2-1/4" wide x 3/4" thick. The significance lies in two custom-designed pieces of steel at each end, in which one has a die-cast "TS" and the other a "TT", in their appropriate measuring heights. Was this the poor man's test set? Not likely, but it did fulfill one function of an important prewar toy train test.

The first postwar test set, the 5C tester, was initially documented in the Lionel Service Manual with pages dated January 1948. The testing concept is similar to that of the prewar models, but with several significant differences. Unlike the multi-gauge 5B unit, the 5C model can test O and O27 Gauges only, with a single track mounted at the top. In addition, the early post-type tester connectors are replaced by several sets of panel jacks. The sets come with leads equipped with battery clips on one end and banana plugs on the other end; the latter for insertion into one of the applicable sets of jacks.

The postwar test sets saw prominent mention in the Lionel Service Manual, beginning with an illustration of the 5C unit in the initial January 1948 edition. A 1949 booklet titled *Information for Lionel Approved Service Stations* has a prominent illustration of the No. 5C tester on page 2. In this informative booklet, Lionel distinctly points out equipment required for the Service Station:

"Dealers who take care of service work on electrical devices need but little specialized equipment for servicing Lionel trains. In addition to the small tools... special electrical testing equipment such as the Lionel Test Set should be installed. This Test Set, designed and assembled by Lionel engineers exclusively for our Service Stations, is sold at $50.00 net, which is less than the cost of manufacturing this fine instrument."

Whereas the Nos. 5, 5B, and 5C units are similar, the No. 5D test set introduced a new generation of testing equipment. Height and depth remained the same as the earlier models, and a full twelve inches in length was added, equating to an extra section of remote-control O Gauge track. Separate whistle/direction and variable voltage controls were added, utilizing handles similar to the 1033 consumer transformer. Separate AC and DC voltmeters were also distinguishing new features.

The final test set carrying the Lionel logo, the No. 5F universal test set, was made available to approved Service Stations after January 1, 1962, at a price of $95 net. This price could be reduced by $25, since Lionel was offering that amount as a credit for a trade-in 5D tester.

While the 5F unit has similar dimensions as the 5D tester (33" long x 7-1/2" deep x 9-1/2" high), the predominant difference is the control panel now made of silk-screened, brushed aluminum, as well as the track configuration. After a two-decade presence, gone was the tinplate O Gauge track, only to be replaced by the gauges of the times: a dual setup of Super O and HO test tracks, flanked by blue bumpers of the same No. 50 gang car vintage.

The various test sets were available for just a quarter century of Lionel's history, yet all models represent creativity and superior engineering techniques. There is little wonder why even today reproduction models are again available under non-Lionel labels to meet collector and operator demand.

The Lionel Riveting Set

One of the most versatile tools Lionel made available to its Service Stations is the ST350 riveting set. The earliest dated instruction sheet for this tool is March 1953, while the author has seen the earliest illustrations of the set identified in the Service Manual as September 1956. The riveter itself is approximately ten inches long by four inches wide and measures twenty inches from the base to the top of the handle.

Lionel's Service Manual states that "this basic machine, built to high precision especially for Lionel Service Stations, will do literally hundreds of riveting and assembly jobs." While certain features may have been designed to Lionel's specifications, the basic riveter predates Lionel's availability by many years.

A silver plate with red lettering on each riveting unit indicates the unit was made for Lionel by the Chicago Rivet and Machine Company, then of Bellwood, Illinois. (The firm is still very much in business, and in the early 1980s moved its facilities to Naperville, Illinois, with its foundry located in Tyrone, Pennsylvania.)

In response to inquiries Chicago Rivet reports that Lionel provided a very small segment of their business, and a similar riveting unit was built to specifications for many other companies. It is believed that the original design of the ST350 set was built under contract for the Caterpillar Tractor Company in the late 1920s or early 1930s. Innovative for its time, the riveter was initially mounted directly to tractor frames and proved especially helpful for on-site repairs of clutches.

Two Lionel riveter versions have been observed, one painted blue and the other red. The blue version is the earlier of the two, and the more desirable. Chicago Rivet has verified that it painted riveters in blue and red. However, there has been speculation among collectors that a green version exists, although this has not been verified. There are design differences between the earlier (blue) and later (red) models, primarily in the base construction. Internally, Chicago Rivet labels the Lionel riveter their "Industrial 915 Version", of which several different castings were made for products ranging from train repair to ski boot construction. A separate "Model 33" was also available for automobile brake and clutch repairs.

Later version red models of the press are no longer inscribed "Made for The Lionel Corporation", but still bear the red on silver plate affixed by Chicago Rivet. Later tool numbers accompanying the press no longer bear the ST350 prefix; rather a "Chicago" number with a "T" prefix is assigned to and engraved in each metal piece.

Originally the set came with fifteen different tools plus a tool block. The tools include seven anvils, seven clinchers, and a knock-out punch, all constructed of rugged steel. The tool block is crude, being cut from common pine wood and painted with a glossy enamel with "Lionel Service" in white block lettering. Unlike the metal tools themselves, these blocks were manufactured by Lionel. The ST375 wheel-mounting tools are also designed to be used with the ST350 riveting press, however these tools were not produced by Chicago Rivet, and were offered separate from the ST350 series.

Other Lionel Tools

What significance can there be in a common screwdriver? This question does not represent a riddle if the screwdriver happens to contain the engraved inscription, "Lionel Service". Again to meet the needs of its Service Stations, Lionel made available a vast array of tools, both common and of a specialized nature unique to the repair of electric trains.

Comparison of Test Set Capabilities

Features:	5	5A	5B	5C	5D	5F
Volts:	115	115	110-115	115	115 (**)	115 (**)
Meter type:	Westinghouse	Beele	Beele	N/A	Marion	General Motors
Test meters:						
AC	Yes	Yes	Yes	Yes	Yes	Yes
DC	No	No	No	No	Yes	Yes
No. of meters:	1	1	1	1	2	2
Test rails:	5	7	8	3	3	5
Variable voltage control:	Yes	Yes	No	Yes	Yes	Yes
Lamp tester:	No	Yes	Yes	Yes	Yes	Yes
Electrical outlet on face:	Yes	Yes	Yes	Yes	Yes	No
Gauges tested:	O, O27, Std.	O, O27, Std.	O, O27, OO, Std.	O, O27	O, O27	O, O27, HO, Super O
Circuit breaker:	No	Yes	Yes	No	Yes	Yes
Face plate colors:	Black	Black	Black	Silver	Silver	Silver
Test connection method:	Posts	Posts F/P (*)	Posts	F/P	F/P	F/P
Separate test track controls:	No	Yes	Yes	No	No	Yes

(*) Female Plug Type

(**) Did a 220 Volt model exist? More information requested.

The ST300 nut driver set contains five socket wrenches, and includes a sturdy metal stand painted in a medium blue color. A companion ST325 screw driver set is also available, and contains five Phillips and regular screwdrivers. A blue metal stand is also available, and contains large holes for the screwdrivers as well as three small holes, apparently for other products of the user's choice, such as the ST302 spring adjusting tool.

Working on a Lionel E-unit, whether replacing the drum or spring contacts, is one of the more challenging aspects of electric train repair. Lionel engineers understood this fact well when they introduced to their Service Stations the E-unit repair tools, consisting of a vise and spreader. The vise, one of the scarcer Lionel tools, is of a somewhat crude design, with its primary components being a rectangular metal strip attached to a blue metal triangular block by means of a tension-adjusting screw. The more common spreader can be used with or without the vise, and three variations of the spreader are known. The earlier tool is made of a heavier metal and with more pronounced lettering as compared to the later-issued aluminum model.

One of the more ingenious — and indispensable — tools made available by Lionel is the wheel puller, available in two distinct models. The early 1951 version, ST301, contains a stubbier, rounded puller jaw compared to the longer jaws of the ST311 version. Another distinct difference between the two models lies in the shaft; the early model shaft measures 11-3/4 mm long whereas the shaft on the later version measures 12-1/4 mm. The ST311 model also has stronger upper and lower brackets and overall is of a more durable construction, in addition to having the advertised feature of small or large forcing pin varieties. It is significant that the ST301 wheel puller receives almost passing mention in the Service Manual, that being a small illustration under the caption, "Removing Wheels", of the 622 and 6220 diesel switcher instructions. The ST311 puller receives a half-page illustrated description under the tools section of the Manual. Recognizing the wheel pullers' popularity with operators, Lionel Trains, Inc. reissued the ST311 version to the consumer in 1988.

One relatively obscure tool available to Service Stations is the ST393 HO Magnetizer. The first mention of this tool appeared in the June 1, 1961 edition of the *Lionel Service Department Bulletin*. Included with the Bulletin is a special two-page feature, *Lionel Service Tools*, assigned a form number ST393-23. It is not specified the

It is regretted that "No Recorded Sale" must be assigned to many of Lionel's ever-popular Service Station tools. If one were to assign relative scarcity factors in each of the major categories, the following would be standouts:

Test Sets: The prewar No. 5 set, of which only one example has been observed by the author, that unit being in the Gordon H. Blickle Collection for many years.

Riveting Set: The early blue riveting press can today be identified as the scarcest, although "rare" is not an appropriate description. If a press other than blue or red is located, and certified to be factory original, this item could be considered in the rare tool category. Since the presses are constructed of rugged cast-iron metal, it would not be difficult to strip the original paint and repaint with a color other than that utilized in the manufacturing process.

Tools: In this category, it is difficult to single out any one item, since most tools with the Lionel name are difficult to locate. In the order of scarcity, the prewar coupler board (although described above under the Test Set section), the HO Magnetizer, and the early wheel puller (ST301) are the most desirable.

Without question all original Lionel tools are highly collectable, with more enthusiasts branching into this collecting arena each year. The fun of collecting tools is the challenge it presents and the joy of locating just one of the few tools made available by Lionel through the years.

form should be an update to the Service Manual, but full instructions for the unit plus a wiring diagram are included. The instructions are quite simple: "No. ST-393 Magnetizer will saturate the Alnico V magnets in Lionel HO motors and similar magnetic field motors made by other HO manufacturers. Because the magnetic field is weakened considerably whenever the motor is disassembled it should be remagnetized after repairs to restore full power." The unit sold for $12.50 net but after late 1961 the tool appears to have disappeared into oblivion.

The final tool worthy of special comment is the track pliers. One of the more common tools found today, this custom-made tool, initially made by the Kraeuter Tool Company, includes a wire-stripping hole, a tinplate rail-framing hole, as well as a pin-crimping nib. The only functional difference between versions is the rail-framing hole for O Gauge versus O27 Gauge. In addition, the earlier version is metal throughout; the later version, metal stamped "ST-384" and "Japan", includes blue rubber sleeves on each handle. That "Made in Japan" designation is significant in the history of the Lionel Corporation: Can the toy train hobby survive the next generation only through the resources of Far East technology? Only time can appropriately answer the question.

G   VG   EXC   NEW

5 PREWAR TEST SET: All purpose tester for Lionel prewar; includes O, O27, and Standard Gauges. Black control panel. 115 volt, single meter. **—   —   800   —**

5A PREWAR TEST SET: All purpose tester for Lionel prewar; includes O, O27, and Standard Gauges. Black control panel. 115 volt, single meter. D. Ely Collection. **NRS**

5B PREWAR TEST SET: All purpose tester for Lionel prewar; includes O, O27, OO, and Standard Gauges. Black control panel. 110-115 volt and 220 volt versions, single meter. R. Otten Collection. **NRS**

5C POSTWAR TEST SET: All purpose tester for all Lionel transformers, locomotives, whistle tenders, rolling stock, and accessories; O and O27 Gauges only. Silver-colored aluminum control panel. 115 volt, single meter. Units may be found with two RCS tracks or one each **UCS** and **RCS** s. I. D. Smith comment.
600   800   900   1000

This is the prewar 5B test set with lid up, showing interior wiring. The lid has track mounted on top to test equipment.

5B test set.

G   VG   EXC   NEW

5D POSTWAR TEST SET: All purpose tester for all Lionel transformers, locomotives, whistle tenders, rolling stock, and accessories; O and O27 Gauges only. The most common of the Lionel test sets. Silver-colored aluminum control panel. 115 volt, double meter. One observed variety has the "115" volt metal etching that appears to be factory-removed, yet the unit does not appear to be a 220 volt version. Are other sets known to have similar numbers removed?
600   800   900   1000

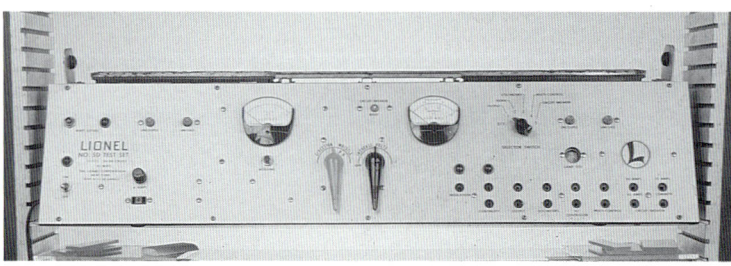

5D postwar test set.

5E ELECTRONIC CONTROL TESTER: Tester for electronic train control, referred to in Lionel Service Manual under "Electronic Transmitter Parts List". Item appears to be a modified voltmeter with four posts, however no actual Lionel label appears on this product. C. Sigadel observation. Additional information requested. **NRS**

5E electronic control tester.

	G	VG	EXC	NEW

5F UNIVERSAL TEST SET: Similar tester as No. 5D, but includes Super O and HO Gauge track. All purpose tester can be used to test all Lionel transformers, locomotives, rolling stock, and accessories. Brushed aluminum control panel. 115 volt, double meter.

750 1000 1200 1500

SE-1 PREWAR COUPLER GAUGE BOARD: Crude tester used to measure coupler height on prewar rolling stock, locomotive, and tender couplers. R. Osterhoff Collection. **NRS**

SE-1 prewar coupler gauge board.

SE-1 coupler gauge board drawing.

ST294 1/8" NUT DRIVER: Component of ST300 nut driver set, tool comes with transparent amber handle inscribed in white embossing "Lionel Service ST-294". **NRS**

ST295 5/32" NUT DRIVER: Component of ST300 nut driver set, tool comes with transparent amber handle inscribed in white embossing "Lionel Service ST-295". **NRS**

ST296 3/16" NUT DRIVER: Component of ST300 nut driver set, tool comes with transparent amber handle inscribed in white embossing "Lionel Service ST-296". This driver is consistently mis-identified in the Lionel Service Manual as a 7/32" inch driver. Measurements distinctly identify this tool as a 6/32" (3/16") tool. **NRS**

ST297 7/32" LARGE NUT DRIVER: Component of ST300 nut driver set, tool comes with transparent amber handle inscribed in white embossing "Lionel Service ST-297". **NRS**

ST298 1/4" NUT DRIVER: Component of ST300 nut driver set, tool comes with transparent amber handle inscribed in white embossing "Lionel Service ST-298". **NRS**

ST301 Lionel Service wheel puller.

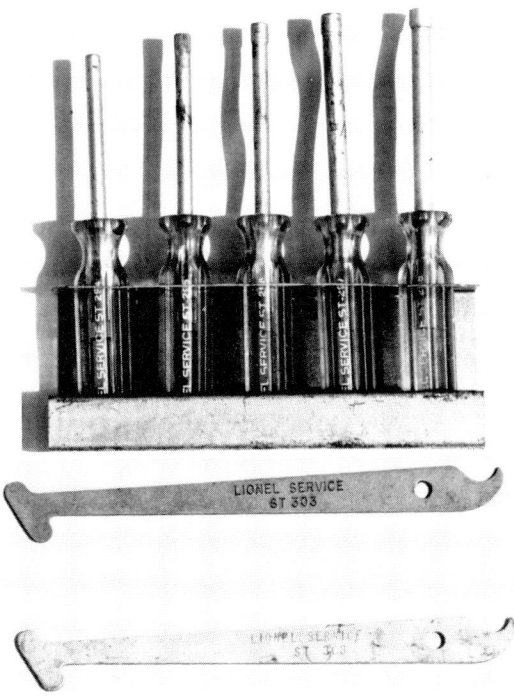

The ST-300 nut driver set came with a convenient tool holding unit. Lionel also sold the ST-303 E-unit spreader tool which permits the much easier insertion or removal of defective E-unit drums.

	G	VG	EXC	NEW

ST299 STAND: Component of ST300 nut driver set, constructed of sheet metal painted medium blue, with openings to insert five nut drivers. No inscriptions can be found on the stand. **NRS**

ST300 NUT DRIVER SET: Set of five nut drivers and stand, these tools are available collectively, or sold separately under individual part numbers. Pieces include ST294 through ST299. It is also believed, but not confirmed, that this set also comes with clear, transparent handles. **NRS**

ST301 WHEEL PULLER: Early double bar model (1951) used to remove wheels from locomotives. Construction of forged steel, gunmetal in color, "No. ST-301" and "Lionel Service" inscribed in sans-serif small letters on lower bracket. **NRS**

ST302 SPRING ADJUSTING TOOL: Double-ended slotted tool for adjusting, with the slotted blades, springs, or contacts, Lionel equipment such as trucks and transformers.
(A) Center handle constructed of yellow transparent plastic. **NRS**

(B) Center handle constructed of amber transparent plastic, darker and curved nose slightly longer than (A). **NRS**

(C) Center handle constructed of clear transparent plastic. Reproductions of this item are available. **NRS**

ST303 E-UNIT SPREADER: Simple hand tool designed to facilitate the separation of E-unit ends.
(A) "Lionel Service ST-303" inscribed in heavy serif lettering; metal is pressed steel. Early model. R. Otten Collection.
—   —   20   30
(B) "Lionel Service ST-303" inscribed in lighter serif lettering; metal is lighter aluminum. Later model.   —   —   8   10
(C) Painted black, block lettering. I. D. Smith Collection. **NRS**

ST311 WHEEL PULLER: Later double bar model used to remove wheels from locomotives. Construction of heavier forged steel, gun-

	G	VG	EXC	NEW

metal in color, "No. ST-311" and "Lionel Service" inscribed in large block lettering on lower bracket.
(A) 1957 model, center shaft measures 5-3/8".
　　　　　　　　　　　　　　25　50　75　100
(B) 1988 model, center shaft measures 5-7/8".
　　　　　　　　　　　　　　10　20　25　30

ST319 PHILLIPS NO. 1 SCREWDRIVER: Component of ST325 screwdriver set, tool comes with transparent amber handle inscribed in white embossing "Lionel Service ST-319". **NRS**

ST320 PHILLIPS NO. 2 SCREWDRIVER: Component of ST325 screwdriver set, tool comes with transparent amber handle inscribed in white embossing "Lionel Service ST-320". **NRS**

ST321 ELECTRICIANS ROUND SHANK SCREWDRIVER: Component of ST325 screwdriver set, tool comes with transparent amber handle inscribed in white embossing "Lionel Service ST321". **NRS**

ST322 SCREW-HOLDING SQUARE SHANK SCREWDRIVER: Two-piece component of ST325 screw driver set, tool comes with transparent amber handle inscribed in white embossing "Lionel Service ST-322". The screw holder fits over the screwdriver shank and is often found missing. **NRS**

ST323 GENERAL UTILITY SQUARE SHANK SCREWDRIVER: Component of ST325 screwdriver set, tool comes with transparent amber handle inscribed in white embossing "Lionel Service ST-323". **NRS**

ST324 STAND: Component of ST325 screwdriver set, constructed of sheet metal painted medium blue, with openings to insert five screwdrivers and three smaller-shanked tools such as the ST302 spring adjusting tool. No inscription can be found on the stand. **NRS**

ST325 SCREWDRIVER SET: Set of five screwdrivers and stand, these tools are available collectively, or sold separately under individual part numbers. Pieces include ST319 through ST324. It is also believed, but not confirmed, that this set also comes with clear, transparent handles. **NRS**

ST342 O27 TRACK PLIERS: Track pliers first available in early 1950s, designed for O27 track use only. Made of shiny forged steel with red rubberized sleeves on pliers handles. Each pliers is inscribed "No. ST-342 Pat Pend" and "Track Pliers — O27 Track" on one side and "Made for Lionel by Kraeuter" on the other. Comes in 2" x 6-3/4" thin cardboard box with instructions. **NRS**

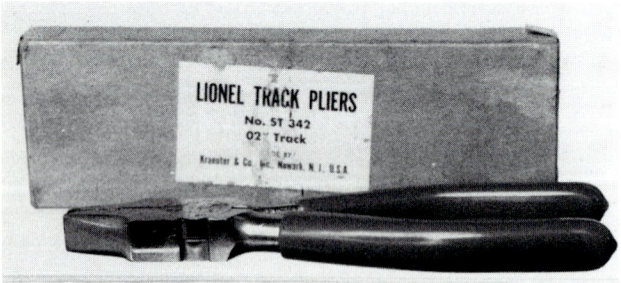

ST342 Lionel O27 track pliers.

ST343 O TRACK PLIERS: Illustrated in (undated) Lionel flyer as Lionel track pliers for O track. More information requested. **NRS**

ST350 RIVETING PRESS: Primary component of riveting set (ST350 series), Chicago Rivet describes as "machine".
(A) Original blue issuance.　　　400　500　600　750
(B) Green; confirmation requested.　　　　　　　**NRS**
(C) Red.　　　　　　　　　　　300　400　550　650

ST350-3 ANVIL HOLDER: (Chicago No. T-793), goes with ST350 riveting press. **NRS**

The ST-350 riveting set includes a rivet press and tools. The tool is very useful in repairing valve gear linkages on Lionel steam engines.

	G	VG	EXC	NEW

ST350-4 ANVIL HOLDER NUT: (Chicago No. T-794), goes with ST350 riveting press; two used. **NRS**

ST350-5 THUMB SCREW: Goes with ST350 riveting press, two used. **NRS**

ST350-6 TOOL BLOCK: Goes with ST350 riveting press, capable of holding 15 riveting tools; made of pine wood with crudely drilled holes.
(A) Red base with orange top. R. Otten Collection. **NRS**
(B) Red base with red top. R. Otten observation. **NRS**

ST350-7 LARGE RIVET ANVIL: (Chicago No. T-809), goes with ST350 riveting press. **NRS**

ST350-8 ROLL CLINCHER (.062"): (Chicago No. T-811), goes with ST350 riveting press. **NRS**

ST350-9 ROLL CLINCHER (.088"): (Chicago No. T-772), goes with ST350 riveting press. **NRS**

ST350-10 ROLL CLINCHER (.098") (Chicago No. T-790), goes with ST350 riveting press. **NRS**

ST350-11 ROLL CLINCHER (.125") (Chicago No. T-771), goes with ST350 riveting press. **NRS**

ST350-12 ROLL CLINCHER (.140") (Chicago No. T-764), goes with ST350 riveting press. **NRS**

ST350-13 STAR CLINCHER: (Chicago No. T-763), goes with ST350 riveting press. **NRS**

ST350-14 BINDING POST ANVIL (.116"): (Chicago No. T-876), goes with ST350 riveting press. **NRS**

ST350-15 BINDING POST ANVIL (.144"): (Chicago No. T-877), goes with ST350 riveting press. **NRS**

ST350-16 BINDING POST ANVIL (.166"): (Chicago No. T-878), goes with ST350 riveting press. **NRS**

ST350-17 SLIDING SHOE ANVIL: (Chicago No. T-879), goes with ST350 riveting press. **NRS**

G VG EXC NEW

ST350-19 SPLAYING CLINCHER: (Chicago No. T-880), goes with ST350 riveting press. **NRS**

ST350-20 KNOCK-OUT PUNCH: (Chicago No. T-881), goes with ST350 riveting press. **NRS**

ST350-21 SMALL RIVET ANVIL: (Chicago No. T-807), goes with ST350 riveting press. **NRS**

ST350-22 KNOCK-OUT ANVIL: (Chicago No. T-882), goes with ST350 riveting press. **NRS**

ST375-1 AXLE MOUNTING TOOL: For use with locomotive axles with ST350 riveting press. **NRS**

ST375-2 UPPER WHEEL CUP: For use with ST350 riveting press in mounting wheels on all diesel locomotives.
— — 10 —

ST375-3 LOWER WHEEL CUP: For use with ST350 riveting press in mounting wheels on all diesel locomotives.
— — 10 —

ST375-4 UPPER WHEEL CUP: For use with ST350 riveting press in mounting wheels on all diesel locomotives.
— — 10 —

ST375-5 LOWER WHEEL CUP: For use with ST350 riveting press in mounting wheels on all diesel locomotives.
— — 10 —

ST375-6 UPPER WHEEL CUP: For use with ST350 riveting press in mounting wheels on all diesel locomotives.
— — 10 —

ST375-7 LOWER WHEEL CUP: For use with ST350 riveting press on locomotives using 2035-type motors.   — — 10 —

ST375-8 SLEEVE: For use with ST375-6 and ST375-7 wheel cups, sleeve used on center wheel of locomotives.
— — 10 —

ST375-9 LOWER WHEEL CUP: For use with ST350 riveting press on locomotives using 2026-type motors.   — — 10 —

ST375-10 UPPER WHEEL CUP: For use with ST350 riveting press on locomotives using 2026-type motors.
— — 10 —

ST378 E-UNIT VISE: Blue metal spring vise used to hold the E-unit drum in place while inserting the contact assembly. This tool, constructed of heavy steel, stands 3-3/8" high and sits on a three inch per side triangular base. L. Connors Collection. **NRS**

ST384 TRACK PLIERS: Universal track pliers illustrated in Service Manual, available in mid-1950s. The pliers are well-constructed of heavy forged steel and are inscribed "Track Pliers — O & O27 Track / ST384 Pat Pend" on one side and "Made for Lionel by Kraeuter" on the other. R. Otten Collection. These pliers have pin-crimping nib. Reproductions are available but do not have this nib. **NRS**

ST384 TRACK PLIERS: Similar in design to Kraeuter model, but inscribed "ST-384" and "Japan". Blue rubber sleeves on plier handles. Later version. **10 15 20 30**

Note: At least one dealer has made available for sale what is identified as a "ST-384 Track Pliers", but with the inscription "KOREA". Although this pliers serves as an excellent tool for working on tinplate track, from a collector standpoint this item, as best as can be determined, has no association with the Lionel name.

ST393 HO MAGNETIZER: Rectangular metal box measuring 9" long x 6" wide x 5" deep, for magnetizing Lionel HO motors. The unit is simple in design and was probably manufactured by Lionel. It is wired to a 12 volt auto battery which in turn is wired to an HO power pack as the final power source. The unit is illustrated in the June 1961 Lionel Service Bulletin, but with two distinct differences from the production model. The production model contains two transformer-type binding posts and the base is a plain metal box. The

ST393 HO Magnetizer.

G VG EXC NEW

Service Bulletin illustration includes a wire strip post and the box bears a distinctive lip for bench mounting. R. Osterhoff and C. Sigadel Collections.   — 150 250 350

Lionel Consumer Tools

Although this chapter is titled by design "Service Station Tools", Lionel did on a few occasions issue what can be loosely classified as a consumer tool category. We list these "tools" here for reference and the fact that they are very collectable of themselves.

773 FISHPLATE WRENCH: 1936, used with fishplate set for mounting scale O Gauge track to ties. Blackened metal, each approximately 3" long.
(A) L shaped wrench. R. Osterhoff Collection. **NRS**
(B) Straight wrench, small grooved handle.
— — 8 10
(C) Straight wrench, coarse grooved handle.
— — 12 15

3109-40 WRENCH: Specialized wrench, comes as part of base parts package for Lionel phonograph assembly No. 3109-45. More information required. **NRS**

3203-139 COMBINATION TOOL: Simple appearance, 3-3/4" tool which comes with all versions of the Electronic Lab Kits, and serves the purpose of a screwdriver, wrench, and wire stripper.
— — — 5

5153 SCREWDRIVER: Part of the 5153 Lionel model motoring track and car cleaner kit, this screwdriver measures 3-1/4" long and has a black plastic handle with no lettering to designate Lionel. If found outside the kit, it is difficult to identify this screwdriver as a Lionel product. Price for entire kit.   — — — 15

6-5817 PORTABLE TOOL KIT: 1987, consumer product, 13-in-1 set stored within handle.   — — — 14

6-5818 MINI MAG LITE: 1987, consumer product, flashlight 5-1/2" long, battery operated.   — — — 22

(NO NUMBER) SMOKE BRUSH: Issued in the early 1950s, apparently for the cleaning of locomotive smokestacks. This small 2-3/4" brush has black bristles in both a straight and circular format. Can any reader establish the origin of these brushes?
— — — 3

Chapter Nine
NON-TRAIN COLLECTIBLES

	G	VG	EXC	NEW

NON-TRAIN AND NAUTICAL PRODUCTS

4L BOAT COMPASS: 1941-43. Smaller compass designed for lifeboats, machine-finished and contains 45% solution of pure grain alcohol, includes 4" compass card. Used in conjunction with No. 4LB-10 wood binnacle box. Price for compass with box.
— — — 650

4LB-10 WOOD BINNACLE BOX: 1941-43. Stabilizer box used in conjunction with No. 4L boat compass. Has not been observed without compass. **NRS**

26 TIMER: Date unknown. While there was a product number assigned to this item, it is widely believed it was produced solely for dealer display use. **NRS**

43 MECHANICAL BOAT: 1933-36, 1939-41. 17" long; red, white, and beige, pleasure boat, admiralty flag, two-man crew.
— — 450 600

44 MECHANICAL BOAT: 1935-36. 17" long; green, white, and brown, racer with large exposed motor, two-man crew.
— — 500 750

49 AIRPORT: 1937-39. Lithographed, 58" diameter circular cardboard base for pylon. — — 125 200

50 LIONEL WARTIME FREIGHT TRAIN: 1943. The ultimate Lionel paper collectible! Packed in box 15-1/4" x 11-1/2" x 1-3/8" deep. Set consists of over 250 pieces, self-assembly fiberboard printed in sheet. Set also contains envelope of wooden axles, sheets of cardboard track, and six-page instruction flyer, "The Best of Everything goes into Lionel Trains". When assembled, set includes locomotive, tender, three cars, railroad crossing, and signal. We list it here because it is not a toy train in the traditional sense.
(A) As described above, original in box. 250 300 350 400
(B) Greenberg Publishing Co. reproduction, no box. — — — 12

Lionel's wartime "paper train."

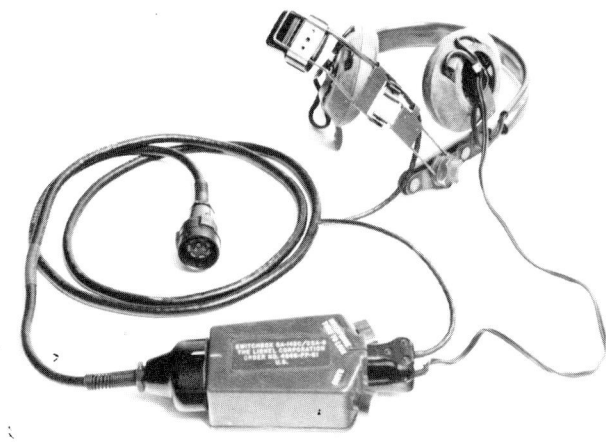

Lionel military H63/U headset microphone with switchbox.

Metal plate identifying the Lionel headset circa 1942-43.

	G	VG	EXC	NEW

50 REMOTE-CONTROL AIRPLANE: 1936. Red with pylon and controls. — — 250 400

51 AIRPORT: 1936, 1938. Lithographed cardboard square for use with No. 50 remote-control airplane. — — 175 300

55 REMOTE-CONTROL AIRPLANE: 1937-39. Red and silver with pylon and control; does not include cardboard base.
— — 300 450

H63/U HEADSET MICROPHONE: Circa 1942-43. World War II tank crew headphones clearly inscribed Lionel. References Army order No. 20054 and Philadelphia. Was designed to attach to Lionel Number SA-142C switchbox. — — 50 —

	G	VG	EXC	NEW

75P COMPLETE PELORUS: 1943. Designed to take ship bearings, comes without stands and measures 7-1/2" in diameter for the card, with a bowl depth of 5-1/2"; comes shipped in a wooden stowage box and weighs approximately 30 pounds. **NRS**

75PS ILLUMINATED PELORUS: 1943. Designed to take ship bearings, includes two stands and measures 7-1/2" in diameter for the card; overall height is 58", with a bowl depth of 5-1/2", comes shipped in a wooden stowage box and weighs approximately 110 pounds. **NRS**

75S PELORUS STAND: 1943. Stand only for No. 75P and No. 75PS pelorus. **NRS**

80 RACING AUTOMOBILE SET: 1912-16. Eight sections of track, 36" diameter; with auto, driver, and starting post. — — 600 1100

81 RACING AUTOMOBILE SET: 1912-16. Eight sections of track, 30" diameter; with auto, driver, and starting post. — — 600 1100

84 RACING AUTOMOBILE SET: 1912-16. Eight sections of curved track, 36" diameter; two automobiles, drivers, and starting posts. — — 1200 2200

85 RACING AUTOMOBILE SET: 1912-16. With two racing automobiles, drivers, eight sections curved track (36" diameter), eight sections curved track (30" diameter), eight sections straight track, and starting post. — — 1200 2200

0106 POWER PACK: 1962. "Racemaster" model for Lionel model motoring, 12 volts DC. 2 4 6 8

110 PHYSICAL SCIENCE SET: 1961. Lionel-Porter kit, explores light, sound, heat, etc. through science of physics. 15 20 30 35

111 CONSTRUCTION SET: 1947. Packed in cardboard box, comes with enough pieces to design 25 different structures, and only tool necessary is a screwdriver, which is provided. 20 30 45 60

120 PHYSICAL SCIENCE SET: 1961. Kit has similar experiments as No. 110, but twice as large. 20 30 40 50

121 CONSTRUCTION SET: 1948. Contents packed in cardboard display container with metal parts box; came with instruction manual. 20 30 45 60

140 LABCRAFT TECHNICIAN LAB: 1961. Kit offers tests for bacteria, water, soil, etc., comes with 750 power microscope. 20 30 40 50

160 BIOCRAFT BIOLOGY LAB: 1961. Kit plus microscope with up to 750 power magnification. 20 30 40 50

162 BIOCRAFT ACCESSORY KIT: 1961. Contains laboratory specimens only, with no microscope. 12 15 18 22

170 INDUSTRIAL SCIENCE LAB: 1961. Kit includes 3-D stereo-vision electric microscope. 20 30 40 50

175 INDIVIDUAL 3-D MICRO SET: 1961. Lionel-Porter kit with No. 175 microscope, but without mineralogy specimens and chemicals. 25 35 50 60

205 MICROCRAFT BEGINNER SET: 1961. Lionel-Porter microscope with 40/75/150 magnification power. 15 20 30 40

210 MICROCRAFT JUNIOR SET: 1961. Lionel-Porter microscope with 70/225/425 magnification power. 20 30 40 50

212L NAVY STANDARD BINNACLE: 1943. A Navy 7-1/2" compass enclosed in metal case (the binnacle), fully illuminated with a height of 59"; total weight exceeds 382 pounds in a packed container. **NRS**

215 ILLUMINATED PELORUS: 1943. A Navy 9" bearing device, fully illuminated and packed in a wooden case; measurements are 56-1/2" high, including dome, with base diameter of 14", and weighs 155 pounds crated. Includes one extra glass dial and extra brass dial for target practice. **NRS**

215S ILLUMINATED PELORUS: 1943. Same as No. 215 model, except pelorus bowl and pedestal base are made of cast iron instead of bronze; weighs 145 pounds. **NRS**

215X ILLUMINATED PELORUS: 1943. Same as No. 215 model, except without rheostat or spare parts. **NRS**

217 MICROCRAFT SENIOR LAB: 1961. Lionel-Porter microscope with 75/180/325/500 magnification power. 20 30 40 50

222 CONSTRUCTION SET: 1947. Set is packed in sturdy metal box with capability to construct as many as 50 different items; includes construction manual. 25 35 50 65

223 MICROCRAFT LABMASTER: 1961. Lionel-Porter microscope with eight magnifications up to 750 power. 20 30 40 50

230 MICROCRAFT SENIOR LABMASTER: 1961. Deluxe microbiology kit with microscope of eight magnifications up to 750 power. 25 35 50 60

232 CONSTRUCTION KIT: 1948. Set is packed in sturdy metal box, and includes an electric motor and instruction manual. 25 35 50 60

255 MICROCRAFT SPECIMEN LAB: 1961. Kit for conducting experiments, without microscope. 12 15 18 22

260 MICROCRAFT JUNIOR RESEARCH LAB: 1961. Lionel-Porter kit includes microscope with up to 425 power magnification. 20 30 40 50

264 MICROCRAFT STUDENT RESEARCH MICROSCOPE: 1961. Lionel-Porter microscope with kit, for up to 750 times power magnification. 25 30 40 55

307 MATHCRAFT SET: 1961. Kit includes slide rule and Chinese abacus instructions. 15 20 25 30

333 CONSTRUCTION SET: 1947. Set packed in heavy cardboard box and includes 10 watt electric motor, instruction manual, and model building book. 30 40 55 70

343 CONSTRUCTION KIT: 1948. Set comes packed in sturdy box with carrying handle and includes a four-speed electric motor, instruction manual, and all-aluminum parts for building such items as a gantry crane and bascule bridge. 30 40 55 70

400 LANTERN: Apparent replica of old-style wick railroad lantern. Inscribed "No. 400 Use Long Time Burning Oil Only", and

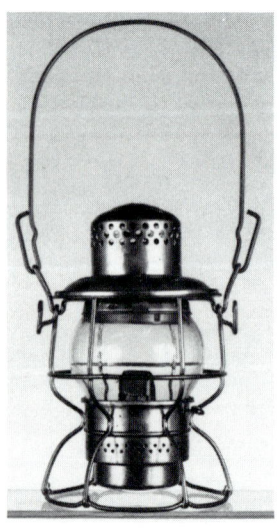

No. 400 lantern.

Non-Train Collectibles • 155

on the side of the wick holder "Adlake 400". Reader date and product information requested. J. Sery Collection. **NRS**

444 CONSTRUCTION SET: 1947. Lionel's top-of-the-line set for 1947, contains a gear-driven 12 watt electric motor, model building booklet, instruction manual, construction pieces in three trays; all contents packed in heavy duty metal box.

G	VG	EXC	NEW
35	50	75	100

453 ELECTRIC RANGE: 1930. Illustrated in the 1930 consumer catalogue without a product number, this range is described as 33" high x 26" deep, and includes five cooking utensils. Additional information requested on this model. **NRS**

454 ELECTRIC RANGE: 1931. Although this model was not listed in the 1931 consumer catalogue, some collectors believe it was actually sold by Lionel in 1931. Reader assistance requested. **NRS**

454 CONSTRUCTION KIT: 1948. Kit packed in oak wooden box, includes a gear-driven motor with built-in transformer, instruction manual, and enough parts to build scores of different models.

| 35 | 50 | 75 | 100 |

455 ELECTRIC RANGE: 1930, 1932-33. Green legs, cream oven and stove sides, two stove top heating units, two units in oven with one for broiling and one for baking, thermometer on oven door, four controls and master switch, pilot light, five cooking utensils; 25" wide x 11" deep x 33" high. A 1932-33 advertising narrative emphasizes that "oven walls are heavily insulated with asbestos." Owners may wish to note this fact in the interest of safety!

| 150 | 300 | 400 | 550 |

502 TOOLCRAFT TOOL KIT: 1961. Junior kit 15" x 7-3/4" x 2"; with hammer, saw, screwdriver, and other basic tools.

| 8 | 10 | 15 | 20 |

503 TOOLCRAFT TOOL KIT: 1961. Kit is 15" x 7-3/4" x 2" and comes in a sturdy blue-colored metal box; contents include hammer, saw, screwdriver, pliers, and other tools.

| 10 | 14 | 18 | 24 |

505 TOOLCRAFT TOOL KIT: 1961. Kit measures 15" x 10-1/2" x 2" and comes packed in a red metal case; contents include more advanced tools such as a carpenter's brace and metal plane.

| 12 | 18 | 25 | 30 |

565 CONSTRUCTION KIT: 1948. Lionel's most comprehensive construction set is packed in a wooden case with drawer and comes with a gear-driven motor with built-in transformer, instruction manual, and enough parts to build the most complex models.

| 40 | 60 | 85 | 120 |

570 LINEX STEREO CAMERA: 1954-56. Die-cast camera body, nylon moving parts, 6-1/2" long x 3" deep x 1-3/4" high, weight about one pound. Camera had brightness control for bright or dull light; fixed shutter operated at 1/50 second. Film came in an oblong magazine which had to be sent to Ansco Laboratories on Long Island for processing. Each magazine yielded eight stereo pairs of slides mounted in special plastic slide holders. Mounted slides meant to be viewed in battery-operated viewer designed expressly for the camera. Approximately 85,000 made; about 65,000 initially sold; the remainder were heavily discounted. For further information, see "The Linex Stereo Camera", Photographic News, May 1985, p. 52.

G	VG	EXC	NEW
75	100	125	150

603 CHEMCRAFT BEGINNER'S SET: 1961. Chemistry set for over 300 experiments.

| 20 | 25 | 30 | 35 |

605 CHEMCRAFT JUNIOR SET: 1961. Chemistry set for over 350 experiments.

| 20 | 25 | 30 | 35 |

608 CHEMCRAFT STUDENT SET: 1961. Chemistry set for over 400 experiments.

| 25 | 30 | 40 | 50 |

610 CHEMCRAFT SENIOR SET: 1961. Chemistry set for 480 experiments.

| 25 | 30 | 40 | 50 |

617 CHEMCRAFT SENIOR LAB: 1961. Chemistry set for over 750 experiments.

| 30 | 40 | 50 | 60 |

623 CHEMCRAFT MASTER LAB: 1961. Chemistry set for over 900 experiments.

| 30 | 40 | 50 | 60 |

634 CHEMCRAFT MASTER DELUXE LAB: 1961. Top-of-the-line Lionel-Porter chemistry set, designed for over 1000 scientific experiments.

| 35 | 45 | 60 | 75 |

634L NAVY-TYPE COMPASS: 1942. 6-3/4" model, U. S. Navy Standard Mark II; can be used in conjunction with certain marine binnacles. **NRS**

712A AZIMUTH CIRCLE: 1943. Precision nautical instrument used with Navy compasses; comes in felt-lined mahogany box. **NRS**

No. 712A azimuth circle, in mahogany box.

712B BEARING CIRCLE: 1943. Precision nautical instrument for measuring compass direction of land or air objects; comes in green felt-lined, polished mahogany box. R. Osterhoff Collection.

| — | — | 150 | — |

712L ILLUMINATED COMPASS: 1940-43. 7-1/2" U. S. Navy Standard Mark I, in wooden box. **NRS**

712LA ILLUMINATED COMPASS: 1940-43. 7-1/2" U. S. Navy Standard Mark I, with azimuth hole in center of top glass. **NRS**

712M ILLUMINATED COMPASS: 1940-43. 7-1/2" U. S. Navy Standard Mark I, same as Model 712L, except for gimbal ring. **NRS**

810 COLLECTOR'S MINERALOGY LAB: 1961. Set contains 30 minerals for studying; no microscope.

| 12 | 15 | 18 | 22 |

The innovative No. 570 Linex stereo camera.

An excellent example of Lionel's wartime production is this No. 712 illuminated compass.

	G	VG	EXC	NEW

817 GEOLOGY LAB: 1961. Kit includes fossil specimens plus rocks and minerals; no microscope included.

	12	15	18	22

825 MINERALOGY LAB: 1961. Set similar to No. 810, but also contains electric microscope.

	20	30	40	50

859 U-DRIVE BOAT: 1964-65. Outside diameter of nine feet, made up of eight curved sections; can hold child up to 50 lbs. Not produced; prototype only created. **NRS**

861 HELIOS 21 SPACESHIP: 1964. "Giant spaceship of the 21st century", packed in a carton which contains the spaceship, antigravity booster, and space controller; No. 5303 power supplier has to be purchased separately.

	—	—	60	85

861 LYTER-N-AIR ROCKET SHIP: 1964. Similar to No. 861, but without "Helios 21" on side.

	—	—	60	85

862 LYTER-N-AIR SPACE STATION: 1964. Kit comes complete with booster tank and electronic control panel.

	—	—	60	85

863 LYTER-N-AIR SELF-LAUNCHING SPACE KITE: 1964. Comes complete with reel controller and space cord.

	—	—	40	50

876 HELIOS 21 SPACESHIP: 1965. "Giant spaceship of the 21st century", packed in a carton which contains the spaceship, antigravity booster, and space controller; No. 5303 power supply has to be purchased separately.

	—	—	60	85

1203L LIFEBOAT BINNACLE: 1943. Binnacle used with No. 4L compass, made of copper with few exceptions, and includes a storage drawer for wicks and matches; shipped in corrugated board box, shipping weight 7-1/2 pounds; No. 214-70A cables have to be purchased separately for use in the binnacle. **NRS**

3100 GUTENBERG, THE PRINTING PRESS: 1961-63. Famous Inventor Series historic science kit in plastic.

	20	30	50	100

3101 GALILEO, THE TELESCOPE: 1961-63. Famous Inventor Series science kit for 8 power telescope.

	20	30	50	100

3102 EDISON, THE ELECTRIC LIGHT: 1961-63. Famous Inventor Series historic science kit in plastic; battery operated.

	20	30	50	100

3103 HERO, THE STEAM ENGINE: 1961-63. Famous Inventor Series historic science kit, produces steam using heating pellets with water.

	20	30	50	100

Top: The loom as mounted in container. *Bottom:* The 3108 Cartwright power loom in original box.

	G	VG	EXC	NEW

3104 MORSE, THE TELEGRAPH: 1961-63. Famous Inventor Series historic science kit in plastic, battery operated.

	20	30	50	100

3105 BELL, THE TELEPHONE: 1962-63. Famous Inventor Series historic science kit in plastic.

	20	30	50	100

3107 HOOKE, THE COMPOUND MICROSCOPE: 1962-63. Famous Inventor Series, includes microscope and bust of Hooke.

	20	30	50	100

3108 CARTWRIGHT, THE POWER LOOM: 1962-63. Famous Inventor Series, allows actual construction of miniature loom.

	20	30	50	100

3109 EDISON, THE PHONOGRAPH: 1962-63. Famous Inventor Series historic science kit in plastic, with Edison bust.

	20	30	50	100

3200 MARK I SET: 1961. Electronics engineering set, introduces principles of electricity; battery operated.

	20	30	40	50

3201 MARK II SET: 1961-63. Electronics engineering set, introduces such principles as switching and circuitry; battery operated.

	20	30	40	50

3202 MARK III SET: 1961-63. Electronics engineering set, teaches the principles of the sensitive relay, allowing for construction of a home burglar alarm; battery operated.

	20	40	60	80

Non-Train Collectibles • 157

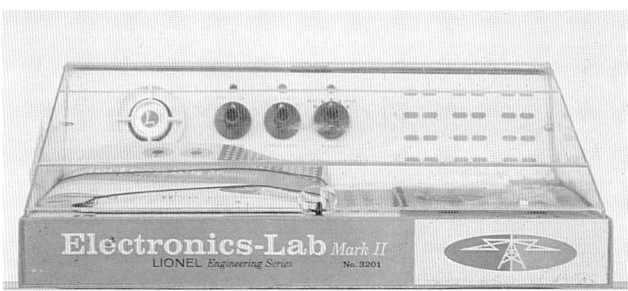

No. 3201 Mark II set.

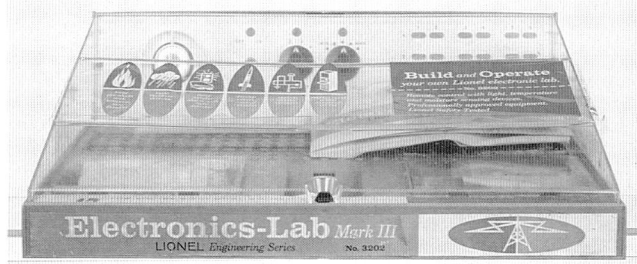

No. 3202 Mark III electronics set.

3203 MARK IV LAB: 1962-63. Electronics lab, allows electrical experiments to be conducted on sensing devices for moisture, light, or temperature; battery operated.   **40   60   80   100**

3210 MARK I LAB: 1962. Electronics lab, provides instructions for building a burglar alarm and electric bell; battery operated.
   20   30   40   50

3225 MARK Ia LAB: 1962. Plastics lab, allows creation of miniature boats through foam casting.   **25   40   50   70**

The more advanced No. 3228 Mark III plastics lab.

3226 MARK I SET: 1961-62. Plastics engineering set, introduces the field of plastics identification.
   20   30   40   50

3227 MARK II SET: 1961-63. Plastics engineering set, allows a molding of speed boats and the Mercury space capsule.
   20   30   40   50

3228 MARK III SET: 1961-63. Plastics engineering set, introduces user to more advanced plastic production techniques, and allows creation of many products.   **25   40   50   70**

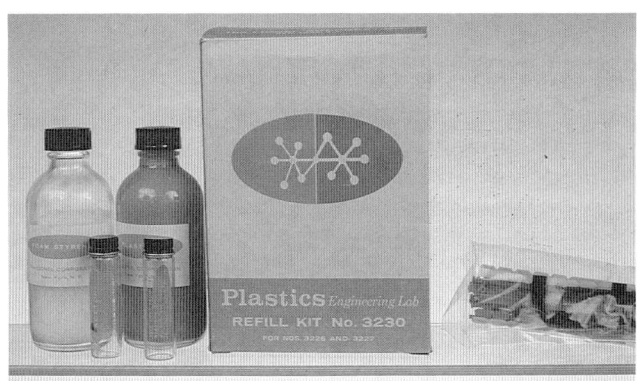

No. 3230 refill kit for plastics lab.

                  G   VG   EXC   NEW

3229 MARK IV SET: 1961-63. Plastics engineering set, most advanced capabilities, allows creation of a chess set, Mercury space capsule, and plastic boat by injection-molding and other methods.
   30   40   60   80

3230 REFILL KIT: 1961-62. For sets 3225, 3226, and 3227.
   —   —   —   20

3231 REFILL KIT: 1961-62. For sets 3228 and 3229.
   —   —   —   20

3251 MARK I SET: 1961. Portable weather station set, basic instructions on predicting the weather; battery operated.
   20   30   40   50

3252 MARK II SET: 1961. Portable weather station set, more advanced meteorological equipment for predicting weather trends, relative humidity, and other functions; battery operated.
   20   30   40   50

3253 MARK I SET: 1962-65. Portable weather station set; used for observing and predicting weather patterns; battery operated.
   20   30   40   50

3254 MARK II SET: 1962-64. Home weather station, includes Telemeter electric indoor wind direction indicator; battery operated.
   20   30   40   50

3255 MARK III SET: 1962-64. Advanced weather station, includes wind direction measurements and allows operator to predict weather without looking out the window; battery operated.
   25   40   60   80

3270 MARK I LAB: 1962-65. Communications lab, explores the wonders of sound, includes seven types of radios; battery operated.
   20   30   40   50

3271 MARK II LAB: 1962-64. Communications lab, allows building of seven types of radios plus public address system; battery operated.   **20   30   40   50**

3272 MARK III LAB: 1962-64. Communications lab, introduces world of condensers, transistors, and speakers; battery operated.
   20   30   40   65

3273 MARK IV LAB: 1962-64. Communications lab, builds radios, an intercom, light beam, and tape recorder; battery operated.
   30   40   60   80

5303 POWER SUPPLY: 1954-65. Used with the Helios 21 spaceship and the Lyter-n-air rocket ship. T. Wagner comment.   **NRS**

16020 AUTO RACING SET: 1963. "Speedway 250" set, includes two cars; 53" x 30" layout.   **30   40   50   60**

16030 AUTO RACING SET: 1963. "Speedway 600" set, includes two cars; 63" x 30" layout.   **30   40   50   60**

16040 AUTO RACING SET: 1963. "Speedway 750" set, includes two cars; 98" x 30" layout, with timer.
   40   50   75   90

	G	VG	EXC	NEW
16050 AUTO RACING SET: 1963. "Speedway 1000" set includes four cars; 59" x 30" layout.	40	50	75	90
16090 AUTO RACING SET: 1965. "Twin Chicane", Standard oval set, includes two cars; 52" x 34" layout.	25	35	45	60
16100 AUTO RACING SET: 1965-66. "Loop-the-Loop" Standard outfit, with over 22' of track, two cars; 45" x 94" layout.	25	35	45	60
16110 AUTO RACING SET: 1965-66. "Skill-Tilt Skyway Leap" Standard outfit, with over 20' of track; 77" x 42" layout.	30	40	50	70
16130 AUTO RACING SET: 1966. "Big 8" Standard set, with over 12' of track, two cars; 30" x 65" layout.	25	35	45	60
17010 AUTO RACING SET: 1963. "Raceway 33" set, with two cars; 40" x 18" layout.	25	35	45	60
17020 AUTO RACING SET: 1963. "Raceway 66" set, container becomes racing platform; 36" x 28" layout.	25	35	45	60
17030 AUTO RACING SET: 1963. "Raceway 99" set, with four cars; 45" x 18" layout.	30	40	50	65
17130 AUTO RACING SET: 1965. "Malibu Twister" model, includes two cars; 27" x 33" layout.	25	35	45	60
17140 AUTO RACING SET: 1965-66. "Loop-the-Loop" model with over 15' of track, comes with two cars; 30" x 60" layout.	25	40	55	80
17160 AUTO RACING SET: 1965-66. "Pretzel Bender" model with over 16' of track, comes with two cars; 52" x 52" layout.	30	45	60	80
17170 AUTO RACING SET: 1965-66. "Monte Carlo" model with over 23' of track, comes with two cars; 88" x 35" layout.	30	45	60	80
17180 AUTO RACING SET: 1965. "Flag-Tag" model, with four cars; 36" x 27" layout.	40	50	60	70
17190 AUTO RACING SET: 1965. Combination HO raceway and train set, includes No. 0055 Minneapolis and St. Louis Husky switcher, freight set plus complete raceway set with figure eight track.				NRS
17200 AUTO RACING SET: 1966. "Matterhorn" model with over 41' of track, four cars, power lift feature; 88" x 40" layout.	40	50	70	90
17515 AUTO RACING SET: 1966. Information on this set, including date confirmation, requested.				NRS
21000 CHEMISTRY SET: 1962. Chemcraft beginner set, includes non-spill lamp and capacity for 309 experiments.	10	15	20	25
21010 CHEMISTRY SET: 1962. Chemcraft junior set, packed in two-panel stand-up cabinet, capacity for 350 experiments.	10	15	20	25
21030 CHEMISTRY SET: 1962. Chemcraft student lab, packed in three-panel stand-up cabinet, capacity for 483 experiments.	20	25	40	55
21040 CHEMISTRY SET: 1962. Chemcraft collegiate lab, packed in four-panel stand-up cabinet, capacity for 640 experiments.	25	30	45	60
21050 CHEMISTRY SET: 1962. Chemcraft senior lab, packed in four-panel stand-up cabinet, capacity for 752 experiments.	25	30	45	60
21060 CHEMISTRY SET: 1962. Chemcraft master lab, packed in six-panel stand-up cabinet, capacity for 915 experiments, includes six manuals and three chemical charts.	40	50	65	85
21070 CHEMISTRY SET: 1962. Chemcraft master deluxe lab, provides for over 1,000 experiments, packed in six-panel stand-up metal cabinet, includes battery-powered chemical agitator.	45	60	75	90
21080 ACCESSORY GIFT PACK: 1962. Comes with a variety of products including a gram balance and hydrometer.	5	8	12	18
21090 ACCESSORY GIFT PACK: 1962. Comes with products such as gram balance, centrifuge, and chemical pen.	7	9	14	20
21100 ACCESSORY GIFT PACK: 1962. Comes with more advanced products including a battery-powered chemical agitator, crime detection kit, and gram balance.	7	9	14	20
21110 CHEMISTRY SET: 1963. Chemcraft beginner set includes non-spill lamp and capacity for 309 experiments.	10	15	20	25
21120 CHEMISTRY SET: 1963. Chemcraft junior lab, with capacity for 350 experiments; packed in two-panel stand-up cabinet.	10	15	20	25
21130 CHEMISTRY SET: 1963. Chemcraft research lab, with capacity for 350 experiments; comes in factory-sealed container.	10	15	20	25
21140 CHEMISTRY SET: 1963. Chemcraft student lab, with capacity for 483 experiments; packed in three-panel stand-up cabinet.	20	25	40	55
21150 CHEMISTRY SET: 1963. Chemcraft senior lab, with capacity for 653 experiments; packed in four-panel stand-up cabinet.	25	30	45	60
21170 CHEMISTRY SET: 1963. Chemcraft master lab, with capacity for 915 experiments; packed in six-panel stand-up cabinet.	40	50	65	85
21180 CHEMISTRY SET: 1963. Chemcraft master deluxe lab, capacity for over 1,000 experiments, includes battery-powered chemical agitator; packed in six-panel stand-up cabinet.	45	60	75	90
21190 ACCESSORY GIFT PACK: 1963-64. Comes with a variety of products including a gram balance and hydrometer.	5	8	12	18
21200 ACCESSORY GIFT PACK: 1963-64. Comes with more advanced products including a crime detection kit and AC-'63 chemical computer.	7	9	14	20
21210 CHEMCRAFT BEGINNER SET: 1964. Provides for over 250 experiments; packed in cardboard box.	12	16	20	25
21220 CHEMCRAFT JUNIOR LAB: 1964. Provides for over 325 experiments; packed in two-panel metal cabinet.	15	20	25	30
21240 CHEMCRAFT STUDENT LAB: 1964. Provides for over 400 experiments; packed in three-panel metal cabinet.	20	25	30	45
21250 CHEMCRAFT SENIOR LAB: 1964. Provides for over 650 experiments; packed in four-panel metal cabinet.	25	30	35	45
21270 CHEMCRAFT MASTER LAB: 1964. Provides for over 900 experiments; packed in six-panel metal cabinet.	35	45	60	80
21280 CHEMCRAFT MASTER DELUXE LAB: 1964. Provides for over 1000 experiments; packed in six-panel metal cabinet.	35	45	60	80
21310 CHEMCRAFT BEGINNER SET: 1965. Set provides for over 250 experiments, with accessories.	15	20	30	40
21320 CHEMCRAFT JUNIOR LAB: 1965. Set provides for over 325 experiments, with accessories.	15	20	30	40

	G	VG	EXC	NEW

21340 CHEMCRAFT STUDENT LAB: 1965. Set provides for over 450 experiments, with accessories; packed in three-panel steel case. **25 35 45 60**

21360 CHEMCRAFT SENIOR LAB: 1965. Set provides for over 650 experiments, with accessories; packed in five-panel steel case. **35 45 55 80**

21380 CHEMCRAFT MASTER LAB: 1965. Set provides for over 1000 experiments, with accessories; packed in six-panel steel case. **40 50 60 80**

21410 CHEMCRAFT BEGINNER SET: 1966-67. Set provides for over 309 experiments, with accessories. **15 20 30 40**

21420 CHEMCRAFT JUNIOR LAB: 1966. Set provides for over 512 experiments, with accessories; packed in two-panel metal cabinet. **15 20 30 40**

21440 CHEMCRAFT STUDENT LAB: 1966. Set provides for over 629 experiments, with accessories; packed in three-panel metal cabinet. **25 35 45 60**

21460 CHEMCRAFT SENIOR LAB: 1966. Set provides for over 749 experiments, with accessories; packed in five-panel metal cabinet. **35 45 55 80**

21480 CHEMCRAFT MASTER LAB: 1966. Set provides for over 967 experiments, with accessories; packed in six-panel metal cabinet. **40 50 60 80**

21710 CHEMCRAFT ELEMENTARY SET: 1967. Set provides for over 309 experiments; packed in two-panel metal box. **15 20 30 40**

21720 CHEMCRAFT JUNIOR OUTFIT: 1967. Set provides for over 429 experiments; packed in three-panel metal case. **20 25 35 45**

21740 CHEMCRAFT STUDENT OUTFIT: 1967. Set provides for over 569 experiments; packed in three-panel metal case. **20 25 35 45**

21750 CHEMCRAFT SCHOLASTIC OUTFIT: 1967. Set provides for over 690 experiments; packed in four-panel metal case. **25 30 40 55**

21760 CHEMCRAFT SENIOR LAB: 1967. Set provides for over 752 experiments; packed in five-panel metal case. **35 45 60 70**

521780 CHEMCRAFT MASTER LAB: 1967. Set provides for over 967 experiments; packed in six-panel metal case. **50 60 75 90**

21800 CHEMCRAFT BEGINNER SET: 1968. Set provides for over 75 experiments. **15 20 30 40**

21810 CHEMCRAFT ELEMENTARY SET: 1968. Set provides for over 345 experiments; packed in cardboard container. **15 20 30 40**

21820 CHEMCRAFT JUNIOR SET: 1968. Set provides for over 429 experiments; packed in cardboard container. **15 20 30 40**

21850 CHEMCRAFT SCHOLASTIC SET: 1968. Set provides for over 639 experiments; packed in four-panel metal box. **25 30 40 55**

21860 CHEMCRAFT SENIOR LAB: 1968. Set provides for over 752 experiments; packed in five-panel metal box. **35 45 60 75**

21880 CHEMCRAFT MASTER LAB: 1968. Set provides for over 967 experiments; packed in six-panel metal box. **50 60 75 90**

21840 CHEMCRAFT STUDENT OUTFIT: 1968. Set provides for over 514 experiments; packed in three-panel metal case. **20 25 35 45**

22000 MICROCRAFT JUNIOR SET: 1962. Built-in battery-powered 75 power Lionel-Porter microscope. **15 25 35 45**

22020 MICROCRAFT SENIOR OUTFIT: 1962. Plug-in electric illumination 75/180/450 power selections, Lionel-Porter microscope. **15 25 35 45**

22030 MICROCRAFT RESEARCH OUTFIT: 1962. Lionel-Porter five-turret microscope includes 30-500 times magnification; electrically illuminated. **20 30 40 55**

22040 MICROCRAFT LABMASTER: 1962. Lionel-Porter five-turret microscope includes 30-750 times magnification, electrically illuminated; packed in three-panel metal box. **30 45 60 75**

22050 MICROCRAFT SENIOR LABMASTER: 1962. Lionel-Porter five-turret microscope includes 30-750 times magnification, electronic stage and power pack; packed in three-panel metal box. **30 45 60 75**

22060 MICROCRAFT SENIOR LABMASTER DELUXE: 1962. Lionel-Porter five-turret microscope includes 30-750 times magnification, mechanical stage, projector viewer, and many accessories; packed in a four-panel metal box. **40 50 65 85**

22070 MICROCRAFT ACCESSORY SET: 1962. Kit provides supplies and instructions for the preparation of microscope slides. **5 8 14 18**

22080 SLIDE KIT: 1962-64. Package of five prepared slides ready for viewing. **1 3 5 7**

22090 MICROCRAFT STUDENT MICROSCOPE: 1962. Lionel-Porter three-turret beginner microscope with 60-425 times magnification capability; packed in two-panel metal box. **15 25 35 45**

22100 MICROCRAFT MASTER MICROSCOPE: 1962. Lionel-Porter five-turret microscope with 30-750 times magnification capability; packed in two-panel metal box. **15 25 35 45**

22110 MICROCRAFT STUDENT SET: 1963. Lionel-Porter three-turret microscope with 75 times magnification capability; packed in cardboard box. **15 25 35 45**

22120 MICROCRAFT SENIOR OUTFIT: 1963. Lionel-Porter three-turret microscope with 75-450 times magnification capability; packed in cardboard box. **15 25 35 45**

22130 MICROCRAFT SENIOR DELUXE LAB: 1963. Lionel-Porter three-turret microscope with 75-450 times magnification capability; packed in two-panel metal container. **15 25 35 45**

22140 MICROCRAFT SENIOR RESEARCH LAB: 1963. Lionel-Porter five-turret microscope with 30-500 times magnification capability; packed in two-panel metal cabinet with many accessories. **15 25 35 45**

22160 MICROCRAFT LABMASTER: 1963. Lionel-Porter five-turret microscope with ten magnifications from 30-750 times; packed in deluxe three-panel metal cabinet with many accessories. **20 30 40 50**

22170 MICROCRAFT SENIOR LABMASTER: 1963. Lionel-Porter five-turret microscope with ten magnifications from 30-750 times; packed in deluxe three-panel metal cabinet with many accessories. **25 35 45 60**

22180 MICROCRAFT ACCESSORY SET: 1963-64. Lionel-Porter set, includes electronic stage and power pack and a variety of other microbiological accessories. **8 12 15 18**

22190 MICROCRAFT STUDENT MICROSCOPE: 1963. Lionel-Porter three-turret microscope with 60-425 times magnification capability; packed in two-panel metal cabinet. **15 20 25 30**

	G	VG	EXC	NEW
22200 MICROCRAFT FOUR-IN-ONE SLIDE KIT: 1963. Lionel-Porter product includes five prepared slides for microscope viewing.	4	7	9	12
22210 MICROCRAFT STUDENT SET: 1964. Includes 75 times magnification microscope plus limited accessories.	15	20	30	40
22220 MICROCRAFT STUDENT OUTFIT: 1964. Includes 75 to 425 times magnification microscope plus limited accessories.	15	20	30	40
22230 MICROCRAFT SENIOR OUTFIT: 1964. Includes three-turret 75 to 425 times magnification microscope plus limited accessories.	20	25	35	45
22240 MICROCRAFT SENIOR DELUXE LAB: 1964. Includes three-turret 75 to 450 times magnification microscope, accessories; packed in two-panel metal cabinet.	25	30	40	50
22250 MICROCRAFT LAB MASTER 1964. Includes five-turret 30 to 500 power microscope, accessories; packed in three-panel metal cabinet.	30	40	50	60
22270 MICROCRAFT SENIOR LAB MASTER: 1964. Includes five-turret 30 to 500 power microscope, accessories; packed in four-panel metal cabinet.	35	45	55	65
22310 MICROCRAFT BEGINNER'S SET: 1965-66. Includes 75 power microscope with limited accessories.	20	25	30	40
22320 MICROCRAFT JUNIOR SET: 1965. Includes 60 to 90 times magnification microscope and limited accessories.	20	25	30	40
22340 MICROCRAFT STUDENT SET: 1965. Includes a 75-675 times three-turret all-metal microscope in steel chest.	20	25	35	45
22350 MICROCRAFT SENIOR LAB MASTER: 1965. Includes a 75-675 times three-turret all-metal microscope in three-panel steel cabinet.	25	30	40	50
22370 MICROCRAFT LAB MASTER: 1965. Includes 75-675 times three-turret microscope in four-panel steel cabinet.	40	50	65	80
22440 MICROCRAFT STUDENT SET: 1966. Includes 600 power three-turret microscope with limited number of accessories.	20	25	30	40
22450 MICROCRAFT SENIOR SET: 1966. Kit includes 675-power, three-turret microscope plus accessories.	20	25	30	40
22460 MICROCRAFT MASTER LAB: 1966. Kit includes 700 power, three-turret microscope plus accessories.	30	40	50	60
22470 MICROSCOPE MASTER DELUXE LAB: 1966. Kit includes 800 power five-turret microscope, many accessories including a shrimp hatchery.	40	50	65	90
22710 MICROCRAFT BEGINNER SET: 1967. Kit includes 60 to 425 times magnification microscope in metal case.	20	25	30	40
22730 MICROCRAFT JUNIOR LAB: 1967. Kit includes 60 to 425 times magnification microscope in metal case.	20	25	30	40
22750 MICROCRAFT STUDENT SET: 1967. Kit includes three-turret 600 times magnification microscope in metal case.	20	25	35	45
22760 MICROCRAFT SENIOR OUTFIT: 1967. Kit includes five-turret 700 times magnification microscope in shrink-wrapped display case.	20	25	35	45
22770 MICROCRAFT MASTER OUTFIT: 1967. Kit includes five-turret 800 times magnification microscope in shrink-wrapped display case.	25	30	40	55
22810 MICROCRAFT BEGINNER OUTFIT: 1968. Kit includes 75 to 450 times magnification microscope.	20	25	30	40
22820 MICROCRAFT JUNIOR SET: 1968. Kit includes 75 to 450 times magnification microscope in shrink-wrapped display case.	20	25	30	40
22830 MICROCRAFT STUDENT SET: 1968. Kit includes three-turret 600 times magnification microscope and various accessories.	20	25	35	45
22840 MICROCRAFT SENIOR OUTFIT: 1968. Kit includes 30-700 times magnification microscope; packed in three-panel metal container.	20	25	35	45
22850 MICROCRAFT MASTER LAB: 1968. Kit includes five-turret 800 times magnification microscope; packed in four-panel metal case.	25	30	45	55
23000 BIOCRAFT ACCESSORY KIT: 1962. Kit includes manual and four animal specimens for use with microscopes.	4	7	12	15
23010 BIOCRAFT ACCESSORY LAB: 1962. Kit includes manual, four animal and three insect specimens for use with microscopes.	6	9	14	18
23020 BIOCRAFT STUDENT LAB: 1962. Lionel-Porter 60-power microscope with dissecting apparatus; packed in two-panel metal box.	15	25	35	45
23030 BIOCRAFT COLLEGIATE LAB: 1962. Lionel-Porter three-turret microscope with 60-425 times magnification; packed in three-panel metal box with specimens.	20	30	40	55
23040 BIOCRAFT SENIOR LAB: 1962. Lionel-Porter three-turret microscope with 75-450 times magnification; packed in three-panel metal box with specimens and accessories.	25	35	45	60
23050 BIOCRAFT MASTER LAB: 1962. Lionel-Porter three-turret microscope with 75-450 times magnification; packed in three-panel metal box with specimens and accessories.	25	35	45	60
23060 BIO-CHEMISTRY LAB: 1962. Lionel-Porter five-turret microscope with 30-750 times magnification, packed in four-panel metal box with specimens, accessories designed for bio-chemistry experimentation.	35	45	65	80
23070 BIOCRAFT STUDENT LAB: 1963. Includes 60 power microscope, accessories; packed in two-panel metal cabinet.	15	20	30	40
23080 BIOCRAFT SENIOR LAB: 1963. Includes 75 to 450 power microscope, accessories; packed in three-panel metal cabinet.	20	25	35	45
23090 BIOCRAFT MASTER LAB: 1963. Includes 75 to 450 power, three-turret microscope, accessories; packed in four-panel metal cabinet.	25	35	45	55
23100 BIOCRAFT SPECIMEN LABORATORY: 1963. Includes three specimens; packed in cardboard container.	12	18	22	28
23110 BIOCRAFT BEGINNER SET: 1964. Starter set includes two specimens.	12	18	22	28
23120 BIOCRAFT JUNIOR LABORATORY: 1964. Includes limited animal specimens, accessories; in cardboard container.	12	18	22	28
23140 BIOCRAFT STUDENT LAB: 1964. Includes 60 power microscope, specimens, and accessories in two-panel metal cabinet.	20	25	30	40
23160 BIOCRAFT SENIOR LAB: 1964. Includes 75 to 450 power microscope, specimens and accessories; packed in three-panel metal cabinet.	25	35	45	60

	G	VG	EXC	NEW
23210 BIOCRAFT JUNIOR LAB: 1965. Introductory set with three animal specimens and accessories.	5	10	15	20
23230 BIOCRAFT STUDENT LAB: 1965. Includes 60 power microscope and accessories; packed in two-panel chest.	15	20	25	35
23250 BIOCRAFT SENIOR LAB: 1965. Includes 30-45 power microscope and accessories; packed in three-panel chest.	20	25	30	40
23310 BIOCRAFT JUNIOR SET: 1966. Includes specimens and accessories to study elementary biology.	10	13	18	25
23330 BIOCRAFT STUDENT LAB: 1966. Includes 60 power microscope with accessories.	20	25	35	45
23350 BIOCRAFT SENIOR LAB: 1966. Includes 700 power magnification three-turret microscope, shrimp hatchery, and many other accessories.	25	30	40	50
23710 BIOCRAFT JUNIOR SET: 1967. Includes specimens and accessories to study elementary biology.	10	13	18	25
23730 BIOCRAFT STUDENT LAB: 1967. Includes 60 power microscope with accessories.	20	25	35	45
23750 BIOCRAFT SENIOR LAB: 1967. Includes 700 power magnification three-turret microscope, shrimp hatchery, and many other accessories.	25	30	40	50
23810 BIOCRAFT JUNIOR SET: 1968. Porter specimen set for basic experimentation.	12	15	18	22
23820 BIOCRAFT STUDENT SET: 1968. Porter set, includes more advanced specimens; packed in three-panel metal container.	20	25	30	35
23830 BIOCRAFT SENIOR LAB: 1968. Porter set, includes 45 power microscope and specimens; packed in two-panel metal chest.	25	30	40	50
23850 BIOCRAFT MASTER LAB: 1968. Porter set, contains 30 to 45 times magnification microscope plus more advanced specimens including a shrimp hatchery; packed in three-panel metal case.	30	35	45	55
24000 MINERALOGY EXPERIMENTAL LAB: 1962. Lionel-Porter lab, includes manual and mineral specimens, plus limited accessories; packed in two-panel metal cabinet.	10	15	20	25
24010 GEOLOGY EXPERIMENTAL LAB: 1962. Lionel-Porter lab, includes manual, mineral specimens, accessories including chemicals, and test tubes with stand; packed in three-panel metal cabinet.	12	17	22	28
24020 GEOLOGY-MINERALOGY LAB: 1962. Lionel-Porter lab, includes manual, mineral, rock, and fossil specimens, and numerous accessories including alcohol lamp with blow torch; packed in four-panel metal cabinet.	20	25	30	40
24030 MINERALOGY COLLECTOR'S LABORATORY: 1963-64. Includes 15 specimens in cardboard container.	12	15	18	22
24040 MINERALOGY SENIOR COLLECTOR'S LAB: 1963-64. Includes 18 specimens, accessories; packed in two-panel metal cabinet.	20	25	30	35
24050 MINERALOGY MASTER COLLECTOR'S LAB: 1963-64. Includes 34 specimens, accessories; packed in four-panel metal cabinet.	30	35	40	50
24110 MINERALOGY COLLECTOR'S LAB: 1965-66. Introductory kit includes minerals and other accessories.	8	12	16	22
24130 MINERALOGY SENIOR COLLECTOR'S LAB: 1965. Kit includes geologist hammer, many specimens, and accessories.	15	20	25	30
24150 MINERALOGY MASTER COLLECTOR'S LAB: 1965. Four-panel kit includes 30-power microscope, specimens, and many accessories.	25	30	40	60
24230 MINERALOGY SENIOR COLLECTOR'S LAB: 1966. Three-panel kit includes specimens, chemicals, and many accessories.	20	25	30	35
24250 MINERALOGY MASTER COLLECTOR'S LAB: 1966. Four-panel kit includes 30-45 power microscope, 27 mineral specimens, and many accessories.	30	40	50	65
24500 GEOLOGY LAB: 1963. Includes fossils, specimens; packed in two-panel metal cabinet.	20	25	30	35
24510 GEOLOGY MASTER LAB: 1963. Includes fossils, specimens, and accessories; packed in four-panel metal cabinet.	25	30	40	55
24710 MINERALOGY JUNIOR LAB: 1967. Includes accessories and specimens for basic experimentation.	10	15	25	35
24730 MINERALOGY SENIOR LAB: 1967. Includes geologist hammer and other accessories and minerals; packed in three-panel metal case.	20	25	35	50
24810 MINERALOGY JUNIOR LAB: 1968. Basic set for beginners; packed in two-panel metal case.	12	18	22	28
24830 MINERALOGY STUDENT SET: 1968. Set includes geologist hammer and 15 specimens; packed in two-panel metal case.	15	20	25	30
24840 MINERALOGY SENIOR LAB: 1968. More advanced set with geologist hammer and 24 specimens; packed in three-panel metal case.	20	25	30	35
25000 MATHCRAFT SET: 1962. Lionel-Porter set includes manual, abacus, and slide rule.	10	15	20	25
25010 MATHCRAFT LAB: 1963-64. Includes manual, abacus, and slide rule in cardboard container.	10	15	20	25
25020 MATHCRAFT LAB: 1963-64. Includes adding machine kit, tools in two-panel metal case.	20	25	35	45
25820 SCIENCECRAFT SCHOLASTIC MICROSCOPE: 1968. 100 to 300 times magnification model.	20	25	35	45
25830 SCIENCECRAFT SCHOLASTIC DELUXE MICROSCOPE: 1968. 600 times magnification model in wood-grain metal chest.	25	30	40	50
25840 SCIENCECRAFT EXPLORER MICROSCOPE: 1968. 100 to 750 times magnification model in wood-grain metal chest.	25	30	40	50
26000 TOOLCRAFT SET: 1962. Lionel-Porter set includes tools for the young carpenter such as hammer and screwdriver.	10	15	20	25
26010 TOOLCRAFT SET: 1962. Lionel-Porter set includes tools for the more advanced "carpenter," and packed in a metal carrying case.	15	20	25	30
26020 TOOLCRAFT SET: 1962. Lionel-Porter set includes more advanced tools such as a plane and brace, packed in a larger metal case than the No. 26010 model.	20	25	30	35
26030 TOOLCRAFT SET: 1963. Includes over eight basic tools packed in metal box.	15	20	25	30
26040 TOOLCRAFT SET: 1963. Includes over ten basic tools packed in metal box.	20	25	30	35
26050 TOOLCRAFT SET: 1963. Includes over ten basic tools packed in larger metal box.	20	25	30	35
26060 TOOLCRAFT SET: 1964. Basic set includes over ten tools packed in metal chest.	20	25	30	35
26810 TOOLCRAFT JUNIOR TOOL-TOTE SET: 1968. Basic tool set in red tote tray.	15	20	25	35

	G	VG	EXC	NEW
26820 TOOLCRAFT APPRENTICE TOOL-TOTE SET: 1968. Red tote tray with wider variety of carpenter tools.	20	25	30	40
26830 TOOLCRAFT MASTER TOOL-TOTE SET: 1968. Heavy duty tote tray with over 20 tools.	25	30	35	45
27000 ELECTRONICS LAB: 1964. Set provides experiments in sound and circuitry, packed in cardboard container.	15	20	25	35
27505 TELESCOPE TRIPOD: 1966-67. Accessory can be used with certain hand-held Porter telescopes.	10	15	20	25
27510 PENSCOPE: 1966-68. Porter combination 10 power telescope and 30 power microscope, size of a fountain pen.	10	15	25	30
27520 HAND TELESCOPE: 1966-67. Porter 30 power hand-held model.	10	15	25	30
27530 ASTRONOMICAL TELESCOPE: 1966-67. Porter 40 power model with tripod and lens mount.	40	50	65	75
27540 HAND TELESCOPE: 1966. Porter 30 power easy-focus hand-held model.	15	20	30	35
27550 HAND TELESCOPE: 1966. Porter 10 to 30 power variable focus hand-held model.	20	25	35	40
27570 HAND TELESCOPE: 1966. Porter 15 to 45 power variable focus hand-held model.	25	30	40	45
27580 ASTRONOMICAL TELESCOPE: 1966-68. Porter 40 power model similar to No. 27530 with wooden tripod and lens mount.	35	45	60	75
27590 TELESCOPE: 1966. Porter 16-1/2 to 50 times variable power model with tripod.	40	50	65	75
27730 ASTRONOMICAL TELESCOPE: 1968. 40 power 40 mm lens scope with tripod in display box.	20	30	40	50
27850 REFLECTOR ASTRONOMICAL TELESCOPE: 1968. 40 power scope with finder scope and metal tripod.	30	40	50	60
27890 REFLECTOR ASTRONOMICAL TELESCOPE: 1968. 65 and 133 power with heavy-duty tripod and finder scope.	40	50	70	90
28000 WEATHER STATION: 1964. Provides accessories to measure humidity, wind speed, other functions.	20	25	35	40
28010 JUNIOR WEATHER KIT: 1964. Provides a basic introduction to weather forecasting; packed in cardboard container.	15	20	25	30
28740 WEATHER STATION: 1967-68. Various instruments allow forecasting of weather; packed in three-panel metal case.	35	40	55	70
29000 COMMUNICATIONS LAB: 1964. Introduces children to transistors, other electronic concepts.	15	20	25	35
29740 COMMUNICATIONS LAB: 1967-68. Various accessories allows experiments in sound. Reader information requested.				NRS
41001 PHONOGRAPH: 1962. Lionel-Spear "Junior Disk Jockey" model, 78 RPM, styled in yellow and blue.	30	35	50	60
41011 PHONOGRAPH: 1962. Lionel-Spear the "Songster" model, 78 RPM, styled in white and red.	20	25	40	50
41021 PHONOGRAPH: 1962. Lionel-Spear the "Prince" model, 78 RPM, styled in turquoise and mallard color.	20	25	40	50
41090 PHONO-VISION PHONOGRAPH: 1964. Combination phonograph with built-in projector allows the playing of records with synchronized slides. Set includes one 78 RPM record and two slides good for fourteen shows.				NRS
41100 PHONOGRAPH: 1963. The "Songster" single-speed model in white and blue case.	20	30	40	50
41110 PHONOGRAPH: 1963. "Junior Disk Jockey" model, 78 RPM, in yellow and blue case.	20	30	40	50
41130 PHONOGRAPH SET: 1963. "Donald Duck" model, 78 RPM, comes with records and record rack.	30	35	40	50
41140 PHONOGRAPH: 1965-66. "The Songster", 78 RPM, children's model in light blue and white case.	20	30	40	50
42001 PHONOGRAPH: 1962. Lionel-Spear the "Travel n' Music" model, 45 and 78 RPM, styled in orange and casaba color.	25	35	45	55
42011 PHONOGRAPH: 1962. Lionel-Spear the "Encore" model, 45 and 78 RPM, in blue vinyl case.	25	35	45	55
42021 PHONOGRAPH: 1962. Lionel-Spear the "Symphony" top-of-the-line model, 45 and 78 RPM, in red and blue carrying case.	30	40	50	60
42100 PHONOGRAPH: 1963-64. "Travel n' Music" two-speed model, orange and casaba case.	25	35	45	55
42130 PHONOGRAPH SET: 1963. Eight-piece set includes two-speed model, records, and record rack, red and white case.	30	40	50	60
42140 PHONOGRAPH SET: 1963. "Mickey Mouse Music Corner" two-speed model, with records and large record stand.	40	60	80	100
42150 PHONOGRAPH: 1964. "Mickey Mouse" two-speed model, red and white case.	40	50	70	80
42160 PHONOGRAPH SET: 1964. "Mickey Mouse" two-speed model, red and white case, with records and rack.	50	60	75	90
42170 PHONOGRAPH SET: 1964. "Mickey Mouse Music Corner" two-speed model with records and large record stand.	40	60	80	100

Lionel-Spear No. 42001 phonograph, yet model is labeled No. 42000.

	G	VG	EXC	NEW
42190 PHONOGRAPH: 1964. "The Merrymaker" two-speed model, green and white case.	30	35	40	45
42200 PHONOGRAPH: 1965. Lionel-Spear "Merry-Maker" model plays 12" 45 and 78 RPM records, set styled in red and white stripes.	30	35	40	45
42210 PHONOGRAPH: 1965. Lionel-Spear "Mickey Mouse Party Maker" model with Dial-a-Matic speed selector; unit in red and white.	30	35	45	55
42220 PHONOGRAPH SET: 1965. Lionel-Spear eight-unit "Mickey Mouse" model, comes with 42210 phonograph plus records, rack in display box.	40	50	60	70
42230 PHONOGRAPH: 1966-67. Lionel-Spear "Winnie-the-Pooh" model, phonograph only; see set No. 42240.	25	30	40	50
42240 PHONOGRAPH SET: 1966-67. Lionel-Spear "Winnie-the-Pooh" nine-piece set in display container. Includes records, recorder rack, and phonograph in orange and white.	40	50	60	70
42260 PHONOGRAPH: 1967. Two-speed "Song 'n Story" model, blue and white case.	25	30	45	55
42270 PHONOGRAPH: 1967. Similar to model No. 42260, but made of heavier weight material.	30	35	50	60
42330 PHONOGRAPH: 1966. Lionel-Spear "Merry-Maker" model, two-speed in blue and white case.	25	30	40	50
42340 PHONOGRAPH: 1966-67. Lionel-Spear "Mickey and Minnie Swinger" two-speed model, red and white case with full color-cartoon in cover.	45	55	70	90
42350 PHONOGRAPH SET: 1967. Same as model No. 42340, packed in large display case, with Mickey Mouse only.	55	65	80	100
42520 PHONOGRAPH: 1966-67. Same as model No. 42340, but features Donald Duck and his nephews, blue and white case.	45	55	70	90
42810 PHONOGRAPH: 1968. Two-speed "Jungle Book" model, blue and white case.	25	30	35	40
42818 PHONOGRAPH SET: 1968. Eight-piece "Jungle Book" model with records and rack, blue and white case.	30	35	40	45
42830 PHONOGRAPH: 1968. Two-speed "Dr. Doolittle" model, magenta and white case.	25	30	35	40
42838 PHONOGRAPH SET: 1968. Same as No. 42830 with records and record rack.	30	35	40	45
42840 PHONOGRAPH: 1968. Two-speed "Mickey and Minnie Mouse" model, red and white case.	40	50	65	80
42848 PHONOGRAPH SET: 1968. Same as No. 42850 with records and record rack.	30	35	40	45
42850 PHONOGRAPH: 1968. Two-speed "Song n' Story" model, blue and white case.	25	30	35	40
43003 PHONOGRAPH SET: 1962-63. Lionel-Spear seven-piece set, includes 78 RPM phonograph, three records, and rack; phonograph styled in blue.	20	25	30	35
43013 PHONOGRAPH SET: 1962. Lionel-Spear eight-piece set, includes 45 and 78 RPM phonograph, records, and rack; phonograph styled in red.	30	35	40	45
43033 PHONOGRAPH SET: 1962. Lionel-Spear 15-piece set, includes 16, 33-1/3, 45, and 78 RPM phonograph, styled in yellow and brown, records, rack, and other accessories.	30	50	60	75
43140 PHONOGRAPH: 1967. Spear "Fun Time" three-speed model, pink and white case.	30	35	40	45
43890 PHONOGRAPH: 1968. Two-speed portable "Sportable" model in aqua and white.	25	30	35	40
44001 PHONOGRAPH: 1962. Lionel-Spear the "Velvet Tone" model, 16, 33-1/3, 45, and 78 RPM phonograph, styled in aqua and white.	30	35	40	45
44011 PHONOGRAPH: 1962. Lionel-Spear the "Modernistic" model, 16, 33-1/3, 45, and 78 RPM phonograph, styled in brush stripe and charcoal color.	40	50	60	70
44021 PHONOGRAPH: 1962. Lionel-Spear the "Swinging Sounds" model, 16, 33-1/3, 45, and 78 RPM phonograph, styled in sahara and avocado with white stripe.	40	50	60	70
44031 PHONOGRAPH: 1962. Lionel-Spear the "Rhythm 'N' Blues" model, 16, 33-1/3, 45, and 78 RPM phonograph, blue case.	40	50	60	70
44053 TALKING TEDDY: 1962-63. Lionel-Spear combination four-speed phonograph and "talking" teddy bear. The bear has a built-in speaker through which the sound from "Talking Teddy" records are played. This innovative toy was among the forerunners of the talking animal toys popularized in the mid-1980s.	50	60	80	90
44090 PHONO-VISION PHONOGRAPH SET: 1964. Set includes four-speed phonograph with built-in synchronized slide projection system, 45 RPM narrated record, and four slides.				NRS
44100 PHONOGRAPH: 1963. "Junior Disc Jockey" model, 78 RPM, yellow and blue case.	25	30	35	45
44130 PHONOGRAPH SET: 1963. "Donald Duck" model, 78 RPM, with records and record rack.	35	45	60	75
44140 PHONOGRAPH: 1963. "Modernistic" model, multi-speed, brush stripe and charcoal case.	30	35	40	50
44150 PHONOGRAPH SET: 1963. "Mouseketeers Treasure of Music" four-speed model, with records and large stand.	35	45	60	70
44160 PHONOGRAPH: 1963. "Swinging Sounds" four-speed model, sahara, avocado, and white case.	30	35	40	50
44170 PHONOGRAPH: 1963. "Rhythm 'n' Blues" four-speed model, blue case.	30	35	40	50
44180 PHONOGRAPH: 1963. "Tandemonic" four-speed model, charcoal and gray case.	30	35	40	50
44190 PHONOGRAPH: 1964. "The Merrymaker" two-speed model, green and white case.	30	35	40	50
44200 PHONOGRAPH: 1964. "Velvet Tone" four-speed model, aqua and white case.	35	40	50	60
44210 PHONOGRAPH: 1964. "Medley" four-speed model, olive and sahara case.	35	40	50	60
44220 PHONOGRAPH: 1964. "Modernistic" four-speed model, red and black case.	35	40	50	60
44230 PHONOGRAPH: 1964. "Swinging Sounds" four-speed model, yellow and sandalwood case.	30	35	40	45
44240 PHONOGRAPH: 1964. "Tandemonic" four-speed model with twin detachable speakers, green and gold case.	35	45	60	70
44250 PHONOGRAPH: 1964. "Maestro" four-speed deluxe model, sunflower and sandalwood case.	30	40	55	70
44270 PHONOGRAPH: 1965. Lionel-Spear "Dance Master" model, sahara and brown case.	30	35	40	45
44280 PHONOGRAPH: 1965. Lionel-Spear "Rhapsody" model, aqua case with white and aqua grill.	35	40	45	50
44300 PHONOGRAPH: 1965. Lionel-Spear "Music Hall" portable model, styled in blue and silver-white.	30	35	40	45
44320 PHONOGRAPH: 1966-67. "Jazz Festival" four-speed model covered with blue fabric, white interior.	40	55	70	80
44350 PHONOGRAPH: 1966-67. "Jet-Set" four-speed model, white and orange-red plastic cabinet.	30	40	50	60

	G	VG	EXC	NEW

44360 PHONOGRAPH: 1966. "Riviera Jet-Set" four-speed model similar to model No. 44350, aquamarine and white case.
30 40 50 60

44390 PHONOGRAPH: 1965. Lionel-Spear "Concerto" model, with two detachable speakers. Styled in sandalwood and white.
45 50 60 70

44700 PHONOGRAPH: 1963. "Concerto" four-speed monaural model, red and black case. 35 40 45 50

44820 PHONOGRAPH: 1968. Four-speed solid-state "Swing Time" model, blue and white case. 35 40 45 50

44830 PHONOGRAPH: 1968. Four-speed "Dr. Dolittle" model, red and white case. 35 40 45 50

44880 PHONOGRAPH: 1968. Four-Speed "Harmonic" model, charcoal and silver deluxe case. 35 40 45 50

44900 PHONOGRAPH: 1963. "Sonata" four-speed stereo model, blue and white case. 35 40 50 60

45003 TAPE RECORDER: 1962-63. Lionel-Spear "Junior" model, basic single speed recording and equipped with two 3" reels and an over-sized microphone. 45 55 70 90

45013 TAPE RECORDER: 1962-63. Lionel-Spear model advertised as a "Sound Studio," record and play back capabilities in addition to the added feature of a two-way intercom system. Came equipped with two 3" reels and an over-sized microphone.
45 55 70 90

48010 RECORD ASSORTMENT: 1964. 24 records in container.
25 40 60 75

48020 RECORD ASSORTMENT: 1964. 24 records in container.
25 40 60 75

48350 RECORD ASSORTMENT: 1964. 24 records in container.
25 40 60 75

48430 RECORD ASSORTMENT: 1964. 24 records in container.
35 45 65 80

48700 RECORD ASSORTMENT: 1964. 24 records in container.
25 40 60 75

A215 CONTROLLER: 1962. Variable speed hand controller for Lionel model motor racing. 3 5 7 10

B1 MODEL RACING MOTORCYCLE: 1962. "Typhoon" model motorcycle racer. 2 4 7 10

C54 MODEL RACING CAR: 1962. "Lotus" model sports car.
2 4 7 10

C55 MODEL RACING CAR: 1962. "Vanwall" model sports car.
2 4 7 10

C56 MODEL RACING CAR: 1962. "Lister Jaguar" model sports car. 2 4 7 10

C57 MODEL RACING CAR: 1962. "Aston-Martin" model sports car. 2 4 7 10

C58 MODEL RACING CAR: 1962. "Cooper" model sports car.
2 4 7 10

C59 MODEL RACING CAR: 1962. "B.R.M." model sports car.
2 4 7 10

C60 MODEL RACING CAR: 1962. "D Type Jaguar" model sports car. 2 4 7 10

C61 MODEL RACING CAR: 1962. "Porsche" model sports car.
2 4 7 10

CD-V-700 GEIGER COUNTER: 1962-1963. One of many products offered by Lionel through its Lionel Electronic Laboratory, Inc., Brooklyn, New York. Model 6B, yellow metal construction for commercial use. — — 70 80

CL-1 CHEMISTRY LAB: 1941. 23-piece set provides for over 175 experiments; packed in cardboard container.
20 25 50 60

CL-2 CHEMISTRY LAB: 1941. 29-piece set provides for over 200

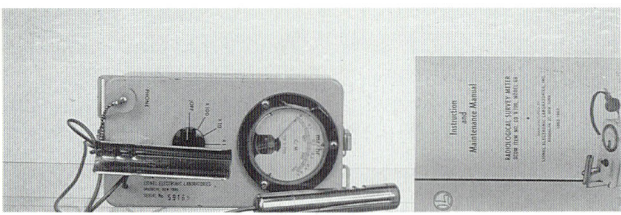

Lionel CD-V-700 geiger counter, without unusual headphones.

	G	VG	EXC	NEW

experiments, packed in chest. This set even provides for chemicals used to make fireworks! 30 40 65 90

CL-3 1/2 CHEMISTRY LAB: 1941. 45-piece set provides for over 500 experiments; packed in hardwood chest.
30 40 65 90

CL-5 CHEMISTRY LAB: 1941. Set provides for over 500 experiments; packed in hardwood chest. 40 50 75 100

CL-7 1/2 CHEMISTRY LAB: 1941. Set provides for over 500 experiments; packed in hardwood chest. 40 50 75 100

CL-10 CHEMISTRY LAB: 1941. Set provides for over 775 experiments; packed in hardwood chest. 50 75 100 125

CL-11 CHEMISTRY LAB: 1942. 23-piece set provides for over 175 experiments; packed in cardboard container.
20 25 50 60

CL-15 CHEMISTRY LAB: 1941. Deluxe set contains the most chemicals and accessories; packed in large hardwood chest.
60 85 110 135

CL-22 CHEMISTRY LAB: 1942. 29-piece set provides for over 250 experiments; packed in chest. 30 40 65 90

CL-33 CHEMISTRY LAB: 1942. 45-piece set provides for over 400 experiments; packed in hardwood chest. 30 40 65 90

CL-44 CHEMISTRY LAB: 1942. Set provides for over 500 experiments; packed in hardwood chest. 40 50 75 100

CL-55 CHEMISTRY LAB: 1942. Set provides for over 650 experiments; packed in hardwood chest. 40 50 75 100

CL-66 CHEMISTRY LAB: 1942. Set provides for over 800 experiments; packed in hardwood chest. 50 75 100 125

CL-77 CHEMISTRY LAB: 1942. Deluxe set provides maximum number of experiments; packed in large hardwood chest that extends five feet when opened. 60 85 110 135

CM3 MODEL MOTORING SET: 1962. Set in Competition Model Series, includes two No. C60 racing cars, track, and other accessories.
40 50 75 90

CM4 MODEL MOTORING SET: 1962. Set in Competition Model Series, includes two No. E1 racing cars with lights, track, and other accessories.
50 60 85 100

E1 MODEL RACING CAR: 1962. "Lister Jaguar" model sports car with lights. 5 8 10 14

E2 MODEL RACING CAR: 1962. "Aston-Martin" model sports car with lights. 5 8 10 14

GP1 MODEL MOTORING SET: 1962. Set in "Grand Prix Series," includes two No. C54 racing cars, track, and accessories.
40 50 70 80

GP 2 MODEL MOTORING SET: 1962. Set in "Grand Prix Series," includes two No. C55 racing cars, track and accessories.
40 50 70 80

GP3 MODEL MOTORING SET: 1962. Set in "Grand Prix Series," includes two No. C58 racing cars, track, and accessories.
40 50 70 80

Non-Train Collectibles • 165

A classic marine product: Lionel's 1943 merchant marine binnacle.

Closeup of the 1943 merchant marine binnacle.

                                                G   VG EXC NEW

MB MERCHANT MARINE BINNACLE: 1943. Large nautical case to enclose a ship's compass, this model was designed for use with Lionel No. 712M compass. Illuminated, constructed of soft cast iron and polished mahogany. Without Flinders bar equipment. Date confirmation requested.   **NRS**

MBF MERCHANT MARINE BINNACLE: 1943. Large nautical case to enclose a ship's compass, this model was designed for use with Lionel No. 712M compass. Illuminated, constructed of soft cast iron and polished mahogany. With Flinders bar equipment. This item was viewed on store display by the author. Also on display was an identical model inscribed "Kelvin-White Co." Perhaps both companies manufactured these models to U.S. Navy specifications, since both binnacles examined were very similar. Date confirmation requested.   **NRS**

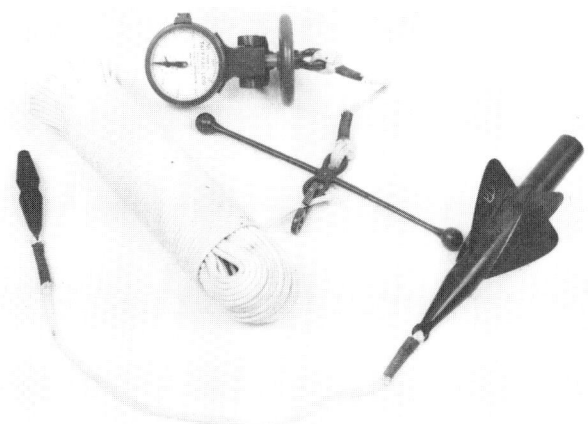

The 1943 TL Taffrail log, removed from wooden crate.

                                      G   VG EXC NEW

M1 MILITARY COMPASS: 1951. "Lensatic M1" model with olive drab case inscribed "U. S." in black. D. DiDio Collection.   **NRS**

TL TAFFRAIL LOG: 1943. U. S. Navy device designed to register the distance traveled by a vessel through the water in multiples of the nautical mile. The set is packed in a wooden crate, and includes two shoes, one hank of 400 foot of rope, and one rotator. The set was also packed with a spare cover glass and, according to Lionel's nautical catalogue, "a tube of lubricant." This tube of lubricant proves to be nothing more than Lionel's standard 2-1/2" train lubricant, with the "Lubriplate" inscription on the reverse. R. Osterhoff Collection.
   NRS

COUPON OFFER: 1963. A "Space Age" science kit was offered for 50 cents in the 1963 science catalogue. Can readers provide information as to the contents of this kit?   **NRS**

PROTOTYPE MICROSCOPE: 1966. 75 through 450 triple-turrent microscope with electric illumination and accessories. No number assigned, but "The Lionel Toy Corporation, Hagerstown, Maryland" inscribed on crude metal box, transparent removable lid. It is believed this prototype was for display purposes at the 1966 Toy Fair.   **NRS**

Airex Fishing Equipment

In the late 1940s, Lawrence Cowen, Lionel's President and an avid fisherman, initiated the partial purchase of the Airex Corporation, which billed itself as "America's first and largest manufacturer of [a] complete line of spinning tackle." Lionel's 1953 catalogue was the first to sport illustrations of fishing equipment, and for many years this fishing gear, although promoted heavily, took a back seat to Lionel's premier model train products.

Very seldom does one find Airex fishing lures, rods, or reels at train shows, but this merchandise is nevertheless an important part of the world of Lionel — and highly collectable. Part of the reason Airex fishing gear has maintained its value is not due to Lionel enthusiasts, but the dedicated following of fishing gear specialists, a rapidly growing hobby in its own right. When train collectors think of rarities, they may think of the 2-7/8 Gauge or 700E classics. Fishing gear enthusiasts think rare when it applies to an early Haskell Minnow lure. Although this rare lure was not manufactured by Airex, one did recently sell for the tidy sum of $8,500!

The following is a sampling of items manufactured by Airex, and known to exist. This list will be expanded as more items are located and collector interest increases. Research has not provided specific dates of issuance for most merchandise, and therefore an "early" or "later" designation is given for those items in the late 1940s and early 1950s (early) versus merchandise which appeared in the late 1950s to early 1960s (later).

110 FISHING ROD: Uslan Tonkin Bamboo spinning rod, two-piece, 6' action rod. **NRS**

115 FISHING ROD: Uslan Tonkin Bamboo spinning rod, two-piece, 6' medium bass action rod. **NRS**

120 FISHING ROD: Uslan Tonkin Bamboo spinning rod, "The Bronzeback" model, two-piece, 7' light action. **NRS**

135 FISHING ROD: Uslan Tonkin Bamboo spinning rod, "The Rainbow" model, two-piece, 7' medium action. **NRS**

140 FISHING ROD: Uslan Tonkin Bamboo spinning rod, "The Steelhead" deluxe model, two-piece, 7-1/2' action. **NRS**

210 FISHING ROD: Solid glass and duraloy spinning rod, two-piece, 6' medium action rod, designed the "Durod" model. **NRS**

220 FISHING ROD: Tubular glass fresh water rod, two-piece, measures 6' 6" long. **NRS**

221 FISHING ROD: Tubular glass fresh water rod, two-piece, measures 6' 6" long; similar to No. 220 but light action. **NRS**

222 FISHING ROD: Tubular glass fresh water rod, two-piece, measures 7' long. **NRS**

230 FISHING ROD: Similar to No. 220, but with fixed reel seat. **NRS**

231 FISHING ROD: Similar to No. 221, but with fixed reel seat. **NRS**

232 FISHING ROD: Similar to No. 222, but with fixed reel seat. **NRS**

235 FISHING ROD: Solid glass and duraloy "Double O" model. 6' long. The name designation of this model is unknown, and one must assume there is no connection with the prewar "OO" trains. **NRS**

250 FISHING ROD: Air-glass heavy duty salt water rod, 6' 9" long. **NRS**

251 FISHING ROD: Air-glass salt water rod designed for long casting, two-piece, 9' long. **NRS**

310 FISHING REEL: Bache Brown Masterreel, for fresh water and light salt water. **NRS**

311 MASTERREEL ARISTOCRAT: Fishing reel. **NRS**

312 LARCHMONT: Fishing reel. **NRS**

314 MASTERREEL ASTRA: Fishing reel. **NRS**

315 FISHING REEL: Bache Brown Spinster, basic all-purpose reel. **NRS**

316 SPINSTER MODEL 5: Fishing reel. **NRS**

317 SPINSTER MARK VI: Fishing reel. **NRS**

318 APACHE MODELS 1 AND 2: Fishing reel. **NRS**

319 APACHE MODEL 3: Fishing reel. **NRS**

320 MASTERKAST: Fishing reel. Model 2. Does this indicate there was also a Model 1 of this item? **NRS**

322 ELDORADO: Fishing reel. **NRS**

324 IMPALA REEL MODEL 1: Fishing reel. **NRS**

325 FISHING REEL: Beachcomber model designed for salt water fishing, the top-of-the-line spinner produced by Airex. **NRS**

328 JUMBO MASTERSPIN: Fishing reel. **NRS**

330 FISHING REEL: 1953 Vagabond Model Spinning Reel, came packed in 5-1/2" square x 3-1/4" silver on blue box with brake dressing. Box includes Airex instruction manual, fuzzy wire, cloth reel container, Authorized Airex Service Station listing (blue and white versions), and Form 325-116 oiling instructions. R. Otten Collection. — — — **65**

350 MASTERREEL: Fishing reel, Model 1. **NRS**
370 MEISSELBACH ABLETTE: Fly reel. **NRS**
371 MEISSELBACH ABLETTE: Fly reel. **NRS**
373 MEISSELBACH ABLETTE: Fly reel. **NRS**
375 MEISSELBACH ABLETTE: Fly reel. **NRS**
377 MEISSELBACH ABLETTE: Fly reel. **NRS**

385 FISHING REEL: Later issue level wind bait casting reel, came boxed with two-page instruction sheet, made in Japan. R. Osterhoff Collection. — — — **25**

No. 385 Airex and 390 fishing reels with original boxes.

390 FISHING REEL: Later issue level wind bait casting reel, slightly larger than Model 385, came boxed with two-page instruction sheet, made in Japan. L. Conners Collection.
— — — **30**

416 SPINNING LINE: Early box of two spools Airex Spinning Line, 4 lb. test lake green, in small box. Box inscribed "No. 7021-G-2" and overprinted by Airex "New Cat. #416". J. Maxwell Collection.
— — **8** —

456 SPINNING LINE: Early box of two spools, 4 lb. test mist green, in small yellow box. This box has affixed to the face an O.P.S. price level label similar to those which appeared on Lionel train merchandise in the 1951 period. J. Maxwell Collection.
— — — **8**

500 FISHING LURE: Preska Perch lure, 1/5 oz. **NRS**
502 FISHING LURE: Vogue lure, red and white, 1/4 oz. **NRS**
504 FISHING LURE: Brown Godart, 1/5 oz., brown head. **NRS**
505 FISHING LURE: Ablette, 3/8 oz. **NRS**
510 FISHING LURE: One-eyed Wobbler, 1/2 oz. **NRS**
512 FISHING LURE: Gold Digger, 1/8 oz. **NRS**
513 FISHING LURE: Wildcat, 1/4 oz., green, yellow, and black eyes. **NRS**
514 FISHING LURE: Devil Dog, 1/2 oz., red metal head. **NRS**
515 FISHING LURE: Twin Spinner Devon, 1/4 oz. **NRS**
516 FISHING LURE: Merry Widow, 1/3 oz., red and yellow. **NRS**
517 FISHING LURE: Merry Widow, 1/3 oz. black. **NRS**
518 FISHING LURE: Preska Perch, 1/5 oz., with nickel blade. **NRS**

	G	VG	EXC	NEW

519 FISHING LURE: Preska Perch, 1/5 oz., with black body and nickel blade. **NRS**

546 FISHING LURE: Later Airex Buggie lure, 1/4 oz., in plastic see-through cylinder container. Red and white color, recommended for all game fish. R. Osterhoff Collection. — — — 15

550 FISHING LURE: Later Airex Popit surface lure, 1/3 oz., in plastic see-through cylinder container. Perch scale color, recommended for bass, pike, and large crappies. R. Osterhoff Collection.
— — — 10

551 FISHING LURE: Later Airex Popit surface lure, 1/3 oz., in plastic see-through cylinder container. Frog finish color, recommended for bass, pike, and large crappies. R. Otten Collection.
— — — 10

570 FISHING LURE: Pixie, 1/2 oz., red perch-scale. **NRS**

571 FISHING LURE: Pixie, 1/2 oz., yellow perch-scale. **NRS**

577 LURE GIFT BOX: Contains ten different lures in plastic see-through container. **NRS**

578 LURE GIFT BOX: Contains four lures, keels, leaders, and snap swivels; packed in see-through plastic container. **NRS**

700 MASTERREEL KIT: Complete spinning outfit includes reel, spools, line, lures, and other accessories. **NRS**

705 SPINSTER KIT: Complete spinning outfit includes reel, spools, line, lures, and other accessories; packed in brown hinged cardboard display container. R. Osterhoff Collection.
— — — 100

No. 705 Spinster kit and examples of fishing lure.

715 SPINSTER KIT: Early kit in blue metal tackle box with Bache Brown Model 4 spinning reel, brake dressing container, extra spools and reel bag with "Airex" indicia. Box measures 11-1/2" x 5" x 3-1/2" deep. R. Otten Collection. — 40 — —

SPINNING REEL: Later unnumbered Bache Brown Spinster spinning reel, marked "Airex Div. of The Lionel Corp."
— 35 — —

SPINNING REEL: Early unnumbered Bache Hamilton Brown spinning reel. One of the first American-made spinning reels, made in Boston and accompanied by reel bag with "Airex" painted on it. Known as Luxor Model A-2. — — — 40

FISHING LURE: Later unidentified lure, red and white tail, chrome weight with red lightning bolt imprinted on weight. R. Otten Collection. — — — 8

LIONEL CORPORATION MEMORABILIA

In identifying the hundreds of individual items associated with the Lionel Corporation over the years, most are relatively easy to classify, especially train-related products. Often these products bear a distinctive number, or come in a container that includes a product description with number. Specialists in Lionel material demonstrate particular enthusiasm for this unique and peculiar area of collecting. The material is neither model trains, nor train-related paper. These items are not Service Station tools, nor something that Lionel offered as part of its product line. **Lionel Corporation Memorabilia** can be defined as ..."those items which represent promotional, non-paper products which are provided free or at nominal charge to Lionel employees, dealers and distributors, or the general public."

The above represents a comprehensive definition, and the items themselves provide yet a different introspective view into the Lionel Corporation, especially into its powerful marketing capabilities. Most of the memorabilia items represent low-cost, trinket-like merchandise provided as part of the many Lionel coupon offers advertised over the years, and are listed as are their associated paper products elsewhere in this reference. In many instances the valuations given do not reflect the true scarcity of the material; when found, many pieces of Lionel memorabilia are not necessarily expensive — these items just do not appear on the market that frequently. Without question, there are certain pieces that are truly rare, and provide more of a collecting challenge than most Lionel trains themselves.

The listing must be provided in a random order, for Lionel often did not assign a product code. Many listings were offered in unknown years, or for a period of several years, and therefore a chronological, year-by-year listing also was not feasible. Nevertheless, the items listed are in effect what true specialized collecting is all about. Be prepared to find identified the truly unusual and unconventional side of Lionel train collecting today.

Clothing and Patches

ENGINEER HAT: Smaller size cotton gray-striped engineer's hat, with flexible band and visor.
(A) Inscribed "Engineer" on visor top, in stenciled yellow paint. Early edition, part of 1952 promotional offer. These hats could be ordered in three sizes: small, medium, and large. Inscription "Engineer" can be found in two shades of yellow. The size label is sewn into the back of the hat with a clear inscription, "Lionel Trains" and the size.
25 40 60 70

	G	VG	EXC	NEW

(B) Inscribed "Lionel Engineer" on visor top, in stenciled yellow paint. Later edition, and frequently illustrated in late 1950s and early 1960s magazine promotional photographs. R. Osterhoff Collection.
25 35 50 60

(C) No inscription on visor top. This hat has appeared with railroad pins and paper items in a 1952 promotional packet. The origin of these packets has not been determined. Hat label does not refer to Lionel, and the authenticity is questionable. **NRS**

CLOTH PATCH: "Lionel Railroader Club" patch in black, yellow, and red picturing embroidered locomotive, 3-1/2" x 2" Fundimensions 1982 version. — — — **5**

CLOTH PATCH: 1975. 4" diameter in silver, red, white, and black, featuring "Lionel — 75th Anniversary" and locomotive front.
— — — **6**

6-5807 SPORT CAP: 1987. One size, features Lionel logo displayed on the front; offered for consumer purchase.
— — — **8**

T-SHIRT: 1987. Lionel logo emblazoned on a blue shirt, offered for consumer purchase.
(A) 6-5813, size 34-36 — — — **11**
(B) 6-5814, size 38-40. — — — **11**
(C) 6-5815, size 42-44. — — — **11**
(D) 6-5816, size 46-48. — — — **11**

6-5809 ENGINEER GLOVES: 1987. Heavy-weight two-tone blue work gloves with "Lionel" imprinted on glove ends; offered for consumer purchase. — — — **9**

6-5825 CLOTH PATCH: 1989-90. 3" patch depicts Lionel "L" in black, red, blue, and white; offered for consumer purchase.
— — — **3**

MEMBERSHIP PATCH: 1976. 3-1/2" x 2" cloth patch inscribed "Lionel Railroader Club", in red, black, and yellow stitching on white background. — — — **6**

MEMBERSHIP PATCH: 1981. 3-1/2" diameter cloth patch illustrating a locomotive in black on white background, with red lettering "Lionel Railroader Club". Patch came with heat seal instruction sheetlet. — — — **6**

6-5832 CARPENTER'S APRON: 1989-90. Two pockets, 10" x 18" in red on white, made of natural cotton duck material; offered for consumer purchase. — — — **7**

6-5835 ENGINEER CAP: 1989-90. One size adjustable, features 2" embroidered Lionel logo sewn onto crown; offered for consumer purchase. — — — **9**

T-SHIRT: 1989-90. Lionel logo emblazoned on shirt; offered for consumer purchase.
(A) 6-5836 blue, child size 6-8. — — — **10**
(B) 6-5837 blue, child size 10-12. — — — **10**
(C) 6-5838 blue, child size 14-16. — — — **10**
(D) 6-5839 white, adult size 34-36. — — — **11**
(E) 6-5840 white, adult size 38-40. — — — **11**
(F) 6-5841 white, adult size 42-44. — — — **11**
(G) 6-5842 white, adult size 46-48. — — — **11**

SWEATSHIRT: 1989-90. Lionel logo emblazoned on red shirt; offered for consumer purchase.
(A) 6-5844 child, size 6-8. — — — **15**
(B) 6-5845 child, size 10-12. — — — **15**
(C) 6-5846 child, size 14-16. — — — **15**
(D) 6-5849 adult, size 34-36. — — — **16**
(E) 6-5850 adult, size 38-40. — — — **16**
(F) 6-5851 adult, size 42-44. — — — **16**
(G) 6-5852 adult, size 46-48. — — — **16**

6-5853 NECKTIE: 1989-90. Navy blue tie with woven Lionel "L" logos in silver, silk blend fabric; offered for consumer purchase.
— — — **22**

6-5854 PERKY BOW: 1989-90. Navy blue bow with woven Lionel "L"ogos in silver, silk blend fabric; offered for consumer purchase.
— — — **22**

Souvenir and Promotional Pins and Jewelry

TIN RAILROAD PINS: 1952. 7/8" diameter pins are fold-over type and typically accompanied or were affixed to Lionel Engineer Hat. Set of five includes Pennsylvania, Union Pacific, Santa Fe, Erie, and C & O Railroads; came in stapled glassine envelope and offered as promotional item in 1952. **35 60 100 125**

LIONEL 5 YEAR TENURE PIN: 1/4" x 1/2" pin in shape of locomotive front, silver with "5" and "Lionel" in blue. No stone on face of pin; comes in 1" square blue/clear plastic box. Presented to Lionel employees only and never offered for sale. — — — **125**

LIONEL 10 YEAR TENURE PIN: 1/4" x 1/2" lapel pin or tie tack in shape of locomotive front, gold with "10" and "Lionel" in blue. No stone on face of pin; comes in 1" square blue/clear plastic box. Presented to Lionel employees only and never offered for sale.
— — — **125**

LIONEL 15 YEAR TENURE PIN: 1/4" x 1/2" lapel pin or tie tack in shape of locomotive front, gold with "15" and "Lionel" in blue, as well as small emerald stone embedded in top. Comes in 1" purple/clear plastic box. Presented to Lionel employees only and never offered for sale. — — — **200**

LIONEL 20 YEAR TENURE PIN: 1/4" x 1/2" lapel pin or tie tack in shape of locomotive front, gold with "20" and "Lionel" in blue, as well as small ruby stone embedded in top. Comes in 1" purple/clear plastic box. Presented to Lionel employees only and never offered for sale. — — — **200**

LIONEL 25 YEAR TENURE PIN: 1/4" x 1/2" lapel pin or tie tack in shape of locomotive front. Presented to Lionel employees only and never offered for sale. **NRS**

TIE CLASP: 1965. 1-1/2" long gold-plated clasp has locomotive attached, but there is no specific reference to Lionel on the item. This can not be considered fine jewelry, but was presented to Lionel guests in attendance at the 1965 Toy Fair. L. Connors Collection. **NRS**

MEMBERSHIP BADGE: 1929-30. 1-1/4" diameter "pinback" with enameled face sent to members only who joined Uncle Don's Lionel Engineer's Club. **NRS**

MEMBERSHIP PIN: 1930s. 3/4" diameter bronze pin inscribed "Lionel Engineers Club", and includes an engraved locomotive front. Offered as a promotional item in 1930s to members in the Lionel Engineers Club, and generally was accompanied by a certificate of membership. A. Rubin and G. Magner Collections. Listing for pin only. — — **55 75**

Lionel engineer hat (later issue); 1980's Lionel pocket watch; 1980 Toy Fair ball point pen.

Non-Train Collectibles • 169

1930s membership pin and certificate of membership for the Lionel Engineers Club.

	G	VG	EXC	NEW

PROMOTIONAL PIN: Late 1950s. 1-1/4" diameter tin pin illustrating Lionel Lion and inscribed "Lionel Lines", brown and red. Information is requested on the origin and distribution of these pins.
                                                                                      1   3   4   5

PROMOTIONAL PIN: Early 1960s promotional item. 1-1/2" diameter tin pin illustrating Lionel "General", diesel and steam locomotives, and inscribed "I am a Lionel R.R. Co. Stockholder".
(A) Original issue, lip of pin inscribed "Keynote Promotions, Inc., New York 1, N.Y."; face of pin is slight oval. R. Osterhoff Collection.
        —   —   60   75
(B) Later reissue, no inscription on lip of pin and face of pin is flat.
        1   2   3   5

PROMOTIONAL PIN: 1975. 3-1/2" diameter tin pin in black, red, and white, featuring "Lionel — 75th Anniversary" and locomotive front.   —   —   —   5

POCKET WATCH: 1980. This pocket watch was given to winners of the Lionel Railroader Club's layout contest. More information on this piece requested. T. Wagner comment.   **NRS**

Various Lionel promotional pins.

	G	VG	EXC	NEW

PROMOTIONAL PIN: 1983. 3-1/2" diameter tin pin inscribed "Lionel — The Inside Track 1983". Blue lettering, orange locomotive on tan background. — — — 5

PROMOTIONAL PIN: 1984. 3-1/2" diameter tin pin inscribed "Lionel" in orange and "The Inside Track 1984" and locomotive in dark blue on buff background. — — — 5

PROMOTIONAL PIN: 1985. 3-1/2" diameter tin pin inscribed "Lionel" in orange and "The Inside Track 1985" in white, with a General locomotive, all against a dark blue and buff background.
    — — — 5

PROMOTIONAL PIN: 1986. 3-1/2" diameter tin pin inscribed "1986 — The Inside Track" in blue, "Lionel" in red, and the "L" insignia against a black background. — — — 5

PROMOTIONAL PIN: 1987. 2" diameter with "Lionel L" logo and caption "Lionel Large Scale". Distributed at 1987 Toy Fair.
    — — 5 7

PROMOTIONAL PIN: 1987. 3-1/2" diameter tin pin inscribed "The Inside Track — 1987 — Lionel" in red, with a black locomotive imaged against a blue and black background.
    — — — 5

PROMOTIONAL PIN: 1988. 3-1/2" diameter tin pin inscribed "The Inside Track — 1988" in blue, "Lionel" in red, with a diesel locomotive, against a red, blue, and black background.
    — — — 5

PROMOTIONAL PIN: 1988. 2-1/2" diameter tin pin inscribed "Lionel-Railroader Club", with image of moving caboose. Sent to club members. T. Patsko Collection. — — — 5

PROMOTIONAL PIN: 1988. 3-1/2" diameter tin pin, undated, has gold Lionel "L" emblem on gold background. This was distributed along with a pair of safety glasses and a pad of Lionel stationery at the October 1988 Factory Seminar, to introduce the 1989 Collector's Series. T. Wagner Collection. **NRS**

PROMOTIONAL PIN: 1989. 3-1/2" diameter tin pin released to promote Lionel's advertising in "Time" magazine, inscribed "Now is the Time — Lionel". Used internally at Toy Fair 1989. Not available to the public. **NRS**

PROMOTIONAL PIN: 1989. 3-1/2" diameter tin pin inscribed "The Inside Track from Lionel 1989" in red, black, and blue on white background. Features drawing of freight set.
    — — — 5

Promotional pin used at Toy Fair 1989 to promote Time magazine advertising.

SERVICE STATION PIN: Mid-1970s, 1985. 1" diameter bronze on black metal pin with clasp on rear, inscribed "Lionel Service" and a locomotive. Issued to Lionel Service Stations in the mid-1970s. Available as late as 1985 on order from Lionel by Authorized Lionel Service Stations. A. Rubin Collection. — — — 7

SERVICE STATION BELT BUCKLE: Mid-1970s, 1985. 2-3/4" diameter bronze on black metal single clasp buckle, inscribed

"Lionel Service" and a locomotive. Available to Lionel Service Stations in the mid-1970s and as late as 1985.

	G	VG	EXC	NEW
	—	—	—	15

ANNIVERSARY BELT BUCKLE: 2-3/8" diameter pewter metal single clasp buckle, inscribed "Lionel — 75th Anniversary" with dates and a locomotive on the face, and "1975" on the back. Available for sale through Lionel Service Department. A. Rubin Collection.
— — — 20

GENERAL BELT BUCKLE: Date unknown. 3-1/2" x 2-1/2" oval buckle, single clasp in bronze, features Lionel "General" locomotive with "Lionel Trains" inscription, in Fundimensions-style logo.
— — — 15

6-5802 LAPEL PIN: 1987-90. Red, white, and blue pin, 7/8" long, made of solid brass and nickel-plated; offered for consumer purchase.
— — — 4

6-5808 BRASS KEY CHAIN: 1987-90. Die-cast medallion with Lionel logo and locomotive in an antique brass finish; offered for consumer purchase.
— — — 8

6-5804 EPOXY KEY CHAIN: 1987. Medal is struck from solid brass and Lionel logo hand-screened; offered for consumer purchase.
— — — 5

QUARTZ WRISTWATCH: 1986. Gold case with black leather strap, the face features the Lionel logo in color, with a circling "General"-type train that acts as a second hand; offered for consumer purchase, this watch comes in a case 2" x 9-5/8".
— — — 110

6-5822 QUARTZ WRISTWATCH: 1987. Gold case with metal band, the face features the Lionel logo in color, with a circling Daylight Special train that acts as a second hand; offered for consumer purchase.
— — — 130

6-5829 LAPEL PIN: 1989-90. Lionel "Circle L" logo is die-struck metal, 1/2" in diameter, 14K gold finish; offered for consumer purchase.
— — — 5

6-5855 SWISS ARMY KNIFE: 1989-90. Victorinox brand army knife includes multi-purpose tools, stored in 2-1/4" handle, with Lionel logo inlaid in nickel; offered for consumer purchase.
— — — 25

6-5856 POCKET WATCH: 1989-90. Nickel-plated watch features red Lionel logo on its face, with a C & A RR General locomotive engraved on the back; offered for consumer purchase.
— — — 26

Consumer Promotional Offers (Non-Paper)

MODEL RAILROAD PRINTING KIT: Includes plastic track templates, plastic ring, and ink pad, with instructions. Comes in a 4-1/2" x 3-1/4" x 7/8" box illustrating a young engineer; first offered in 1952 as a coupon promotion.
10 20 30 40

Lionel printing kit, with templates and ink pad.

Plastic Locoscope with accompanying 16mm filmstrip.

	G	VG	EXC	NEW

LOCOSCOPE: Black plastic locomotive, measuring 5-3/4" x 1-1/2" with "Lionel" inscribed on cab, and accompanied with a 16 mm filmstrip. The filmstrip, consisting of 75 views of "the world's most famous railroad pictures," is fed through the locomotive boiler and the viewer looks through the headlight directly at a light source for actual viewing. Offered free for a two-year subscription to *Model Builder* magazine. The locomotive and filmstrip come packaged in a box measuring 6-3/8" long x 2-1/4" wide x 1-7/8" deep.
(A) Filmstrip of World's Most Famous Railroad Pictures. (Reproductions of this filmstrip exist.) W. Mekalian Collection. **NRS**
(B) Filmstrip of New York World's Fair Locomotives. Assigned product code of No. 1500 by Lionel, although this code is not referenced in any advertised or printed media. This version comes in an attractive red and blue on white box measuring 7-7/8" long x 3-1/2" wide x 1-1/4" deep, with a locomotive and the World's Fair Trylon and Perisphere dominating the front. Included in the contents of the box examined by the author was a small brochure titled "Romance of Lionel Trains," with a dating of 1939. (See separate 1939 listing under Prewar Paper, Chapter II.) While version (A) of the Locoscope was heavily advertised by Lionel as a promotional item at no charge, it appears version (B) might have been available for sale, perhaps on the grounds of the 1939-40 New York World's Fair. Reader comments would be welcomed. A. Rubin Collection. **NRS**

LOCOMOTIVE SHED: Kit form by Skyline Kits reproduced by silk-screen process on heavy board and when assembled measures 21-1/2" long x 7-1/4" high x 8-3/4" wide. Was offered free in 1942 as a promotion for a two-year subscription to *Model Builder* magazine. Shipped unassembled in cardboard box measuring 7-1/2" x 9-1/4" x 1-1/4" deep, also includes a printed instruction sheet. R. Osterhoff Collection.
20 30 45 60

Promotional Phonograph Records

BILL STERN RECORD: 1947. Features the famous sports commentator, 4" diameter "Lionel Trains in Action" on one side and "Lionel Trains Whistle Signals" on the other. Records are not identified but play on 78 rpm record players. These records were part of a consumer coupon promotion.
(A) Red and white center, black record. R. Otten Collection.
— 20 25 35
(B) Red and purple center, blue record. L. Connors Collection.
— — 35 45

Left: Bill Stern records in blue and black. *Right:* 1955 "Toot Toot" promotional record. Promotional records.

Lionel sound effects record and folder, available to the general public.

Promotional sound effects record.

	G	VG	EXC	NEW

PROMOTIONAL RECORD: 1947(?). 10" shellac record Lionel issued with train sounds. More information on background and date confirmation of this record requested. B. Lazarus Collection. **NRS**

PROMOTIONAL RECORD AND FOLDER: 1949. "Whistles and Bells" clear flexible plastic record, 5-1/2" diameter, 78 RPM, inserted in four-page card stock folder. Folder measures 5-3/4" square when closed, black and dark red on golden paper, with cover inscription "Whistles and Bells and Puffing Lionel Trains".
                              20   30   40   50

PROMOTIONAL RECORD AND FOLDER: 1951-54. Clear flexible plastic record, 78 RPM, 5-1/2" in diameter, with printed circular insert. Side 1 depicts a Santa Fe freight with the lettering "Lionel Train Sound Effects"; side 2 features a steam locomotive freight set with "Lionel Train Sound Effects" printed on top. Folder measures 5-5/8" square when closed, printed red and gray on yellow paper, inscribed "Lionel Sound Effects". The reverse cover includes the caption "We all like Lionel Trains and Accessories because they are real and big and powerful". We would also like to know how variations differ between years.
(A) "Printed in U. S. A." in three small oval lines in left corner of page where record is inserted. L. Connors Collection.
                              10   20   30   40
(B) "Printed in U. S. A." on one line in right corner of page where record is inserted. L. Connors Collection. 10   20   30   40
(C) "Printed in U. S. A." on one line in right center of page where record is inserted. L. Connors Collection. **NRS**

PROMOTIONAL RECORD: 1955. "I'm a Lionel (Toot Toot) Engineer" record, 78 RPM, 4-5/8" diameter, red, black, and white. Printed one side only and glued to large promo catalog "... and Away We go for Record Sales in 1955". Record illustrates Lionel lion. L. Connors Collection.   —   —   30   40

SOUND EFFECTS RECORD: 45 RPM record listed with Lionel merchandise in Sears 1962 catalogue. Reader assistance requested to establish if this was released by Lionel. **NRS**

JOHNNY CASH DESTINATION VICTORIA STATION: 1976 (record originally released 1975). 78 RPM record in stereo, featuring radio commercials from the Victoria Station restaurant chain. The record itself does not have ties to Lionel, except for the fact Lionel affixed a 3-3/4" x 1-1/2" black and white label to the outside cellophane wrapper. The printing on the wrapper reads "Hear the great songs from Johnny Cash's Ridin' the Rails Special. Brought to you by Lionel." This record was sent to dealers in October 1976 as part of a large promotional pack. A. Rubin Collection. **NRS**

(**Editor's Note**: Lionel-Spear phonograph records are not included in the above listing since they were offered exclusively as a non-train, nonpromotional Lionel consumer product.)

Promotional Films

One of the most fascinating aspects of train collecting is viewing a film short or television commercial featuring Lionel products from past decades. Years ago this experience was remotely possible by viewing either the original programs or old 16 mm films — if one was fortunate enough to locate a copy. Today's video recorders make viewing of Lionel films a pleasant and inexpensive experience. Many of these films survive today as video cassette recordings or as a 16 mm print made from original studio copies. The following list, compiled from research by William Mekalian and A. Rubin, is provided for reference only; prices are not provided since what appears on the market today are copies only. Since this is the first attempt to classify Lionel films, additions and clarifications to this list from readers are especially welcome.

1916: Industrial film, length unknown, referenced on page 4 of the 1916 catalogue.
1925: Industrial film, 5,000 feet, 150 minutes, referenced on page 4 of the 1925 catalogue.
1938: "4's a Crowd", 91 minutes, produced by Warner Bros., directed by Michael Curtiz, and starring Errol Flynn, Olivia de Havilland, and Rosalind Russell.
1948: "Tales of the Red Caboose", a series of 12 serials, all 15 minutes each. First aired in the 7:30 p.m. time slot on ABC Network October 22, 1948, with the last episode January 14, 1949. Dan McGee was host of this prime time show.
1949: "Manhattan Special", 15 minute television show with Arthur Raphael. Additional information on this series requested.
1949: Television commercials, eight minute film with twelve 40 second spots.
1949: "Iron Ponies", 350 feet, 11 minute film featuring Lionel products.
1949: Television commercials, length unknown, features Joey at Madison Hardware.

	G	VG	EXC	NEW

1950: Twelve specials featuring baseball great Joe Di Maggio, 15 minutes each. Additional information on this series requested.

1950: "So You Want a Model Railroad", 380 feet, 12 minute film featuring Joe McDoaks. This is the popular film featured at the TCA Museum.

1951-52: "Railroad Story", 330 feet, 10 minute Lionel feature.

1951-52: "Iron Ponies", 430 feet, 12 minute film featuring Lionel products.

1953: Lionel commercials on 170' reel, four minutes total, consisting of three 60 second and three 20 second spots.

1954: "Adventures of Ozzie & Harriet", 30 minutes; details on this television production requested.

1959: Television commercial, 50 feet, one minute in duration, features Lionel products.

1959: Television commercial, 50 feet, one minute in duration, features details on Lionel's Colgate train contest.

1960: "Wonderful World of Trains", 1000 feet, 30 minutes of commercial footage of Lionel products.

1962: "Cavalcade of Trains", 400 feet, 12 minutes, featuring various Lionel products.

1963-64: Television commercial, 60 feet, one minute in duration, features various Lionel products.

1965: Television commercial, 60 feet, one minute in duration, features Lionel Helios "21" non-train product.

1988: Promotional Video Tape, 1/2-inch VHS, 15 minutes. Includes RailScope demonstration and Double Crossing game featurette, repeats three times. Came with 3-3098 dealer display.

1989: Promotional Video Tape, 1/2-inch VHS. Features commercials available to media advertising current products.

Miscellaneous

PRINTERS TYPEFACE: Metal typeset mounted on wooden block, illustrating "Lionel Trains Approved Service" logo. Logo is 5/8" in diameter. Prior to modern offset printing, illustrations and virtually all printing had to be set in metal typeface. It cannot be assumed this came from Lionel, as paper copy was probably converted to "cold type" through chemical processes. — — — **10**

DEALER SAMPLE CASE: Custom-made suitcase measures 29-3/4" long x 16-1/2" wide x 6" high when closed. Case opens to a small O27 layout with mounted track, board measures 50-3/4" x 28-1/2". Professionally constructed, with space for storing a locomotive and small transformer. Circular track is mounted to a fold-in board, attached to the case. Brown with plastic carrying handles; origin in early 1950s. Reader information requested. R. Osterhoff Collection. **NRS**

COASTER: Promotional item issued by Lionel on the occasion of its Fiftieth Anniversary in 1950. It is believed this item was presented to Lionel employees and dealers, came in sets of four and was produced for Lionel by Lenox. Thus far only single coasters have been located. This item, which some collectors believe is an ashtray, came with the outer rim in black-painted brass. It is not known when the paint was applied. A. Rubin Collection and comment.
The coaster was originally packaged individually with cellophane seal along with engraved note on white stock from J. L. Cowen. Add $100 for box and note, which reads, "with my personal compliments on the occasion of the Golden Anniversary of the Lionel Corporation." G. Magner Collection. **75 100 130 170**

PAPERWEIGHT: Promotional souvenir distributed by Lionel, not available commercially, depicting in brass a City of Portland streamliner and mounted to a 4" x 5" marble base. Perhaps issued on Lionel's 35th anniversary but unconfirmed. This piece is definitely of prewar origin, however reader information is requested.
— — — **200**

Lionel 1950 Golden Anniversary Coaster.

	G	VG	EXC	NEW

BEVERAGE COASTER: 1975. 3-1/4" diameter white plastic coaster with Lionel printed adhesive attached, featuring "Lionel — 75th Anniversary" and locomotive front. — — **5 7**

6-1076 CLOCK: 1976. Illuminated 17" x 12" electric clock, red, white, and black plastic; offered to Lionel dealers.
25 50 75 100

MECHANICAL PENCIL: Lionel was reported to have made available as a promotional item a mechanical pencil which contained a locomotive immersed in liquid. This locomotive would move as the user would move the pencil. Confirmation of its existence requested. **NRS**

BALL POINT PEN: Parker pen issued by Lionel for 1980 Toy Fair, inscribed in silver on a blue base "Fundimensions — 1980 — Take a Closer Look". As the pen is "clicked," a window changes sequentially to "Lionel", "MPC", "Craft Master", and "Electronics". Pen packed in card stock box. A. Rubin Collection. **NRS**

PLAYING CARDS: Issued in mid-1980s. Deck of playing cards printed in black and red on white glossy card stock with "Lionel" imprinted diagonally in alternating colors.
— — — **5**

SUMMER PACKAGE: 1988. Includes 9" blue plastic frisbee, two colder holders, and sun visor; offered for consumer purchase.
— — **15 20**

6-5801 LIGHTER: 1987. Cigarette lighter in white with "Lionel Lines" logo in red, blue, and black; offered for consumer purchase.
— — — **4**

6-5803 LICENSE PLATE: 1987. Colorful plate in full color with caption "I'd Rather be Running my Lionel Trains"; offered for consumer purchase. — — — **4**

6-5805 ASH TRAY: 1987-90. Glass ash tray, 3-1/2" triangular design with red, blue, and black Lionel logo in center; offered for consumer purchase. — — — **7**

6-5806 COFFEE MUG: 1987-90. 12-ounce Ironstone coffee mug with gold trim and Lionel logo in gold; offered for consumer purchase.
— — — **8**

| | G | VG | EXC | NEW |

6-5818 PEN/PENCIL SET: 1987-90. Offered as a consumer item, Garland pen and pencil is black matte finish with engraved "Lionel Trains", plus a "Circle L" logo in the crown; offered in 1989 as a 6-5819 product item. — — — 20

6-5820 TRAVEL ALARM: 1987. Plastic clock with "General"-type train going around tracks that act as a second hand; outside case is red; offered for consumer purchase. — — — 25

6-5821 COASTER SET: 1987. Set of four die-cast coasters surrounded by a leather insert and displayed in an oak tray, center of each coaster features Lionel logo; offered for consumer purchase. — — — 70

6-5826 PENNANT: 1989-90. Lionel logo displayed on 9" x 24" felt pennant; offered for consumer purchase. — — — 5

6-5828 LICENSE PLATE: 1989-90. Poly-formulated plate with insignia "I brake for Lionel Trains"; offered for consumer purchase. — — — 5

6-5831 COLDER HOLDERS: 1989-90. Pair of polyurethane holders issued in blue and red with white Lionel insignia; offered for consumer purchase. — — — 6

6-5834 FROSTED BEVERAGE MUG: 1989-90. Engines illustrated next to "Circle L" Lionel logo, white 13 oz. container; offered for consumer purchase. — — — 9

6-5847 TOTE BAG: 1989-90. Water-repellant, red nylon bag 10" x 18" with Lionel insignia; offered for consumer purchase. — — — 16

6-5857 WELCOME MAT: 1989-90. Blue heavyweight mat 18" x 27" with Lionel logo; offered for consumer purchase. — — — 30

6-5858 DIRECTOR'S CHAIR: 1989-90. Varnished frame with white seat and back, desk size. Seat back has red Lionel logo imprinted. Offered for consumer purchase. (For the record, similar larger bar-type director's chairs were used at the 1988 Toy Fair, however, these were not offered to the public.) Prices for consumer item only. — — — 60

Lionel 25th anniversary paperweight featuring Lionel No. 402 engine.

| | G | VG | EXC | NEW |

SAFETY GLASSES: 1988. Yellow plastic safety glasses that came in a red plastic protector. Protector has inscribed gold lettering "Lionel Trains, Inc. / Champions For Success / October 6, 1988". This was distributed along with a pad of Lionel stationery and a gold "L" promo pin at the 1988 Factory Seminar that was held in October 1988 to show off the 1989 Collector's Series trains. T. Wagner Collection. **NRS**

PAPERWEIGHT: Promotional souvenir distributed by Lionel, not available commercially, depicting in pewter a Lionel No. 402 electric cast on a pewter stand. The inscription reads "LIONEL 25th ANNIVERSARY 1900-1925". A Rubin Collection. **NRS**

MIRROR: Made for Lionel between 1925 and 1930, shows a child playing with early electric and passenger cars, possibly a Lionel 402 with a set of 100 series passenger cars. Mirror is approximately 18" x 24", has a dark wood frame, and has a green border with silver trim. Different variations have been reported. Confirmation of variations requested. A. Rubin Collection. **NRS**

Chapter Ten
DEALER DISPLAYS

1953-54 dealer display No. D-103 featuring Lionel sign, shelves for set displays, and layout without landscaping. E. Dougherty Collection.

There is nothing more impressive in a train room than to have trains mounted on an actual dealer display unit, in much the same manner as in a toy store of yesteryear. Dealer displays enjoy a peculiar buyer/seller market. Certain collectors drive hundreds of miles to examine and hopefully purchase a display of their liking. Other displays appear periodically at major train meets, sitting attractively on tables but not sold until the later hours of the show. This phenomenon is not fully understood, but one point is clear: The demand for displays definitely outweighs the supply, with the difference being the high prices often requested for these merchandising masterpieces. Due to their relative scarcity, collectors are content with eyeing displays in the printed media. Display illustrations frequently appear in scarce dealer advance catalogues or price lists. But displays *do* appear on the market.

As can be expected, displays were never a consumer commodity, nor advertised in the mass-distributed consumer catalogue. Often the merchandise display was available to Service Stations or other vendors of Lionel equipment at or below cost. When equipment was included with the display, the equipment alone was sold to the dealer at a price substantially less than the merchandise plus the display together. Dealer displays were designed as attention-getters, and often exceeded expectations in attracting would-be buyers to the train areas of a massive toy department.

Hundreds of different displays were produced by and for Lionel over the years, although exact numbers are not known. The question of the final disposition of these displays makes for an interesting discussion.

First, to the business owners selling toy trains these displays were nothing more than promotional gimmicks. Storage of the displays often required large amounts of valuable space, and upon completion of the Christmas selling season, were given to someone for the asking or disposed of in the trash bin. There were also occasions when stores sold Lionel displays to interested buyers. Lionel occasionally encouraged this practice, or at least the merchandise on display. The 1941 displays Nos. 1A, 2, and 8 advertise specifically that "cartons for each of the items are shipped with the display so that the merchandise may be sold toward the end of the season." Despite the cost involved, some displays were stored year after year for reuse, and perhaps these too now reside in private collections. Most displays were not so fortunate, and were relegated to destruction.

To find an original display in excellent condition is difficult; to locate a display in the original box is rare. (For an interesting story of a 1940 dealer display "find," that of a 15' No. 15 located in a Toledo hardware store, we invite readers to refer to the Fall 1981 issue of the *Train Collectors Quarterly*.) Often pieces of displays appear on the market; for instance, shelves without signs, no layouts, missing support dowels, etc. Enterprising collectors take what they can find, and then improvise. They have signs reproduced, or replace shelves with fabricated duplicates. Certain displays were manufactured by Lionel using crude, painted two-by-fours, and it is relatively easy to complete a display in one's own workshop. That also lends a certain frustration to the purist collector, who desires only original display pieces. Unfortunately only a few experts can tell the difference, and therefore probing into a display's origin prior to purchase may be a safe precaution.

The evolution of Lionel's dealer displays is a study of art, architecture, and merchandising techniques. It can also be a study of advertising cost vs. product acceptance by the public. Just as Lionel engineers were pioneers in the development of innovative electric trains, Lionel's advertising department excelled in capturing the hearts of America and bringing the consumer in touch with model railroading and the train display counters. The physical dealer displays continued the advertising task where the frequent Lionel ads, appearing in the pages of *Life, Look,* and *Coronet* magazines, finished.

Lionel made effective use of a combination of visual media: blinking red lights, speeding locomotives, and moving gatemen. Splashes of color abounded on each display. Rounded corners with gradually sloping, contoured steps provided artistic pleasure, all of which gained a subliminal attraction to the potential toy train operator. From the toy departments of major department stores to the smallest hobby shop, Lionel demonstrated an aura of Madison Avenue at its best!

Displays were majestic in many respects. The No. 15 display of 1939-1941 provided art deco treatment to the 15' silk-screened station background. One of the more popular displays of which numerous examples have appeared on the market, the 1949 No. 10 display, used four Kodachrome slides with a light to project the visual effects of train products from that year. A popular display from 1961, the No. D-288, used a standard battery-operated motor field to power a swinging lantern. Whether it was artistic or engineering genius, each of these displays provided a different and effective method of the ultimate in advertising, captivating people's attention.

In compiling a reference of Lionel dealer displays, the primary sources are advance catalogues, price lists, and the actual items in those instances where no catalogue reference is known. By definition, an item is considered a display, for purposes of this listing, if it meets three criteria: 1) Offered with the purpose of promoting Lionel products in any manner, 2) manufactured or authorized for manufacture by the Lionel Corporation, and 3) not available for sale to the general public. The latter qualification is important, in that in 1959 Lionel began packaging several select train sets such as the set No. 1800 General Frontier Pack in display-like boxes for counter top display. This numbered 1800 sequence also included dealer displays Nos. 1801 and 1802 in 1959, so one could argue that the gift packs were indeed dealer displays. We do not know why Lionel chose the same series for both gift packs and dealer displays. We do know the gift pack numbering system was short-lived; only four sets were assigned the 1800-series designation. Regardless of this argument, Lionel sets are not included in this listing simply because they were offered in their display cases direct to the general public as opposed to only Lionel authorized dealers and distributors. Since advance catalogues were a primary reference for this chapter, there may be certain displays illustrated and offered in a catalogue which were not available. Consequently, we have added the notation "display confirmed" to indicate that a prototype or production example is currently owned by an individual collector or a museum. A listing without that designation does not indicate that the item does not exist; we are simply waiting confirmation.

Our goal for future editions is to confirm existence of all known display merchandise offered by Lionel. Reader assistance is requested in confirming further listings. To provide a basis for our confirmation we would ask that the reader provide a clear photograph of the item or arrange for a physical examination by the editors. The final question is always, "What is the value of a display?" Very few displays have changed hands often enough to establish a reliable market valuation for most items. Similar to Lionel tools and other scarce collectibles, many displays exchange ownership privately between two parties rather than at a public train meet. In the case of a display value, the usual rule of price/value relationship applies: the value of a display is whatever a seller will accept and a buyer will offer.

DEALER SIGN: Circa 1940, No number, round with white face, lighted black picture of 700E Hudson on face, "Lionel Trains" in curved white fluorescent tube below face, curved yellow fluorescent tube circles face. Provided to early Lionel Authorized Service Stations as a promotion. Only a few known left in existence. One may be seen

in perfect working condition at Lionel Service Station No. 7, Downtown Lock and Electric in Washington, D.C. R. Lord comments.
NRS

1A DEALER DISPLAY: 1940-41. Contoured display; for promoting track, switches, transformers, and accessories; wired for operations; measures 53-3/4" long x 24" deep x 14" high. **NRS**

2 DEALER DISPLAY: 1940-41. Accessories display, includes 28 different accessories; all wired for operation; measures 51-1/4" long x 20" wide x 29" high. **NRS**

3 DEALER DISPLAY: 1940-41. Basic two-section display with three shelves and dual tunnel, intended for smaller stores; measures 60" long x 11-1/2" deep x 12" high. Display confirmed. **NRS**

3 SCALE MODEL STAND: 1937. Stand for displaying the scale Hudson; has T-rail track, switches, fishplates, ties, bolts and nuts, and wrenches; top of display has a swivel stand for the 700EW Hudson. This display was given free to dealers with a purchase of three 700EWs; measures 42-1/2" long x 7" wide x 17-1/2" high. T. Wagner comment. **NRS**

4 DEALER DISPLAY: 1939. Similar to No. 8, with addition of No. 97 coal loader; features four shelves plus operating O27 layout; display measures 54" long x 37" deep x 35" high. **NRS**

5 DEALER DISPLAY: 1932. Reader information requested. **NRS**

LT-5 DISPLAY: 1947. 3-D papier-mache sculpture simulating 671 locomotive with tender; measures 15' long x 48" high x 14" deep. Available for $385 from W. L. Stensgaard & Assoc., Chicago, Illinois. **NRS**

LT-5 DISPLAY: 1948. Same as 1947 version, however priced at $250 in 1948 dealer price list. **NRS**

6 ACCESSORY DISPLAY: 1939. Designed to demonstrate 27 popular accessories, wired for operation; measures 52" long x 20-1/2" wide x 26-1/2" high. **NRS**

7 DEALER COUNTER DISPLAY: 1937-40. Features operating accessories and rolling stock and includes circular "Lionel Accessories" sign; measures 52" long x 17-3/4" deep x 23" high. **NRS**

8 DEALER DISPLAY: 1938-41. O27 operating display with four shelves, designed to demonstrate new six-wheel drive steam locomotives. **NRS**

8 DEALER DISPLAY: 1940-41. Different from the previously-listed display, and designed to demonstrate popular accessories, such as the 313 bascule bridge and 164 lumber loader. Attractive island display concept; measures 56" long x 20-1/8" wide x 20" high. Some literature states that the No. 8 is 21-1/2" wide and other literature states 20-1/8". It is not known which was actually produced. **NRS**

9 DEALER DISPLAY: 1939. Operating car demonstration; includes rolling stock 3651, 3652, and 3659; measures 27-1/2" long x 9-1/2" deep x 14-1/2" high. **NRS**

10 DEALER DISPLAY: 1932-33. Constructed of veneer lumber, contains six shelves for Standard and O Gauge outfits, measures 5' 8" wide x 2' 1" high x 2' 7" deep. **NRS**

10 DEALER DISPLAY: 1940-41. Displays five O27 outfits on shelves plus operating oval with accessories; measures 54-1/2" long x 41-1/4" deep x 37" high. **NRS**

LT-10 DISPLAY: 1948. Comuras display with locomotive, 2332 GG1, measures 15' long each side, total 45 feet. Available for $409.50 from W. L. Stensgaard & Assoc., Chicago, Illinois. **NRS**

10 DISPLAY: 1949. Illuminated with four colorful Kodachrome transparencies above four-shelf display with oval layout; measures 60" wide. Display confirmed. **— — 750 1000**

10M DISPLAY: 1948. Four-shelf display with base finished in green imitation grass, came with merchandise; measures 29-1/2" high x 37-1/4" deep x 59-3/4" wide. **NRS**

11 DEALER DISPLAY: 1932-34. Three-tier display for accessories, with "Lionel" prominently illustrated in front; fully wired; includes Nos. 56, 57, 58, 83, 92, and other accessories. **NRS**

11 DEALER DISPLAY: 1940-41. Platform with accessories 97, 164, 165, and 313; measures 33-1/2" x 26-3/4". T. Wagner comment. **NRS**

11 DEALER DISPLAY: 1950. Oval layout with four wooden shelves and side tower with lights, does not include trains or accessories; measures 4' x 6'. Display confirmed. **200 400 600 900**

13 DEALER DISPLAY: 1939. OO Gauge railroad exhibit, operating layout features OO two-rail and three-rail and includes track and accessories; measures 97" long x 57" wide. Display confirmed. **— — 1000 —**

14 DEALER DISPLAY: 1939-41. Dealer display, arranges five different transformers on steps; measures 36" long x 8-1/2" wide x 7" high. Display confirmed. **NRS**

15 DEALER DISPLAY: 1939-41. One of the most impressive of Lionel's displays, this massive product was designed to project a complete train department. Includes two banks of steps and a silk-screened background of a train station; measures 15' x 17" x 63" high. For 1939 it was advertised to dealers that the No. 15 display could be used in conjunction with display No. 6; in 1941 the No. 15 display included the center platform which was the previously labeled No. 6 display. In total, it appears this display actually comprised two No. 10 displays, a No. 6 display, and a No. 14 display, in addition to the silk-screened background. Display confirmed. **— — — 3500**

18 DEALER DISPLAY: 1939. Car loading and unloading display, designed to demonstrate operating cars and the No. 97 coal loader; contains three shelves plus lower tier of operating controllers; measures 52" long x 19" deep x 23-1/2" high. **NRS**

19 DEALER DISPLAY: 1939-40. O Gauge train display, with the capability of displaying six complete outfits and operating another two sets; measures 76-1/2" long x 40" deep x 24" high **NRS**

20 DEALER DISPLAY: 1950. Step-up type display which shows off the 58, 71, 88, 145, 151, 153, 154, 252, 394, 395, 455, and 1045 accessories, which are included. T. Wagner comment. **NRS**

21 DONALD DUCK DISPLAY: 1936. Includes 3' base and 42-1/2" Donald Duck action display that features bobbing head. Base intended to display circular Donald Duck handcar. **NRS**

21 DEALER DISPLAY: 1941. Display of popular accessories; includes locomotive illustration and operating 152, 153, and 154 accessories; measures 21-1/2" long x 3-1/2" wide x 11" high. **NRS**

21 O27 TRACK DISPLAY: 1950. Wooden panel sporting the 26, 1013, 1018, 1021, 1024, 1121, 6019, and CTC lockon O27 track items; measures 24" x 30". T. Wagner comment. **NRS**

22 O GAUGE TRACK DISPLAY: 1950. Wooden panel; features the OC, 1/2-OC, OS, 1/2-OS, UCS, 26, 020, 020X, CTC lockon, 022, and 042 O Gauge track items; measures 24" x 30". T. Wagner comment. **NRS**

22 MICKEY MOUSE DISPLAY: 1936. Three-foot base operates Mickey Mouse handcar and includes 32-1/2" display that features a movable Mickey arm. **NRS**

23 DEALER DISPLAY: 1936. Six tiers feature mechanical trains, displayed on steep stairs and topped by a silhouette of the Lionel "Torpedo." The train includes an engineer whose hand pulls a cord with each blast of the whistle; measures 49" long x 17-3/4" deep x 37" high. **NRS**

24 DEALER DISPLAY: 1937-38. 42" cutout display of trainman that swings an arm holding a lantern, comes in sets of two. **NRS**

51 DEALER DISPLAY: 1943. Lithographed cutout, displays the Paper Train, comes with the display unit itself, plus one fully- assem-

| | G | VG | EXC | NEW |

bled paper train; measures 49" long x 5-1/2" wide x 26" high. T. Wagner comment. **NRS**

70 LABSTOCK RACK: 1961. Lionel-Porter wire rack, capable of containing 36 different chemicals; dealers were required to purchase six each of these chemicals. **NRS**

72 LABSTOCK DISPLAY BOARD: 1961. Lionel-Porter display board, contains a selection of popular laboratory glassware and other apparatus, all mounted with the board; measures 32" x 32" x 4". **NRS**

74 APPARATUS & GLASSWARE ASSORTMENT DISPLAY: 1961. Lionel-Porter assortment of stock, not a display per se, but starter backup stock for the No. 72 display board. It is listed here for reference only.

76 BOOK-SPECIMEN ASSORTMENT RACK: 1961. Lionel-Porter wire display rack stands 36" high and contains 42 science manuals and 30 biological specimens. A "Porter Science" sign is displayed prominently at the top. **NRS**

77 HOBBY SCIENCE MERCHANDISER: 1961. Complete Lionel-Porter floor display cabinet, features self-service for inexpensive items; measures 5' 10" high x 3' wide x 18" deep. **NRS**

78 TOP UNIT CABINET: 1961. This unit consists only of the top portion of Lionel-Porter display No. 77, designed for the merchandiser with limited floor space; measures 32" high, and essentially an owner of a No. 77 Lionel-Porter display would also have a No. 78 display. **NRS**

79 BASE UNIT DISPLAY: 1961. Consists only of the bottom unit of display No. 77, designed for the merchandiser who owns the No. 78 display and now wants the top unit. **NRS**

D-101 DISPLAY: 1953. Accessory display, pre-wired, back plus base to mount various accessories, all included in promotional price. **NRS**

D-102 DISPLAY: 1953-54. Small accessory display and stock cabinet; back of cabinet holds stock; measures 16" high x 12" wide x 7-1/2" deep. **NRS**

D-103 DISPLAY: 1953. Train display, landscaped, built of wood with oval "Lionel" sign at top above four shelves, wired, but includes no merchandise; measures 4' x 6'. **NRS**

D-104 TRAIN DISPLAY: 1953. Display, landscaped, no mountains; includes accessory merchandise, plus KW transformer; measures 4' x 8'. **NRS**

D-105 TRAIN DISPLAY: 1953. Display, landscaped with mountains, two-train operation; includes accessory merchandise, plus ZW transformer; measures 5' x 9'. **NRS**

D-106 TRAIN DISPLAY: 1953. Display, fully landscaped with mountains, multi-tier, three-train operation; includes accessory merchandise, plus ZW transformer; measures 8' x 8'. **NRS**

111 LAMP ASSORTMENT DISPLAY: 1935. Individual packed bulbs in cardboard and wooden containers were included in this larger display box for merchandising purposes. Display confirmed. **NRS**

122 LAMP ASSORTMENT DISPLAY: Date confirmation requested. Total of 92 bulbs in an orange and blue display box; measures 13-1/2" long x 7-1/2" wide x 1-1/2" deep. Listing begins with No. 27-3. Display confirmed. Price for display without bulbs.
25 35 50 60

123 LAMP ASSORTMENT DISPLAY: 1959. Orange and blue display box with lamps and locomotive front illustrated on cover; box measures 13-1/2" long x 7-1/2" wide x 1-1/2" deep.
(A) Listing on back of lid begins with No. L51 bulb. Display confirmed. Price for display without bulbs. **25 35 50 60**
(B) Listing on back of lid begins with No. L12 bulb. Display confirmed. Price for display without bulbs. **25 35 50 60**

123-60 LAMP ASSORTMENT DISPLAY: 1960-62. Orange and blue box; measures 5-3/4" long x 3-1/4" wide x 4-1/4" deep unopened. When opened for display purposes the top flap extends the

| | G | VG | EXC | NEW |

box height to 6-3/4". The outer box contains 12 smaller bulb box assortments, although the bulb description identifies only ten types. Display confirmed. Price for display without bulbs.
25 35 50 60

D-130 DISPLAY: 1954. Train display, landscaped platform, completely wired, no mountains or shelves, with KW transformer; measures 4' x 8'. **NRS**

D-131 DISPLAY: 1954. Display, landscaped platform, completely wired, with mountains, no shelves, with ZW transformer; measures 5' x 9'. **NRS**

D-132 DISPLAY: 1954. Display, multi-tier landscaped platform, completely wired, with mountains, no shelves, with ZW and RW transformers; measures 8' x 8'. **NRS**

D-133 TRAIN DISPLAY: 1954-55. Display, "Lionel Trains", lettering is illuminated; includes four shelves for display purposes plus oval layout; measures 4' x 6'. **NRS**

D-134 DISPLAY: 1954. Accessory display, completely wired and includes many accessories; measures 36" x 21" x 34" high; states No. 50 gang car can be operated on track at front of fixture. **NRS**

145 DISPLAY: 1930-33. Consists of platform 10' long x 4-1/2' wide, upon which is mounted a superstructure of steps 3' 2" high and is completely illuminated. One of Lionel's most comprehensive displays of trains and accessories of all gauges available during that era.
NRS

146 DISPLAY: 1930. Equipped with a Standard and O Gauge layout, features a large arch bridge spanning the entire layout; measures 10' long x 4-1/2' wide. **NRS**

146-1 DISPLAY: 1930. Features layout only from No. 146 display. Track is completely wired. **NRS**

146-2 DISPLAY: 1930. Features bridge only from No. 146 display; measures 9' 9" long x 3' 4" high x 1' 2" wide. **NRS**

146-3 DISPLAY: 1930. Consists of low bridge version of that described as the 146-2 display; measures 10' long x 13" high. **NRS**

D-146 DISPLAY: 1955. Train display, landscaped platform, wired, and includes KW transformer and many accessories but no trains; measures 4' x 8'. One-train operation possible. **NRS**

D-147 DISPLAY: 1955. Train display, fully landscaped; includes ZW transformer, accessories; measures 5' x 9'. Two-train operation possible. **NRS**

D-148 DISPLAY: 1955. Train display, fully landscaped and wired; includes mountain, accessories, and both ZW and LW transformers; measures 8' x 8'. Three-train operation possible. **NRS**

D-149 ACCESSORY DISPLAY: 1955. Display; includes accessories and track, but no cars; No. 50 gang car or No. 60 trolley can be demonstrated; measures 36" x 21" x 34" high. **NRS**

D-159 OPERATING CAR DISPLAY: 1957. Highlights 3356, 3359, 3360, 3361, 3651, and 3662 cars, not included on original display; measures 26" long x 20" deep x 17" high. **NRS**

D-159X OPERATING CAR DISPLAY: 1958. Similar to 1957 display; but includes wiring for the following cars: 3650, 3424, 3359, 3361, 3662, and 3356. Cars not included. **NRS**

D-160 DISPLAY: 1956-57. Accessories display; highlight includes No. 50 gang car with signals, track, etc.; measures 30" long x 28" high x 13" deep. **NRS**

D-161 DISPLAY: 1956-58. Four-step display with "Lionel Lion" at top, space for five train sets, not included; measures 31" high x 12" deep x 72" long. **NRS**

D-161 DISPLAY: 1958-60. Similar to 1956-58 display, however "Lionel Lion" illustrated differently, showing a side view versus the earlier frontal view. **NRS**

D-162 DISPLAY: 1956. Dealer display, Lionel operating layout; includes track and switches only; measures 4' x 6'. **NRS**

                                        G   VG   EXC NEW

D-163 DISPLAY: 1956. Display, operating layout; includes KW transformer, track, and several accessories; measures 4' x 8'. **NRS**

D-164 DISPLAY: 1956. Display, Lionel operating layout; includes ZW transformer, mountain, track, and several accessories; measures 5' x 9'. **NRS**

D-165 DISPLAY: 1956. Large display, operating layout; includes ZW and LW transformers, mountains, track, and several accessories; measures 8' x 8'. Capable of three-train operation. **NRS**

173E DISPLAY SET: 1933-34. This display was believed sold to the general public and although not a true dealer display, it is listed here for information only. **NRS**

D-186 DEALER DISPLAY: 1957-58. Three-tier circular display features two circular O Gauge and one circular Super O tracks. The illustrated lion in the center of display is different for each year; measures 45" high x 39" wide. This display was also advertised separately as an HO display, which was logical, since the plain circular shelves could appropriately contain any Lionel product.
NRS

D-187 FERRIS WHEEL ACTION DISPLAY: 1957-58. Display; can accommodate 12 different freight cars, but display came without cars; measures 29" high x 12-1/2" deep. Display confirmed.
NRS

D-189 DISPLAY: 1957. Board display; with track and switches, wired for accessories; measures 4' x 6'. Display confirmed. **NRS**

D-190 DISPLAY: 1957. Board display; with ZW transformer, track, and full complement of accessories, completely wired; measures 4' x 6'. **NRS**

D-191 DISPLAY: 1957. Board display; with ZW transformer, mountain, track, and accessories, completely wired; measures 5' x 9'.
NRS

D-192 DISPLAY: 1957. Board display; with ZW and LW transformers, track, mountains, and several accessories. **NRS**

D-0200 OPERATING HO DISPLAY: 1960. Display layout; capable of demonstrating up to five train sets, and includes a No. 0100 and 0101 power pack plus many HO accessories; measures 4' x 6'. In the advertising for this display appearing in all versions of the 1960 advance catalogue, there is a rare reference by Lionel for disposing of custom built layouts: "You will find a ready market for this display...sell it at the end of the season." **NRS**

D-0205 OPERATING HO DISPLAY: 1961. Layout, fully landscaped and wired, and designed to operate up to two trains for demonstration purposes; includes 0100 and 0103 power packs, ample track, and switches, but few accessories; measures 4' x 6'. **NRS**

D-206 COLOR MURAL: 1958-59. Illustrates diesel and steam locomotives with heading "Lionel Trains and Accessories"; measures 6' wide x 3-1/2' high. Lionel indicated these posters would be available after September 1 of both years. **NRS**

D-206 COLOR MURAL: 1960-62. (Revised), illustrates family (and perhaps a first for Lionel: includes father, mother, son, and daughter, and even the family dog!) overlooking an operating layout; measures 6' wide x 3-1/2' high. Was free to dealers with the purchase of any Lionel operating layout. Display confirmed. **NRS**

D-220 OPERATING ACCESSORY DISPLAY: 1958-61. Highlights operating accessories and automatic signals; measures 25" high x 16" deep x 48" long. Lionel recommended placing several of these displays together for maximum effect. **NRS**

D-221 ISLAND DISPLAY: 1958-60. Chipboard two-level multi-purpose display for use with 920-2 tunnel portals; display includes no train items. **NRS**

D-222 DISPLAY: 1958. Operating display; includes display D-221, plus track, switches, and controller; measures 4' x 6'. **NRS**

                                        G   VG   EXC NEW

D-223 SUPER O DISPLAY: 1958. Super O operating display; includes ZW transformer, many accessories; fully wired; measures 4' x 8'. **NRS**

D-224 SUPER O DISPLAY: 1958. Super O operating display; includes ZW transformer, accessories, and landscaped mountain, all fully wired; measures 5' x 9'. **NRS**

D-225 SUPER O DISPLAY: 1958. Super O operating display; most impressive of the year and capable of presenting three trains operating simultaneously; includes ZW and LW transformers, accessories, landscaped mountain, all fully wired; measures 8' x 8'. **NRS**

D-226 HO DISPLAY: 1958. Metal wire dispenser with full-color two-sided sign at top, and capable of containing 64 HO cars; measures 33" high x 16" wide. **NRS**

D-227 HO STEP DISPLAY: 1958-60. Display, with five steps and capable of showing off five different HO train sets; measures 28" high x 12" deep x 60" long. At the top of the display is an attractive colored sign depicting an engineer, locomotives, and a caption "HO...By Lionel". **NRS**

D-260 CIRCULAR DISPLAY: 1959-60. Two-level display, for use with all gauges of track, including HO; measures 26" high x 39" wide and when two are joined together a figure eight results. **NRS**

D-260 HO DISPLAY: 1959-60. Low-cost two-level display; features a sign reading "HO By Lionel" at the top; measures 26" high x 39" wide. Both tiers are circular in design, and mounted on furniture legs. **NRS**

D-261 OPERATING DISPLAY: 1959-60. Basic display, with a simple oval of track and 1043 transformer; measures 30" x 40". Display confirmed. — — — **100**

D-262 OPERATING DISPLAY: 1959. Two-part display; includes a 4' x 6' dual train operating layout as well as four shelves overhead with a painted sign in the shape of a semaphore. The sign, with the legend "Lionel Trains and Accessories", marks a similarity in design of the early 1950s style. **NRS**

D-263 OPERATING DISPLAY: 1959. Super O display, came fully wired; includes a ZW transformer as well as numerous accessories; measures 4' x 8'. **NRS**

D-264 OPERATING DISPLAY: 1959. Super O display, fully wired; includes landscaped mountain, ZW transformers, and numerous accessories; measures 5' x 9'. **NRS**

D-265 OPERATING DISPLAY: 1959. One of the largest displays offered by Lionel, this is actually two 4' x 8' layouts assembled together, fully landscaped and wired. The display, which sold for $350 to dealers in 1959, includes ZW and LW transformers and several major accessories, but dealers were still instructed to take locomotives and cars from their personal stock. **NRS**

D-266 HO DISPENSER DISPLAY: 1959. With minor changes in the top sign only, this display is very similar to the D-226 model of 1958. This display was free when dealers ordered a certain assortment of the 64 cars the display could contain, and therefore another major difference between the two years were the cars offered that were eligible for the free display. **NRS**

D-287 DISPLAY: 1960. Designation of a special offer in 1960 in which dealers who ordered a variety of popular accessories received display No. D-220 at no charge. This was therefore a promotional designation rather than a newly-designed display.

D-288 AUTOMATED LION DISPLAY: 1960. Animated lion in full color, with swinging lantern powered by battery-operated magnetic field motor; measures 36" high x 21-1/2" wide. **NRS**

D-288 AUTOMATED LION DISPLAY: 1961-62. Similar to 1960 display, however lantern swings on left of display and the three locomotives illustrated are now distinctly facing to the right. The display when fully assembled measures 36" high x 21-1/2" wide; unassembled displays still in the box have been examined, and each was shipped in a cardboard container measuring 22" x 3-1/2" x 20",

	G	VG	EXC	NEW

with a "Lionel Display Instruction Sheet" included. Display confirmed. **200 450 800 1200**

D-289 OPERATING DISPLAY: 1961. Two-part display; includes a four-shelf unit plus operating layout for demonstration of up to two trains; measures 4' x 6'. Display is fully wired but includes minimal merchandise such as track and switches. **NRS**

D-290 OPERATING DISPLAY: 1960. Super O display; includes ZW transformer, several popular accessories, and detailed, landscaped mountain; measures 4' x 8'. **NRS**

D-291 SUPER O DISPLAY: 1960-61. Super O display; includes ZW transformer, many popular accessories, fully landscaped tunnel, and provisions to operate three trains with the aid of a block signal; measures 5' x 9'. **NRS**

D-292 SUPER O DISPLAY: 1960. Super O display; includes ZW transformer, many popular accessories, fully landscaped tunnel, and the capability to operate four trains; measures 8' x 8'. This display represents one of the most elaborate available from Lionel in the postwar era. **NRS**

D-325 OPERATING DISPLAY: 1961. Combination O27 and HO display; includes some accessories, fully landscaped mountain, and fully wired, ready-to-run layout; measures 4' x 8'. **NRS**

D-326 OPERATING DISPLAY: 1961. Combination Super O and HO display; includes basic accessories such as the No. 145 automatic gateman and No. 151 automatic semaphore, but little else besides the usual track and switches. The display does include a ZW transformer and landscaped mountain, but unlike the prior years' busier and more dynamic displays, this is rather spartan for its size; measures 8' x 8'. **NRS**

D-400 OPERATING DISPLAY: 1962-63. Combination O27 and HO display; includes four display tiers, completely wired, and comes with minimal products; measures 4' x 6'. **NRS**

D-401 OPERATING DISPLAY: 1962-63. Exclusive HO display, comes completely wired with a number of accessories and a landscaped mountain; measures 4' x 6'. **NRS**

D-402 OPERATING DISPLAY: 1962. Fully wired and landscaped combination O27 and HO display; can operate up to three trains, sidings are also provided to demonstrate operating cars; measures 4' x 8'. Display confirmed. **NRS**

D-403 OPERATING DISPLAY: 1962. Combination Super O, O27, and HO; capable of operating up to five trains simultaneously; measures 8' x 8'. The display is landscaped on one 4' x 8' board, and includes numerous accessories, including a ZW transformer. **NRS**

D-404 COMPACT TRACK MERCHANDISER: 1962. Display was provided free to dealers when an order for a specific merchandise assortment was placed. Display primarily intended to sell track and small consumer parts such as contactors, controllers, and smoke fluid. Display is floor model made of wood, approximately 5' tall. **NRS**

D-466 OPERATING DISPLAY: 1963. Combination O27 and HO display; fully wired and includes mountains and a wide assortment of track, accessories, and two transformers; measures 4' x 8'. **NRS**

D-476 OPERATING DISPLAY: 1964 or 1965. Oval of O27 track similar to D-261; measures 30" x 40". Display confirmed. **— — 65 100**

DO-492 DEALER DISPLAY: 1965. Combination O27 and HO layout with four-shelf super structure; measures 4' x 6'. Top of shelves is a sign headed by the caption "Lionel Trains and Accessories" plus their features. Layout is completely wired. **NRS**

DO-494 DEALER DISPLAY: 1965. Combination O27 and HO layout with four-shelf super structure; measures 4' x 8'. Top of shelves is a sign headed by the caption "Lionel Trains and Accessories" plus their features. Layout is completely wired, and comes with several accessories. **NRS**

DO-502 OPERATING LAYOUT: 1966. Inexpensive display, allows operation of two train sets; completely wired and comes with minimal minor accessories; measures 3' x 5'. **NRS**

DO-503 DEALER DISPLAY: 1966. Layout with four-shelf product display, topped by sign which reads "Lionel Trains and Accessories" and description of Lionel features; fully wired and comes with accessories and two transformers; measures 4' x 6'. Display confirmed. **— — — 550**

DO-504 DEALER DISPLAY: 1966. Layout with four-shelf arrangement similar to display No. DO-503; includes more accessories, two transformers, including the ZW model, fully landscaped and wired for immediate operation; measures 4' x 8'. Display confirmed. **— — — 600**

DO-507 DEALER DISPLAY: 1966. This display does not appear in any printed Lionel reference, and perhaps it was an internally-used product number. The display apparently was identical to No. DO-504, except operating cars 3662 and 3356 were not included. This information was learned only from a margin notation in the 1966 dealer display booklet "To Help You Sell", and obtained from a Lionel sales manager. **NRS**

925 LUBRICANT DISPLAY: Confirmation of date requested. Orange and blue box for displaying tubes of No. 925 Lionel lubricant; measures 6-1/2" wide x 2" deep x 8-1/4" high when display flap is extended. Display confirmed. **15 30 40 60**

930 ACCESSORY STAND: 1936-38. Three-step dealer display designed to highlight the more popular accessories of the prewar era; completely wired; measures 17" x 49-1/2". **NRS**

932 MURAL PHOTOGRAPH DISPLAY: 1936. Features Lionel Union Pacific train mounted on linen back; measures 14' x 4'. **NRS**

933 MURAL PHOTOGRAPH DISPLAY: 1936. Features Lionel Pennsylvania "Torpedo" train, mounted on linen back; measures 14' x 4'. **NRS**

950 KIT DISPLAY: 1938. A kit 700K model mounted on six-panel display with scale Hudson and tender illustration featured on top of display. All scale Hudson parts are mounted individually to board. **NRS**

1053 DISPLAY SET FOR O27: 1933. This display was believed sold to the general public and although not a true dealer display, it is listed here for information only.

1057 DISPLAY SET FOR O27: 1934. This display was believed sold to the general public and although not a true dealer display, it is listed here for information only.

1254 DISPLAY MERCHANDISER: 1965-66. Three-tier revolving metal rack contains track and switches; at top is a sign "Lionel Train Accessories". **NRS**

1255 DISPLAY MERCHANDISER: 1965-66. Four-tier revolving metal rack contains basic accessories plus smoke fluid, controllers and similar merchandise; at top is a sign "Lionel Train Accessories". **NRS**

1256 DISPLAY MERCHANDISER: 1965-66. Four-tier revolving metal rack contains track, switches, and minor accessories; at top is a sign with the caption "Lionel Train Accessories". **NRS**

1801 ROLLING STOCK DISPLAY: 1959. Easel-type counter top display; features operating cars 3419, 3435, 3512, and 3540; measures 27" high x 13" wide. For some reason all dealer displays in 1959 contained the prefix "D", with the exception of displays 1801 and 1802. This continued into 1960, and the question is, why? Reader comments requested. **NRS**

1802 ROLLING STOCK DISPLAY: 1959. Easel-type counter top display; features operating cars 6470, 6650, 6819, and 6826; measures 27" high x 13" wide. **NRS**

1803 ROLLING STOCK DISPLAY: 1960. Easel-type counter top display; features operating cars 6361, 6475, 6530, and 6544; measures 27" high x 13" wide. **NRS**

	G	VG	EXC	NEW

1804 ROLLING STOCK DISPLAY: 1960. Easel-type counter top display; features operating cars 3330, 3419, 3535, and 3830; measures 27" high x 13" wide. **NRS**

1807 ROLLING STOCK DISPLAY: 1961. Easel-type counter top display; features rolling stock cars 6445, 6448, 6544, and 6822; measures 27" high x 13" wide. **NRS**

1808 ROLLING STOCK DISPLAY: 1961. Easel-type counter top display; features operating cars 3370, 3419, 3519, and 3665; measures 27" high x 13" wide. **NRS**

1811 OPERATING ACCESSORY DISPLAY: 1961. This "display" is more accurately a special dealers offer, whereby quantities of Nos. 140, 163, 252, and 452, when ordered, would include a free No. D-220 operating accessory display. This listing is included for information purposes only.

1812 ROLLING STOCK DISPLAY: 1962. Easel display provided free to dealers for ordering quantities of four different O Gauge cars; includes Nos. 3413, 3419, 3665, and 6512. **NRS**

1813 ROLLING STOCK DISPLAY: 1962. Easel display provided free to dealers for ordering quantities of four different O Gauge cars; includes Nos. 3357, 3370, 3376, and 6445. **NRS**

1814 ROLLING STOCK DISPLAY: 1962. Easel display provided free to dealers for ordering quantities of four different O Gauge cars; includes Nos. 3619, 6413, 6448, and 6501. **NRS**

1815 ROLLING STOCK DISPLAY: 1962. Easel display provided free to dealers for ordering quantities of four different O Gauge cars; includes Nos. 3349, 3470, 3519, and 3830. **NRS**

1816 DEALER DISPLAY: 1962. Display; features the Lionel Lion with nine different accessories; measures 25" high x 16" deep x 48" long. **NRS**

3000 DEALER DISPLAY: 1970. Oval layout with provisions for one-train operation; measures 4' x 8'; track, accessories, trees, and scrubs come mounted to board; train and transformer to come from dealer stock. T. Wagner comment. **NRS**

3000 ROLLING STOCK DISPLAY: 1960. Easel-type counter top display; features ten different cars, and provided free to dealers with a purchase of 26 total cars; measures 27" high x 20" wide, with "Lionel HO Rolling Stock" sign at top. **NRS**

3001 ROLLING STOCK DISPLAY: 1960. Easel-type counter top display; features five different cars, and provided free to dealers with a purchase of 16 total cars; display measures 27" high x 12" wide. **NRS**

3001 DEALER DISPLAY: 1970. Figure eight layout for one-train operation; comes fully landscaped, track mounted to board; measures 4' x 6'. Accessories, train, and transformer to be taken from dealer stock. T. Wagner comment. **NRS**

3002 HO ROLLING STOCK DISPLAY: 1961. Easel-type counter top display; features ten different cars, and provided free to dealers with the purchase of a total of 22 cars of the ten-car assortment; measures 27" high x 20" wide. **NRS**

3003 HO ROLLING STOCK DISPLAY: 1961. Easel-type counter top display; features rolling stock HO cars 0039, 0319, 0333, 0337, and 0366; measures 27" high x 12" wide. **NRS**

3004 HO OPERATING CARS DISPLAY: 1962. Single-tier display; features five different HO cars arranged vertically; measures 27" high x 12" wide. **NRS**

6-3004 DEALER DISPLAY: 1972. Layout for one-train operation; comes fully landscaped, track mounted on board; measures 4' x 8'. Accessories with display and pre-wired. **NRS**

3005 HO ROLLING STOCK DISPLAY: 1962. Double-tier display; features ten different HO cars arranged vertically in each tier; measures 27" high x 20" wide. **NRS**

6-3005 DEALER DISPLAY: 1972. Layout for one-train operation; comes landscaped, track mounted on board with minimal minor accessories; measures 4' x 6'. **NRS**

6-3006 DEALER DISPLAY: 1973. Layout for one-train operation; comes fully landscaped, track mounted on board; measures 4' x 6'. Has no provisions for accessories except for streetlights. Train and transformer to be taken from dealer stock. T. Wagner comment. **NRS**

6-3007 DEALER DISPLAY: 1973. Layout for one-train operation; comes fully landscaped with track and accessories mounted on board; measures 4' x 8'; train and transformer to be taken from dealer stock. T. Wagner comment. **NRS**

3095 DEALER DISPLAY: 1977. Measures 68" x 42". Layout for one-train operation, constructed of heavy styrene; comes with track, girder bridge, lighted station and crossing gate. T. Wagner comment. **NRS**

3-3098 RAIL SCOPE DISPLAYER: 1988. Full-color cardboard display, with easel and plastic miniature man placed over television for promotional purposes; measures 14-1/2" x 13-1/2"; comes with consumer television and video tape cassette. Display confirmed.
— — **200 225**

3-3099 RAIL SCOPE DISPLAYER: 1988. Same as 3-3098, but comes without television. Display confirmed. T. Wagner Collection.
— — — **100**

5180 RACING EQUIPMENT MERCHANDISER: 1965. Three-tier revolving metal rack, contains racing track and cars in packaged blister packs; at top of the stand is a sign with the caption "Lionel Action Packed Racing". **NRS**

5577 RACING EQUIPMENT MERCHANDISER: 1965-66. Three-tier revolving metal rack, contains racing track and track accessories in packaged blister packs; at top of the stand is a sign with the caption "Lionel Action Packed Racing". **NRS**

5578 RACING CAR MERCHANDISER: 1965-66. Two-tier metal rack, contains space to display eight different products arranged four to each tier; at top of the stand is a sign with the caption "Lionel HO Racing". **NRS**

5579 RACING CAR MERCHANDISE PACKAGE: 1965. Although this package is not advertised with a rack, its contents can be placed on the No. 5578 merchandiser. **NRS**

D-58-52 CATALOG COUNTER DISPENSER: 1959. Cardboard dispenser, intended for use in making the current consumer catalogue visible to the public; measures 15-1/2" wide x 20-1/2". **NRS**

11415 DEALER DISPLAY: 1963. Although this is the number assigned to a low-priced set, "The Trendsetter", Lionel advertised in the 1963 advance catalogue that a colorful, pilfer-proof heavy gauge display was available with this outfit. Reader assistance in providing additional information on this display is requested. **NRS**

DO-16100 RACEWAY DISPLAY: 1965-66. The Loop-the-Loop Speedway; includes 22 different products and the criss-cross lane change accessory. **NRS**

DO-16110 RACEWAY DISPLAY: 1965-66. The Daredevil Speedway; includes 26 different products and demonstrates the Skyway Leap optional accessory. **NRS**

DO-16130 RACEWAY DISPLAY: 1966. The Big 8 Raceway; features 12' of track and automatic lap counter, and includes 15 different raceway products. **NRS**

DO-17130 RACEWAY DISPLAY: 1965. The Malibu Twister Raceway; includes 19 different products and demonstrates the automatic lap counter. **NRS**

DO-17140 RACEWAY DISPLAY: 1965-66. The Stunt Rider Raceway; includes 25 different products and demonstrates Lionel's new accessory, the Loop-the-Loop. **NRS**

	G	VG	EXC	NEW

DO-17160 RACEWAY DISPLAY: 1965-66. Two cars can race on the same track on this raceway; includes 21 different Lionel products. In 1966 this display was designated "The Pretzel Bender". **NRS**

DO-17170 RACEWAY DISPLAY: 1965-66. The Daredevil Monte Carlo Raceway; includes 34 different products and features the Skill Tilt and Skyway Leap accessory options. **NRS**

DO-17180 RACEWAY DISPLAY: 1965. The Combination Four-lane Flag Tag Relay Set, allows four people to race simultaneously; includes 29 different Lionel racing products. **NRS**

DO-17200 RACEWAY DISPLAY: 1966. The Matterhorn Raceway; features Lionel's new Mystery Route Selector and a power lift to raise the cars to the top of a mountain. Set includes 33 different raceway accessories. **NRS**

DO-19335 OPERATING DISPLAY: 1965. An inexpensive dealer display allows demonstration of the basics through a no-frills 3' x 5' double layout. **NRS**

25510 CHEMICAL ASSORTMENT DISPLAY: 1966. Three-shelf metal display rack with space for 24 different chemicals arranged six-deep; includes a sign which reads "Lionel-Porter Chemicals — Buy Yours Today". This display is the same as the unnumbered 1965 version. **NRS**

25520 SCIENCE ACCESSORIES DISPLAY: 1966. Four-tier display single-pole rack, with space to mount 24 different science products. This display is the same as the unnumbered 1965 version. **NRS**

48010 COUNTER DISPLAY: 1963. Lionel-Spear record assortment of favorite children's songs and stories on 12" 33-1/3 rpm records. Each record pack of four records is inserted into a cardboard container. **NRS**

48020 COUNTER DISPLAY: 1963. Lionel-Spear record assortment of 24 Talking Teddy stories on 12" 33-1/3 rpm records. Each record pack of four records is inserted into a cardboard container. **NRS**

48350 COUNTER DISPLAY: 1963. Lionel-Spear record assortment of 24 nursery tunes, folk songs, and others on 45 rpm records. Each record is inserted into a cardboard display container. **NRS**

48430 COUNTER DISPLAY: 1963. Lionel-Spear record assortment of 12 each 45 rpm and 78 rpm dance, Christmas, and other songs. Each record is inserted into a cardboard display container. **NRS**

48700 COUNTER DISPLAY: 1963. Lionel-Spear record assortment of 78 rpm records of various types. Each record is inserted into a cardboard display container. **NRS**

48710 COUNTER DISPLAY: 1963. Lionel-Spear record assortment of 45 rpm and 78 rpm records. Each record is inserted into a cardboard display container. **NRS**

UNNUMBERED DISPLAYS

WINDOW TRIM DISPLAY: 1930. Base of display is a roundhouse, topped by engineer holding a Standard Gauge locomotive and states "Lionel Trains are Real — Like Mine"; measures 39" long x 36" high. **NRS**

WINDOW TRIM DISPLAY: 1930. Cutout incorporates a raised platform for product display; includes a Lionel industrial background consisting of the "Lionel Locomotive Works" and "Lionel Steel Works"; measures 5' long x 5-1/2" wide x 32" high. **NRS**

CUTOUT DISPLAY: 1933. Cardboard lithograph cutout; features the 400E and the cutouts contain platforms on which a locomotive and a car may be displayed. **NRS**

DEALER DISPLAY: 1933. Illustrates Lionel No. 43 Lionel craft on cardboard display simulating water. More information requested.

	G	VG	EXC	NEW
				NRS

SWINGING DISPLAY: 1934. Fits into a 40" x 40" display area and swings on a turntable base to display four sides of trains and accessories. Display came with 84 items and each of four sides is devoted to cars, signals/lamps, track, and bridges. **NRS**

DEALER SIGN: 1934. Assimilated neon sign; measures 14" x 21" and illuminates lettering "Authorized Dealer — Lionel Trains". **NRS**

MAGAZINE DISPLAY RACK: 1940. Solidly-constructed, enameled metal rack with multicolored descriptive display sign for selling Lionel's *Handbook for Model Builders*. This rack was sent free to dealers with every order of ten copies of the *Handbook*. **NRS**

STEP DISPLAY: 1947. Display 60" wide with "Lionel" in large letters at top, with four shelves for trains. Available for $21 from Lionel in 1947 price list. **NRS**

TRIPLE ACTION DISPLAY: 1949. Center display; measures 12' long x 57" high x 21" deep. Single AC motor turns displays to depict three separate scenes, a GG-1, Santa Fe diesel, and 671 steam locomotive. Available for $275 from Lionel. **NRS**

DEALER DISPLAY: 1950. Unnumbered dealer train layout used for demonstrating Magne-Traction. Layout comes with locomotive, 14 cars, track, and landscaping; measures 4-1/2' x 8'. The train enters a tunnel pulling all 14 cars and emerges from the other side seemingly pulling only two cars. This is accomplished by a loop running beneath the layout. This layout is supposedly the origin of the 1002 gondola in red, silver, and yellow. Reader assistance on this layout requested. T. Wagner comment. **NRS**

POINT-OF-SALE MICROSCOPE DISPLAY: 1959. Features plug-in microscope and live specimens in action. Reader information requested. **NRS**

SCIENCE MERCHANDISER: 1965. Unnumbered four-tier wire display rack is topped by a sign with the caption "Lionel-Porter Science Accessories"; includes 24 different Lionel-Porter science products, each mounted on a single pole supported by four legs. **NRS**

CHEMICAL ASSORTMENT DISPLAY: 1965. Three-shelf rack; contains an assortment of 24 different chemicals, includes a sign at the top which reads "Lionel-Porter Chemicals — Buy Yours Today". **NRS**

FABRIC BANNER: 1965-66. Unnumbered 48" x 30" white plastic-like fabric with black border, long loops in each corner, "LIONEL" in black lettering in center, circle of two arrows, orange and blue surround "LIONEL". Below arrows is "A Lifetime Investment in Happiness". R. Lord Collection **—   —   250   300**

SCALE HUDSON MOUNTING BOARD: 1966. During 1966, there were discussions among Lionel's sales management concerning the feasibility of providing a display board for mounting Lionel's classic 773 scale Hudson, which had been reissued two years prior. Based on an observation of the size of the original Lionel shipping box, a total of three prototype boards were produced, but only two are accounted for today.
(A) 28" x 8" with white label "Mahogany — Sample / 28" 3.50 / 14" 2.50". Packed in cardboard box sent from Hillside, New Jersey October 1966, with Lionel mailing label. Display confirmed. **NRS**
(B) 28" x 8" with white label "Walnut — Sample / 28" $4.75 / 14" 3.75". Without box. Display confirmed. **NRS**

BIG TRAIN ACCESSORY CENTER DISPLAY: 1977. Two accessory centers and two bonus centers available, each with a different amount of shelves, no identifying product numbers. All accessory centers come with a red, black, and white 36" x 6" header card with the legend "Lionel Big Train Accessory Center". T. Wagner comment. **NRS**

ADD-CESSORIES CENTER DISPLAY: 1978. Four different accessory centers available, each with a different number of shelves, and none with identifying product numbers. All displays are topped

	G	VG	EXC	NEW

by a red, black, and white 26" x 15" header card with caption "Expand Your Train Set with Lionel Accessories". **NRS**

SUPER CENTER DISPLAY: 1979. Features three shelves of assorted Lionel products, topped by a sign depicting a locomotive and various sports motifs. **NRS**

LOCOMOTIVE SIGN: 1984. Formed plastic mounted on a hardboard back, black with silver engine and red "LIONEL" lettering; measures 35-1/2" x 29-1/2". **NRS**

DEALER DISPLAY: "RailScope Video Contest", 1989, two-sided cardboard A-frame, 8-1/2" x 6-3/4" each side when assembled, announcing the contest to "Show Off Your Train Layout". One side blue letters against a red background; other side red letters against a blue background. **NRS**

DEALER SIGN: 1989. "Lionel Large Scale" circular sign for hanging from a ceiling. Circular sign 12" diameter, thick fibre card stock, black with large "L" and lettering in gold, printed both sides. Sign is packaged in clear plastic sealed packet with metal hanger and wire. Display confirmed. **NRS**

BANNER: Undated, no number. Approximately 3' x 6', dark blue with dark red border, white lettering "HEADQUARTERS / FOR / LIONEL TRAINS". Banner fastens to rod or wire with white upper hanging strip. Upper right has black monkey figure in orange circle, black lettering "(obliterated) BUNTING", and orange lettering "DYED WITH OUR EVERLASTING DYES". Also includes "DETTRAS / FLAG" in black shield. It is believed this banner is from the early to mid-1950s; it is not known if this is actually a Lionel-approved item. E. Mancinelli Collection. **NRS**

DEALER NEON SIGN: Date unknown. Chromium plated, illustrates "Lionel Trains" with handles and space for adjustable chain suspension, measures 6" x 30". **NRS**

1989 RailScope video contest dealer display.

ABOUT THE AUTHOR

Robert J. Osterhoff

Robert Osterhoff was born in Dubuque, Iowa in 1947. After graduating from Loras College with a Bachelor's Degree in Accounting, Bob joined the Xerox Corporation in Rochester, New York in 1969. Bob also holds a Masters Degree in Business Administration from Rochester Institute of Technology.

Bob's introduction to model trains came in 1950 when he received his first Lionel set for Christmas. He remembers well the enthusiasm with which he used to peruse Lionel's annual catalogues. In addition to his interest in Lionel's paper and non-train collectibles, Bob is a serious collector and operator of Lionel's trains from prewar to the modern era.

Bob and his wife Laura are the parents of three children — Michael, Marissa, and Meredith . He is currently National Quality Manager for Xerox Corporation, and also serves on the Board of Examiners of the Malcolm Baldrige National Quality Award.

More Books for Your Enjoyment

Create Your Own Expert Layout

with "Lionel Wizard" Roland LaVoie. Learn the ins and outs of track layout and design as you build your own railroad empire. This essential guide includes advice on simple repairs, building platforms, restoring old track, and avoiding the pitfalls of layout building. 144 pages, many color illustrations. Soft cover, #10-6745, **$19.95**. Hard cover, #10-6745LE, **$28.95**.

Build the Ultimate Reference Library

with Greenberg's Lionel Catalogue books. Lionel pioneered the use of lavishly-illustrated catalogues in the toy train world and went to great lengths to provide the most exciting, captivating "wish books" that a boy could have. Now, you can have this wealth of data in a handy multi-volume set. Each book contains reproductions of the original catalogues presented in a long-lasting hardcover binding.

1902-1922 Volume I, #10-6910, available in 1990. **$100.00**.

1923-1932 Volume II, #10-6915, October 1989. **$110.00**.

1933-1942 Volume III, #10-6920, January 1990. **$110.00**.

1945-1954 Volume IV, #10-6925, October 1989. **$110.00**.

Note that the 1945 and 1946 catalogues are provided in a separate packet with Volume IV. Because of their vertical format, they do not fit with the other catalogues.

Put Prices and Inventory Information in Your Pocket

with *Greenberg's Pocket Price Guide and Inventory Checklist to Lionel Trains*, 1901-1942 & 1945-1988. This complete, handy reference fits in your pocket or glove compartment so you can take it any where! All items are listed by number, with a concise description, current values, and blanks where you can check off your inventory. Don't be caught without your "want list" — use *the* Pocket Guide. 80 pages, 4" x 8", #10-7290, **$6.95**.

3 1880 0205418 9

```
621.19 O
Osterhoff, Robert.
Greenberg's guide to Lionel
 paper and collectibles
```

DATE DUE			

JAMES PRENDERGAST LIBRARY ASSOCIATION

JAMESTOWN, NEW YORK

Member Of

Chautauqua-Cattaraugus Library System